# Performance-Based Assessment for Middle and High School Physical Education

## Second Edition

**Jacalyn Lea Lund, PhD**
Georgia State University

**Mary Fortman Kirk, PhD**
Northern Kentucky University

**Human Kinetics**

## Library of Congress Cataloging-in-Publication Data

Lund, Jacalyn Lea, 1950-
  Performance-based assessment for middle and high school physical education / Jacalyn L. Lund, Mary Fortman Kirk. -- 2nd ed.
     p. cm.
  Includes bibliographical references and index.
  ISBN-13: 978-0-7360-8360-7 (pbk.)
  ISBN-10: 0-7360-8360-X (pbk.)
  1. Physical education and training--Study and teaching (Secondary)--Examinations. 2. Educational tests and measurements. I. Kirk, Mary Fortman, 1946- II. Title.
  GV362.5.L86 2010
  613.7'0712--dc22

                              2009046820

ISBN-10: 0-7360-8360-X (print)
ISBN-13: 978-0-7360-8360-7 (print)

The Web addresses cited in this text were current as of October 2009, unless otherwise noted.

**Acquisitions Editor:** Sarajane Quinn; **Developmental Editor:** Melissa Feld; **Assistant Editor:** Rachel Brito; **Indexer:** Betty Frizzéll; **Permission Manager:** Dalene Reeder; **Graphic Designer:** Joe Buck; **Graphic Artist:** Dawn Sills; **Cover Designer:** Keith Blomberg; **Photographer (cover):** Human Kinetics/Neil Bernstein; **Photographer (interior):** Human Kinetics; **Photo Production Manager:** Jason Allen; **Art Manager:** Kelly Hendren; **Associate Art Manager:** Alan L. Wilborn; **Illustrators:** Dick Flood (line drawings), except pages 5 and 6 Tim Offenstein; Alan L. Wilborn (diagrams); **Printer:** Sheridan Books

Printed in the United States of America    10  9  8  7  6  5  4  3  2  1

The paper in this book is certified under a sustainable forestry program.

**Human Kinetics**
Web site: www.HumanKinetics.com

*United States:* Human Kinetics
P.O. Box 5076
Champaign, IL 61825-5076
800-747-4457
e-mail: humank@hkusa.com

*Canada:* Human Kinetics
475 Devonshire Road Unit 100
Windsor, ON N8Y 2L5
800-465-7301 (in Canada only)
e-mail: info@hkcanada.com

*Europe:* Human Kinetics
107 Bradford Road
Stanningley
Leeds LS28 6AT, United Kingdom
+44 (0) 113 255 5665
e-mail: hk@hkeurope.com

*Australia:* Human Kinetics
57A Price Avenue
Lower Mitcham, South Australia 5062
08 8372 0999
e-mail: info@hkaustralia.com

*New Zealand:* Human Kinetics
P.O. Box 80
Torrens Park, South Australia 5062
0800 222 062
e-mail: info@hknewzealand.com

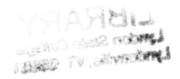

E4836

To Mom—you are missed!

Jackie

In memory of my Aunt Edna Epstein, for always making me
feel so special! In memory of my parents, Joseph and Lois
Fortman, who were always my greatest fans and supporters.

Mary

# Contents

# Preface

After years of teaching others how to assess, we have concluded that learning how to assess is not so much a discrete experience with distinct starting and finishing points; it is, rather, a journey. In fact, the more we learn about assessment, the more complex we recognize it to be. We published our first book on performance-based assessment 8 years ago. Since that time, we have continued on our personal assessment journeys and we wish to share some of our insights with you in this second edition of the book. We know that learning how to assess is not an easy journey. However, we feel that this book will provide you with guidelines for developing assessments that are practical and useful to those of you who are teaching the next generation how to be physically active.

This book is governed by the following beliefs:

• The primary purpose of assessment should be to enhance student learning. Assessments provide feedback to students, letting them know what they have accomplished and where they still have work to do. Assessments that enhance student learning are not punitive but positive; teachers and students should use them as they work together toward a goal of competence.

• Assessment should not be considered a separate entity but rather it is a part of instruction, woven into the instructional process. The best instruction includes assessments that help document student learning and let teachers know their next steps for teaching. Assessments that are not a part of instruction do not support the belief expressed in the previous item—that the primary purpose of assessment is to enhance student learning.

• Teachers must use a variety of assessment tools in order to accurately measure student learning. Learning is different for each activity. One assessment instrument cannot or should not be used exclusively. Assessments used for a dance unit, for example, are different from those used in a soccer unit. Teachers need to look at movement in different ways depending on the content being taught. Teacher educators must prepare their students to use appropriate assessments for various types of learning.

• Learning should be assessed in a variety of ways to develop a complete picture of student achievement. One-shot testing can give a distorted picture of students' abilities. Students should have as many opportunities as possible to demonstrate what they know and can do. It is only when teachers look at student achievement from a variety of perspectives and through several different lenses that they grasp a full understanding of what their students have learned.

• Doing good assessment requires a lot of hard work. Assessments must be planned prior to the start of instruction and implemented at several intervals during a unit. Each assessment should be examined and the information gained from the assessment used to help increase student learning. Preparing good assessments takes a lot of time and energy.

• Doing assessment well is worth the effort! Nothing is more satisfying than observing the change in a youngster or young adult who enters a class unable to perform a certain skill or activity but experiences success at the completion of the unit. Assessments administered during instruction keep both the teacher and the student focused on the ultimate goal of competence and are worth every single minute spent doing them.

Our combined 26 years of experience in public schools taught us about the problems that physical educators face while working in the trenches. We try addressing these problems as we discuss various assessment formats in this book. Obstacles such as large class size, poorly skilled students, and time shortages can make it difficult to do assessments—but not impossible. The examples offered in this book are meant to be modified for your own situation. Assessing students must be a highly contextualized endeavor. Our descriptions of how to do assessments will help you make the necessary changes to implement the assessment in your gymnasium, with your students. We present our ideas as a starting point and challenge you to take the plunge into assessment-based teaching. To help get you started, we provide models of continuous performance-based assessment in chapters 7, 8, 9, and 10.

You will also find additional forms and charts to use with performance-based assessments on the enclosed CD-ROM. The CD-ROM also includes all of the material marked with a CD-ROM icon in the book. To see the complete contents for the CD-ROM, view the start page on the CD-ROM.

Grant Wiggins offers the following advice: "Nothing worth understanding is mastered the first time, the first year, or the first course of study" (Wiggins 1998a, 15). We encourage you to use this philosophy as you begin changing your assessment practices. Change takes time, good change takes even longer. You will no doubt at times experience frustration when things do not work as they should. However, if you keep working at the process that we present in this book, you will begin to experience satisfaction as you see how assessment can enhance instruction. We encourage you to begin your journey to change your assessment practices with small steps. Thinking big but starting small makes the task both worthwhile and possible. Remember that improvement entails change and if you want to be a better teacher, changing assessment practices is one way to accomplish your goal. It won't be easy, but you can do it.

We hope that you enjoy this book and that it encourages you to expand your assessment horizons. The power of assessment came alive for one of us during a field experience involving a preservice elementary classroom teacher. After teaching a series of lessons, the prospective teacher arranged assessments to show students how much they had progressed. At the conclusion of her lesson, she spoke of her success and finished by stating: "I never realized how motivational assessment could be." Her high rate of time on task and the excitement generated when students could see evidence of their progress was a huge *aha!* moment for her. We encourage you to make a similar discovery and become just as excited about the instructional potential that effective assessment holds. We wish you good luck on your new assessment adventure!

# Acknowledgments

Many thanks to our friends, colleagues, and families who have supported us throughout this project. Bill, thanks for all the love and support you have provided during my latest assessment adventure. Jan Montague, thanks for your encouragement, patience, and understanding, and for taking on my share of the "household chores."

Additionally, we'd like to recognize many individuals for the following contributions:

Our colleagues, who inspire and challenge us

Margaret Pentecost and Darren Clay, who contributed assessment examples

Tara Scanlan and her students, who created the brochure for chapter 2

Our students and student teachers, who have taught us much about assessment and who continue to challenge and inspire us

Our cooperating teachers, who have shared information about the assessment process

# Introduction to Performance-Based Assessment

This section gives an overview of performance-based assessment and introduces some of the terminology used throughout the book. Performance-based assessments can enhance student learning when teachers systematically measure student ability to apply the skills, knowledge, and dispositions that they are taught in class. This type of assessment can be used as both formative and summative assessments, allowing teachers to focus on student learning in new and exciting ways.

# The Need for Change

*It is not our classroom assessments that draw all of the news coverage and editorial comment. All the visibility and political power honors go to our large-scale standardized tests. Nevertheless, anyone who has taught knows that it is classroom assessments—not standardized tests—that provide the energy that fuels the teaching and learning engine. For this reason, our classroom assessments absolutely must be of high quality (Stiggins 1997, vi).*

One of the purposes of education is to prepare students to be successful as adults. A school's curriculum and its system for delivering instruction must be attuned to the society for which its students are being prepared so that they develop the skills and knowledge needed to negotiate the pathways and pitfalls that they will encounter as adults. If there is one word to describe today's world, that word is probably *change*.

The changing world has dictated that schools must do things differently to prepare students for a globalized economy. It is no longer possible for a student to memorize all the facts needed for success as an adult. Students need skills that allow them to access information and apply it in their own situations. The Internet has led to the creation of a huge network of information that allows users to research everything from academic topics to installing a floor for a do-it-yourself remodeling project. Physical education teachers can access many Web sites that show lesson plans and assessments for teaching almost any sport or activity, and students can see videos of professional athletes performing a wide variety of sport skills and providing instruction on the finer points of performance. The available information is almost limitless; the problem becomes one of deciding whether a given piece of information is accurate or misleading.

Collaboration (typically called teamwork in physical education and sport) is also a valued skill. Many of the projects that adults undertake are too complex to be completed by a single individual. Although the ability to support and work with others is invaluable, the extensive use of computers in schools often discourages the development of this skill.

# THE CALL FOR CHANGE IN PHYSICAL EDUCATION

The global economy has led to academic comparisons between the achievement levels of students from various countries. Comparing the performance of children from the United States with those of children in other countries has been a primary factor fueling the educational reform efforts in the United States. Although many factors have contributed to calls for change in education, some seem more significant than others. In the early 1980s, a report titled *A Nation at Risk* was issued that stated that the country's educational system was in serious decline (National Commission on Excellence in Education 1983). Some students were unable to perform basic functions that were assumed to be standard for capable high school graduates, such as the ability to read, write, and solve math problems. A high school diploma, in some cases, merely represented "seat time"—that is, students had attended school for enough days to satisfy attendance requirements while acquiring rather minimal knowledge and skills. For some students, a diploma simply meant that the student had attended school for 12 years.

Those in power began calling for the establishment of standards in many subject areas after reports critical of education were issued. "The major reason that national and state leaders have coalesced around the need for defining content and student performance standards is that the quality of American education must be improved, and the current system of relying on local decision-making power over curriculum is failing to bring about that improvement" (Jennings 1995, 768). Surprisingly, the call for reform did not originate with educational leaders. Rather, people from the world of business noted a lack of skills and called for the establishment of accountability to increase the quality of education; thus, they were calling for a business model to govern educational policy. In response to these criticisms, national content organizations put together teams to write standards in subject areas such as math, social studies, science, and language arts. In 1995, standards for physical education were released in a National Association for Sport and Physical Education (NASPE) publication titled *Moving Into the Future: National Standards for Physical Educa-*

*tion: A Guide to Content and Assessment.* These physical education standards were accepted by many states while others used them as the basis for state physical education standards. The standards were revised in 2004 (see figure 1.1).

So what are standards in relation to education? The term *standards* generally represents the minimal amount of information that all students should know and be able to do in relation to a given subject. When people use the term standards they are typically talking about either content standards or performance standards. **Content standards** specify what students should know and be able to do (National Association for Sport and Physical Education 2004). They "establish what should be learned in various subjects . . . [and] emphasis is apt to be on learning content more through critical thinking and problem solving strategies than through rote learning of discrete facts" (Lewis 1995, 746). Content standards incorporate the most important and enduring ideas that represent the knowledge and skills necessary to the specified discipline. The NASPE physical education standards are content standards, as are most state standards.

---

A physically educated person:

1. Demonstrates competency in motor skills and movement patterns needed to perform a variety of physical activities.
2. Demonstrates understanding of movement concepts, principles, strategies, and tactics as they apply to the learning and performance of physical activities.
3. Participates regularly in physical activity.
4. Achieves and maintains a health-enhancing level of physical fitness.
5. Exhibits responsible personal and social behavior that respects self and others in physical activity settings.
6. Values physical activity for health, enjoyment, challenge, self-expression, and/or social interaction.

**Figure 1.1**   Content standards in physical education.

Based on NASPE, 2004, *Moving into the future: National standards for physical education*, 2nd ed. (Reston, VA: National Association for Sport and Physical Education).

**Performance standards**, on the other hand, seek to answer the question "How good is good enough?" They define a satisfactory *level* of learning (Lewis 1995). A performance standard indicates both the nature of the evidence that is acceptable for documenting student achievement and the quality of student performance that is necessary to satisfy the performance standard. Grant Wiggins (1998a) uses the high jump to illustrate the difference between content and performance standards (see figure 1.2). If one thinks of the high jump as the content standard, then the performance standard is where the teacher places the bar. Jumping a bar placed at 3 feet is much less demanding than jumping one placed at 6 feet. Performance standards for physical education have not yet been written at the national level, but NASPE is developing assessments for each of its six national standards under a program called PE Metrics. The elementary assessments for standard 1 were released in 2008, and the assessments for the other standards and grade levels will follow.

The establishment of standards has given schools a way of comparing students' performance with a standard for learning rather than with the work of other students. In **standards-based instructional formats**, students are required to demonstrate competence in a variety of subject areas. With standards-based education it doesn't matter how well students perform in comparison each other because standards are criterion-referenced (based on a set standard) rather than **norm-referenced** (see figure 1.3). Many national achievement tests are norm-referenced. In physical education, FitnessGram is a criterion-referenced test while The President's Challenge is an example of a norm-referenced fitness test. Many of the standardized physical education skill tests from the 1960s and 1970s were norm-referenced. Norm-referenced tests tell teachers and administrators how the performances of students in a given school compare with those of others taking the same test.

Another form of norm-referenced testing is grading on a curve, wherein a student's performance is compared with the performances of other students. Since the standard set by the curve depends on performance, it can change what the teacher expects students to know. The use of a curve makes the goal for learning a moving target because the performances

**Figure 1.2** If one thinks of the high jump as the content standard, then the performance standard is where the teacher places the bar.

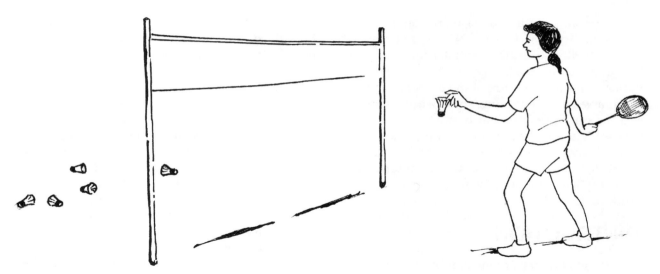

**Figure 1.3** In standards-based education, it doesn't matter how well students perform in comparison with others because standards are criterion-referenced (based on a set standard) rather than norm-referenced (based on comparison of one's performance with those of a certain population).

of other students determine the standard for a given student's learning. The best students get the best grades (e.g., top 5 percent) and the poorest students get the lowest grades (e.g., lowest 5 percent), but no one is really sure how much students learn. Comparing students with one another isn't always bad, especially when top student performances are of high quality. However, when student performance is not generally of a high caliber, comparing mediocre students with one another doesn't provide much information about their level of achievement.

Standards provide teachers with measuring sticks that they can use to assess students' learning more accurately and determine the additional work that students must do to reach the specified level of achievement. Standards make learning expectations clear to both students and teachers. When students are judged via a criterion-referenced score or standard, there is no limit to the number of students who can reach the goal. If the teacher sets a criterion score or standard for the badminton serve, all students who reach that standard have achieved the desired goal or developed the desired competence. It doesn't matter how they place in a rank ordering of the class because they are competing to meet a criterion-referenced score instead of against one another.

This paradigm represents a philosophical shift in the way many teachers plan and conduct classes because with a standards-based approach teachers select activities or sports so that students can meet the standards. The standards do not specify which sports or activities must be taught. Instead, they identify meaningful concepts that are important for being a physically educated individual.

## STANDARDS-BASED INSTRUCTION

This book focuses on improving students' learning and achievement in physical education through the use of **standards-based instruction** and performance-based assessments for students. In standards-based instruction, the teacher identifies unit goals based on state or national standards and uses these goals to set expectations for student learning. Assessments are developed based on these expectations prior to the start of instruction. Formative assessments are given regularly so that the teacher can determine students' progress toward final goals. When students are unable to reach the expectations for learning, teachers modify instruction to support student learning. The goal at the completion of the unit is that every child will meet the criteria for performance set prior to the beginning of the unit. Planning assessments before implementing the unit helps ensure that assessment is systematic and thorough. If teachers don't plan assessments ahead of time, they may end up doing it in a piecemeal manner or not at all. Chapters 7, 8, 9, and 10 provide examples of developing standards-based units of instruction and assessments that support student learning.

# TYPES OF ASSESSMENT IN STANDARDS-BASED INSTRUCTION

The standards movement has brought with it new ways to document student learning. For many years, schools were dominated by a behavioral approach, wherein a learning unit was divided into a series of tasks and learning was sequenced according to an accepted teaching progression. This approach to teaching is analogous to the assembly-line method of producing cars. The process begins with a frame, followed by the motor, then a body is added, the exterior shell, and so on. Assessment in this behavioral approach was focused on achievement of discrete skills and learning of factual knowledge (Lambert 2007). Many of the valid and reliable skill tests that exist for sport skills were developed between 1950 and 1970 (Strand and Wilson 1993). They focus on the evaluation of skills associated with a variety of sports and activities. The cognitive assessments associated with this model were typically selected-response questions (e.g., true-false, matching, multiple-choice) that measured students' recall of information rather than requiring them to think critically. The emphasis was on the parts of the game—not the whole.

Some educational researchers found this approach lacking and began experimenting with a different methodology. In the early 1990s a constructivist approach to learning began to be widely accepted. With the constructivist approach a student's individuality is recognized as well as a need for the student to make sense of information and link it to prior learning. Facts memorized for a test will quickly be forgotten if they are not applied and reinforced. These tests typically measure knowledge and comprehen-

sion, which are lower levels of learning. Educators who take a constructivist approach value higher-level thinking in students. The need to document this different type of learning (i.e., application rather than recall of information) led educators to develop new, alternative forms of assessment. Grant Wiggins (1989b) called for the use of authentic tests that approximate tasks done by people in the real world. Performance-based assessment is closely associated with both the standards movement and the need for students to measure application of knowledge while demonstrating mastery of content material. Because much of physical education is already based on observable performance or behavior, physical educators have been very comfortable with using these new forms of assessment.

Two instructional models are quite compatible with the constructivist philosophy of education. The first, Teaching Games for Understanding (TGfU), emphasizes game play and game-play strategies over skill development. Games are classified into four types: invasion games, net or wall games, target games, or field games. In this instructional model students are engaged in a game from one of the four categories to learn strategies that are important to success in that game category. When a new skill is needed with which to work on a more complex strategy, the skill is introduced within the context of the game. Thus students are able to see how the skill is used during the game and construct their knowledge of the skill in an applied setting. The second model, Sport Education, also emphasizes achievement in an applied setting. Students are divided into teams at the beginning of the unit and then learn various roles considered essential to playing the game. Team roles can include coach, fitness trainer, equipment manager, statistician, and publicist. When engaged in a tournament, students who are not playing in the game are assigned to duty-team roles such as referee, line official, scorekeeper, and timer. Both the TGfU and Sport Education models emphasize the application of skill in an authentic setting instead of only skill development as measured by a skill test.

Performance-based assessments are compatible with either of these two instructional models as well as other instructional models common to physical education because they focus on application of skill and knowledge. Performance-based assessments are also compatible with the standards movement. Lambert defines **standards-based assessment** as "the process of determining whether and to what degree a student can demonstrate, in context, his or her understanding and ability relative to identified standards of learning (2007, 12; emphasis in original). If students are to demonstrate their understanding and knowledge, some type of observable action or tangible product is required. Although traditional forms of assessment can be part of the assessment process, standards-based assessments involve students doing something to process the information and being assessed using predetermined criteria rather than just selecting a correct answer or achieving a certain score on a skill test.

The alternative assessments discussed in this book are referred to as **performance-based assessments**. Many authors use this term interchangeably with **alternative assessment** and **authentic assessment** (Herman, Aschbacher, and Winters 1992), while others (Marzano, Pickering, and McTighe 1993) use these terms to define different types of assessment. In this book, the terms are used synonymously. Performance-based assessments require students to generate rather than select a response (Herman, Aschbacher, and Winters 1992). They include two essential parts—the performance tasks or exercises that students are asked to do and the criteria by which the product or performance will be judged. Although some authors have made a rather liberal interpretation of the term *performance-based assessment*, this book uses a more conservative definition that requires the assessment to be complex and to involve integrative tasks to determine whether students have reached desired outcomes or standards. The key elements or dimensions of performance are called performance criteria. Clear criteria are essential to the assessment process.

Teachers should not confuse performance-based assessments with assessments of performance. Performance-based assessments are complex and often measure learning in more than one domain. In contrast, skill tests, such as those used to measure students' competence in a sport skill, are considered assessments of performance but not performance-based assessments.

# EFFECT ON TEACHING WHEN STANDARDS ARE USED

When many teachers plan instruction, they target students with average abilities. Standards-based learning means that all students will achieve a stated level of competence. Those students who are more capable should be expected to achieve more than is required by the standards. The following are key tenets of standards-based instruction:

- Set goals for instruction that identify what students should know and be able to do.
- Plan units so that every child can learn.
- Inform students about the criteria for evaluation.
- Develop assessments and instruction that work together.
- Connect assessment with real-world tasks.
- Identify an audience outside the realm of the school.
- Use assessments to document students' ability to apply learning and demonstrate higher-level thinking skills.

The next section discusses ways that standards-based learning can change the methods that teachers use when planning for and delivering instruction to students.

## Determining Goals for Instruction

Many beginning teachers plan lessons on a day-to-day basis, resulting in lessons that may keep students engaged but lack a sense of purpose or learning. Such lessons resemble children's exploration of the interesting sights and sounds of the neighborhood as they make their way home instead of walking directly from point A to point B. People following either path arrive at the same destination, but the person on the direct path gets there in far less time. When teachers focus on a final learning goal or outcome, they design lesson content to reach that destination directly and stay clear of extraneous activity that can be confusing to students and irrelevant to the final goal (see figure 1.4).

**Figure 1.4** When teachers know where they are headed, students' paths to learning are much more direct.

With standards-based instruction, teachers begin the planning process by identifying what students should ultimately know and be able to do. Lesson planning with standards-based instruction begins with establishing solid educational goals and then developing assessments that measure whether these goals are met. By clearly defining what the final outcomes or products should look like, the teacher can build all instruction around getting students to reach these goals. Teachers choose criteria for meeting these goals before instruction starts and inform students of the final objectives and activities so that students can work purposefully toward fulfilling the established goals. Teachers use a technique referred to as **backward mapping** to plan instruction by looking at what they ultimately intend to accomplish and then determining the best path for getting there. When teachers consider the impact that an instructional task has on reaching the goals for the unit, they avoid frivolous lessons and focus instead on those activities that contribute to student learning.

One example of choosing activities before identifying goals was witnessed by one of this book's authors when a group of preservice teachers was planning a badminton unit. One young man, a baseball coach, had access to a radar gun. His planned badminton lesson revolved around using the radar gun to time the speed of badminton strokes by beginning students. Although this might serve as a novel way to motivate advanced players, it is an inappropriate approach for students who are just learning the game. After considering his goals for the unit, the teacher candidate changed the lesson to one that emphasized the process or correct form of the stroke rather than racket speed.

In standards-based assessment, the unit goal is selected first. Unit activities that will lead to students reaching that goal are chosen next. Activities that do not contribute to student learning are not included in the unit. All instruction is built around helping students reach criteria for student learning established by the teacher.

In secondary schools, many teachers want students to be competent in game play, dance, or some other movement form. Teachers define what competence means through assessments and the criteria established for them. Because teachers identify ahead of time what students must know and be able to do to demonstrate competence in a unit, teachers create a clear picture of the final outcome or product. By clearly identifying the assessments and criteria, teachers are forced to think through the teaching and learning process, making lessons purposeful and meaningful for students.

## Planning Units

Even in ideal teaching conditions (with small classes and adequate time, equipment, and teaching space), students would not have enough time to learn every sport or activity found in physical education classes. For this reason, teachers must carefully select activity and sport units that help their students meet the standards that define a physically educated person (see table 1.1). Additionally, because of the limited time available to teach physical education, teachers cannot afford to waste any time during class. Too many teachers go to convention sessions to get new ideas for lesson activities without

**Table 1.1**   Differences in Planning Between Traditional and Standards-Based Assessment

| Traditional assessment | Standards-based assessment |
| --- | --- |
| Select the activity or unit (e.g., dance, badminton). | Select a goal or target; it may already be selected for you. |
| Determine goals. | Precisely define the targeted standards and indicators. |
| Decide what will be taught. | Choose an appropriate course of study. |
| Assess. | Determine how you will know whether the standards have been met (i.e., assessment). |
| Move to the next unit. | Write the rubric. |
| | Choose an activity. |
| | Practice continuous assessment and instruction to reach the goal or target. |

considering whether it contributed to curricular or unit goals. Teachers need to be wise consumers of new ideas and ensure that any new ideas are aligned with standards-based goals.

When planning lessons, some teachers plan to spend a certain amount of time teaching a skill (e.g., teach the set on day 1, teach the forearm pass on day 2, teach the service on day 3, and play volleyball on day 4). Time is not the key factor in deciding what to teach; student learning is the primary consideration. Some students may need additional or remedial instruction, while others learn skills quickly. Assessment for student learning can help teachers make appropriate decisions regarding the allocation of time for teaching the skills and knowledge necessary for student success.

## Informing Students of Criteria

When practicing standards-based instruction, teachers inform students of the evaluation criteria. When teachers clarify what they want students to know and be able to do as a result of instruction, they eliminate guessing games and give students a clearly defined target at which to aim. Students can then work toward reaching the established goals without the false starts and wasted effort that come from pursuing the wrong path due to confusion about the unit's primary goals.

These benefits were verified in a high school class during a badminton unit. In this study, the teacher informed students about the assessments she would use and the level of performance they would be expected to achieve at the beginning of instruction (Shanklin 2004). Because the students knew the criteria in advance, they were able to work toward meeting them. Students of all skill levels demonstrated dramatic improvement (e.g., increasing the number of strokes performed with correct form) with the lower-skilled students showing strong gains with their responses. Students in the control class that did not have prior knowledge about how they would be assessed showed only slight improvement using the same drills and activities.

## Linking Assessment to Instruction

Many physical education teachers complain that assessment requires too much time to complete, especially with large classes. With performance-based assessment, instruction and assessment are linked. For example, game play allows students to apply the information and skills learned during a unit and increase their levels of competence. While students are playing, the teacher can assess components such as students' knowledge of rules, use of strategy, selection and execution of psychomotor skills, and teamwork. By creating criteria for assessing various aspects of student performance, teachers can assess game-play skills while students continue to learn. Assessment results are used to provide feedback to students, enabling them to further enhance their performance. By the conclusion of the unit, students have achieved competence. When assessment is used to support instruction, students are more likely to achieve competence.

Teaching and assessment sometimes become so intertwined in performance-based assessment that it is impossible to distinguish between the two. Students have the opportunity to work on meaningful projects and tasks that are later assessed. For example, choreographing a dance allows students to apply knowledge of dance composition elements as they create different levels, shapes, and patterns of movement while combining various dance steps and locomotor movements. When the dance is completed, the teacher evaluates it to determine whether students understand and can apply the principles of choreography, while at the same time assessing their ability to dance. Thus the task is both a learning experience and a way to assess students' performances. Teachers could also use an affective-domain rubric to assess students' ability to work with one another while they are choreographing the dance. Because the students have the criteria, they can self-assess during the instructional process, and the role of the teacher changes to a more supportive one as he or she works to help every student reach the criteria established for the project.

## Making Real-World Connections

When teachers use standards-based assessments, they attempt to connect them with real-world tasks. For example, instead of taking a written test covering the rules of a game, students might demonstrate their knowledge of the sport by creating a coach's playbook, officiating a game, keeping statistics, or writing a report about the game (as a publicist would do in Sport Education). Since these assessments are perceived as meaningful, students are often willing to devote more time to complete them.

## Identifying the Audience

Naming a target audience gives the assessment a focus. Writers are constantly aware of their audience when they consider the purpose of a paper or product they are creating. Similarly, to make assessment more authentic, teachers should try, when possible, to identify an audience outside the realm of the school. An audience contributes to the meaningfulness of the

assessment and gives students an opportunity to extend their knowledge beyond the walls of the gymnasium. During the culminating round of game play, a teacher might invite parents or students from other classes to view the tournament. A real audience is always preferred, but a contrived audience can also help students focus their intent for the product and gear it to a more specific knowledge base. The dance rubric for the talent scout (figure 1.5) is an example of adding a real-world context to an assessment task.

## Dance Rubric

You are a talent scout looking for new pieces for an upcoming 10-city modern dance tour. Today, several dancers will be auditioning in hopes that you will select the dance they have choreographed for your tour. You are to watch the dancers perform and use the following criteria to evaluate their performance:

- The dance uses both locomotor and non-locomotor movements.
- The elements of good dance performance are present (e.g., force, time, space).
- The dance was well rehearsed and smoothly performed.
- Members of the group worked together.
- The dancers moved in time to the rhythm or musical accompaniment.
- The dancers demonstrated creativity in movement combinations.

A quantitative analytic rubric uses the following descriptors for rating the performance on each of the stated criteria:

0—No dance was performed.

1—The dance did not demonstrate this element.

2—The dance element was present some of the time.

3—The dance element was clearly present.

4—The use of this dance element was outstanding; it took your breath away.

**Figure 1.5**  Adding a real-world context to an assessment task makes the assessment more authentic.

**R**ecently, while teaching a badminton unit, I used skill tests to assess performance on some of the skills, along with performance-based assessments to measure playing ability, content knowledge, and affective-domain dispositions. At the end of the unit, I asked students which type of test best measured their abilities. The overwhelming response was that the performance-based assessments were better indicators of their ability to play the game than were the more traditional tests. Students preferred being evaluated with an assessment that provided opportunities to demonstrate multiple dimensions of skill and learning.

## Higher-Level Thinking Skills

Many written tests for physical education ask questions that evaluate knowledge or comprehension. **Bloom's taxonomy** (figure 1.6) identifies higher-order thinking skills that students use as their knowledge and learning become more complex. Standards-based instruction calls for the use of higher-order thinking skills—such as analysis, synthesis, and evaluation—and performance-based assessments provide students with an opportunity to develop and demonstrate these skills. For example, a game-play scouting assignment can develop a student's ability to analyze an opponent's strengths and weaknesses and synthesize or create plays to give his or her own team a playing advantage. Similarly, serving as a judge for a class gymnastics meet requires students to use established criteria to evaluate the performance and decide whether the desired characteristics were present.

## NEED FOR MORE ASSESSMENT IN PHYSICAL EDUCATION

In 1987, the American Federation of Teachers, the National Council on Measurement in Education, and the National Education Association published a set of standards for evaluating teachers' competence in conducting student assessment (Cunningham 1998). The standards were based on two fundamental assumptions: First, student assessment is a key part of a teacher's role. Teachers must determine, through evaluation, whether students have met the goals that the teacher has set for them. Second,

effective teaching and effective evaluation go together. Assessment should inform instruction and determine the pathways that teachers follow to make learning most effective. In other words, effective teachers use assessments to increase the quality of instruction.

Assessment is a key component of standards-based learning. Educators cannot merely say that a student has learned something or met a standard; district and state officials want proof. Providing documentation of student learning requires teachers to engage in some type of measurement. Increased testing of students to obtain this proof was inevitable in the standards movement because assessment was seen as essential for promoting change and educational reform. Administrators and those encouraging change wanted to document improvement in concrete ways rather than rely on subjective or anecdotal information.

The current No Child Left Behind (NCLB) legislation puts the focus on basic skills and knowledge that can be measured with a standardized test instead of using assessments that stem from a constructivist philosophy. Many of the NCLB assessments measure the type of learning that is popular with the behavioral strategies described earlier in this chapter. Although the current emphasis on academic achievement and the omission of physical education from the accountability formulas have led many administrators to shortchange the time allotted to physical education, NCLB has not regulated physical education, which means that teachers can change assessment practices and implement more performance-based assessments to measure student achievement.

Physical educators have not always done a good job of using assessments to document student learning. In 1987, approximately 1,400 physical educators (98 percent of the respondents) reported that participation was the most frequently used factor in determining student grades (Hensley et al. 1987). Slightly fewer than

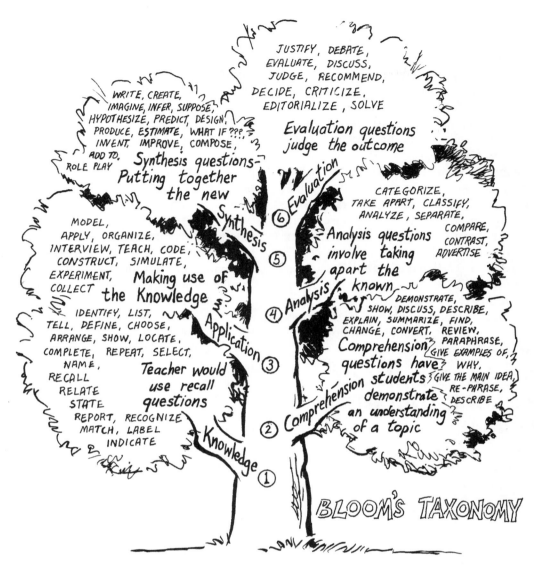

**Figure 1.6** Bloom's taxonomy. The level of student learning required for completing an assessment is impacted by the type of question asked and the verbs used when asking it.

half of those surveyed reported using written tests with their classes. Other subjective factors used to determine grades included attitude, effort, improvement, and potential. The article noted the heightened demand for accountability and the need to develop and use better evaluation techniques. The authors stated: "It is likely that the survival of our profession may, to some extent, depend on the efficacy of our measurement and evaluation efforts" (Hensley et al. 1987, 61). Despite this call for assessment reform some 20 years ago, many physical educators still rely on dressing for class and attendance data when calculating student grades.

Unfortunately, many new physical education teachers were socialized into the profession as students in physical education programs that did not use assessment to increase student learning. Those teachers have a difficult time envisioning an effective assessment system that works in tandem with instruction. It is critical that members of the next generation of physical education teachers learn to use assessment regularly in their classes to document student learning. As beginning teachers establish their instructional protocols, assessment must be woven into instruction so that it becomes a habitual routine.

Another reason for seeking to change the assessment paradigm in physical education is that some physical education teachers administer assessments only when they need to determine a grade. This use of assessment only for grading was exemplified when a student teacher was asked to administer skill tests during a field experience. She replied that she was unable to give skill tests because the district in which she was teaching required physical education teachers to grade students only on attendance and written tests. When assessments are viewed from this narrow perspective, they lose their potential to become powerful instructional tools. If physical education is to be considered a viable part of a school curriculum, teachers must ensure that it is taught with the same rigor and expectations for learning that are applied in other subjects. Holding physical education to a lesser standard diminishes its potential to contribute to students' education.

# ROLE OF ASSESSMENT IN PHYSICAL EDUCATION PROGRAMS

Assessments have many purposes in physical education programs. Physical education teachers can use them to do the following:

- Measure students' progress to plan future instruction
- Measure students' learning to show progress and motivate students
- Provide feedback to students
- Document program effectiveness
- Formalize the observation process
- Document students' learning for parents and administrators

Assessment can enhance instruction because it increases teachers' effectiveness. The following section explains how teachers can use assessment to improve the quality of their physical education programs.

## Plan Future Instruction

One of the current trends in educational assessment is to use assessment for learning. With this philosophy, formative assessments are used to improve student performance. Assessment for learning can help teachers identify gaps in students' learning and use the information to plan future lessons. Assessments let teachers know which concepts students have grasped and what needs to be presented again in a different manner.

Much of instruction tends to be progressive with each lesson building on the preceding one, thus moving students toward a teacher's final goal or outcome. For teachers, planning for the next lesson without measuring student progress is like trying to hit a target without knowing where to aim. Although physical education teachers are constantly watching student performance during instruction to provide feedback, without recording student performance, it is impossible for them to remember everything that students accomplish and determine whether all students are learning. This is not to imply that teachers must evaluate every student every day; with large classes, teachers must sometimes use systematic sampling procedures. If it is not possible to do an assessment of every student on every day, the teacher can use a system that looks at highly skilled students, average-skilled students, and low-skilled students on a rotating basis to gather evidence of what is happening in the class. Without some way to assess students and record results, determining the content for the next lesson is merely a guessing game.

## Measure Student Learning

For students, assessment provides a means of documenting progress. In the process of acquiring motor skills or learning how to play various sports, progress often occurs in minute steps. Progress can be slow, and students can become discouraged. This frustration is especially true for lower-skilled students, who may have difficulty learning motor activities, and a lack of success can lead to lack of motivation. Measuring progress along the way can motivate students because it allows them to see concrete evidence of their improvement; that is, assessments allow students to track their improvement and see their gains. Measurement becomes a powerful means for improving student learning.

## Provide Feedback

The primary reason to assess should be to give feedback to students about their progress toward meeting the learning goals set by the teacher and the program. Because of the overt nature of physical activity, teachers frequently give feedback verbally to students to help them improve their performance. Written feedback from assessments is more powerful than verbal feedback alone, because it signals to students that the material is important and that the teacher is holding the students accountable for learning it. For many students, if it is tested, it is considered important. Using written assessments to measure students' learning provides concrete feedback to students and informs them of what they must do to achieve mastery and competence. This feedback can be given either by the teacher or by other students using **peer assessments**.

## Document Program Effectiveness

It is no longer sufficient to say that students have learned simply because they have attended a given class (i.e., seat time). Accountability is currently a concern in education, and learning must be documented. People in charge (e.g., state officials, school board members, district superintendents, district curriculum specialists, principals) are held accountable by states for documenting students' learning. Therefore, assessment and record keeping are no longer just options; they are necessary.

As academic requirements increase, physical educators must be prepared to justify the time that students spend on physical activity in a school curriculum. Classes must be educative rather than recreational, and learning must be documented. School leaders are not asked to show direct evidence of effective teaching; instead, effective teaching is determined by seeing evidence of students' achievement. Physical educators must be prepared to document students' learning by using appropriate assessments if the field is to survive in today's educational climate.

Although physical education has not been held accountable through a rigorous testing format like that found in math, reading, or science, it has faced accountability in terms of decreasing physical education requirements for secondary students. Many states have decreased the high school graduation requirement for physical education. According to a 1996 surgeon general's report, only 25 percent of all high school stu-

dents are enrolled in physical education classes (U.S. Department of Health and Human Services 1996). Illinois and Massachusetts are the only states with a K–12 physical education requirement, and Illinois (which does allow exemptions) is the only state to mandate daily K–12 physical education (National Association for Sport and Physical Education 2006). Additionally, even without a K-12 mandate, one-third of the states allow exemptions or waivers regarding physical education time requirements. One-half of the states allow students to substitute other activities for physical education, and one-quarter offer online physical education (National Association for Sport and Physical Education 2006).

## Formalize the Observation Process

Physical education teachers have used observation for years to provide feedback to students. Assessments give teachers a means of recording this feedback and documenting students' performance to help both teacher and students during future lessons. When they use assessments, teachers have records, or proof, with which to document students' improvement and achievement to parents and administrators. Informal (unwritten) feedback can be fleeting and is not always accurate. By formalizing observation, teachers can concretely identify student behaviors that they sensed were occurring but could not necessarily document. In addition, when a teacher watches a class systematically during an assessment, it may become evident that not all students are participating equally. Some aggressive students may take more opportunities than passive students to respond. Similarly, students who play certain positions may have more opportunities than others to respond (e.g., In softball, compare the number of responses for a right fielder with those for a catcher). Sometimes competent bystanders appear to be engaged and on task, but when viewed through an assessment lens, they rarely have opportunities to respond (Tousignant 1981).

## Inform Others

Assessments of learning are summative assessments used for determining a grade thus providing a way to inform parents and administrators about students' achievement. Grades are probably the most common use of assessment. At the secondary level, physical education teachers are usually required to give students a grade, which is meant to symbolize the degree to which students have met either the teacher's or the program's learning objectives. Grading is an important function of assessment, and teachers must use certain methods to ensure that it is done validly and reliably. The grade should represent the student's learning and should be determined in the same manner for all students. Chapter 11 discusses grading in depth.

# THE SWITCH TO PERFORMANCE-BASED ASSESSMENT

For many years, the only types of assessment taught to physical education majors in test and measurement classes—and then used in physical education classes—were skill tests, fitness tests, and written tests that consisted of selected-response questions. Many beginning teachers had only these tools in their rather limited arsenals as they started their first teaching job. As a young teacher, I struggled with wanting to assess differently but not knowing how. My students would do well on skill tests and written tests but couldn't play the game. I was frustrated but didn't know how to fix the problem. In some physical education classes, the goal was simply for students to pass the tests. Instead of being the means to an accomplished performance, the tests became the final performance or the outcome of instruction. Although this was not the case for me, the available assessment tools still fell short of measuring what I wanted my students to learn.

My introduction to performance-based assessment was like letting a person with asthma breathe pure oxygen—I finally had the means to assess what I had wanted to assess all along. I hope your journey through this book will be equally enlightening, especially if your prior experience has primarily involved using traditional assessment, or even no assessment.

Because several books are available that explain how to develop written tests and administer skill and fitness tests, this book does not delve into those areas. Each of those tests does have a place in improving student learning if used appropriately. The purpose of this book,

however, is to focus on performance-based assessments and to encourage teachers to start incorporating them into their assessment repertoires. It is not suggested that teachers abandon all other types of assessment but rather start integrating these new assessments with the old. Although some physical education teachers do a good job of using assessment to augment learning in their classes, many teachers could improve their current practices. This next section points out some of the shortcomings of traditional assessments so that teachers can see how performance-based assessment can help them assess the types of student learning that they want students to achieve.

## Written Tests

Many of the written tests used in physical education measure basic knowledge of rules and definitions. The questions evaluate students' recall of knowledge and sometimes their comprehension (levels 1 and 2 of Bloom's taxonomy, respectively). It is difficult to write questions that assess the upper levels of Bloom's taxonomy, which is probably why most teachers don't include them on written tests. Although it is important for students to know basic facts, it is also important for them to know other things related to skill performance. Performance-based assessments can be used to determine students' ability to use knowledge that has been presented in class in an applied setting. They typically require students to use higher-order thinking skills.

Written tests offer an effective way to measure students' knowledge and comprehension, especially when teachers have large classes. If teachers want to make sure that students know basic safety procedures before allowing them to hit real golf balls, a written test can verify this information. When developing written questions, teachers should avoid tests that cover only the handout provided for the class. Teachers present a wealth of information in a unit of instruction, and written tests are a way to hold students responsible for listening to instructions and learning. Teachers should also avoid questions that focus on basic facts (e.g., court dimensions and net height) that are memorized for the test. Instead, written tests should cover important information that students should know 20 years from now, such as the basic rules, strategies, and techniques of a game or activity. Performance-based assessments can complement these written tests and help teachers determine whether students can use information in an applied context.

## Fitness Tests

Many physical education teachers administer fitness tests every fall and spring, only to let the results sit on the shelf for the remainder of the year. Fitness test results can tell teachers whether students are fit or unfit and thus can be used in planning future lessons. For example, if the members of a class generally have poor flexibility, then a yoga or gymnastics unit might be taught. Unless teachers use the results of fitness testing to improve students' learning, testing should not be done. Fitness tests are also a good complement to performance-based assessments that require students to create an improvement or maintenance plan based on personal fitness test results. This type of assignment can be helpful to students not only at the present time but also when they become adults. Figure 1.7 discusses some appropriate uses of fitness tests.

## Skill Tests

Skill tests, can be used as part of the instructional process as they typically require students to perform skills in a closed environment. When students are given skill tests and told the criteria, they can practice the targeted skills and show dramatic improvement. Still, skill tests should be viewed not as an end in themselves but as a means to an end (i.e., the ability to use skills in a game). If skill assessments are used, it is recommended that teachers use a mastery approach and allow students several opportunities to pass them (see chapter 11 for an explanation). This approach eliminates the issue of a student having a bad day and producing a substandard performance on a one-shot assessment. If students see the skill assessments early in the unit, they can practice them during non-instructional time (i.e., before class begins or while others are engaged in game play). Additionally, teachers can build drills and skill practices around testing protocols.

Many standardized skill tests are onerous to administer when normative tables are used for scoring. They are time-consuming to set up

## Appropriate Uses of Fitness Tests

• A teacher uses test results from various classes to determine which units to teach. For example, if students are not meeting flexibility standards, then the teacher might include units on gymnastics, dance, and martial arts in the program. Similarly, students with little upper-body strength might benefit from gymnastics and strength training with medicine balls and Dyna-Bands.

• A teacher organizes testing stations so that the assessment can be completed in 2 days. Parents or student aides who have been taught the test protocols monitor the stations to ensure that the test is administered correctly. Students use their test results to set goals for health-related fitness.

• Students are tested by adults or trained test administrators during the fall and spring. Test results are used to set goals for students to improve their level of fitness. Students have an opportunity to self-test during the year (every 4 to 6 weeks), completing the entire battery of tests in 1 day, to determine whether their efforts are helping them reach their personal goals or whether their goals or workout plans need adjustment (i.e., made either more or less demanding).

• A teacher provides test results to parents, along with activity suggestions for helping each child improve his or her current fitness level. The teacher also includes activity log sheets and encourages parents to monitor their child's weekly participation in various physical activities by signing the log sheet.

• Students learn how to self-administer fitness tests and use this ability to assess the fitness levels of family members. The students' knowledge of fitness is used to encourage the family to become more active by participating in those activities that will help increase current fitness levels.

**Figure 1.7**  Fitness tests are a good complement to performance-based assessments.

and administer when test protocol is followed. For instance, if a volleyball serving test is to be valid, the net must be set at an exact height, which presents problems in schools with unofficial equipment; in addition, the server must stand at a certain distance from the net, and the ball must fall within certain zones in the opposite court. Some standardized tests are not developmentally appropriate for children, since weaker students have insufficient strength to perform the skill as described in the assessment and thus end up with a score of zero, which is more representative of their strength than of their ability to play the sport (French et al. 1991).

Although skill tests do have their place—measuring students' performance of skills that are necessary for game play—some teachers do not use them effectively in the instructional process. Figure 1.8 presents examples of how skill tests are used *in*effectively.

Skill assessments are useful for documenting students' performance of the discrete skills involved in a game, whereas game-play assessments require students to use the skills in a real-life environment. When performance-based assessments and skill assessments are used together, a complete picture of student achievement is possible.

The authors do not claim that performance-based assessments will cure all of the problems associated with assessment in physical education. However, when used appropriately, performance-based assessments can address many of the concerns detailed in this chapter.

# CONCLUSION

Education is usually a reflection of society. Just as society is experiencing great change today, reformers are calling for change in the educational system as well. New criteria are being written to specify what students should know and be able to do, and reformers are urging the development of better methods of teaching and assessing. Accountability is being mandated for both teachers and students, and much of the pressure is coming from groups outside the field of education. If physical education is going to survive, changes in current assessment practices need to occur to enhance its status with other educators, as well as with students, parents, and administrators.

Many of these needs can be addressed through performance-based assessments, which differ from traditional assessments in that they require students to actively apply

## Ineffective Uses of Skill Tests

• Teachers typically administer skill and written tests at the completion of the unit, which makes the tests summative. Since instruction is completed, any feedback gleaned from the test about deficiencies in students' learning or performance is not used in the instructional process.

• Teachers show test protocols to students for the first time on the same day that the testing is completed. This approach gives students no chance to practice and improve their performance of those skills under testing conditions.

• If a teacher uses skill tests as part of a student's grade and the student has a bad day on the date of the tests, his or her grade for the unit suffers. Thus, even despite stellar performances in other parts of the unit, poor test scores can adversely affect the student's grade.

• Teachers don't always explain what they are looking for in skill tests. For instance, one teacher was observed skill-testing the volleyball set and forearm pass by giving students 10 chances to return a tossed ball to him. Students assumed that the number of balls returned to the teacher determined their score. When interviewed after the testing, the teacher revealed that he was evaluating process, or correct form, and 10 opportunities gave him ample chance to determine a given student's ability. The number of balls returned successfully had nothing to do with the final grade.

**Figure 1.8**   Unless properly administered, skill tests do not assess students' learning or achievement.

their skills and knowledge while performing a meaningful task. This chapter outlined the benefits of using performance-based assessments; it also pointed out ways to avoid problems that can occur while using them. This book is designed to help physical educators incorporate performance-based assessment into their instructional formats. By understanding the advantages of using performance-based assessment—and learning how to do so effectively—physical educators can incorporate new instructional tools into their programs for both assessment and learning.

Students must be given choices in what they learn and how they demonstrate their learning. Current assessment practices must change, shifting the focus from the evaluation of learning to the enhancement of it. Many good programs have a difficult time demonstrating that they do meaningful work. Assessment is the key to making positive changes in physical education programs—and documenting those changes.

# What Is Continuous Performance-Based Assessment?

*In our concern for the well-being of students, however, we must not make the mistake of lowering our academic standards merely to make school easy. On the contrary, a classroom environment centered on each student's academic well-being must hold those students accountable for the attainment of high academic standards that are both clearly articulated and not negotiable. . . . Just trying hard, while critical for success, is not enough. Our classroom assessments should define for students precisely what we expect of them—they must define the truly important achievement targets (Stiggins 1997, vi).*

With various parties—state officials, school board members, district superintendents, district curriculum specialists, and principals—holding teachers accountable for documenting students' learning, assessments play an important role in the educational process. Failure to document learning leaves a program vulnerable to the claim that little is actually learned in physical education classes. Thus, if physical education is to be considered a legitimate part of a school curriculum, physical educators must develop effective ways to document students' learning. Because few

states have adopted statewide assessments for physical education, it often falls to individual teachers or district-level curriculum specialists in physical education to decide which assessments provide the best indication of students' learning.

Because physical education typically involves a performance rather than a concrete product or artifact, documenting learning in physical education can be problematic. For many years, physical educators relied on three types of tests for assessing students: written, fitness, and skill. Written tests usually consisted of selected-response questions (multiple-choice, true-false, matching), fill-in-the-blank questions, or short-answer essay questions. Questions typically assessed recall or factual knowledge (i.e., Who invented basketball? What is a foul? When was volleyball invented?) but did not ask students to apply this information. Skill tests measured individual skills in a controlled or closed environment but did not look at a student's ability to apply or combine skills during game play. Fitness tests (e.g., Fitnessgram, President's Council on Physical Fitness, local or district fitness assessment) measured health-related or motor skill fitness.

Classroom teachers also had difficulty with selected-response questions. Too often, students who scored well on selected-response items were unable to use the information in a real-world setting. Higher-levels of thinking—identified in Blooms' taxonomy as analysis, synthesis, and evaluation—were often not required of students when teachers used selected-response questions to evaluate students. In particular, classroom teachers had difficulty with selected-response questions.

In 1989, Grant Wiggins outlined several alternative types of assessment in an article titled "A True Test: Toward More Authentic and Equitable Assessment" (1989a). Wiggins proposed that students be required to apply information in a more performance-based type of assessment. Specifically, he proposed having students do tasks and solve problems similar to those that adults face in everyday life. According to Wiggins, testing should represent central experiences in learning and give students an opportunity to showcase their learning in areas where they should be competent. With Wiggins' proposed assessments, students complete real-world tasks, requiring them to know facts and understand concepts well enough to apply them. The culminating event or performance would consist of a task similar to those used in the field that represents mastery of a body of knowledge. As noted assessment authority Richard Stiggins has observed, "Performance assessments can be based on observations of process while skills are being demonstrated, or on the evaluation of products created" (1997, 77).

Wiggins and McTighe (1998) identified three basic types of assessment: quiz and test items, academic **prompts**, and performance tasks and projects. Assessments can be placed on a continuum (see figure 2.1). At one end are selected-response tests, which have a single correct answer and give the teacher a good deal of control. At the other end are performance-based assessments that evaluate learning while giving students choice in how they wish to demonstrate mastery or competence. Performance-based assessments often incorporate human judgment into the evaluation process. Along with assessing student learning, performance-based assessments are designed to increase students' interest and prepare students for life after school. Of course, teachers must provide parameters and guidelines for assessments in which students are given more choice, but students have input and freedom about how they choose to approach their final product and performance. Part III of

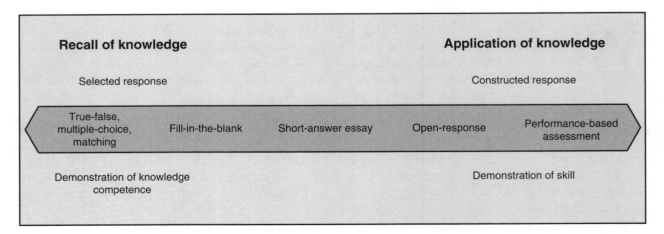

**Figure 2.1**   Assessments can be placed on a continuum.

this book gives numerous examples of performance-based assessments that demonstrate how such assessments can be woven into a unit of instruction in order to measure learning.

# CHARACTERISTICS OF PERFORMANCE-BASED ASSESSMENT

Performance-based assessments are typically open-ended, complex, and authentic. They are used in units that are long enough to allow in-depth learning. Although they require more time to administer, they can be combined with instruction to enhance students' performance. Performance-based assessments give teachers new ways to look at student achievement; figure 2.2 presents characteristics typically associated with performance-based assessment in physical education (Lund 1997).

Performance-based assessments satisfy many of the changes specified in reports calling for educational reform. The following are the key components of performance-based assessment. A thorough understanding of these characteristics will help teachers begin to develop their own assessment tasks.

## Worthwhile Tasks

Observation of what an expert in the field does on a regular basis serves as an excellent source of ideas for performance-based assessments. In physical education, these assessments can include projects (e.g., designing a school fitness center); products (e.g., a magazine or newsletter about a sport or activity); and performances, such as game play, dance or gymnastics routines, and competitions such as track-and-field or swim meets (see figure 2.3 for other examples). Just as professionals associated with physical activity—such as coaches, officials, sportswriters, broadcasters, and critical reviewers (e.g., of dance performances)—must demonstrate knowledge and understanding of various aspects of performance, students involved in performance-based assessment are called on to demonstrate similar expertise. Thus, the tasks that these professionals perform on a regular basis can provide ideas for performance-based assessments (see figure 2.4).

## Higher-Level Thinking and Complex Learning

Since performance-based assessments require students to apply facts in a meaningful way,

---

## Characteristics of Performance-Based Assessments

- Require the presentation of worthwhile or meaningful tasks designed to be representative of performance in the field
- Emphasize higher-level thinking and more complex learning
- Articulate criteria in advance so that students know how they will be evaluated
- Embed assessments so firmly in the curriculum that they are practically indistinguishable from instruction
- Expect students to present their work publicly when possible
- Involve the examination process as well as the products of learning

**Figure 2.2** Performance-based assessments require a different approach to teaching than do traditional assessment practices.

---

## Examples of Performance-Based Assessments

- Announcing an in-class ball game
- Creating a script for announcing an imaginary game
- Officiating during game play
- Keeping statistics during game play
- Writing a critique of a dance performance of peers performing live in class or of a video shown in class
- Reporting on a class tournament for the school's newspaper or morning announcements
- Coaching a team during a sport or activity unit

**Figure 2.3** Performance-based assessments often represent tasks that a professional in the field would perform.

**Figure 2.4**  Announcing a game in class requires students to demonstrate many types of game-related knowledge.

they give teachers a means for incorporating higher-level thinking skills (e.g., analysis, synthesis, and evaluation) into physical education. Consider the many complex decisions that participants must make about choice of skill and strategy during game play or gamelike situations. Using game play assessments, teachers evaluate their students' ability to make appropriate choices. Teachers use this information to give feedback to students to help them improve their performance. Creating a dance routine (which requires synthesis) is more complex than identifying different levels on which a dancer can move on a written test. Assessments that require students to engage in higher levels of critical thinking are far more challenging—and more meaningful. When students are required to *use* information, teachers can better determine students' understanding of it and determine misunderstanding or incomplete learning of a concept or topic.

## Articulation of Criteria in Advance

If a teacher gives students assignments without giving a detailed explanation of expectations, students complete those assignments on a trial-and-error basis, hoping that they guess correctly what the teacher intends for them to do. With performance-based assessments, teachers explain their expectations to students by giving them the criteria along with the assessment. Writing down their expectations for students also helps teachers clarify the assessment, which in turn helps students understand exactly what is expected of them. Writing criteria frequently causes teachers to go back to the assessment and

revise part of it. (*Note:* This step occurs before giving the assessment to students.) Providing students with criteria helps demystify the assessment and allows them to focus on important components and factors while completing the assessment. Teachers can further clarify their expectations for an assessment by showing examples of past student performances or products made in response to the assessment.

## Assessments Firmly Embedded in Instruction

Some physical education teachers say that the reason they don't assess students is that it takes too much time. Because performance-based assessments have an instructional component, learning and assessment can occur simultaneously. For instance, when doing a dance unit, students might choreograph a dance sequence to show their understanding of certain dance concepts and principles; in doing so, students learn about elements such as shape, effort, flow, and levels. The dance they present is then evaluated through the use of a rubric that explains the criteria the teacher expects to see demonstrated. Because students know the criteria, they can self-assess or peer-assess as they complete the assignment. Teachers can provide additional feedback while coaching students on criteria that they will use to evaluate the final product and further explain expectations to students as the project is completed. Thus the learning task and the assessment become seamless and difficult to separate.

Assessment and instruction can be combined by means of various instructional styles, including practice, reciprocal, or self-check. For example, the reciprocal teaching style requires students to analyze the performance of a partner and compare the performance with the criteria provided by the teacher. The recipient of the feedback benefits from having someone watch his or her performance individually, and the person giving the feedback gets to see what fulfillment of the criteria looks like when someone else is performing. The Peer Teaching Instructional Model requires students to use information provided by the teacher to teach someone else. With this instructional model, each class member is placed into a dyad, which consists of a learner and a tutor (each student is arbitrarily assigned to one of the two roles). The teacher begins by instructing the tutors, while the learners are engaged in a practice task. Following the teacher's instruction, each tutor then joins the learner designated as his or her partner and relates the information that the teacher provided. The two then practice the task, and the tutor provides feedback to the learner. After the students have finished practicing the task, the learners go to the teacher for instruction in order to assume the role of tutor; meanwhile, the former tutors continue to practice the previous task. After receiving the teacher's instruction, the new tutors rejoin their partners to teach the new information and present the new practice task that the teacher has just provided. The rotation continues in this manner; that is, each student alternately assumes the role of learner or tutor. To determine a student's learning on the subject being taught, the teacher can assess his or her ability to convey information to a peer.

## Public Presentation of Students' Work

Given the overt nature of physical education, in which game play and other athletic activities are often done while others watch, this characteristic is familiar to physical educators. Performing in front of an audience can affect assessment in two ways. First, an audience usually holds people accountable for doing their best work. Second, performing for different audiences may change the focus of an assessment. For example, a magazine project about community sport would feature different articles if written for North Dakota than if written for California. Similarly, a fitness calendar for elementary children would differ considerably from one for college students.

Performance-based assessments can be shared with an audience in many ways. For example, as part of one fitness unit, a student teacher worked with a classroom teacher to create a brochure about a healthy heart (see figure 2.5). The brochure was handed out during a parents' night event, and students explained how the heart functions and guided family members and adults through an obstacle course representing the various parts of the circulatory system. Sharing written assignments with others is an excellent way for students to show off their hard work. Dance performances and gymnastics routines can also be presented for others, and audiences can participate in the culminating game event of a Sport Education unit.

Wiggins (1989a) noted that even a simulated audience adds an element of authenticity. Of course, for something like a dance performance,

**Figure 2.5** This brochure about a healthy heart was created by students using information from a fitness unit and distributed to adults at a school open house.

a real audience is preferred, but video recordings of student dance performances done for an imaginary situation or for an imaginary audience also carry an element of authenticity.

## Importance of Both Process and Product of Learning

In performance-based assessment, the process of learning—that is, *how* students complete an assessment—is just as important as the final product. Since performance-based assessments are often intertwined with instruction, the process that students use to complete the assessment task must be included in the criteria, because how the students complete the task is an important part of the learning process. For example, in adventure education, teamwork and cooperation are key elements of the process, and students who do not demonstrate teamwork and cooperation can fail the assessment despite completing the task. Since shortcutting a process merely to obtain an identified product negates the strength and value of performance-based assessments, process is included in the evaluation criteria for performance-based assessments. Thus students are required to identify the processes they use while solving problems given to them.

## TYPES OF PERFORMANCE-BASED ASSESSMENT

A variety of performance-based assessments can be used to evaluate student learning, and this section describes several of the most common types. Chapters 5 and 6 provide additional information on open-response questions and student portfolios, and part III of the book provides several examples of how these performance-based assessments can be used during an activity unit.

Traditional testing formats, such as skill tests and selected-response written tests, do have their place in physical education. Specifically, they provide an efficient and effective way to measure factual knowledge or skills in a closed environment. This book is not intended to downplay their importance, but many other sources explain them in detail, and since the focus of this book is performance-based assessment, they are not explained in this text.

## Teacher Observation

Many teachers use observations to make assessments about students' learning. When watching skill practice, teachers make judgments about the quality of students' performances and usually provide feedback to students. Simply observing students and providing oral feedback does not constitute an assessment; an assessment must result in some type of written record. Writing an evaluation gives a teacher a concrete way to document a student's learning, thus formalizing the observation. Beginning teachers often make the mistake of watching only a few members of the class. If they focus on the most skilled students, they assume that the class in general has learned the skill and therefore is ready to move on to more difficult skills or activities. By doing purposeful evaluations and focusing on a variety of students with different ability levels, teachers can determine which students are learning and which ones need additional instruction.

In large classes, it is difficult, if not impossible, to do a written assessment of every student every day, but teachers can systematically target students for observation (some lower-skilled students, some with average skills, and some higher-skilled) to determine whether students have met learning goals and are ready to move on to more difficult tasks. If teachers rotate their observations so that every student is evaluated, they can eventually use these observations to calculate student grades. It is helpful for teachers to bring these observations to parent-teacher conferences for use in explaining what children have accomplished in the class. Such documentations provide concrete proof of students' achievements when teachers talk to others about the success of a program and about students' development of skills.

## Peer Observation

When properly taught how to do so, peers can assess one another. Peers can use **checklists** or simple rubrics to serve as personal teachers or fitness trainers as they evaluate and provide feedback about each other's performances (see figure 2.6). Peer observations can become part of a student's portfolio, either to demonstrate his or her competence in conducting the **peer evaluation** (i.e., knowing what correct performance looks like) or to show mastery of a particular skill as verified by a classmate. Teachers might even have students develop the checklist itself as a way to check their understanding of factors such as game-play elements or critical elements of a skill. Some caveats, however, are in order. First, students must be taught how to do these assessments and must know which criteria are important. Too often, teachers assume that students know how to do peer assessments when in fact they do not. Second, if an assessment is to be beneficial, it must be done accurately and objectively. Teachers must encourage students to evaluate performances as honestly as possible, reminding them that the purpose of assessment is to provide genuine feedback to improve performance. Finally, peer observation of skill performance should *not* contribute to another student's grade because this can lead to dishonesty. Also, the student is not a professional and his or her judgment should not contribute to the grade of another student.

**Figure 2.6** Peer evaluation can be used to assess higher levels of learning, as students are required to evaluate the performance observed on the basis of the characteristics of skilled performance.

## Self-Observation

Adults rarely have someone around to provide feedback about their performance. Thus, teaching students to conduct self-observations can help them to both improve their performance now and start developing a skill that is important in adult life. Again, it is imperative that teachers educate students about this process and not just assume that students know what they are doing. Teachers also need to give students specific criteria for the assessment to provide guidance to them as they move toward being self-sufficient learners. As with peer observations, self-observations are not appropriate for determining student grades.

## Game Play and Modified Game Play

**Game play** refers here to a performance-based evaluation done while students are playing a sport or activity. Various aspects of game play can be evaluated—psychomotor skills, knowledge of rules, use of strategy, teamwork—each dependent on the purpose of the assessment and the criteria specified in the rubric or scoring guide. Assessing game play allows teachers to inform students both about their strengths and about those areas in which they still need practice; in fact, providing students with this information is an important first step toward improving game-play performance. Game play is very complex, and evaluating several aspects of game play gives the teacher a clear picture of which concepts students understand. Small-sided games (e.g., 1v1, 2v2) also present excellent assessment opportunities both for experienced teachers and for those just beginning to use performance-based assessment. Small-sided games are often easier to evaluate because there are fewer people to observe at one time.

## Role Plays

Role plays are simply scenarios developed by teachers to assess certain components of physical education or physical activity (see figure 2.7). They are especially valuable for examining components of the **affective domain**, such as those associated with sensitivity to diverse

## Examples of Role Plays

- A discussion between a coach and a player: The player doesn't feel that he or she is receiving a fair amount of playing time.
- After meeting in a restaurant, a discussion between two friends on rival swim teams following a competition between their teams: One person was beaten by the other in a race and the winner qualified for the state meet.
- An interview with a coach who knows the game was won by cheating.
- A discussion between two students: One was spotting the other and laughing and fooling around; the student being spotted fell and is now paralyzed.
- A discussion between two dancers trying out for the dance team: One dancer is trying to decide how much help and feedback to give to the other dancer. The feedback might help one of the dancers make the squad, while the other giving the feedback might not make the team.
- An athlete of Native American heritage talking with a coach about his or her difficulty in playing for a team whose mascot is derogatory to Native Americans.
- An interview with a referee after he or she booted a player from a game because of poor sporting behavior.
- An interview with a referee who allowed an overly physical player to continue playing, which led to another player being injured.
- An interview with a coach who knowingly allows players to continue playing despite risk of serious injury because he or she feels the team cannot win without them.

**Figure 2.7** Teachers can assess students' learning in the affective domain by using role plays that put students into simulations of commonly encountered situations.

learners, promotion of teamwork and cooperation, and creation of a safe and nourishing environment. Through role plays, teachers can present students with a challenging, real-world problem and evaluate the decisions they make as the scenario develops. Role plays may be live, video-recorded, or written out. Students can work individually or in small groups to develop a solution to the presented problem. Role plays can be used as components of student portfolios.

## Event Tasks

**Event tasks** are performance tasks that can be completed within a single class period or less (NASPE 2004) and usually include psychomotor activity in physical education (see figure 2.8). Some examples of event tasks include game play, dance compositions, and gymnastics routines. Having students create a novel game using certain pieces of equipment assesses whether students know the elements or strategies of a game. Requiring that the game involve certain manipulative or locomotor skills allows teachers

the opportunity to evaluate those elements in an applied setting. Teachers can use **adventure education event tasks** to evaluate problem-solving, cooperation, and team-building skills. Event tasks are popular assessment options for physical education. (For a sample event task rubric, see figure 2.9.)

## Interviews

In certain situations, teachers might choose **interviews** as a way to evaluate students' knowledge. When a student explains the reasoning behind his or her choice of a game-play strategy, the teacher often gains considerable insight into whether the student really understands how best to use that strategy. After game play, a student might do a self-analysis of personal game play or an assessment of game play as related to other members of the team (e.g., teamwork or elements of fair play). With a large class, an in-depth interview is not an appropriate method of assessment, but in situations where a short interview is appropriate, interviewing provides an excellent means of

## Beach Ball Traverse

Activity is suitable for 8 to 12 participants.

### Equipment Needed

- Beach ball
- 100-foot (30.5 m) rope

### Statement of Problem

Students at a local school in Indiana do not have a beach ball. The students at a Kentucky school are willing to share their beach ball, but no nearby bridge crosses the Ohio River, which separates the two states. The students must work together to get the ball across the river using only the two ropes that were strung across the river (represented in the activity by a space of about 45 feet [14 m]). It is very important that the ball not fall into the river because the current will carry it away, and no one will have a beach ball.

### Solving the Problem

Give students 5 to 7 minutes of planning time to come up with a solution. Students can plan together how to move the ball from one side of the river to the other, but actual implementation takes place as follows:

Place the two groups of students about 45 feet (14 m) apart. Draw lines on the ground (or place tape on pavement or the gym floor) to indicate the banks of the river. Double the rope and place it on the ground so that it lies across the "river" between the two groups of students. Place the beach ball on the "Kentucky" side. Now, students must figure out a plan to move the ball from one side to the other without letting it fall into the river. Of course, students are not allowed into the river.

### Possible Solutions

1. Spread the ropes wide enough to make tracks for the ball to roll across to the other side. Students will have to elevate the ropes on one side, hold them taut, and then let the ball roll slowly across.
2. Students can tie the ball to the rope in some manner and make a conveyor belt.
3. There may be other solutions. Students are pretty ingenious.

### Assessment

The assessment involves measuring cooperation and whether students get input from all members of the group. Ideas must be shared, and group members must be open to accepting all viable solutions. Comments such as "That's a stupid idea!" are inappropriate. No single student should be the boss; rather, all students should offer suggestions, ideas, and other types of assistance. Rubric criteria should address cooperative attitudes and acceptance of ideas from others.

**Figure 2.8**   Example of an event task.

Reprinted, by permission, from Margaret Pentecost.

assessment. Teachers can also use interviews when they wish to sample students' knowledge rather than assess every individual in class, and they can use the information they gather to help them plan subsequent lessons. This assessment option also benefits students for whom English is a second language, and those with learning disabilities or writing deficiencies, since it may allow a student to demonstrate higher levels of analysis and synthesis that would be difficult or impossible to assess using conventional assessment techniques.

## Essays

**Essays** as performance assessments are not the typical compositions one writes for English classes. These performance-based assessment usually represent some type of product used by a person in the field (e.g., a brochure, flyer, a review or critique) and are written for an audience. These written compositions are open-ended, complex, and authentic and are typically used to evaluate **cognitive knowledge.** Figure 2.10 illustrates examples of essays that could be

## Rubric for Beach Ball Traverse Rubric

### Distinguished ("Let's Do Mount Everest Next")

Members of the group brainstorm before beginning to solve the problem so that everyone's voice is heard before the group starts to move. Members of the group not responding initially are solicited for their ideas and opinions. It is difficult to identify a leader because the group is working in harmony and as a team. Positive and supportive comments come from all members of the group leading to an enthusiastic and positive climate. At the conclusion of the exercise, all members of the group have a sense that they contributed to the solution.

### Proficient ("Pikes Peak, Here We Come")

All members of the group are encouraged to give their ideas. Positive and supportive comments come from various members, and everyone receives at least one compliment. Group members have a sense that a team effort led to the final outcome or solution.

### Satisfactory ("Together We Can Make It")

Group members solve the problem through trial and error. Several different students assume leadership roles as the problem unfolds. Opinions of group members are accepted. Students cooperate with each other to develop a solution.

### Unsatisfactory ("Backyard Adventurers")

One or two students assume leadership roles and address the problem without input from other members of the group. Derogatory comments are heard (e.g., "That's a stupid idea!"). Ideas from some students are rejected without exploring their merit. Students may or may not successfully complete the task.

**Figure 2.9** Event task rubric for beach ball traverse.

Reprinted, by permission, from Margaret Pentecost.

## Examples of Essay Topics (With Assessment Rationale)

- Write a speech, to be given at a school board meeting, outlining the benefits of physical education (to assess students' knowledge of the benefits of physical education).
- Create a brochure, to be handed out to parents during an open house or back-to-school night, explaining a concept learned in class (see figure 2.5).
- Write a dialogue between James Naismith (the inventor of basketball) and Luther Gulick (Naismith's teacher, who gave him the assignment that led to his creation of the sport) explaining what a good game should include (to assess students' knowledge of what constitutes a game).
- Create the broadcast dialogue for a sports announcer during an inning of the World Series or part of any championship game or culminating event of a sport (to assess knowledge of rules, depth of understanding of strategy, etiquette, and other factors important to the game or sport).
- Create a pregame interview with a famous coach discussing the strategy to be used in an upcoming game (to assess understanding of game-play strategy and when it is best used).
- Write a review or critique of a dance performance (either an in-class presentation or a video recording of a performance) for the local newspaper (to assess knowledge of the elements of dance choreography and performance).
- Write a letter to a dance department or coach outlining your skills and how they could benefit the program so that you will be recruited as a dancer or player (to prompt self-assessment of performance skills).

**Figure 2.10** Essays can demonstrate students' ability to apply their knowledge of a sport or activity in a creative format.

used for physical education, along with indicating the knowledge that is assessed.

With essay performance-based assessments, students are given a realistic task, an audience is identified, and a product is created. When tasks are open-ended, students can choose from a variety of ways to answer them. In writing the rubric for such assessments, teachers must remember to accommodate the breadth of possible responses by allowing for student creativity while at the same time focusing students on the objectives of the assessment.

## Open-Response Questions

**Open-response questions** give teachers additional written alternatives for assessing how students use or apply knowledge outside the world of the gymnasium. Although at first glance they resemble essay questions, a key difference is that an open-response answer usually begins with the phrase "It depends." In other words, the answer tends to vary by situation, which means that there are several ways to respond to the question correctly. An open-response question presents students with a real-world scenario or problem and gives them an opportunity to solve it. These questions require complex higher-order thinking, because students usually analyze something (e.g., compare X and Y), propose a resolution for a scenario, or solve a problem. Open-response questions are discussed in greater detail in chapter 5.

## Journals

**Journals** provide an excellent opportunity for teachers to assess students' learning in the affective domain. By providing students with a specific question or focus, teachers can gain insight on whether a student struggles to learn new skills, feels competence during instruction, feels a sense of teamwork or fair play during class, and so on. In addition to affective-domain evaluation, teachers might use journals to have students self-assess certain skills. Students' assessments of their own abilities can also include cognitive knowledge if the teacher requires them to articulate the critical elements of a skill and indicate which are most important for optimal performance. Students can also be asked to indicate whether they experienced problems while trying to perform skills, which

ultimately helps the teacher plan future lessons.

When having students write about feelings, a teacher should not evaluate the responses for affective-domain components or quality of thought. Doing so may cause students to stop being honest because they may fear that honesty will adversely affect their grade. The teacher can, however, hold students accountable for completing the journal entry, using correct spelling, and demonstrating mastery of cognitive content.

## Student Projects

**Student projects** generally require considerable time to complete and may involve work outside of the regularly scheduled class. Most projects call for students to apply knowledge gained in class in order to create a concrete product that can be submitted for evaluation (see figure 2.11 for a list of sample projects). The projects typically apply to real-world settings.

Because student projects require time and effort outside of class, they extend students' engagement with physical education content. Students are usually willing to spend the extra time necessary to complete the assessment because the projects are engaging and interesting. These projects call for students to use higher levels of thinking by creating new products, analyzing a situation or performance, or making an evaluation or determination. When establishing criteria for evaluation, teachers must not penalize students with limited outside resources. For example, students who don't have access to color printers or clip art should not be penalized for submitting black-and-white written projects. Teachers should also weigh content and student learning more heavily than format or spelling.

## Student Performances

**Student performances** are often used as culminating events in performance-based assessment. When using this type of assessment, instruction is geared toward helping students develop the skills necessary to complete the performance and providing several days for them to practice the performance to achieve competence. Using the objectives established for a unit, teachers design the parameters for the **culminating performance** before beginning the unit, and all instruction for the unit is geared

## Examples of Student Projects

- Students choreograph a dance and film their performance. This project demonstrates student knowledge of various elements of dance design and of concepts such as level, shape, and other dynamics associated with dance performance.
- Students create a piece of equipment designed to exercise a muscle group or body part (e.g., abdominal muscles, upper body, quadriceps).
- A student creates a workout video that covers all components of health-related fitness (whether for personal use after school or for use by other members of the family).
- Students research the history and rules of a playground game (e.g., four square, jacks, tetherball, hopscotch) and then teach it to children from a neighboring elementary school. Products could include a summary of the history, rule sheets, artifacts used for teaching, and a video of game play.
- A student shadows an adult for a day (preferably in a career that the student hopes to pursue) and identifies possible ways to increase this person's level of physical activity. The goal is for this person to engage in at least 30 minutes of moderate activity during a normal workday.
- Students develop a playbook for use in a sport such as softball, basketball, or soccer to demonstrate their knowledge of strategies and rules for that game.
- Students develop a WebQuest, which is an "inquiry-oriented lesson . . . in which most or all the information that learners work with comes from the [World Wide] Web" (Dodge 2009)—for a topic related to physical education (e.g., a sport, a fitness concept, stretching to prevent injury).

**Figure 2.11**    Many student projects are developed from the challenges faced by people working in the fields of physical education and sport.

toward having students successfully complete this final task. Examples of culminating events include gymnastics routines performed for the class gymnastics meet, a class tournament, a dance choreographed by a group of students over the course of several weeks, training for a cross country run, or a synchronized swimming performance that takes several weeks to learn.

To complete such performances, students are often required to use higher-level thinking skills and learn new skills that push them to higher levels of achievement. These student performances are labor-intensive both for the teacher and for the students, but they frequently yield a product that makes both students and teachers very proud.

## Student Logs

To evaluate standard 3 of the National Standards for Physical Education ("Participates regularly in physical activity"; National Association for Sport and Physical Education 2004), teachers might require students to keep track of practice trials or time spent doing various activities. One method of doing so is to keep a **student log**. For example, some teachers post an instant activity for students to do as soon as they enter the gymnasium for class, and if the same skill or activity is repeated for several days in a row, students can use logs to document their improvement. If a log does not indicate improvement, the teacher can then explore whether the student was making errors while practicing or was demonstrating a lack of effort. The teacher can then provide additional attention or instruction as needed.

Students can also use logs to document practice or activity done outside of class. For example, if a student needs increased flexibility during a gymnastics unit, the teacher can prescribe appropriate exercises for the student to perform on his or her own. If the student fails to develop improved flexibility, the teacher knows to look either for a failure on the student's part to complete the designated tasks or for an error in his or her own choice of which tasks to prescribe in the first place. Student logs can be used for documenting effort in various types of physical education homework, practice, and activity outside of the physical education class.

## Portfolios

**Portfolios** are collections of materials or artifacts that, when considered collectively, demonstrate students' competence in or mastery of a given subject area. Generally, portfolios are used to document improvement or growth over time. Portfolios are often used for assessing students over a significant time frame, such as in a six-week sport education unit or fitness improvement during a semester. For example, a teacher might have students document their growth in the ability to play games and participate in activities during a semester. The units may have included tennis, lacrosse, and gymnastics. Since several different types of knowledge and skill are involved, different types of assessments are used to document the student's competence, thus making a portfolio an ideal assessment. Portfolios provide an excellent way for students to gather evidence and display it in a meaningful manner. Figure 2.12 lists some artifacts that might be required in a fitness portfolio.

There are two types of portfolios. Students use **working portfolios** to gather diverse information that demonstrates mastery of learning objectives, whereas **evaluation portfolios** are submitted for assessment by the teacher. A working portfolio might contain a potpourri of student work and multiple examples of achievement in a given area. Although the working portfolio does not get evaluated by the teacher, teachers may evaluate individual artifacts as part of other assignments or assessments before placing them in the working portfolio.

Teachers typically limit the number of artifacts that students can place in an evaluation portfolio to force students to select the items that *best* represent their competence according to specific criteria. This approach leaves the teacher with fewer pieces to evaluate, thus

## Possible Artifacts for a Fitness Portfolio

- Research paper comparing various training techniques
- Log of cardiorespiratory workouts
- Analysis of cardiorespiratory workouts (indicating which type is most effective), optimal training schedule, and intensity variations (caused by working out on different surfaces or terrains)
- Analysis of current activities (times when they occur, length, and type of activity engaged in) and identify ways to increase time spent doing these activities (taking into account current obligations)
- List of excuses (personal or those provided by friends) for not exercising and then a proposal that identifies ways to address the excuses so that levels of activity are increased
- Develop a list of current activities and then set realistic goals for improving the health-related fitness components over a period (e.g., 9 weeks or a semester). The student sets weekly targets for gradually reaching these goals, and a way to document whether the intermediate goals are met
- Lifting log
- Pre- and posttraining measurements of body fat composition
- Pictures taken during a local road race
- Discussion of a pacing strategy for a 10K road race
- Training program based on analysis or testing of fitness components
- Analysis of a health spa or fitness facility to determine which provides the most benefit for the money spent per visit
- Interview questions for a personal trainer
- Graphs noting improvement in strength and flexibility measurements
- Charts depicting muscles used during workouts and stretching

**Figure 2.12** A fitness unit might encompass a variety of student learning that can be evaluated holistically by means of a fitness portfolio.

saving him or her considerable time during the evaluation of the portfolios. Evaluation portfolios are geared toward a specific set of criteria, set by the teacher, in which students must demonstrate competence, but students can select the specific pieces they use to meet the criteria. Students write **narratives** or reflections to accompany the artifacts that explain why they chose each piece to demonstrate their competence. Some portfolios specify the kinds of artifacts to include but allow students some options in choosing their specific items; others give students total choice in the selection process. Portfolios are a popular approach to evaluating student learning, and are discussed further in chapter 6.

# HOW PERFORMANCE-BASED ASSESSMENTS CHANGE INSTRUCTION

Beyond the shift to different types of assessment, the move toward performance-based assessment often requires a philosophical shift as well. For many teachers, *assessment* is synonymous with *evaluation* and implies the assignment of a grade. Many physical education teachers do assessments only when they are trying to determine grades for students. The main purpose of assessment, however, should be to document student learning. Therefore, instead of assuming the role of a judge who determines whether and how well a student has learned, performance-based assessments encourage teachers to *coach* students so that they reach a given level of excellence. This approach entails several changes in teaching philosophy.

## Teacher as Coach

When teachers evaluate student learning, they often view themselves as gatekeepers, but performance-based assessment allows them to act as coaches who help students get the most out of their abilities and achieve optimal levels of performance. The word *assessment* comes from the French *assidere,* which means to sit beside (Herman, Aschbacher, and Winters 1992). With performance-based assessments, teachers and students work together to enhance students' learning. Instead of being limited to lectures and direct instruction as the only methods of presenting new information, teachers can use projects or assessments as learning experiences and then coach students as they work to achieve excellence. This approach lets teachers discard the old analogy of the teacher as a hose delivering information to students who soak it up like sponges. As a result, learning can be measured in terms of the content that students master rather than how well they score on a written exam.

With performance-based assessments, teachers no longer serve as the only source of students' knowledge since students learn from others and learn through experience while completing the assessments. With some assessments students are expected to obtain knowledge from references or external sources to complete it. Students are expected to demonstrate *application* of knowledge rather than regurgitation of facts. Furthermore, students' performance continues to improve during the assessment process as a result of support given by the teacher.

## Greater Use of Formative Assessment

There is evidence that formative assessment improves learning and that low-achieving students benefit the most (Black and Wiliam 1998, 2004). Popham defines **formative assessment** as "a planned process in which assessment-elicited evidence of students' status is used by teachers to adjust their ongoing instructional procedures or by students to adjust their current practices" (2008, 6). Formative assessment provides information that teachers use to adapt instruction for meeting student needs *as instruction progresses* rather than at the completion of the teaching unit. In every study reviewed by Black and Wiliam (1998), formative assessments produced significant learning gains in the classroom.

When students make errors on summative assessments, they have no chance to correct them to improve performance or increase learning. Such tests serve a purely evaluative quality, and when students do poorly on them there is no second chance. Formative assessments, on the other hand, allow students multiple opportunities to demonstrate competence. If a student performs poorly on one day, formative assessment gives him or her the opportunity to practice and have a second chance for success at a later date. According to many studies, students' learning increases substantially when a teacher (a) is selective about what students should know and be able to do, (b) focuses instruction on that information, and (c) gives feedback regularly through formative assessment.

Assessments should provide evidence that there is room for improvement and alert students and teachers to areas of incomplete learning. Unfortunately, with summative tests, this information arrives too late to be of value to either the teacher or the student; the unit is over, and there is no chance for reteaching and clarification of misunderstandings. Formative assessments, on the other hand, are given throughout instruction and therefore function as feedback for the learning process. Formative assessments are typically given more than once and thus allow students additional chances to demonstrate mastery of materials and content.

## Improved Feedback

Because formative assessments are given during instruction, they provide feedback to both students and teachers about possible gaps in learning and allow teachers to evaluate the degree to which students use feedback to improve their performance (Wiggins 1998a). After formative assessments, teachers can go back to material that students just didn't get and teach it in another manner. Students receive feedback about their performance and can also work to correct any errors. Once students understand where they are in relation to final goals for learning, they are more likely to improve. "The aim of assessment is to educate and improve student performance, not just audit it" (Wiggins 1989a, 707). Teachers and students must understand that assessments can do more than evaluate learning—they can also improve it.

## Progressively More Difficult Assessments

As you move through a unit, both performance-based assessments and learning activities should become progressively more complex. **Progressive assessment** is a term used to describe a process whereby students progress from the performance and assessment of simple to more complex skills in increasingly complex situations

and settings. The assessments themselves also increase in complexity to reflect the progressive nature of the learning activity or required performance. For instance, in the early stages of learning new skills, the focus may be on learning and demonstrating the correct critical performance elements or correct form in a controlled or closed setting. Assessment in this stage of learning focuses on students' demonstration of the skill in a highly consistent situation, such as bumping a volleyball tossed softly and directly to them by a partner; the assessment and scoring guide in this case could be an observation checklist of the critical performance cues arranged in sequential order. Either the teacher or the student's peers could use the checklist to assess the student's performance; the student could also use a video recording to assess his or her own performance. The next learning activity or assessment might involve having students receive a ball tossed directly to them by a partner, which they pass back in a high arc to the partner, who is 15 feet (about 4.5 m) away, so that the person who tossed the ball can set it to a target.

An appropriate measure for success in these tasks would be a criterion-referenced assessment in which the student is expected to use correct form to accomplish the task 8 out of 10 times before going on to another task. If the unit goal is to have students demonstrate and apply learned skills and strategies in tournament games near the end of the unit, then an appropriate progressive assessment would be to keep statistics documenting how each student performs and applies the skills and strategies in a gamelike situation. This approach might involve having either teachers or students design an appropriate game-statistics form that can be used easily during game play. On the form, the recorder would count the number of attempted bumps, those that were accurate passes, and those that were errors so that the recorder could calculate a percentage of accurate passes. These game performance statistics might be kept over time so that students can see if they are improving in game situations. Many examples of this assessment philosophy in action can be found in chapters 7, 8, and 9.

To truly reflect the progressive nature of the skill performance, most progressive assessments must be authentic or performed in situations that are as close to real life as possible. Because progressive, continuous assessments are repeated, they can be used to track students' performance of a particular skill, strategy, or skill combination across trials and across time (days or weeks). That way, student and teacher can monitor progress and intervene if necessary before the student gets too far behind. These assessments are referred to as **progress checkpoints** or simply **checkpoints** (Graham, Holt-Hale, Parker 2007; Lambert 2007).

When assessment is progressive, it can be very motivating to students because they are able to track their skill development and their progress while performing skills in increasingly more complex environments while working to achieve established goals throughout the unit. The teacher may identify specific progress checkpoints throughout the unit or semester so that students can see how they are progressing toward goals. Again, progressively more complex assessments must be planned before beginning instruction for the unit. The final (or culminat-

ing) performance, product assessment, or experience should require students to apply knowledge and skills in an *authentic* final performance or product in that allows them to demonstrate their achievement of unit goals and movement toward targeted standards.

## Learning and Progress Seen Through Multiple Lenses

In much the same way as it takes several situations to come to know a person's ability and potential, multiple assessments are needed to get a clear picture of a student's abilities and potential. This is a strength of performance-based assessment: Students are evaluated many times and through many lenses so that it is possible to develop a full and complete picture of each person's skills. By looking at a composite of multiple assessments, the teacher gets a better idea of what each student has achieved during the unit.

It is important to note that no test is comprehensive enough to address all the material covered in a course. This concern is often voiced regarding the No Child Left Behind legislation (Popham 2001, 2005). Tests merely cover a representative sample of the material that teachers want students to know. Several types of assessment are needed to verify students' learning. Many teachers use written tests to measure cognitive ability in a sport (e.g., volleyball). Although such assessments can measure students' basic knowledge, students' ability to *apply* knowledge is very difficult to assess, and written assessments are rarely used for that purpose. A teacher can develop a better, more complete

A checkpoint assessment could be implemented, for example, in a badminton unit in which the unit goal is for students to demonstrate the ability to play successfully in a singles and doubles badminton tournament. During the first 2 days of the unit, the teacher introduces the short and long serves. Serving is a complicated skill that must be performed with accuracy on a consistent basis. At the beginning of class each day, the teacher provides 10 minutes for warm-up practice, during which students serve 10 long and 10 short serves on an official court. Students record the number of successful serves out of 10 for each type of serve. Thus they gather data throughout the unit and can graph their serve percentage data using the daily checkpoints. Each student, or his or her peers, could also collect data about serve placement and about returns to provide additional information about serving progress. If the data indicate that no progress is being made, or that the student is regressing, then the teacher can plan an intervention, such as (a) peer observation of the serve's critical elements based on a check sheet or rating scale or (b) a video recording of the student's serve for self-analysis. During remedial instruction, students perform without undue pressure because they are not graded on the assessment. They know that this instruction is conducted simply to help them improve their performance; the assessment is integrated with learning activities as part of the daily practice activity.

picture of a student's ability to use cognitive knowledge by requiring him or her to officiate games played by classmates; by observing a student's demonstration of knowledge of rules, play selection, and strategy during game play; and by having students analyze a skill to help a classmate improve his or her performance.

It is also important to remember that no single assessment form is sufficient for measuring the complex material covered in a physical education unit. Performance-based assessment allows teachers to evaluate the many types of learning involved in an activity or unit. By doing several types of assessment, thus creating a total picture of each student's abilities, the teacher gets a clearer idea of what the student has learned and accomplished. Just as the blind men who were describing the elephant had many different ideas about what an elephant looked like (e.g., one man described the trunk, another an ear, and another a tail), teachers can develop a more accurate picture of students' competence by taking multiple looks at their achievements.

# ADVANTAGES OF USING PERFORMANCE-BASED ASSESSMENTS

Many of the things that physical educators do during an instructional unit can be easily turned into performance-based assessments. By making a few modifications, writing out criteria for the performance, and gradually including performance-based assessments throughout a unit, a teacher can begin to transform current assessment practices into performance-based assessments.

Performance-based assessments provide several instructional advantages in physical education and can greatly increase the effectiveness of instruction and evaluation systems. This section considers some advantages of using performance-based assessments.

## Direct Observations of Student Learning

Performance-based assessments allow teachers to assess areas of learning that traditional assessments do not address. Many traditional assessments do not directly measure progress toward the teacher's final learning objectives. For example, at the secondary level, a physical educator's goal is usually to teach a student how to play a game or do an activity. However, while skill tests may evaluate performance of discrete skills in a fairly closed (unchanging) environment, they do not evaluate a student's ability to use these skills and "put it all together" during game play. Additionally, game play, involves making decisions about which skill to use and thus requires students to evaluate a complex environment. Skill tests are merely an approximation of what a student must be able to do. Although they do represent a first step in learning, obtaining high scores on a skill test is usually not the teacher's ultimate goal for the unit.

Direct observation of students performing in a real-world setting provides a powerful way to measure both their knowledge and their ability to apply it. Traditional assessments are designed to measure students' learning indirectly. For example, when students take a test about tennis rules, the teacher assumes that the test measures the degree to which a student knows the rules, and if the questions are valid then this is a reasonable assumption. However, a student might know the rules of tennis and demonstrate that knowledge on a written test yet be unable to apply them during a game. Skill tests and written tests give teachers a useful way to sample students' learning during instruction, but actual assessment of game play allows teachers to see whether students can combine the pieces into a meaningful entity.

Thus performance-based assessments allow teachers to access information not available through traditional testing. Assessments must measure how well students meet the teacher's goals or targets for the unit. When a teacher's goals include game play or some type of student performance, then performance-based assessments provide an excellent way to determine whether students have achieved those goals.

## Good Instructional Alignment

Put simply, **instructional alignment** means that teachers test what they teach. Cohen's research (1987) revealed the power of instructional alignment strategies. Teachers in his study demonstrated a significant difference in student

**A**s a teacher, I remember my frustration when teaching activity units. I felt like I was not assessing progress toward my ultimate objective—that of getting students to play the game. Students would score well on skill tests but remain unable to use the skills during game play. Unfortunately, when I first began teaching, I didn't know of a way to assess students during game play because I was taught how to use traditional skill tests to evaluate psychomotor skills. With a game-play assessment, I could have evaluated students' ability to *use* the targeted skills and thus identified the gaps between their skill acquisition and their ability to play a game.

learning when their assessments matched student learning. When applying instructional alignment principles, teachers decide on a target, then test what they teach. This approach may seem logical, but the fact is that not all teachers use it. Some teachers use written tests to evaluate learning for activity units. Too often, the material covered by a test comes from a one- or two-page handout on the history or rules of a game or sport, which means that the test ignores all the skill and game-play instruction involved in the unit. In performance-based assessment, in contrast, the assessment can *be* the instructional task. Students know exactly what is expected of them and are given multiple opportunities to meet preannounced teacher expectations and criteria. Thus instruction and assessment work together in performance-based assessments, which leads to strong instructional alignment and enhances students' learning.

## Interesting Assessments

Since performance-based assessments usually involve real-world tasks, students tend to find them more engaging and challenging. Rather than studying just enough to get a good grade on a test, students spend many hours engaged in their projects and often explore and use sources beyond the teacher and textbook. In addition, when an assessment simulates what a person in the field might do, students have several role models to emulate (e.g., announcing a game like Harry Caray, doing basketball analysis like Pat Summitt, or dancing like Michael Flatley or Julianne Hough). When an assessment results in a product or performance, students accomplish something they can be proud of.

## Instructional Feedback

Because they have a formative component, performance-based assessments provide high-quality feedback to students throughout the assessment. Since students have access to the rubric that is used to judge the final product, they can self-assess and peer-assess as they move through the assessment and receive additional feedback. The overall purpose of assessment should be to enhance learning, and the primary reason to assess should be to give feedback to students about their progress. The second reason for doing assessments is to provide information to the teacher that can be used to shape instruction. Thus, instead of doing assessment at the end of the unit, teachers can enhance students' learning by integrating assessment throughout the instructional process.

## Measurement of Multiple Objectives and Concepts

These days, physical education is often squeezed into an instructional curriculum loaded with classes that students were not required to take 10 years ago. As a result, physical education teachers must make every minute count. Because performance-based assessments are linked with instruction, the two can be accomplished simultaneously, thus increasing instructional efficiency. Game play provides opportunities for teachers to assess students' skill, use of strategy, knowledge of rules, and affective-domain attributes. Additionally, physical education teachers can often work with other teachers to do assessments that display competence in multiple areas. For example, written assessments could be used to evaluate learning in both English and physical education, and fitness assessments could also be used to measure biology content knowledge. Assessments involving other subject areas can be completed outside the gym, which maximizes time available for activity.

## Active Student Learning

Performance-based assessments can empower students by giving them freedom to make choices, within parameters set by teachers, about the direction that their learning should take. Giving students this kind of ownership of their learning process can be a powerful motivator. In addition, because students understand what their learning should look like, students are more likely to experience success with performance-based assessments. Not only do the lessons have a more lasting effect—performance-based assessments require students to *do* something, which makes them more likely to retain the knowledge they use—but also may lead students to other projects and activities. Indeed, whether they involve writing or the use of psychomotor skills, performance-based assessments should encourage students to go outside the confines of the class for additional learning. As a result, an assessment may not be the end or culmination of learning so much as it is the beginning of engagement with a newfound area of interest.

## Higher-Order Thinking Skills

Higher-order thinking skills, which are important for success as an adult, must be nurtured and developed throughout a student's school career. Performance-based assessments prompt students to use higher-order thinking skills such as analysis, synthesis, and evaluation. The more opportunities students are given to practice these skills, the more proficient they become at using them. For example, a teacher might call on students to use higher-order thinking skills in physical education by giving them a scouting assignment in which they analyze the skills and strategies of future opponents in a badminton tournament. Another option would be to have students create a dance for an upcoming performance or design a play for use in an upcoming game.

## Multiple Chances to Get It Right

Some educators see assessment in a purely evaluative light: students have one chance to prove that they have learned the required material. In contrast, because of its formative focus, performance-based assessments give students multiple chances to succeed. Indeed, in life out-side the classroom, people often have multiple chances to demonstrate competence without penalty. Did you pass your lifesaving exam the first time you took it? If you didn't, that setback did not mean that you could never become a lifeguard. It just meant that more work was necessary before you met the criteria. In much the same way, performance-based assessments allow students multiple opportunities to meet the criteria or standard of excellence set by the teacher.

When game-play assessments are used during a tournament, the grade should be determined not by averaging a student's early performance with that from later games but by using results from his or her best performance. Errors made during a game in the early stages of learning should not be held against the student because improvement with experience is the expectation. When dancers make errors while performing for their video recording, they can do another take. When a student's written work misses the mark, he or she is allowed to rewrite. Educators who administer an assessment only once must recognize that in the world outside the classroom people often have multiple chances to demonstrate proficiency. Athletes compete in many contests, dancers put on many shows, and skaters perform in numerous competitions. Thus, giving students multiple opportunities to achieve success provides more of a real-world experience than a one-shot evaluation provides.

## Students' Enjoyment

Because assessments are challenging and simulate real-world experiences, students find them interesting and engaging. Time on task in class tends to be high and students are willing to spend additional time outside of class to complete their projects. Afterward, when students consider their accomplishments, they have a strong sense of satisfaction and pride, since the product or performance provides a tangible, concrete demonstration of their achievement.

# WHAT TO AVOID WHEN USING PERFORMANCE-BASED ASSESSMENTS

Despite the many benefits that performance-based assessments bring to the evaluation arena, several concerns have emerged about their use. Performance-based assessments are still relatively new to the scene, and procedures for using them are still evolving. As teachers continue to expand the use of performance-based assessments, the following issues should be kept in mind.

## Concerns About Reliability and Validity

**Reliability** and **validity** are always of concern, regardless of the type of test one uses. With performance-based assessment, validity is high because the teacher makes direct observations of students performing the skills that the teacher is trying to teach. Problems with validity usually arise when a rubric uses inappropriate criteria for assessment. In selecting traits for a rubric, teachers should consult many sources to ensure that the most important items are selected for the evaluation.

Reliability can be problematic in the scoring of performance-based assessments because an evaluator must use his or her judgment in determining whether specified criteria have been met. However, with training in using performance-based assessments, an evaluator can achieve high levels of reliability. As with all forms of assessment, teachers must address concerns about validity and reliability when they use performance-based assessments. Fortunately, with proper care both issues can be resolved.

## Failure to Set Criteria for an Assessment

When creating a performance-based assessment, the teacher must determine what criteria to use. If there are no criteria then there is no way to evaluate the task or project. In this case, the "assessment" is merely an instructional task, not an assessment. Failing to establish criteria for performance is a common error for those using performance-based assessments.

Teachers should look at what they want students to know and be able to do (i.e., the essential questions) to determine the criteria for an evaluation. The first time a teacher uses an assessment, criteria might need some adjustments. For this reason an assessment should not have high stakes for students when it is used for

the first time. After a teacher has done an assessment once, he or she can look at student work to revise criteria when the assessment is used again. It is not enough for students to go through the motions and just complete the assessment; they must understand that a level of excellence is expected and the criteria will establish this expectation.

## Teaching to the Test

Educational reform has triggered an explosion of testing over the past several years. In some states, testing involves high-stakes accountability, ranging from cash awards for schools and teachers to the closing of schools with substandard performance. Given the importance placed on these tests, teachers have narrowed the curriculum, focusing on areas included on "The Test." As a result, **teaching to the test** has come to carry a negative connotation because some think that when teachers instruct students with the sole purpose of helping them pass a test, important concepts are no longer taught.

These concerns notwithstanding, performance-based assessments are often designed so that the teacher teaches to the test. Wiggins (1989a) points out that if the test is worthwhile, then teaching to the test is not always a bad thing. For instance, if the test represents a culminating performance in which students are expected to "put it all together" and indicate mastery of a content area, then teaching to the test allows students to be successful in achieving the overall unit objective. Wiggins (1989a) also notes that no one complains when a coach teaches to the test. Coaches prepare their athletes for competition against opponents who will *test* them. Similarly, having students engage in game play in a sport unit or complete an adventure education course can make teaching to the test a worthwhile educational endeavor.

## Assessment Is Time Consuming

It takes teachers more time to develop and evaluate performance-based assessments that require students to create a product or complete a project. For this reason, teachers must make careful choices when deciding to have students do certain types of performance-based assessments. The assessment should involve a meaningful task and be the best method for assessing how well students have achieved the teacher's goals. Teachers should also determine whether the time required to complete the assessment will constitute a worthwhile investment in learning for both the students and the teacher. Teachers should use performance-based assessments when they are the best way to motivate students or measure learning. If a program's goals can be adequately assessed using other assessment techniques, then teachers should consider using those methods. In short, teachers must use available time as efficiently as possible, which includes making wise choices when selecting assessments.

## Completion of an Assessment by Parents

Given the current prevalence of childhood obesity, some teachers are reluctant to do anything in physical education that detracts from activity time. Since performance-based assessment projects can require a great deal of time, some physical education teachers assign part of the project for completion outside of class. When work is done at home, parental help is a possibility. Although this problem is not unique to performance-based assessments, it can surface more often due to the complexity of some performance-based assessments. As a result, physical education teachers sometimes face the dilemma of having to choose between using an assessment that may not be completed by the

student and using in-class time to complete a nonactivity assessment. Teachers can avoid or minimize this problem by building safeguards into assessments that are completed outside of class. For example, a teacher might verify student learning by integrating an in-class piece into the assessment that addresses another dimension of the assessment, thus using multiple sources to document learning. Another way to address the issue is to require students to add an oral component to the assessment in which they explain the process they used to complete the task outside of class. With a little planning, teachers can resolve the issue of protecting activity time while ensuring that students do their own work—thus maximizing students' learning.

## Focusing the Assessment on Irrelevant Content

Performance-based assessments should be open-ended, complex, and authentic. As teachers create performance-based assessments, they must keep them open enough that various interpretations or products can satisfy the requirements. At the same time, a task that is too open might be approached using a pathway that fails to demonstrate understanding of the intended content (see figure 2.13). Thus teachers must exercise caution in writing performance-based assessments. They must focus the assessments on the desired learning yet leave them open enough to be answered in a variety of ways.

**Figure 2.13** If performance-based assessments are not focused on a specific subject or on specific content, then the desired student learning might not be demonstrated—thus, it cannot be assessed.

## CONCLUSION

Performance-based assessments offer a new set of options for physical education teachers as they evaluate student progress. This form of assessment gives teachers the opportunity to assess students' learning in an applied setting where students often demonstrate competence by doing real-world or authentic tasks. Given the nature of physical education, these assessment techniques have been embraced by many teachers. Since physical education tends to be very performance based, creating performance-based assessments for physical education is sometimes easier than creating them for other areas that focus only on cognitive learning.

Performance-based assessments can include a wide variety of activities—for example, emulating the performances of sports and activity professionals (e.g., announcers, sportswriters, dance reviewers, coaches, choreographers) or actually playing games or performing dance production pieces. When teachers use performance-based assessments, their role shifts from that of a gatekeeper or evaluator to that of a coach interested in improving students' knowledge and skills. Instructional alignment tends to be strong because teachers are assessing what they teach, and all lessons are focused on helping students meet instructional goals. Because assessments are formative, students have multiple opportunities to meet the criteria that teachers convey to them before the assessment begins.

As with any form of assessment, teachers must take care to create both valid and reliable assessments. Performance-based assessments are time consuming to develop, time consuming for students to complete, and time consuming for teachers to score. In addition, teachers must write criteria for these assessments that distinguish between levels of learning. All of this requires much of a teacher's time and energy.

We have witnessed the positive changes in student learning that performance-based assessments enable, and this is why we endorse them. We have seen students become interested in learning rather than just doing enough to pass the test and students who were on the academic fringes become enthusiastic learners. When teachers use performance-based assessments, students know what is expected of them and work hard to meet the expectations and challenges set forth by their teachers. Assessment is interwoven throughout the learning process, which relieves the pressure on teachers to get evaluations done during the last days of a unit. In addition, teachers have multiple lenses through which to evaluate students' learning, thus providing a far better idea of what students really know and can do. These lenses also provide many opportunities to adjust teaching content as lessons progress.

The following chapters go into greater detail about how to create performance-based assessments and incorporate them into the curriculum. By gradually introducing these assessments into the curriculum, teachers can avoid feeling overwhelmed while making changes. We hope that you are starting to see the benefits to students' learning that performance-based assessments provide and are ready to start using them in your program.

# Components of Performance-Based Assessment

Part II explains the nuts and bolts of using performance-based assessments. Rubrics are necessary for performance-based assessments, so an entire chapter is dedicated to explaining how to create them. Also included is a chapter of ideas that will help with the development of various performance-based assessments for physical education classes. Two types of performance-based assessment are discussed in their own chapters. The first type—the open-response question—is being used more frequently in education. Traditionally, they have not been widely used in physical education. A chapter is devoted to explaining them in depth because of their potential for assessing higher levels of thinking. A chapter is also devoted to portfolios, which are gaining widespread acceptance in physical education. The final chapters in this part walk teachers through the planning process for developing performance-based assessments. The examples demonstrate the use of a five-step plan for assessment and also illustrate the integration of learning and assessment in the instructional process.

# Rubrics

*We as teachers make judgments about students all the time. Since these judgments are based on criteria, whether we can articulate them or not, we have only two choices: we can either make our criteria crystal clear to students, or we can make them guess (Arter 1996, p. vi-2:2).*

Personal preference is generally the deciding factor in a person's choice of which brand or style of an item to buy. For example, when purchasing shoes, many people have discovered that some brands fit their feet better than others do, and they make their selections from their preferred manufacturers. Other people just want the latest style of shoe and are willing to sacrifice comfort for style. For some, longevity is the most important factor; they want shoes that will hold up under duress. The person selling shoes has no idea what type of shoe a potential buyer wants until there is an exchange of information. Unless the customer tells the clerk what he or she is interested in, the clerk could end up bringing out hundreds of shoes before satisfaction is reached.

This analogy suggests a reality that many students experience in school: They often have no idea what the teacher deems adequate, since the teacher has not fully communicated that information to them. Communication of expectations to students is a very important part of the assessment process because it will enhance students'

learning and tremendously improve the quality of their performances. This chapter explains how teachers can communicate their expectations for performance-based assessments.

## WHAT IS A RUBRIC?

Before starting any significant task, one should know the criteria that will be used to judge the result. The more significant the event, the more important it is to have the criteria in advance. For example, if baking a cake for one's own family, the stakes are relatively low. If, however, that same cake is being prepared for a national bake-off with a grand prize of $100,000, then it is crucial to know how it will be judged. Criteria for judging student performance have been called scoring criteria, scoring guidelines, rubrics, and scoring rubrics (Herman, Aschbacher, and Winters 1996). In this book, the term **rubric** refers to the criteria used for judging student performance.

Rubrics are guidelines by which a product is judged (Wiggins 1996). These guidelines make public what is judged and in some cases explain the standards for acceptable performance (Herman, Aschbacher, and Winters 1996). There is general agreement that the term *rubric* has its origins in the Latin language, but it has been attributed to various specific origins. Some authors (Wiggins 1996; Popham 1997) claim that *rubric* derives from the Latin word meaning *red*. The set of instructions for a law or liturgical service, typically written in red, was a rubric; thus, a rubric provided guidelines for lawfully judging a performance. Another source, Marzano, Pickering, and McTighe (1993), places the roots of the word in the Latin *rubrica terra*, which refers to the practice (centuries ago) of indicating the importance of something by marking it with red earth. Much like this ancient practice, rubrics point out what is significant or important in learning and assessment.

Writing a rubric is probably the most difficult part of creating an assessment. Some teachers develop assessments for their classes but fail to specify criteria or expectations for students' performances. Such assessments are actually pseudo-assessments. These assessments may serve as excellent tasks for promoting student learning, but without an indication of the criteria for performance, they do not state a required level of performance. Without stated criteria, they leave one to assume that any student attempt at completing the task is acceptable. Chapter 2 explained that performance-based assessments have two parts—a task or exercise for students to do and the criteria by which the performance will be judged. Without a standard of evaluation, assessments are really just instructional tasks. In reality, teachers make judgments about students all day, every day, when they look at students' performances and decide whether a student can really perform a given dance or execute a skill sequence. Rubrics are ways for teachers to communicate their expectations for student performance and establish the criteria that will be used to judge the assessment task.

## BENEFITS OF USING RUBRICS

Rubrics offer several benefits for scoring performance-based assessments. First, rubrics increase the consistency of scoring, because teachers have the criteria in writing and can refer to them in the case of questionable student performances. Having the criteria in writing helps prevent the fluctuation that sometimes characterizes assessment when assessing a sizeable number of students in large classes. Second, the use of rubrics can improve instruction itself. Writing a rubric requires teachers to clarify expectations and remove the fuzziness from their instructional goals. When teachers establish a clear notion of what they intend to teach, their teaching tends to be more focused on the targeted learning.

Students benefit from having a rubric because they know what is really important. A good rubric will contain the most important criteria for an assessment, thus helping students see how instruction supports and fits with these goals. For learning to be most effective, students must filter information and determine the most important content. Rubrics help filter this information by pointing out what is most important, which helps students make sense of their learning. Students understand the teacher's expectations and what they must do to demonstrate their achievement of the learning goals. They no longer need to guess about what to learn; it is clearly stated for them in the rubric.

## CRITERIA FOR RUBRICS

In education, rubrics include the criteria used to inform students about desired standards and **levels** of quality. Clear criteria are essential in performance-based assessments, so that students' work can be judged consistently (Arter 1996). Unlike selected-response questions (i.e., multiple-choice, true-false, matching) for which a single correct answer is identified, performance-based assessments require an evaluator to make a professional judgment about the quality of student work. Rubrics identify the criteria that the person scoring a performance-based assessment should use when doing evaluations.

In addition to helping teachers evaluate student performance, performance-based assessments help teachers provide specific feedback to students about how to improve their performance. Just as specific cues are necessary for improving athletic performance, specific criteria are vital to improving students' performance in physical education. When both teachers and students have a clear vision of what an ideal performance looks like, mastery of the desired criteria is much more likely to occur. Students are capable of achieving desired targets, as long as they know what those targets are (Stiggins 2001), and the specific criteria found in rubrics help students understand what they must do to achieve mastery of content.

According to the literature, teachers can use three types of criteria to evaluate student performance (i.e., to determine grades): product, process, and progress (Guskey and Bailey 2001). The term **product criteria** simply refers to what students produce, or what they are able to do at a particular point in time—for example, creating a concrete artifact such as a project, like a pamphlet or brochure. In physical education, product criteria are frequently stated in terms of student performance. Thus a student might be expected to play a game, create a dance, or perform a dance routine. Product criteria can also specify actions, such as shooting and making a basketball shot a certain number of times or executing a tennis serve that lands in the proper service court.

Merely stating student performance outcomes in terms of products says nothing about a student using correct form. When physical educators require students to use correct form, they must specify **process criteria**, which are those elements that are critical to correct performance. Classroom teachers use the term *process criteria* when they refer to effort, class participation, or homework—in other words, the *processes* that students use to learn (Guskey and Bailey 2001). Physical education teachers often evaluate process criteria on a checklist when they use self-check or peer evaluation techniques or when they require students to have correct form when performing skills.

Guskey and Bailey (2001) report that teachers also use **progress criteria** to determine the level of a student's achievement. Progress criteria do not look at a student's current level of achievement but rather at how much he or she has improved or progressed along a learning curve. When teachers use progress criteria, they must administer assessments more than once.

Knowing where to set the criteria for performance is difficult because many factors affect what students are capable of learning and doing, including prior experience in a sport or activity, resources available to the teacher (e.g., equipment, time, space), class size, and students' physical maturity. The book *Moving Into the Future*, produced by the National Association for Sport and Physical Education (NASPE) in 2004, provides benchmarks for grades kindergarten through 12. NASPE is also developing a series of assessments that can be used to evaluate students' achievement for each standard. The PE Metrics program will give teachers an excellent starting point as they develop rubrics for their assessments.

n many cases, teachers should use multiple types of criteria to judge the same performance. Once, when I was teaching a tennis class, the first set of lessons focused on teaching correct form for the serve. Students' serves were videotaped, analyzed by peers, and analyzed by the teacher, and by then end of that section their form was wonderful. However, when we moved into a product assessment, requiring students to serve the ball into the proper court, the *process* criteria (e.g., correct form) were not specified. As a result, students reverted to the toss-and-dink serve typically used by people with limited tennis experience Because teachers are not supposed to change the rules midway through an assessment, I let the students get by with that type of serve, but the experience taught me to specify all criteria that I expect students to meet—and never to assume anything!

## SIMPLE SCORING GUIDES

**Checklists** contain a list of criteria that must be seen for a performance or product to meet expectations. Some authors refer to these lists as performance lists (Arter and McTighe, 2001). When teachers use checklists, they decide whether the product or performance demonstrates a given characteristic without making a judgment about the quality of that characteristic. Checklists are commonly used as skill assessments of correct form with psychomotor skills (e.g., skipping, throwing, executing a forearm pass). Checklists are also useful in peer assessment and self-assessment, since students can use them to ensure that a project includes all of the required components. Checklists used in peer assessments of psychomotor skills reinforce critical elements both for the observer and for the performer, and they make excellent tools for encouraging perfect practice of skills.

Checklists are scored as yes-or-no ratings (Herman, Aschbacher, and Winters 1992). Scorers decide whether the students demonstrate the characteristic in the product or performance. Figure 3.1 shows a checklist for appropriate sporting behavior during games. In this example, the teacher is interested only in whether the student demonstrates the desired behaviors during game play; the teacher makes no determination about the degree to which the trait is present. Rather than explicitly offering *yes* and *no* options, some checklists list the traits and provide the scorer with a place to make a check mark if the behavior is present. Since the absence of a check mark beside a given trait could mean either that the performer failed to demonstrate the trait or that the evaluator simply failed to look at the descriptor and make the evaluation; this format is discouraged.

Some teachers use student journals to assess students' feelings or reactions to tasks or activities. The teacher can use a checklist to indicate the presence of various points without making a judgment about the quality of the student's response. Students are assessed on whether they include a specific element in an entry or meet certain standards of writing. Judging the quality of journal content about the affective domain can be problematic, since it sometimes leads students to begin writing what they believe teachers want to hear rather than expressing their genuine feelings. Because checklists identify the desired characteristics, they provide students with guidelines for successfully completing these assessments.

Checklists generally contain more traits or descriptors than are typically found in other types of scoring guides. This level of detail is helpful to students as they first learn to perform a motor skill or activity. Although teachers must provide enough characteristics to be diagnostic, they should not include so many that the checklist becomes cumbersome or difficult to use. When too many characteristics are included, a key element of performance may be undervalued or neglected because the scorer focuses on less important characteristics. Checklists for younger students should include fewer items—probably no more than three—whereas older students might be able to look at five critical elements when doing peer evaluations of skill. When checklists are used for motor skills, teachers must remember to list the critical elements in the order in which students will observe them (e.g., follow-through would not be listed first on the list of critical elements).

When checklists are used for peer or self-assessment, teachers must teach students how to do the assessments. Students must understand explicitly what the various terms on the checklist mean and what the performance should look like before marking a characteristic as present.

| Yes | No | |
|-----|-----|---|
| _____ | _____ | Plays within the rules of the game |
| _____ | _____ | Does not argue with others |
| _____ | _____ | Shares in team responsibilities |
| _____ | _____ | Gives others a chance according to the rules |
| _____ | _____ | Follows the coach's instructions |
| _____ | _____ | Respects the other team's efforts |
| _____ | _____ | Offers encouragement to teammates |
| _____ | _____ | Accepts officials' calls |
| _____ | _____ | Accepts the outcome of the game—win or lose |

**Figure 3.1** A checklist rubric is designed to assess the presence of listed characteristics or traits.

When teachers use checklists to look at student skills, it is very time consuming to check off each element. Because a teacher has more experience in evaluating skills, he or she is able to see whether a skill has been performed correctly. If it has not been then the teacher can pick out any elements that the student is doing incorrectly. Figure 3.2 shows a checklist that a teacher can use to evaluate a class. Skill element descriptors are listed at the top, and space is provided for the teacher to indicate whether the student is performing the skill correctly. If the whole skill is done correctly, the teacher simply checks the box in the first column for that student and moves on to evaluate the next student. If the student is performing the skill *incorrectly*, the recording sheet is used to indicate which of the critical elements the student is *not* performing correctly. If several members of the class are making the same error, the teacher can then provide additional instruction. If an error is limited to a few students, then those students can be instructed on an individual basis.

# POINT SYSTEM SCORING GUIDES

Point system scoring guides are very similar to checklists, except that they call for the scorer to award points for each of the various criteria on the list. As with checklists, the scorer is not required to make a judgment of quality; if the characteristic is present, then the student is awarded a set number of points for it. Also as with checklists, point systems provide feedback to students, who can quickly see whether they were awarded points for a given dimension or trait. Because point systems usually include more descriptors than does either an analytic or a holistic rubric, they can provide additional feedback to students. An advantage of using a point system scoring guide is that teachers can total the points earned and convert the result into a grade. When a teacher wants to emphasize a certain trait or dimension, he or she can assign more points to it (i.e., give it more weight).

A caution is offered when using point systems: In cases where several traits are listed under a main characteristic, either every listed trait must be present to award points for that characteristic or the teacher must assign points individually for the various subcomponents (those points equal the total allotted for that characteristic overall). This latter approach is illustrated in the rubric shown in figure 3.3. If, for example, a student's performance does not contain some of the points listed under the heading "Fitness evaluation," then the student will earn fewer than the total of 15 points allocated to that characteristic.

# CHOICES IN WRITING RUBRICS

Teachers face several choices when developing rubrics. This section will help teachers make those decisions by providing information about the types of rubrics (analytic and holistic) and explaining the differences between task-specific and generalized rubrics. The section will conclude with a discussion about the number of levels to include in a rubric.

| Student name | All correct | Assume ready position | Tuck chin | Raise hips | Stay curled | Stand to finish |
|---|---|---|---|---|---|---|
| Darius Ulmer | | | X | X | | |
| Andrea Stacy | | | X | | X | |
| Hannah Jackson | | | | X | | |
| Lamon Williams | | | | X | X | |
| Charity Johnson | X | | | | | |

**Figure 3.2**  Teacher checklists help teachers evaluate a class by marking if each student has done the skill correctly.

## Fitness Portfolio

_____ Fitness evaluation (15 points)

    _____ Abdominal strength (2 points)

    _____ PACER or other test of aerobic endurance (4 points)

    _____ Flexed-arm hang, pull-ups, push-ups (2 points)

    _____ Sit-and-reach (2 points)

    _____ Body fat (2 points)

        _____ Triceps

        _____ Calf

    _____ Resting heart rate (1 point)

    _____ Height (1 point)

    _____ Weight (1 point)

_____ Fitness plan (25 points)

    _____ Calculation of target heart rate (2 points)

    _____ Calculation of body mass index (2 points)

    _____ Needs analysis (5 points)

    _____ Proposed workout plan (16 points)

        _____ Warm-up and recording chart (3 points + 1 point for chart)

        _____ Strength workout and recording chart (3 points + 1 point for chart)

        _____ Flexibility program and recording chart (3 points + 1 point for chart)

        _____ Aerobic program and recording chart (3 points + 1 point for chart)

_____ Nutritional analysis (15 points)

    _____ Food record sheet for 1 week (5 points)

    _____ Analysis of food intake according to basic food groups (3 points)

    _____ Average caloric consumption per day (2 points)

    _____ Proposed nutritional action plan (5 points)

_____ Results (45 points)

    _____ Completed workout charts (10 points)

    _____ Weekly journal entries for exercise and nutrition (10 points)

    _____ Analysis of fitness improvements (10 points)

    _____ Discussion of nutrition results (5 points)

    _____ Analysis of fitness and nutritional products (10 points)

Student's choice of visiting a local fitness center and evaluating its services, offerings, and so on or doing one of the following:

    _____ Food label analysis for five favorite foods (5 points)

    _____ Food analysis for favorite fast-food meal (5 points)

    _____ Analysis of a commercial diet plan of the student's choosing (5 points)

    _____ Video analysis of weightlifting technique for two stations (5 points)

    _____ Analysis of the value of a popular piece of fitness equipment advertised to the public (5 points)

**Figure 3.3** When assigning points to broad categories in a point system scoring guide, teachers must also indicate the number of points that the subcategories receive.

## Analytic and Holistic Rubrics

The type of rubric chosen for an assessment depends on the task being evaluated and the needs of the assessor. The following discussion introduces teachers to analytic and holistic rubrics and explains when each can be used most effectively.

### Analytic Rubrics

**Analytic rubrics** require the scorer to use his or her judgment about the level of quality demonstrated in a product or performance for each trait or dimension included in the rubric. With analytic rubrics the scorer can indicate when a descriptor is present but not demonstrated to the point of showing competence or mastery. Because each dimension is scored independently of the others specified in the rubric, students can easily identify the areas in which they must improve.

The two types of analytic rubrics are quantitative and qualitative. **Quantitative analytic rubrics** (also called **numerical analytic rubrics**) require the scorer to give a numerical score (e.g., 3 out of 4) for each trait evaluated. On the surface, quantitative rubrics resemble checklists, because the traits are listed, but they differ from checklists in that the product or performance is evaluated for the *quality* of the traits (see figure 3.4). With a checklist, the trait must be fully present if the scorer is to credit the student for demonstrating it, whereas an analytic rubric allows the scorer to note the presence of a characteristic in rudimentary form. Because analytic rubrics require a decision about the degree of quality for each trait listed, they take longer to score than do checklists or point system scoring guides.

Words that give a verbal indication of the degree of quality—such as *never*, *sometimes*, *usually*, and *always*—are often included with the numerical score so that the numbers carry a specific meaning. It is more effective, however, if teachers use more than one word to describe a level—for example, "the performer is equally likely either to make a mistake or to perform the skill correctly." The same descriptors are used to evaluate every trait on the rubric. These verbal indicators give the scorer an idea of the quality of performance that each number represents. Without them, reliability could be low, if a scorer shifts the expectations that he or she associates with different numbers as the evaluation process evolves. Verbal indicators also help ensure consistency when more than one person is doing the scoring.

**Qualitative analytic rubrics** provide verbal descriptions for each level of the various traits or characteristics to be evaluated (see figure 3.5). The evaluator decides which description or level best describes the student's work in terms of each trait. Writing descriptive statements for each of the various traits is a laborious task. The difficult part is determining various levels of performance and writing the descriptions so that the differences between them are clear. Several rubrics are presented in chapters 7, 8, 9, and 10. Teachers can use those, along with the ones presented in this chapter, as a blueprint for writing their own rubrics so that they do not have to start from scratch. Several books (Arter and McTighe 2001; Marzano, Pickering, and McTighe 1993) contain rubrics written for various kinds of products or student work outside of physical education. Additional sample rubrics are available on many Web sites. These resources can provide ideas for descriptive terminology that teachers can use in writing qualitative rubrics.

When deciding whether to use a quantitative or qualitative analytic rubric, consider that people tend to remember numbers more easily than verbal descriptions—as long as it is clear what each number means. Qualitative rubrics provide the scorer with more complete and thorough descriptions of the desired quality for a given level, thus making it more apparent how to evaluate the performance or product (Herman, Aschbacher, and Winters 1992). These descriptions also improve the consistency of scoring with a qualitative rubric. Because qualitative rubrics are more detailed and require more time to use, they generally have fewer characteristics or traits than a quantitative rubric.

Analytic rubrics are usually used with formative assessments for two reasons. First, because the student receives a score for each individual trait, he or she can readily see areas of strength and those where further improvement is needed. Second, analytic rubrics are difficult to convert to grades. The various traits usually have different levels of importance in the assignment, which makes it unfair to simply assign each level a point value and then add the total points and

## Game-Play Assessment for Doubles Tennis

| The student: | Never | Inconsistently | Often | Usually |
|---|---|---|---|---|
| 1. Uses correct form on the forehand. | 1 | 2 | 3 | 4 |
| 2. Uses correct form on the backhand. | 1 | 2 | 3 | 4 |
| 3. Uses correct form on the lob. | 1 | 2 | 3 | 4 |
| 4. Uses correct form on the volley. | 1 | 2 | 3 | 4 |
| 5. Uses correct form on the first serve, making solid contact. | 1 | 2 | 3 | 4 |
| 6. Second serve—when needed—has correct form and lands in the service court. | 1 | 2 | 3 | 4 |
| 7. Uses specific shots at appropriate times. | 1 | 2 | 3 | 4 |
| 8. Places shots rather than just returning the ball. | 1 | 2 | 3 | 4 |
| 9. Moves into position quickly and prepares to play the ball. | 1 | 2 | 3 | 4 |
| 10. Returns to base position after making a play. | 1 | 2 | 3 | 4 |
| 11. Approaches the net for offensive play. | 1 | 2 | 3 | 4 |
| 12. Covers the entire court with partner. | 1 | 2 | 3 | 4 |
| 13. Communicates with partner. | 1 | 2 | 3 | 4 |
| 14. Hits shots to open spots on opponents' court. | 1 | 2 | 3 | 4 |
| 15. Play is balanced and somewhat even between partners. | 1 | 2 | 3 | 4 |
| 16. Recognizes good performance by partner and opponents. | 1 | 2 | 3 | 4 |
| 17. Calls shots correctly. | 1 | 2 | 3 | 4 |
| 18. Knowledge of rules is evident. | 1 | 2 | 3 | 4 |

Never = the skill is not attempted.

Inconsistently = the performer is equally likely either to make a mistake or to perform the skill correctly.

Often = the performer is consistent but does make an occasional error.

Usually = the performer is very consistent, rarely making an error.

**Figure 3.4** Quantitative analytic rubrics are useful for providing feedback to students and assessing their ability to use discrete sport or activity skills in an applied setting.

# Qualitative Analytic Rubric for Tennis Play

| | Shot execution |
|---|---|
| 4 | Executes all shots taught with good form using them at appropriate times. Footwork is correct. Student knows in advance which shot to use and begins preparation for that shot while moving into position. Can read spin. Shot is unhurried. |
| 3 | Utilizes most shots taught with good form, usually using them at appropriate times. Feet are set when making the shot. |
| 2 | Uses several of the shots taught but not always at the appropriate time. Some form breaks are apparent but form is mostly correct. Student arrives in position to play the ball just in time. |
| 1 | Relies on one or two shots for the entire game. Incorrect form causes shots to be misplaced or ineffective. Student is not in position when shot is attempted. |

| | Court movement |
|---|---|
| 4 | Moves around, covering all parts of the court, and consistently attempts to return to home position. Feet appear to be in constant motion, and weight is on the balls of the feet to enable quick movement. Student is in position to play all shots. Always anticipates where the opponent will place the next shot and moves into position to play it. |
| 3 | Covers court, usually attempting to return to home position. Weight is on the balls of the feet to enable quick movement. Student is usually in position to play shots and can anticipate opponent's shot. |
| 2 | Covers court but is occasionally out of position. Must shift weight to the balls of the feet, delaying arrival to the ball to make the shot. Student attempts to return to home position but may not always get there. Makes some attempt to anticipate opponent's return shot. |
| 1 | Moves to play the ball after the ball comes over the net and then remains there. Parts of the court remain uncovered at times. Weight is usually back on the heels, slowing the ability to respond to the shot. Student tends to reach to play the ball rather than being in position. |

| | Service |
|---|---|
| 4 | Always uses correct form while executing the serve. The serve is placed in the corners of the opponent's service area. The first serve is powerful and occasional aces result. The second serve, when necessary, is always in and is also very strong. |
| 3 | Usually uses correct form while executing the serve. The first serve is very strong, usually landing within the service area. The second serve usually lands in. |
| 2 | Demonstrates several elements of correct form while executing the serve, although does commit some errors. The second serve is consistent and usually lands in. Student may not use a full swing on the second serve using more of a "punch" shot. |
| 1 | First serve is usually not in. There is little difference between first and second serve with regard to power. Student may not use a full swing for either serve. |

*(continued)*

**Figure 3.5** Qualitative analytic rubrics provide verbal descriptions of the teacher's expectations and can be used for providing formative feedback about several elements that are important to playing a game or performing well.

| Rules | |
|---|---|
| 4 | Shows evidence of thoroughly knowing and applying rules. Partners rotate up and back for service. Can play a tiebreaker without instruction. Can answer any question when asked. |
| 3 | Shows evidence of usually knowing and applying the rules. Serving order and rotation are correct. Can answer most questions when asked. |
| 2 | Shows some evidence of knowing rules. Serving order and rotation are correct. May make a few errors. Struggles with some questions. |
| 1 | Is unfamiliar with rules and depends on opponents or partner for guidance. Is unsure of serving order and rotation. Struggles with most questions. |
| **Strategy** | |
| 4 | Demonstrates much evidence of using strategy against an opponent. Hits shots to open places on the court. Uses lob and volley shots to gain an offensive advantage. Tries to anticipate opponent's shots by moving into position to play them. Communicates well with partner. Consistently works with partner to cover the court. Serving order and rotation benefits own team. Court positions are based on his or her team's strengths. Hits to opponent's weaknesses. |
| 3 | Demonstrates evidence of using strategy against an opponent. Usually hits shots to open places on the court. Communicates with partner, cooperating to cover the court. Uses lob and volley shots to gain an advantage. |
| 2 | Uses some strategy against the opponent. Attempts to hit the open places on the court. Some communication with partner. Some evidence of working with partner to cover the court. |
| 1 | Hits shots directly back to the opponent so that they are easy to return. Does not talk to partner. At times, both players go after the ball. Little evidence of teamwork or cooperation. |
| **Fair play** | |
| 4 | Consistently recognizes good play by others. Congratulates opponents for a good game regardless of the game's outcome. Works well with partner to cover the court at all times. Shows strong evidence of cooperation and teamwork. Does not try to play the entire court alone. Calls all shots honestly and fairly. |
| 3 | Usually recognizes good play by others. Works with partner to cover the court most of the time. Shows evidence of cooperation and teamwork. Does not try to play the entire court alone. Calls shots honestly and fairly. |
| 2 | Occasionally recognizes good play by others. Shows some evidence of working with partner to cover the court. May dominate court play from time to time. Calls shots honestly and fairly. |
| 1 | Rarely talks with others. Does not work as a team with partner. Complains constantly about line calls made by the opponent. Makes incorrect calls to benefit self. |

**Figure 3.5** *(continued)*

divide by the number of traits to get an average score. To use an analytic rubric for grading in a manner that is fair to students, teachers must develop a weighting system and a method for calculating grades so that the grades represent the true level of student learning.

## Holistic Rubrics

**Holistic rubrics** consist of paragraphs written to describe various levels of performance, and each paragraph includes several dimensions and traits (see figure 3.6). Whereas analytic rubrics require scorers to evaluate the quality

# Holistic Rubric for Doubles Tennis

**Level 4:** Executes all shots taught with good form using them at appropriate times. Footwork is correct. Student knows in advance which shot to use and begins preparation for that shot while moving into position. Can read spin. Shot is unhurried. Moves around, covering all parts of the court, and consistently attempts to return to home position. Feet appear to be in constant motion, and weight is on the balls of the feet to enable quick movement. Student is in position to play all shots. Always anticipates where the opponent will place the next shot and moves into position to play it. Always uses correct form while executing the serve. The serve is placed in the corners of the opponent's service area. The first serve is powerful and occasional aces result. The second serve, when necessary, is always in and is also very strong. Shows evidence of thoroughly knowing and applying rules. Partners rotate up and back for service. Can play a tiebreaker without instruction. Can answer any question when asked. Demonstrates much evidence of using strategy against an opponent. Hits shots to open places on the court. Uses lob and volley shots to gain an offensive advantage. Tries to anticipate opponent's shots by moving into position to play them. Communicates well with partner. Consistently works with partner to cover the court. Serving order and rotation benefits own team. Court positions are based on his or her team's strengths. Hits to opponent's weaknesses. Consistently recognizes good play by others. Congratulates opponents for a good game regardless of the game's outcome. Works well with parner to cover the court at all times. Shows strong evidence of cooperation and teamwork. Does not try to play the entire court alone. Calls all shots honestly and fairly.

**Level 3:** Utilizes most shots taught with good form, usually using them at appropriate times. Feet are set when making the shot. Covers court, usually attempting to return to home position. Weight is on the balls of the feet to enable quick movement. Student is usually in position to play shots and can anticipate opponent's shot. Usually uses correct form while executing the serve. The first serve is very strong, usually landing within the service area. The second serve usually lands in. Shows evidence of usually knowing and applying the rules. Serving order and rotation are correct. Can answer most questions when asked. Demonstrates evidence of using strategy against an opponent. Usually hits shots to open places on the court. Communicates with partner, cooperating to cover the court. Uses lob and volley shots to gain an advantage. Usually recognizes good play by others. Works with partner to cover the court most of the time. Shows evidence of cooperation and teamwork. Does not try to play the entire court alone. Calls shots honestly and fairly.

**Level 2:** Uses several of the shots taught but not always at the appropriate time. Some form breaks are apparent but form is mostly correct. Student arrives in position to play the ball just in time. Covers court but is occasionally out of position. Must shift weight to the balls of the feet, delaying arrival to the ball to make the shot. Student attempts to return to home position but may not always get there. Makes some attempt to anticipate opponent's return shot. Demonstrates several elements of correct form while executing the serve, although does commit some errors. The second serve is consistent and usually lands in. Student may not use a full swing on the second serve using more of a "punch" shot. Shows some evidence of knowing rules. Serving order and rotation are correct. May make a few errors. Struggles with some questions. Uses some strategy against the opponent. Attempts to hit the open places on the court. Some communication with partner. Some evidence of working with partner to cover the court. Occasionally recognizes good play by others. Shows some evidence of working with partner to cover the court. May dominate court play from time to time. Calls shots honestly and fairly.

**Level 1:** Relies on one or two shots for the entire game. Incorrect form causes shots to be misplaced or ineffective. Student is not in position when shot is attempted. Moves to play the ball after the ball comes over the net and then remains there. Parts of the court remain uncovered at times. Weight is usually back on the heels, slowing the ability to respond to the shot. Student tends to reach to play the ball rather than being in position. First serve is usually not in. There is little difference between first and second serve with regard to power. Student may not use a full swing for either serve. Is unfamiliar with rules and depends on opponents or partner for guidance. Is unsure of serving order and rotation. Struggles with most questions. Hits shots directly back to the opponent so that they are easy to return. Does not talk to partner. At times, both players go after the ball. Little evidence of teamwork or cooperation. Rarely talks with others. Does not work as a team with partner. Complains constantly about line calls made by the opponent. Makes incorrect calls to benefit self.

**Figure 3.6** Holistic rubrics are useful for summative evaluation of student performance and for determining students' grades.

of each trait, holistic rubrics call on the scorer to assign a single score by deciding which level best describes the overall quality of the product or performance. Because the scorer makes only one decision about the quality of the student product or performance, holistic rubrics generally require less time to use. Holistic rubrics are also useful for assigning grades because a single overall score is given. The descriptions within a level and the number of levels used can correspond with a teacher's grading scale.

Teachers begin the process of developing a holistic rubric by combining the traits listed for a given level from an analytic rubric into a single, integrated paragraph. Holistic rubrics address only the major characteristics to determine the overall quality of a product or performance. Therefore, when teachers convert traits from an analytic rubric into a holistic rubric as described in the previous paragraph, some adjustments to clarify the levels and the descriptors must be made.

Holistic scoring can sacrifice validity and reliability for efficiency (Wiggins 1996). Problems with validity arise when two students get the same score for different reasons. Because the product or performance is considered as an entity—with several dimensions contributing to the final score—the scorer's reasons for rating the product or performance at a certain level are not always apparent, and students don't always know specifically why they were given a certain score. In contrast, an analytic rubric allows students to see a score for each characteristic or dimension. Validity and reliability can also be threatened when a holistic rubric is used by two or more evaluators. Unless scorers are trained to know which dimensions or criteria are most important (i.e., to agree on a hierarchy), one scorer might emphasize one or two traits that are of relatively little importance to another scorer, thus threatening reliability. For instance, in using a game-play assessment, the first scorer might value skill execution whereas the second scorer considers strategy and court position most important. When a hierarchy of traits exists, it must be indicated in the rubric and scorers must be trained to use the rubric appropriately.

If a student product or performance falls between levels—that is, it includes characteristics from each of two levels—the dilemma of how to score it can be resolved in several ways.

The first is simply to state that all traits must be demonstrated for the score to be at that level. A second approach is to identify the key elements and those traits considered most important determine the level at which to score the product or performance. Another possible solution is to allow scores of 1.5, 2.5, and 3.5 to indicate the presence of characteristics from more than one level. This issue should be addressed when training scorers. Teachers who score their own assessments would make their own decisions about how to handle mixed levels prior to scoring the assessment.

Because holistic rubrics assess overall student performance, teachers should not use them to diagnosis strengths and weaknesses of the individual traits. Problems arise when they are used for student self-assessment. Holistic rubrics are more likely to be used for summative (final) evaluations and large-scale testing (e.g., state-level tests), because, in both of these situations, students are not expected to improve performance and therefore do not need the diagnostic detail that an analytic rubric provides. Some teachers choose to use holistic rubrics because they are more conducive to determining a student grade or because the teacher prefers to evaluate work as an entity rather than considering components individually. If teachers use holistic rubrics to evaluate student work, they might use markers to highlight the characteristics that place a performance or product at a particular level. Using another strategy, teachers might highlight characteristics that were at a higher level than the overall score to acknowledge student achievement.

Both analytic and holistic rubrics distinguish between levels of student performance. When using a rubric to score student performances or products, teachers should make sure that the differences are obvious between different levels of achievement or student understanding. Analytic rubrics require more time to use for scoring than are holistic rubrics because the scorer must make a decision regarding each dimension or trait. One rule of thumb is to use analytic rubrics *during* instruction (i.e., for formative assessment) because they give diagnostic information. Holistic rubrics, on the other hand, are best used if projects or performances from many students must be scored or if the assessment represents a final product or performance for an activity unit.

## Generalized and Task-Specific Rubrics

The next choice that one must make before starting to write a rubric is whether to write a task-specific or generalized rubric. **Generalized rubrics** are used in a variety of assessments. They are popular in statewide assessments that evaluate a broad concept such as writing ability. They are useful for assessments that contain many different types of performance or products as found in portfolios. Generalized rubrics tend to look at big-picture characteristics that are common to all assessments rather than at specific traits relative to the assessment task. They use more universal descriptors (see figure 3.7 for an example involving invasion games) and evaluate conceptual learning. A generalized rubric for gymnastics, for example, would focus on characteristics (e.g., amplitude, elegance, lightness, rhythm) that are important in every gymnastics routine, from floor exercise

## Game-Play Rubric for Invasion Games

### Base or Home Position

**Level 4:** Consistently returns to base or home position between skill attempts. Feet are constantly moving, even when ball or projectile is not on his or her side of the net. Is always in position, whether making a play or supporting teammate.

**Level 3:** Frequently returns to base or home position between skill attempts. Keeps feet moving to position self to make a play or support teammate. May occasionally be out of position.

**Level 2:** Attempts to return to base or home position between skill attempts. Often takes up correct position to make a play or support teammate. Occasionally stops on the court or field.

**Level 1:** Occasionally returns to base or home position between skill attempts.

### Adjusts to the Movement of Others

**Level 4:** Consistently adjusts to movement by other players, either offensively or defensively. Is aware of changes and moves made by an opponent. Anticipates opponent's movements. Weight is always forward and on the balls of the feet, making the player ready to move.

**Level 3:** Frequently adjusts to movement of other players, either offensively or defensively. Is aware of changes and moves made by an opponent. Weight is usually forward, making the player ready to move.

**Level 2:** Attempts to makes adjustments to movement of other players, either offensively or defensively. Weight is often forward, making the player ready to move.

**Level 1:** Tends to wait to move until after opponent has completed shot or play. Slow in reacting to movement of teammates or opponents.

### Appropriate Choices

**Level 4:** Consistently makes appropriate choices about what to do with ball or projectile. Shows no hesitation or latency when getting ready to make a play. Decision about how to make the play is based on response from opponent and seems to be automatic. Seems to anticipate opponent's response.

**Level 3:** Frequently makes appropriate choices about what to do with ball or projectile. Decision on how to play the ball or projectile is made well before the object arrives, making the response deliberate. Shows little hesitation or latency on the response.

**Level 2:** Makes appropriate choices about what to do with ball or projectile more often than does not. Decision about how to play the ball or projectile is made shortly before the object arrives, making the player appear to scramble at times.

**Level 1:** Makes a play on the ball or projectile, but it may not be appropriate considering court position, opponent's position, or game strategy. May show some hesitation or delay in play or shot selection.

*(continued)*

**Figure 3.7** This generalized game-play rubric could apply to several different invasion games.

## Skill Execution

**Level 4:** Consistently uses correct form while executing and performing a skill. Movement is smooth, seemingly effortless, and deliberate. Is in position before making the play and shows follow-through when appropriate.

**Level 3:** Frequently uses correct form while executing and performing a skill. Movement is smooth and deliberate. Positioning is correct before making the play and player follows through when appropriate.

**Level 2:** Uses correct form much of the time while executing and performing a skill. Occasionally has to rush into position to make the play.

**Level 1:** Student's movement approximates the appropriate skill but is hesitant or choppy. Form breaks are apparent.

## Support

**Level 4:** Consistently provides support off the ball or projectile, positioning self to receive it when a teammate has the object. Player positioning reflects the use of sound strategy being in an optimal position to make the subsequent play.

**Level 3:** Frequently provides support off the ball or projectile, positioning self to receive it when a teammate has the object. Use of strategy is apparent.

**Level 2:** Attempts to provide support off the ball or projectile when a teammate has the object. May occasionally find self in a nonadvantageous position.

**Level 1:** Fails to position self to receive a pass or provide support to a teammate. Frequently is behind the play rather than in position to enhance current play status.

## Cover

**Level 4:** Consistently provides defensive help for a player making a play on the ball or projectile, or moving toward the ball or projectile. Teammate is able to make an appropriate play, as opponent is unable to interrupt. Provides support by creating a player advantage (e.g., three-on-two, two-on-one) for teammate. Teammate is successful with intended play because of this support.

**Level 3:** Frequently provides defensive help for a player making a play on the ball or projectile, or moving toward the ball or projectile. Support for teammate is apparent and facilitates the play. Teammate is usually able to make intended play because of this support.

**Level 2:** Attempts to provide defensive help for a player making a play on the ball or projectile, or moving toward the ball or projectile. Support for teammate is noticeable.

**Level 1:** May attempt to provide defensive help for a player making a play on the ball or projectile, or moving the ball or projectile, but in fact impedes the play or progress. Positioning is not timely and may be inappropriate.

## Guard or Mark an Opponent

**Level 4:** Consistently covers the opponent, making it impossible for opponent's teammates to pass to player. Maintains position between an opponent and the goal when opponent is in control of the ball. If the guarded opponent has the ball, the player is in position to intercept an attempted pass. Maintains a wide base of support, low center of gravity for balance, and thus can move rapidly in any direction. Focuses on opponent's midsection to better stay with the opponent.

**Level 3:** Frequently is in position to cover player being marked to prevent a pass or score. Maintains a wide base of support to move in any direction, keeping a lowered center of gravity. Usually maintains defensive position, staying with the opponent.

**Level 2:** Attempts to cover the player being marked to prevent a pass or score. When loses position on player being marked, attempts to regain it.

**Level 1:** Is often behind the opponent and unable to intercept a pass or keep the player from scoring. May know correct position, but opponent is usually able to move quickly and put the player guarding the opponent out of position.

**Figure 3.7** *(continued)*

and tumbling to those that involve gymnastics apparatus. In another example, a **game-play rubric** for net games might look at elements (e.g., skill execution, strategy, shot placement, court movement) that are common to all net games (e.g., badminton, pickleball, volleyball).

One advantage of using a generalized rubric is that the person creating the assessment does not have to develop a rubric for every assessment task. Because generalized rubrics are used to score multiple tasks, teachers save time by not needing to write multiple rubrics. Another benefit is that after a scorer receives initial training in how to use the generalized rubric, no further training is necessary for later assessments. In addition, since teachers using a generalized rubric are looking at a standard set of criteria, scoring consistency between teachers tends to be better (Arter and McTighe 2001). Reliability tends to be lower at first for generalized rubrics, but once a person has been trained on scoring using a generalized rubric, reliability increases (Arter 1996) to a level equal to that of task-specific rubrics.

When creating a generalized rubric, one must look for the elements that the tasks have in common, then identify relevant and explicit criteria for those elements. The generalized rubric for game play shown in figure 3.7 uses game-play performance criteria identified by Mitchell, Oslin, and Griffin (2006) as the source of its descriptors. This analytic rubric was developed from seven categories identified for game analysis and describes levels of performance for each of these areas. The components included in the rubric are important in many games, especially those classified as invasion and court games. Because generalized rubrics need to look at broad concepts, they may not have the detail found in a task-specific rubric. What is scored depends on the purpose of the assessment. In generalized rubrics, dimensions can be either emphasized or downplayed, according to assessment needs, as long as this aspect of the rubric is communicated to all people scoring the task.

**Task-specific rubrics** contain criteria unique to the assessment and thus are created for individual assessment tasks (see figure 3.5 for an example of a qualitative analytic rubric that is task-specific). Task-specific rubrics are generally easier to create than generalized rubrics because one can focus on a specific activity area or sport rather than having to consider characteristics that are universal to several activities or sports. The benefit of a task-specific rubric is that it can target specific knowledge or behaviors that the teacher wants to see students demonstrate. The disadvantage is that a task-specific rubric is sometimes so transparent that students are not required to think through the process they will use to complete the assessment (in the case of a written assessment).

Because task-specific rubrics address a single task, it is easier and faster to get consistent scoring with them. Teachers must practice using each task-specific rubric before being able to use it competently. Task-specific rubrics can often be modified, with little effort, to apply to another sport. Figure 3.8 illustrates how a tennis rubric could be modified for badminton. When a task-specific rubric is preferred, the teacher might create a rubric that combines characteristics from a generalized rubric with characteristics specific to a task or assessment. The broad criteria that generalize across performance could form the basis for the rubric, requiring the teacher to only add criteria specific to the assessment being used. This approach saves time for the teacher and results in a solid rubric for the assessment.

## Deciding How Many Criteria to Include

A question arises here: "How many characteristics should a teacher include?" The answer to this question lies with the type of rubric being created along with the complexity of the assessment. Obviously, simpler assessments require less complex rubrics. Having too many criteria to consider usually leads to an unreliable rubric; the evaluation process can be slowed down to the point that it is inaccurate, and the assessor may actually forget to consider some of the criteria. Deciding what and how many criteria to include is similar to making a salad—you have to determine which ingredients are essential and which are meaningful but not essential to the making of a good final product. A rule to thumb to follow when writing a rubric is to include all essential elements but hold the extras.

The elements included in a rubric to define excellence are referred to by several names: **descriptor**, **trait**, and **characteristic** (Herman, Aschbacher, and Winters 1992; Wiggins 1998a). They reflect the elements of good performance

## Modification of an Existing Task-Specific Rubric

| From tennis (doubles) | To badminton (doubles) |
|---|---|
| 1. Uses correct form on the forehand. | 1. Uses correct form on forehand shots. |
| 2. Uses correct form on the backhand. | 2. Uses correct form on backhand shots or around the head shots. |
| 3. Uses correct form on the lob. | 3. Uses clear shots before moving to the net to gain offensive position and advantage. |
| 4. Uses correct form on the volley. | 4. Uses correct form on change of pace shots, such as the drop, smash, underhand drop (hairpin), and so on, making it difficult to determine which shot the player is using. |
| 5. Uses correct form on the serve, making solid contact. | 5. Uses correct form on serves. |
| 6. When necessary, makes good second serve that lands in. | 6. Uses both short and long serves when appropriate, placing them on the court where the opponent is not standing. |
| 7. Uses various shots at appropriate times. | 7. Uses various shots at appropriate times. |
| 8. Places shots rather than just returning the ball. | 8. Places shots rather than just returning the bird. |
| 9. Moves into position quickly and prepares to play the ball. | 9. Moves into position quickly and prepares to play the bird. |
| 10. Returns to ready position after making a play. | 10. Returns to ready position after making a play. |
| 11. Approaches the net for offensive play. | 11. Uses a variety of shots to alter the pace of the game and add deception. |
| 12. Covers the entire court with partner. | 12. Covers the entire court with partner. |
| 13. Communicates with partner. | 13. Communicates with partner. |
| 14. Watches opponent and hits shots to open spots on opponent's court. | 14. Watches opponent and hits shots to open spots on opponent's court. |
| 15. Play with partner is balanced and even. | 15. Play with partner is balanced and even. |
| 16. Recognizes good performance from partner and opponents. | 16. Recognizes good performance from partner and opponents. |
| 17. Calls shots correctly. | 17. Calls shots correctly. |
| 18. Knowledge of rules is evident. | 18. Knowledge of rules is evident. |

**Figure 3.8** In some cases, an existing task-specific rubric can be modified for a similar sport by changing the skills being evaluated.

and become the criteria by which a presentation is judged. Teachers can evaluate student performance from a variety of perspectives. Criteria must distinguish between useful indicators and genuine criteria (Wiggins 1998a). With some rubrics a criterion is used across the levels with different levels of difficulty or quality. Another strategy for writing rubrics is to use a cumulative approach where additional criteria are added to those described at the lowest level so that the difficulty for the characteristic becomes increasingly more demanding.

When writing a qualitative or holistic rubric, related criteria can often be used to describe the different levels of performance on the rubric. Criteria for effective rubrics should do the following:

- Include all important components and aspects of performance
- Avoid details that are insignificant
- Be written in language that the user understands (which may require separate rubrics for scorers and students)
- Take into account any contextual variable that has the potential to affect performance
- Link to instructional objectives
- Reflect best practice or professional opinion
- Address every task and component of the assessment

Consulting resources can help avoid the problems with validity that arise when a rubric addresses incorrect criteria. Expert opinion, rather than personal preference, should be used to determine criteria. A teacher must be aware of his or her bias and avoid selecting criteria that are not important. Rubric criteria should be derived logically from analysis of what students must know and be able to do to demonstrate competence.

Again, the trick is to include all essential criteria without getting bogged down in details. If a rubric does not include all the important criteria, it will be invalid. If, during a pilot use of a given rubric, a student meets all the specified criteria and still produces a substandard performance, then the criteria are inappropriate. With qualitative or holistic rubrics, 4 to 6 characteristics will generally suffice, whereas the list for a quantitative analytic rubric may include up to 15 characteristics. The more criteria included in a rubric, the more time required to score the product or performance. When looking at game-play performance, teachers should plan to use the rubric on more than one day to accurately evaluate student performance. Another strategy is to evaluate only a few of the characteristics listed on the rubric during any given class period.

When several people are going to use the same rubric, a brainstorming session helps to determine the list of criteria. Consulting with colleagues about essential elements can help avoid omitting key criteria. Another useful approach is to generate a list of many possible items for inclusion and ask someone with content knowledge to rank-order them. When writing rubrics, leave out the trivial elements and make sure to include the important ones. A rubric must represent a balance between too little and too much. Including too little detail can make it difficult or even impossible to accurately evaluate student work. On the other hand, too much detail can cause confusion because scorers have too many items to consider and may lose sight of what the final overall performance or product should demonstrate or look like.

## Deciding How Many Levels to Write

Teachers frequently want to know how many levels to include in a rubric. The best way to answer this question is to consider the purpose of the assessment. When a teacher merely needs to distinguish between acceptable and unacceptable performance, then only two levels are required. In other instances, teachers will develop five levels of performance—one to represent each grade (e.g., A, B, C, D, F). Some state assessments have up to 10 levels of performance.

When outside requirements do not dictate the number of levels (e.g., five categories for grades), a rubric should have at least three levels: one to indicate desired student performance, a second to indicate the cut score (i.e., the cutoff for an acceptable or passing grade), and a third to describe unacceptable student performance. The authors recommend adding a fourth level, at a higher level of performance than the expected level, so that teachers have a way to recognize and reward exceptional student work or performance. This fourth level should represent the ultimate performance (e.g., of a level equal to Tiger Woods or Annika Sorenstam), something that only 1 or 2 percent of the students will achieve over the course of a teaching career. With this ultimate level, ceiling effect is avoided thus giving teachers a way to challenge exceptional students who go beyond the normal expectations. By writing this ultimate level, teachers encourage students to raise their expectations and broaden their horizons. Even if students never reach this level, they have a sense of what is "out there." If grades are a consideration, the level below this ultimate level represents A level performance.

**Developmental rubrics** are used with all grade levels (K–12; see table 3.1 for an example) and include several performance levels; when taken together this rubric represents a continuum of performance quality. Developmental rubrics may be used for statewide assessment tasks such as those for writing or literacy. The national curriculum for the United Kingdom uses developmental rubrics to assess students in physical education (DfEE/QCA 2000). Additionally, this type of scoring is used in some sports. For example, gymnastics routines for beginners through those performed at the Olympics are judged on a 10-point scale.

A rubric with an even number of levels force scorers to exercise more care in judging (Wiggins 1996). If a rubric includes an odd number of levels, teachers sometimes tend to score the product or performance toward the middle. An even number of levels removes the option of a middle score and forces the user to make a decision about the quality of the work or performance. Also consider adding a level to use when a student fails to attempt the task (i.e., to indicate nonperformance). If awarding points, it is suggested that this level be given a point value of zero.

# HOW TO CREATE RUBRICS

Writing rubrics is one of the most difficult parts of creating performance-based assessments. The following basic steps are offered to guide the reader through a process for developing rubrics:

1. Identify what needs to be assessed.
2. Envision the desired student performance.
3. Identify the main characteristics.
4. Develop descriptors (for quantitative rubrics).
5. Pilot the assessment and rubric.
6. Develop levels (for qualitative rubrics).
7. Create a separate rubric for students (for qualitative rubrics).
8. Administer the assessment.
9. Revise the rubric.

## Step 1: Identify What Needs to Be Assessed

Educators who create performance-based assessments are sometimes guilty of failing to align curriculum and assessment. In an attempt to be "authentic" and "real-world," an educator may start by creating an assessment that is germane to the subject area, then look for a standard or objective that it could be used to assess. The result is a fun, nifty, assessment that doesn't address or evaluate the desired content. Another common problem occurs when a teacher knows that a lesson should include an assessment but doesn't stop to consider what information needs to be obtained from the assessment. The result is an ineffective assessment that wastes both the teacher's and the students' time.

The first questions to consider when writing an assessment are: What is the purpose of this assessment? What am I assessing? What information do I need from this assessment? These questions require teachers to go back to their instructional goals. If these questions are not addressed, assessments will not align with the curriculum. Although this step may appear to be a rather simple and logical one, all too often it is left undone.

Some rubrics are written for behaviors rather than for an assessment task. In the case of a disposition or affective-domain rubric, no specific task is associated with the assessment; the rubric is used instead to evaluate whether students have demonstrated appropriate behaviors. The expected behaviors must be stated and defined in concrete, observable terms. Similarly, generalized rubrics are written conceptually and can be applied to a multitude of tasks. Regardless of the content that a rubric will be used to evaluate, if the teacher fails to clearly identify the content, the purpose of the assessment, and the information that the assessment needs to provide, then the resulting rubric will be deficient.

## Step 2: Envision the Desired Student Performance

An idea of expected student performance on this assessment should emerge after considering the instructional goals and the assessments used to measure student learning relative to these goals. Teachers must decide what they will accept as evidence that students have met their instructional goals or objectives. Along with determining the type of assessment, teachers also must envision an acceptable level of quality.

Regardless of the type of rubric written, establishing a target for the final product or

**Table 3.1** Developmental Rubric for Soccer

|  | Kindergarten | Grades 1–2 | Grades 3–5 | Grades 6–8 | Grades 9–12 |
|---|---|---|---|---|---|
| Dribbling | Is able to touch the ball with various parts of the foot. When touching the ball with one foot, can maintain balance while switching from one foot to the other. | Is able to use the dribble to advance the ball toward the target. Can move in different directions while following different pathways. | Is able to maintain possession of the ball against a light defense. Makes a smooth transition from receiving a pass to dribbling, to advance the ball toward the goal. Can pass the ball to others while dribbling. | Is able to use the dribble to maintain possession while playing small-sided games against moderate level of defensive pressure. | Is able to maintain possession and use the dribble effectively during game play. Can transition smoothly from receiving a ball from another player to advancing the ball, to passing the ball to a teammate or shooting it to score. |
| Shooting and passing | Can kick a stationary ball, causing it to advance in the intended direction. | Can kick a stationary ball from a moving approach and hit a target 10 feet (3 meters) away. | Is able to shoot or pass the ball from a dribble and can receive a pass from another teammate during game play. | Is able to maintain possession of the ball by passing to a teammate. Can hit the target when doing penalty kicks. | Can shoot the ball from a dribble or pass to score. Passes the ball to teammates, advancing the ball toward the goal or to an open player. |
| Trapping and volleying | Is able to stop the ball using a foot trap. | Can trap the ball with either foot and with parts of the lower body. | Traps the ball with various parts of the body. Is able to begin dribbling with some hesitation after the initial stop. | Traps the ball with a variety of body parts and settles it to initiate the next play. Is able to direct a volley kick with some accuracy. | Is able to trap the ball and control it regardless of the incoming level. Is able to score using a volley kick. |
| Offensive skills | Knows that the dribble is used to advance the ball toward the goal and that a team needs to shoot the ball into the goal to score. | Is able to dribble and move the ball toward the goal. | Moves to an open area to receive a pass from a teammate. Can create a scoring situation when up a player (e.g., 2v1). | Maintains possession of the ball with the dribble or pass. Understands how to create space and find open space. | As first attacker, knows when to pass, dribble, or shoot while playing a game. Switches the point of attack when appropriate. |
| Defensive skills | Knows that the way to keep the other team from scoring is to position oneself between the ball and the goal area. | Can move down the field while mirroring an opponent. Is able to back shuffle while moving to face an offensive player. | Works to delay opponents' advance of the ball while forcing the dribbler in one direction. | Is able to gain control of the ball from the dribbler with a tackle. Can force the dribbler to a player giving cover. | Fills passing lanes to prevent opponent from scoring. Is able to block shots as a player or goalkeeper. |

performance is easier if teachers develop a mental picture of the expected student performance or behavior. If teachers are working as a team to develop the rubric, it is necessary to spend some time discussing expectations for student achievement to clarify the vision for all members of the writing team. If a teacher is working alone to develop the rubric, discussing ideas with colleagues is helpful. Some teachers also gather ideas by raising the topic in an Internet chat room. Whatever the approach, having a clear picture of final expectations will make the subsequent steps much easier to implement.

## Step 3: Identify the Main Characteristics

After envisioning the desired student performance, teachers must capture these ideas in writing. Too often, teachers have mental expectations regarding an assessment but fail to articulate those expectations for students. They rely on the idea that "They will know it when they see it." When teachers fail to write down their criteria, students have little idea about what their performance must be to satisfy teacher expectations. The process of capturing expectations in writing begins with brainstorming several words that represent student achievement. These words describe a clear explanation of the teacher's goals and objectives and could become descriptors or traits for the rubric. After identifying several ideas, teachers use them to write short sentences or phrases that describe student competence. Along with envisioning acceptable student performance, errors can also provide valuable information for the rubric. Teachers can clarify their expectations in parts by thinking about what students should *not* do.

After developing these phrases, evaluate the entire list and see which items fit together; some

of the elements collapse nicely into others. Since this may not be the final list, teachers should remain open to change. If developing a quantitative rubric, this list of phrases represents the criteria to include in the rubric. If several statements describe the qualities of a given characteristic, this characteristic will probably be a primary trait on the rubric. These additional statements can be used when developing the descriptions of levels for qualitative rubrics.

## Step 4: Develop Descriptors (for Quantitative Rubrics)

In this step, teachers develop a quantitative analytic rubric. The descriptors written in the previous step must be modified into sentences or phrases that capture what is expected of students. Some people use single words (e.g., *sometimes, often, always, never*) to describe the various levels of the rubric. Another strategy is to attach a percentage to single words; for example, *sometimes* might mean that the statement is true about 25 percent of the time. Yet another strategy is to use a descriptive phrase (see table 3.2 for examples).

To use the rubric, the teacher must develop a score sheet on which to record students' scores. It is helpful to have a sheet that lists the entire class, but in the case of large classes this might not be possible. If possible, it is helpful to group students together on the recording sheet so that the teacher doesn't have to spend a great deal of time looking for students' names (e.g., list students by teams). If the names of the students are listed alphabetically, the teacher might consider highlighting the rows containing the names of the students chosen for a given observation. If the teacher will be evaluating several groups during a single class period, he or she can use different colors to easily find the names of

**Table 3.2**    Descriptive Phrases for Levels of a Quantitative Rubric

| Level | Beginning | Developing | Competent | Sound |
|---|---|---|---|---|
| Phrase describing the level | This is a bare beginning. Student is attempting to complete the task or do the skill. | There is need for improvement. The level of performance is inconsistent but correct about half of the time. | Overall, the student demonstrates correct performance more often than not, but some weaknesses are still evident. | The student demonstrates control and consistent performance, and many strengths are apparent. |

students in any given group. When assessing a single item, some people prefer to list the trait at the top of the score sheet, then simply check the appropriate column once they have decided which level to assign to a given student performance (see figure 3.9 for an example).

Another type of score sheet lists *several* traits across the top with the class roster listed in the column at the left of the page (see figure 3.10). Each level of the rubric is assigned a number (e.g., 1 = beginning), and for each trait the teacher writes the number that corresponds with the student's level of performance in the appropriate box for that student and trait. Teachers who use personal digital assistants (PDAs) or small handheld computers can use Excel to create a score sheet on a regular computer, then load it onto the PDA. After the assessment is completed, they can download it to a computer with a larger screen.

## Step 5: Pilot the Assessment and Rubric

The next step in developing the rubric is to pilot it. One of the key components of performance-based assessment is to give students the assessment criteria to help guide them as they respond to and complete the assessment task. When developing a rubric, it is advisable to use it initially for an assessment that does not serve as a major part of a student's grade. In fact, using a rubric only to provide feedback to students is an excellent way to pilot it. Knowing the level at which to set the criteria for an assessment is not easy the first time an assessment is used (i.e., how high to place the bar). The best assessments require students to work hard to achieve the listed criteria but are not so difficult that students give up on the task. A rubric should

## Recording Sheet

| Assessment | Levels of badminton court movement | | | |
|---|---|---|---|---|
| Student name | Beginning | Developing | Competent | Sound |
| Shamika Smith | | | | |
| Darius Davids | | | | |
| Michelle Robbe | | | | |
| Shaina Wister | | | | |
| Chris Bradley | | | | |

**Figure 3.9**   Recording sheet for a single trait.

## Recording Sheet

| Student name | Serve | Court position | Knowledge of rules | Return to base position after shot |
|---|---|---|---|---|
| Shamika Smith | 1 | 2 | 2 | 3 |
| Darius Davids | 3 | 3 | 3 | 2 |
| Michelle Robbe | 2 | 2 | 3 | 2 |
| Shaina Wister | 4 | 4 | 3 | 4 |
| Chris Bradley | 3 | 3 | 4 | 4 |

**Figure 3.10**   Recording sheet for multiple traits.

require students to work hard and make them feel that they have conquered the challenge that the assessment presented.

The pilot will help determine if the correct descriptors were chosen, whether the criteria have been set at an appropriate level of difficulty, and whether all of the correct traits have been identified. If a rubric is valid, the best students should receive the top scores and less skilled students should receive lower scores. Additionally, a pilot of a quantitative rubric provides the teacher with examples of student work or performance to use when developing levels for qualitative or holistic rubrics.

## Step 6: Develop Levels (for Qualitative Rubrics)

If teachers are developing a quantitative rubric, they will skip this step. If teachers are developing a qualitative rubric, the next step is to condense the list of descriptors used on the quantitative rubric, group together those that are alike, and come up with the essential categories for the qualitative rubric. Ideally, a qualitative rubric targets about six characteristics that are considered most critical to evaluating students' performances.

Effective rubrics facilitate the evaluation and scoring process by differentiating levels of aptitude and performance. After looking at many performances or analyzing many student products, the person writing a rubric has a solid idea of what is acceptable and what is not.

A teacher might ask the following questions: What does an excellent product or performance look like? What about a poor product or performance? What are the characteristics that distinguish levels of performance? In other words, before determining which criteria to include, teachers must determine how good is good enough to meet their expectations for student performance.

The pilot administration of the assessment in step 5 provides teachers with a performance or product to examine when writing levels of performance for the rubric. In the case of rubrics used for assessing student performance (e.g., game play, dance performance), video recordings of student activity and game play provide excellent sources of information for writing levels of student performance. When

teachers look at a truly excellent performance, noting the characteristics that set it apart from others will help them write descriptions for the rubric levels. Weak descriptors neither clarify scoring nor provide students with insight into the quality of their performance. Rubrics must clearly point out and differentiate between levels of performance and degrees of understanding.

The easiest qualitative rubric to develop is one in which the levels emerge from the student products or performances obtained from the pilot. When teachers have a product or performance that they think is appropriate, they should look for characteristics to use to describe it. Sometimes teachers cannot identify the evaluation criteria distinctly before looking at student work, but they can recognize these characteristics when they see them. By noting what skilled players do (and thus what lower-skilled players do not do), teachers can write descriptions of the different levels of student performance.

Level descriptors for a rubric should do the following:

- Distinguish between the best possible performance and the least successful
- Use words that provide a true distinction between performance levels
- Explain to students what is expected rather than dwelling on omissions
- Focus on quality, not quantity
- Avoid comparison words such as *more, better,* and *worse*

Because writing clear descriptions of levels of student performance is difficult and time-consuming, some people resort to using comparison words or phrases such as *better, more than,* and so on as they develop various levels of performance. Teachers should avoid using language that makes comparisons between different levels. Descriptive words that have stand-alone meaning and are independent of other descriptors or levels help clarify a rubric, thus facilitating its use. Using comparison words creates arbitrary differences between the levels and leaves the scorer to decide whether a given product or performance is better than something else. Descriptive words with independent meaning lead to valid assessments of students' learning (Wiggins 1996).

An effective rubric also differentiates between a sophisticated understanding of the material and a naïve understanding. Students with a naïve understanding of a concept tend to simplify it rather than address higher levels of meaning and more sophisticated factors. Similarly, some students know a lot of facts but do not truly understand a concept or see the big picture (Wiggins 1998a).

Rubrics can predict and anticipate errors; they can also uncover misunderstandings and alert scorers to these mistakes. For example, a student might know a given offensive strategy but not understand when to use it most effectively in game play. Another student might know the critical elements of an overhand throwing motion yet not see the connections between it and other similar movement patterns and skills, such as a tennis or volleyball serve.

The unacceptable level of a rubric is usually the one that is written least effectively. Too often, the unacceptable level is simply listed as the absence of a trait. However, when students perform insufficiently, they are still doing *something*, even though it is wrong. Identifying these errors sometimes gives teachers a way to write a more meaningful description of unsatisfactory performance. For instance, when playing volleyball, a novice typically reaches for the ball, rather than moving into position behind the ball and facing the target. If teachers include this characteristic of novice performance in a volleyball rubric instead of merely stating that the player fails to make the play, they will make a valuable clarification for the person scoring the performance.

Teachers must also decide how many levels a rubric will contain. In some cases the school district or state may designate the number. If the teacher can make that decision, the discussion on page 61 will help when completing this step.

## Step 7: Create a Separate Rubric for Students (for Qualitative Rubrics)

Sometimes it is necessary or beneficial for student learning to create a separate rubric for students. This step can be omitted if a rubric is easy for students to understand or if it does not contain information that teachers are trying to assess in the response.

Deciding whether to create a separate rubric depends on the complexity of the assessment. In most cases, one version of the rubric will suffice, but complex assessments usually require two versions. Both versions contain assessment criteria, but the scorer's version also lists items that scorers should look for to document student learning (if students were given this version of the rubric, they would have the information that the teacher is seeking to assess). For example, if an assessment measures students' knowledge of the components of health-related fitness, the scorer's version of the rubric would list the components so that there is no confusion about them. If students were given the list, it would reveal to them the knowledge that the assessment is designed to measure. The discussion about transparency on page 69 in this chapter gives further insight about this issue.

The students' version of the rubric should give students a clear understanding of what they are required do without revealing the information that is being assessed. Teachers may either write the students' version for them or have them write their own. Having students write their own rubric offers several benefits. When students put criteria into their own words, they are more likely to understand and internalize them. In many cases, the discussion required to create a student rubric also clarifies the teacher's expectations and requirements for the assessment, and the teacher may be alerted to misunderstandings that students have about the requirements for the assessment. This step is not meant to suggest that students should develop the actual rubric used with the assessment. That remains the responsibility of a person who has in-depth content knowledge (i.e., the teacher).

## Step 8: Administer the Assessment

The next step is to administer the assessment to students to evaluate their achievement. The student rubric should be attached to the assessment so that students can self-assess or peer-assess as they complete their work.

## Step 9: Revise the Rubric

After using the qualitative rubric for scoring an assessment, teachers should examine at students' performances and look for ways to strengthen the rubric. Rubrics evolve over time, and teachers should not expect to create a perfect rubric on their first attempt. Even after teachers have written what they consider to be a finished product, they should continue revisiting the rubric and the criteria used in it to refine and improve the rubric. Rubrics should be considered works in progress, and teachers should mentally write the word *draft* on them. Continual attempts to improve the quality of rubrics are worthwhile uses of teacher time.

## SPECIAL CONSIDERATIONS IN CREATING RUBRICS

When creating a rubric, it is essential to look closely at validity, reliability, transparency, and subjectivity. Without attention to these items, the quality and value of the assessment can be jeopardized. The following section addresses these issues.

### Validity

To evaluate students, teachers must select assessments that will allow them to make an accurate conclusion about whether students learned. A valid assessment allows the teacher to make an accurate or valid judgment about whether and how much a student has learned (Popham 2003). For teachers to make an accurate decision about learning, the assessment must be

a valid measure of this learning and it must align with what the teacher is trying to assess. For example, a written test that consists of selected response items can be used to measure student knowledge about the rules of a game. However, if a teacher wants the student to be able to apply knowledge of the rules during the game, a performance-based assessment has the potential to be a better indicator of student ability to apply the rules because it will allow a direct observation of that ability. When a *direct* observation of student ability is not possible, teachers must use assessments that measure student competence indirectly. With this indirect measurement, teachers must infer from looking at student responses on the assessment whether the student has learned the skills or knowledge specified for the lesson or unit.

Performance-based assessments are criticized by some for having poor validity. An assessment is considered valid if it measures what it purports to measure (Baumgartner & Jackson 1999). Although a performance-based assessment is potentially a valid measure of student achievement, this validity can be negated by a poorly written rubric. Validity problems arise if the rubric includes the wrong characteristics, omits important items, or has vague or unclear directions for use. In such instances, the teacher would reach invalid conclusions about students' mastery of the desired content and learning despite having an assessment tool that had the potential to measure the desired student learning. Validity is also impacted when some elements are more important than others and are given extra consideration or weight on the rubric. If this is the case, the rubric should clearly indicate this weighting so that both the students and the evaluators clearly understand the relative importance of each factor.

A teacher told students to develop a trifold brochure advertising a tennis camp to show their content knowledge of tennis. Students in one group got excited about the project and decided to meet over the weekend to make it really nice. Unfortunately, they did not have access to a computer and ended up handwriting the information and hand-drawing some of the diagrams. These students were disappointed when others with less content knowledge received higher scores because they were able to use home computers and color printers. The content of the handwritten brochure was superior, but the teacher gave the other students more credit despite the fact that she had never stated that the brochure should be produced with the aid of a computer. Teachers must remember that the main purpose of an assessment is to measure students' learning. Although some credit can be given for format, grammar, and visual attractiveness, these factors should not overshadow the credit given for students' learning and demonstration of content knowledge.

Validity is a concern regardless of the type of assessment used. When using performance-based assessments teachers must be careful to select an assessment that is aligned with the learning goals and use a rubric that will allow an accurate judgment about this learning. The quality of a rubric is in part judged by its ability to reduce bias in scoring and therefore minimize errors in judgment about whether students have learned the desired content.

## Reliability

When an assessment is reliable, it consistently produces the same results. In other words, when several people score a performance or product, the scores from the various evaluators are similar. To ensure that performance-based assessments are reliable, teachers must establish clear and complete criteria. A clear and concisely stated rubric is more likely to be reliable (Wiggins 1996).

When several people use the same assessment rubric, training them is essential so that they understand the assessment criteria (Fredrickson and Collins 1989). Training the scorers will calibrate how people doing the scoring interpret the criteria, ensuring that all people who use the rubric are interpreting the criteria in the same way. With proper training, evaluations using performance assessments can produce scores with reliability similar to that of standardized test scores (Fredrickson and Collins 1989).

Problems with intrarater reliability occur when the scorer changes how the criteria are applied. This change is referred to as drift because the scorer moves away from the original criteria to a different interpretation as the evaluation process continues. As a result, elements of student performance that were not acceptable in early performances or products may be allowed in later ones. In a sense, performances or products are receiving a given score because of when they were evaluated, not because of the actual content or quality.

A reliable rubric helps avoid the problem of drift because the scorer has something concrete to refer to when a question arises as to how to evaluate a product or performance. The order in which student work is scored should not matter. Each student must be evaluated fairly and consistently, which is one of the goals of evaluation and assessment.

Some rubrics reward quantity of work instead of quality of work (Wiggins 1996). It is easy to count events as they occur, and there is little judgment involved in determining the number of times that something happens. A rubric that counts events is likely to be reliable, but this is not necessarily a valid measurement of performance. For example, if a badminton rubric specified that the player needed to use four types of shots during the game, the person scoring the evaluation could easily keep count and determine whether the goal is met. The scorer would not, however, be evaluating whether the shots were used at an appropriate time or whether they were effective (i.e., led to a point for the player or a loss of serve by his or her opponent). Too often, when frequency is included as a criterion in a rubric, the issue of *quality* of response is not addressed.

Frequency should not be used to determine the level of performance unless it improves the quality of the response. If, during game play, one student makes the majority of the responses, this does not necessarily make him or her the better player. Teachers must consider other factors, such as teamwork and quality of response (e.g., correct form, use of strategy) to determine how well a student plays. When writing a rubric, teachers must select the criteria that relate most directly to the purpose and nature of the task. The rubric should look for the quality of response, not just how many times the student does something.

## Transparency

Rubrics must include sufficient detail or **transparency** to enable scorers to do their job reliably. Criteria for assessments must be transparent, or clear enough, to students so that they can assess themselves and others with roughly the same reliability achieved by scorers (Fredrickson and Collins 1989). Providing this information may require teachers to put some of the answers in the scoring guide. For example, if teachers are writing dance assessments, they would include elements of good choreography in the scoring guides. However, if part of the assessment is students' knowledge of the elements of good choreography, then giving students the same rubric would be counterproductive.

Although transparency is an important element of an effective rubric, it can also cause problems with written assessments (Cunningham 1998). When a rubric provides too much information, students know exactly what they must do to meet the criteria for the assessment without going through the critical thinking process that the teacher intends for them to implement. Because part of any assessment is to evaluate students' knowledge, those who create rubrics must ensure that their attempts to be clear do not go so far as to effectively solve the problem described in the assessment for the student.

To avoid problems with transparency, a teacher should create a separate scoring guide for students when the scorer's rubric contains too much information. The student rubric should outline key criteria and explain the teacher's expectations, but it should not contain the detail found in the scorer's rubric. Letting students know how an assessment is evaluated is a key part of performance-based assessment. However, the scoring guide cannot be so thorough that students are not required to demonstrate desired skills and knowledge to complete the assessment.

tion before the assessment can be evaluated (Fredrickson and Collins 1989). By their very nature, performance-based assessments involve a certain amount of subjectivity. Despite their subjectivity, performance-based tasks are valuable in physical education because they relate to real-world demands and are meaningful for students. They allow teachers to directly assess certain aspects of student knowledge. Because they require a professional judgment about the quality of performance, subjectivity does enter into the evaluation.

A critical point to remember here is that the people making these decisions have credible expertise in the relevant subject matter. Danielson (1992) notes that the evaluation decisions are made by experts in the field (e.g., teachers, judges) who exercise professional judgment to render these decisions. Performance-based assessments require scorers to make decisions based on *professional* judgment. Therefore, the term *professional judgment* is more accurate than the term *subjectivity* to describe evaluation of performance-based assessments.

Teachers use professional judgment when they do any type of evaluation. With traditional tests, professional judgment comes into play before the scoring begins—in determining what to assess, in writing questions to sample students' knowledge of the material covered, and in deciding on the best answers for those questions. Thus, professional judgment is involved in both traditional and performance-based assessments; the difference is simply the timing of when this professional judgment is used.

A beginning teacher recently required students to teach a sport skill to others in the class. She used the assignment as an indicator of the students' knowledge of process criteria (e.g., critical elements) for the sport skills taught in the class. She based her rubric, not on content but on effective teaching behaviors—developing a practical plan, using informative visual aids, asking appropriate questions, and checking for understanding. Because the rubric focused on effective teaching practices and presentation skills, it could have been used as an effective way to evaluate students' learning, but it did not assess the students' knowledge of the sport. A valid rubric must specifically assess the targeted area of student learning.

## Subjectivity

Performance-based assessments have been criticized by measurement specialists for having a lot of subjectivity and therefore being invalid and unreliable (Hensley et al. 1987). **Subjectivity** refers to the degree of judgment used in assigning a score to a student's test performance. Subjective assessments require the scorer to exercise judgment, analysis, and reflec-

The issues of validity and reliability raised about performance-based assessments stem, in part, from lack of training. With proper training, "there is no reason that subjective evaluation cannot be valid, reliable, efficient, and as objective as possible" (Hensley et al. 1987, 61).

With training, people can use professional judgment to evaluate performance-based assessments in a valid and reliable manner.

Gymnastics scoring is very subjective, but training on the criteria makes the judges reliable. A gymnastics judge is required to make a series of judgments concerning several specified elements. That a panel of judges can score routines within an acceptable range of one another confirms that training can make reliable judgments about physical performance possible.

# RUBRIC HINTS AND GUIDELINES

Writing rubrics can be difficult, even for veterans who have written many of them. Rubrics are typically less than perfect when initially developed, but can be improved through refinements and fine tuning. The following ideas will help teachers avoid some common speed bumps as they travel the road of learning how to write rubrics.

## Use Samples of Student Work

One characteristic of performance-based assessments is that they can be answered using a variety of approaches. Conveying this acceptable variety via a rubric is difficult. One solution to this dilemma is to use **exemplars** or anchors, which are samples of student work that demonstrate either an acceptable or unacceptable performance. Exemplars help explain why a particular score was assigned (Fredrickson and Collins 1989). When evaluators compare the piece being evaluated with another product or performance, it is easier to determine an appropriate score. The term *anchor* is also used to represent student work, since it gives evaluators something on which to ground or base their evaluations. Samples of student work or performance at various levels provide scorers with concrete examples with which to compare the student work that they are evaluating.

Some of the out-of-the-box thinking that teachers wish to encourage in students can be demonstrated with the inclusion of a wide variety of exemplars. Rubrics that use a single anchor can stifle creativity (Wiggins 1996). Samples of diverse or divergent models of excellence show scorers a range of possible acceptable answers, and teachers can use these diverse exemplars to encourage students' creativity. Because one advantage of performance-based assessment is that it encourages students to think creatively and engage in higher levels of thinking, allowing diversity in students' responses is important.

Video recordings of acceptable student performance can also be used as exemplars. Consider the wide variety of dance pieces that could be used to satisfy a choreography assessment. Video-recorded examples of the various levels of game-play performance can help students understand the levels described in a rubric.

One caveat is in order: Using an exemplar at the top level can limit students' products and performances unless the exemplar is truly exceptional. Teachers should use anchors for the highest level only if they fully exemplify exceptional quality. For example, when teachers use an excellent paper to illustrate the top level of a rubric, that paper creates, in essence, a norm-referenced rubric. If Venus Williams was in a physical education class, she might be used to anchor the top level of a tennis rubric. Short of that talent level, teachers should indicate that what they are showing represents good quality but also that higher levels of performance are possible. Exemplars should show students what is possible, but they should not place a ceiling on their potential for excellence.

## Give Rubrics With the Assessment

One key characteristic of performance-based assessments is that the teacher gives students the criteria that he or she will use to evaluate their work when the assessment task is presented. Sharing rubrics with students helps them understand a teacher's expectations for the task, and students tend to achieve more when they know what to expect before beginning the task (Lazzaro 1996).

When students have the criteria used to judge an assessment, they can self-assess or peer-assess the product before submitting their work for evaluation by the teacher. Self-assessment is an important life skill that performance-based assessments can help students develop. Although performance-based assessments require a lot of time to create and evaluate, when students raise their own quality of work through self-assessment, teacher time is saved since better products and performances are easier and faster to assess. The teacher's time is also saved when students refer to the rubric for feedback rather than seeking clarification from the teacher.

Failing to give a rubric with a performance-based assessment can decrease students' clarity about the assessment and limit the quality of their performances. Even if the rubric is rudimentary, it should be presented with the assessment.

## Have Students Rewrite the Rubric

Discussing and clarifying an existing rubric (sometimes referred to as "unpacking the rubric") is an excellent instructional strategy for demystifying a rubric. Discussing rubrics with students can clarify the level of quality expected. Having students develop checklists to use for self-assessment or peer evaluation helps them understand a teacher's expectations for the assessment.

Teachers with high levels of subject-matter expertise sometimes struggle to decide which dimensions to include and where to set the standards. Some teachers let students write a rubric for an assessment. When teachers allow students to write their own rubrics for major

assessments, they are, in a sense, passing the buck. Anyone who designs a rubric must consider a multitude of factors, and using the wrong criteria jeopardizes the validity of the assessment. If an assessment contributes to a major part of a grade, it must be valid and have a well-developed rubric. Students do not have the necessary understanding of the material being evaluated to create a valid rubric for a major assessment. A teacher should not bypass his or her responsibility to provide expert judgment regarding the evaluation of an assessment. Teachers who use complex assessments should write the scoring guides themselves and interpret them for students.

## Allow for Multiple Correct Answers

Selected-response assessments involve questions designed to elicit responses that are either right or wrong. With performance-based assessments, there are multiple ways to address the task, and one is not necessarily more correct than another. Frequently a response begins with the words "It depends." As such, the rubric must allow for this variation, and the teacher must be willing to accept alternative interpretations and performances that are within the scope of the guidelines and criteria established in the rubric. Rubrics written in broad terms allow for this range of acceptable student responses.

Sometimes, a teacher's biases or limited experience can constrain a response. When a teacher fails to consider the potential breadth of an assessment, the range of acceptable responses is curtailed or narrowed. Brainstorming with a colleague to explore alternative responses may help ensure that a rubric allows for potential diversity of acceptable answers. Piloting an assessment and the accompanying rubric also helps point out varied ways in which students can address the task. In some cases, the pilot generates anchors or exemplars useful for giving scorers an idea of what constitutes an acceptable answer when the assessment is used again.

Rubrics should never mandate the process, format, method, or approach that students are to use in completing an assessment (Wiggins 1998a). Allowing students to make choices in these areas forces them to think critically while formulating their responses. Furthermore, when students address an assessment in a variety of ways, their thinking is enhanced, and their responses show greater insight into their knowledge and understanding.

This is not to say that a student can respond in any way and it will be correct. Teachers must set boundaries and help students understand that there is a range of acceptable answers—and that not just anything will be accepted.

## Limit the Scope of the Assessment

Sometimes assessments ask questions that are very broad, resulting in a rubric that is too long and cumbersome to use. Overly broad assessments can also create problems with reliability because the range of acceptable responses is virtually limitless, which makes the rubric quite complicated to use. When a question is vague or overly broad, students may respond in ways that do not require them to display the learning that the teacher wants to assess.

Teachers creating assessments must limit them so that the rubric captures the range of correct responses without allowing just any answer to be appropriate. When a rubric becomes complex to the point of being cumbersome, the scope of the assessment should be narrowed. When student learning outcomes are clearly delineated, the assessment is far more effective.

## Avoid Hypergeneral Rubrics

When the evaluative criteria of a qualitative rubric are so general that it is impossible to distinguish levels, the rubric is of little value. Hypergeneral rubrics (Popham 2003) do not help students learn and are susceptible to reliability problems. In many cases, hypergeneral rubrics are nothing more than restatements of the trait for which they are written and leave much room for subjectivity and personal preference. For example, a recently published rubric used these levels to evaluate the descriptor "evaluation of lesson":

Target = thorough evaluation of the lesson

Acceptable = substantial evaluation of the lesson

Incomplete = partial evaluation of the lesson

Unacceptable = unclear evaluation of the lesson

The rich descriptions associated with qualitative rubrics increase reliability. When hypergeneral descriptions of the levels are used, the rubric is really just a quantitative rubric without the numbers.

The unacceptable level in a rubric is usually the place where people have a tendency to develop hypergeneral descriptions. Even in an unacceptable performance, students are doing something, even though they may be doing it incorrectly. To develop a descriptor for this level, it is often useful to think of errors that students make in an unacceptable performance. See step 6 in the discussion of how to create a rubric (page 65 in this chapter) for more information.

## Writing Levels of Difficulty for Cognitive Assessments

When writing a rubric for a written assessment or product, one technique for determining levels is to sort the work into piles. Sometimes the quality of the work allows the piles to emerge naturally; at other times, the number of piles created depends, in part, on how many levels the teacher needs to create. For example, when grading on a scale of A through F, five piles are necessary for the grades, as well as a sixth pile to serve as a non-response category.

Teachers must address each level needed when writing a rubric. The more levels written, the smaller the differences will be between levels. Smaller differences make it harder to distinguish between levels and thus reliability decreases (Wiggins 1996; Herman, Aschbacher, and Winters 1992). When creating rubrics for written performances, teachers should not use more levels than necessary. If the teacher has a choice about how many levels of performance to include, using examples of student work student work can help make this determination.

## Adjust the Rubric After— Not During—the Scoring of the Assessment

Despite all the care taken in writing a rubric, it sometimes becomes painfully clear when a teacher begins using it to score an assessment that omissions and errors have been made. Although the rubric can be improved, a teacher must continue evaluating student work for this task based on the criteria given to students with the assessment. Students should not be penalized for a rubric's inherent problems. In some cases, the students' grades turn out much higher than deserved due to a poorly written rubric. For example, if a teacher neglects to include change of level or change of direction as a criterion for a dance choreography assessment, then that area should not be used as a factor in grading despite its importance.

Problems with rubrics accentuate the need to pilot the assessment before using it for a major student grade. Anyone who has ever written rubrics has probably created at least one bad one. When this happens, teachers should simply swallow their pride, use the rubric as it is, and revise the assessment or the rubric before the next use.

On the other hand, during an extended unit, teachers might begin with a basic rubric and, as students' skill level increases, increase the difficulty of the rubric as well. For example, in a dance unit, the rubric for the first piece might emphasize change of levels, pathways, and direction. In contrast, the dance choreographed for the culminating event of the unit should be much more complex, since the teacher will have raised his or her expectations for students' learning throughout the unit. Changing one's expectations or demands for student mastery of content is acceptable as long as students are informed of the new criteria before they start a given assessment task.

## CONCLUSION

Rubrics make public the criteria used to evaluate students' performance. When criteria are made public, students know what teachers expect and are more likely to meet those expectations. Rubrics enhance student learning; they focus students on desired outcomes and help remove the mystery that too often surrounds assessment. Rubrics are helpful for teachers, as well, because they force teachers to define their expectations for achievement before beginning an assessment. Frequently, after a rubric is written, teachers return to the assessment and provide additional detail or instruction that improves students' performance. Creating a guide for scoring the assessment forces teachers to think through the assessment process and, to some extent, streamline it.

There are several types of rubrics that teachers can use to remove the veil that can cover up evaluation expectations. I admit that I sometimes get pressed for time and give performance-based assessments that are not accompanied by a rubric, and students' performances on these assessments are almost always below my expectations. When I do use a rubric, students' work is measurably better. And when I show exemplars, the results amaze me.

Teachers should give their students an opportunity to shine. The may not create the perfect rubric or select the optimal type of scoring guide the first time an assessment is used, but it is much easier to edit an existing rubric than to create one from scratch. With this in mind, the authors encourage teachers to take the first step by beginning to shape criteria into a rubric with the knowledge that, through revision and reuse, a worthwhile means of scoring students' achievements emerges. The sample rubrics provided in this chapter can help beginning teachers jump start their assessment journey.

**4**

# Developing Performance-Based Assessments

*Good teaching is inseparable from good assessing (Wiggins 1996, v-6:8).*

This book identifies many types of performance-based assessment, and this chapter offers you useful hints about developing and implementing various kinds of performance-based assessment in physical education. The assessments covered here include observation (by teacher, peer, and self), game play, modified game play, role play, event tasks, student performances, journals, student projects, and student logs. Two other types of performance-based assessment—open-response questions and portfolios—are not covered in this chapter, but are covered in greater detail in chapters 5 and 6.

## OBSERVATIONS

Because so much of physical education learning involves overt skill performance, observation is one of the best assessment tools available in physical education settings. Teachers, peers, and students themselves can observe skills and provide assessments of performance that are designed to improve learning. Although teachers typically create observational tools based on per-

sonal knowledge of the activity, subject-specific activity books (e.g., for tennis, golf, social dance, weightlifting) are excellent sources for developing observational assessment tools (see table 4.1).

Some teachers think that they are assessing students when they provide feedback during instruction. Feedback, however, is not assessment; it is an instructional technique designed to improve students' performance. To serve as an assessment, a teacher observation must include some type of form on which the results can be recorded. A written observation form helps ensure that students receive congruent feedback from the assessment. The following sections provide ideas for using assessments based on observation by the teacher, one's peers, or oneself.

### Teacher Observation

Teacher observation is the most basic assessment used in physical education. After giving students a task to perform, the teacher watches to determine whether students have achieved mastery of the task or whether more instruction

75

**Table 4.1** Sources for Skill Sheets

| Title | Authors or editors | Publisher |
|---|---|---|
| *Advanced Golf: Steps to Success* | Owens and Bunker | Human Kinetics |
| *Advanced Swimming: Steps to Success (3rd Edition)* | Thomas | Human Kinetics |
| *Alpine Skiing: Steps to Success* | Yacenda | Human Kinetics |
| *Archery: Steps to Success (3rd Edition)* | Haywood and Lewis | Human Kinetics |
| *Australian Football: Steps to Success (2nd Edition)* | McLeod and Jaques | Human Kinetics |
| *Badminton: Steps to Success (2nd Edition)* | Grice | Human Kinetics |
| *Basketball: Steps to Success (2nd Edition)* | Wissell | Human Kinetics |
| *Bowling: Steps to Success* | Strickland | Human Kinetics |
| *Fencing: Steps to Success* | Cheris | Human Kinetics |
| *Field Hockey: Steps to Success (2nd Edition)* | Anders and Myers | Human Kinetics |
| *Golf: Steps to Success* | Schemp and Mattsson | Human Kinetics |
| *Ice Skating: Steps to Success* | Kunzle-Watson and DeArmond | Human Kinetics |
| *Netball: Steps to Success* | Shakespear | Human Kinetics |
| *Nordic Skiing: Steps to Success* | Guillon | Human Kinetics |
| *The Physical Education Handbook* | Schmottlach and McManama | Allyn & Bacon |
| *Racquetball: Steps to Success* | Kittleson | Human Kinetics |
| *Rugby: Steps to Success* | Biscombe and Drewett | Human Kinetics |
| *Self-Defense: Steps to Success* | Nelson | Human Kinetics |
| *Soccer: Steps to Success (3rd Edition)* | Luxbacher | Human Kinetics |
| *Social Dance: Steps to Success (2nd Edition)* | Wright | Human Kinetics |
| *Softball: Steps to Success (3rd Edition)* | Potter and Brockmeyer | Human Kinetics |
| *Sport and Recreation Activities* | Mood, Musker, and Rink | WCB/McGraw-Hill |
| *Squash: Steps to Success* | Yarrow | Human Kinetics |
| *Swimming: Steps to Success (3rd Edition)* | Thomas | Human Kinetics |
| *Table Tennis: Steps to Success* | Hodges | Human Kinetics |
| *Teaching Cues for Basic Sport Skills for Elementary and Middle School Students* | Fronske and Wilson | Benjamin Publishing |
| *Teaching Cues for Sport Skills* | Fronske | Allyn & Bacon |
| *Team Handball: Steps to Success* | Clanton and Dwight | Human Kinetics |
| *Tennis: Steps to Success (3rd Edition)* | Brown | Human Kinetics |
| *Volleyball: Steps to Success* | Viera and Ferguson | Human Kinetics |
| *Weight Training: Steps to Success (3rd Edition)* | Baechle and Groves | Human Kinetics |

is necessary. Prior to using the observation form, the teacher has watched students and provided them with feedback. The observation form is used to formalize the assessment process and provide the teacher a way to document students' performances.

When observing the performance of skills, teachers can focus either on process criteria (i.e., correct form) or product criteria (e.g., the number of times a student serves the tennis ball into the proper service court). When teachers evaluate process, they must identify the critical elements most important to correct performance. The observation is much more efficient if only a few items are targeted. In some cases, a teacher can use a category such as "ready position" that, if broken down, would include several smaller components. Instead of listing the various components of ready position, the term is used to represent two or three subitems. When doing an observation, a good rule of thumb is to observe the starting position, the initiation of the skill, the performance of the skill, and the follow-through. These components may not be present in every skill, but they will work for most skills.

When creating the recording form, it is most efficient to list all of the students who will be observed on a single page or screen. When recording product-type scores (i.e., those based on product criteria, such as 10 tennis serves or 5 free throws), teachers should still require good form for the skill attempt to count. When recording observations from product assessments, teachers should allow enough space to record the results. If students are being timed and are allowed multiple opportunities or trials, the recording form should have the appropriate number of boxes along with another box to indicate the best score. The space for recording the best score on the observation form should be closest to the student's name if teachers will be transferring this information into a permanent record or grade book. This is not an issue for teachers who use PDAs with Excel software as they can sort data after downloading it onto a computer with a larger screen.

At this early stage of skill development, assessments are useful for the teaching and learning process. At the end of a lesson, if teachers give students a task to keep them engaged in practicing the skill, teachers can circulate

among the students, observe their performance, and record assessment results. Options for recording results range from a low-tech process (e.g., recording scores on a paper form held by a clipboard) to the use of modern technology (e.g., using a handheld computer). Whatever process used, consider recording the errors that students make rather than the critical elements they perform correctly, since the number of errors is usually smaller. If using this strategy, reserve one column of the recording form as a place to note that a student is executing the skill with correct form—that is, making no critical errors in form—since simply leaving all error columns blank could be interpreted as meaning that the student was not observed. For an example of this type of recording form, see figure 3.2 on page 49.

Keeping a written record of student performances offers several advantages over merely providing oral feedback. By writing down the criteria, teachers become more focused on the quality of performance that they expect from students. Also, knowing what students can do helps teachers plan effectively for subsequent lessons. By doing daily assessments, teachers can document or verify learning and improvement in such a way that the results can be shared with students, parents, and administrators. In addition, because observation is performed more systematically when written down, it helps teachers ensure that all students are learning. Some students learn to avoid performing in physical education; these students are generally not highly skilled and are usually not successful with their skill attempts. Often they avoid responding to avoid the embarrassment of performing poorly in front of peers. Siedentop and Tannehill (2000) refer to these students as **competent bystanders**. They are not students who present behavior problems, but neither are they learning and acquiring the correct skills. These students can be very clever in their nonresponses and sometimes go unnoticed by the teacher. When students are systematically assessed, however, these competent bystanders are detected.

Sometimes it is impractical to assess every student. If a teacher is simply trying to get a sense of whether the class has learned the concept or skill being taught, he or she can select certain students prior to the start of class and assess these "representatives" of the class in order to gain a sense of whether the class overall is learning the material. To get a feel for the performance of students at various levels of skill, a teacher might select two lesser-skilled students, two with average skills, and two with higher skill levels. Identifying these representative students before the class period allows the teacher to systematically observe different students each day. By looking at six to eight students per day, the teacher can effectively evaluate the learning progress for every member of an entire

> Once, while doing a research project, my target students were two of those with more skill than most members of the class, and two students with less skill than most. The teacher had identified a certain young woman, who in the teachers' view had a lower level of skill, as my target student. As it turned out, the target student was actually a competent bystander. In a 3-week volleyball unit, she touched the ball 41 times. Competent bystanders behave just as the name implies—they are competent at avoiding participation in an activity without drawing the teacher's attention to their pattern of nonresponse. While systematically doing teacher observations, competent bystanders become obvious very quickly. If teachers become aware of these students' patterns of behavior, they can consciously monitor them on a regular basis and encourage them to begin participating.

class during an instructional unit. Teachers can use the results of these observations in planning future lessons. However, if the assessment is part of the students' grade, then every student must be evaluated.

Teachers may also use observation results to group students by ability for instruction or feedback. For example, observation could help identify students who are struggling with a concept. They can then receive additional instruction or tutoring. Or, if a teacher wanted to mix abilities within a group (e.g., for forming a team or practice group), teacher observation can provide essential information about students' ability levels.

Teacher observations can be used to assess student *behavior* as well. One strategy for doing this is to notify students that they will be randomly observed throughout the unit and that the results of these observations will be factored into their final grades (the teacher should provide

the criteria and his or her expectations before initiating this practice). Since students do not know who will be observed on any given day, all students are encouraged to display proper behavior because their actions may be evaluated at any time for grading purposes. Students are not given the results of these observations until every member of the class has been observed and the next observational cycle begins. This approach helps ensure on-task behavior from the entire class. Because students eventually see the results, this assessment also provides feedback on performance.

When teacher observations are included in the grading system, teachers should observe students at multiple times during the unit to make sure that a given student does not get evaluated only on an atypical day (e.g., when the student doesn't feel well or is paired with an extremely low-skilled or high-skilled partner). Conducting multiple observations over a period of time allows the teacher to develop a more accurate picture of overall student performance.

## Peer Observations

Peer observations also provide an excellent way to do assessments that inform students about their performance, especially in large classes where it is difficult for the teacher to provide individual feedback to students frequently. Peer observations increase feedback by having each student serve as a teacher for one of his or her peers. Teachers can also use peer observation to verify or reinforce cognitive learning related to a skill or activity.

To create a peer observation instrument, teachers must (as with teacher observation) decide what they want students to know and be able to do, then create a set of criteria for assessing students' capacity in those areas. Peer observation is especially useful when students are first learning a skill. During the initial learning phases, it is critical that students engage in high-quality practice so that they do not learn errors that must later be corrected. After initial instruction, the teacher can distribute a list of criteria for performing the skill correctly. The teacher must also show students how to use the list. Too often, teachers merely distribute the list without demonstrating or explaining to students how to use it. Students being observed must understand that the purpose of the observation is to encourage correct practice—not to be punitive if errors are made—and that the results will not count toward a grade. The feedback received from a peer is intended solely to help each student improve his or her performance, and students must understand this purpose clearly when they give feedback to a peer. They are trying to help their partner(s) perform skills correctly with the goal of improving performance. Peer assessments are invaluable when the Sport Education Instructional Model is used to teach a sport, especially if students understand that their teams will be only as good as their weakest players.

Students doing the observations must also be taught what good performance looks like so that they can give correct feedback. When creating worksheets for use in peer evaluations, teachers must remember that they are usually dealing with novice performers and observers. If students are taught to observe certain phases of performance using a set protocol, they become more skilled at assessing others' performances. After learning the protocol, students can apply it to all skill observations.

When developing a peer observation, teachers should list the cues they want students to use on a recording sheet (for an example, see figure 4.1). The cues or critical elements should be listed in the order in which they should occur, starting from the feet and moving up the body. The following order is suggested for peer observation:

1. Ready position
2. Preparation (preparatory action)
3. Execution
4. Follow-through

Teachers can organize the cues under these categories. Since beginners are not able to observe too many things at once, teachers should limit the cues being observed to five or fewer and allow students multiple opportunities to view performances by peers. Teachers should participate in several observations along with their students so that students learn how to observe.If students compare their own observation results with the teacher's results, the training helps improve the accuracy of their observations.

A recording form is needed for the observation. If paper or printing is a problem, teachers can create erasable forms by laminating a paper copy or covering it with clear contact paper. Whiteboards can be made by obtaining a sheet of whiteboard from a lumber store and having it cut into lapboards that measure 8 by 10 inches (about 20 by 25 cm). Teachers can then list the elements on a poster and use a cue word to represent the critical element. After students record the cue words on their whiteboards, they are ready to begin the observation. The teacher then collects the forms after class, notes what students wrote down, and then erases the boards in preparation for use by the next group of students. The results of student observations give teachers useful information about the quality of students' skill performances. A comparison of students' observation results with teacher observation results will provide insight into how well students are understanding what good skill performance looks like.

Beginners have a difficult time seeing all that is happening during a live performance. Video recordings, on-line movies, or DVDs allow students many opportunities to observe the same skill. Some teachers set up an observation station and give students the opportunity to record and watch their performances. Figure 4.2 presents an example of a peer evaluation that uses video recording; the assessment was designed for video analysis, but a similar one could be used to evaluate student performance in the gymnasium.

Although the purpose of the sample assessment is to provide feedback to peers, teachers could also, by changing the format slightly, use it to evaluate the observer's cognitive knowledge of the skills. By assessing students' accuracy for their use of cues and their evaluations, teachers can determine students' knowledge of the critical elements and their ability to apply that knowledge. If the same video is used for all

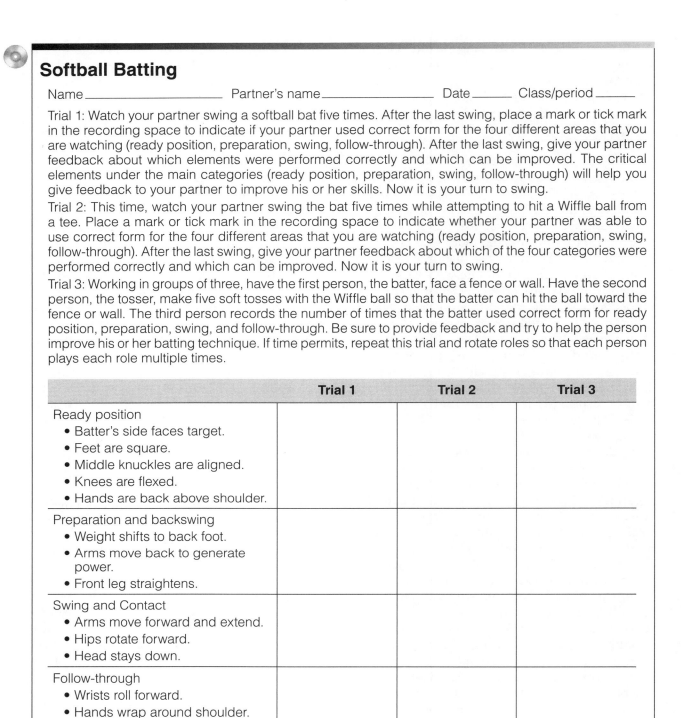

## Softball Batting

Name_____ Partner's name_____ Date_____ Class/period_____

Trial 1: Watch your partner swing a softball bat five times. After the last swing, place a mark or tick mark in the recording space to indicate if your partner used correct form for the four different areas that you are watching (ready position, preparation, swing, follow-through). After the last swing, give your partner feedback about which elements were performed correctly and which can be improved. The critical elements under the main categories (ready position, preparation, swing, follow-through) will help you give feedback to your partner to improve his or her skills. Now it is your turn to swing.

Trial 2: This time, watch your partner swing the bat five times while attempting to hit a Wiffle ball from a tee. Place a mark or tick mark in the recording space to indicate whether your partner was able to use correct form for the four different areas that you are watching (ready position, preparation, swing, follow-through). After the last swing, give your partner feedback about which of the four categories were performed correctly and which can be improved. Now it is your turn to swing.

Trial 3: Working in groups of three, have the first person, the batter, face a fence or wall. Have the second person, the tosser, make five soft tosses with the Wiffle ball so that the batter can hit the ball toward the fence or wall. The third person records the number of times that the batter used correct form for ready position, preparation, swing, and follow-through. Be sure to provide feedback and try to help the person improve his or her batting technique. If time permits, repeat this trial and rotate roles so that each person plays each role multiple times.

|  | Trial 1 | Trial 2 | Trial 3 |
|---|---|---|---|
| Ready position <br> • Batter's side faces target. <br> • Feet are square. <br> • Middle knuckles are aligned. <br> • Knees are flexed. <br> • Hands are back above shoulder. |  |  |  |
| Preparation and backswing <br> • Weight shifts to back foot. <br> • Arms move back to generate power. <br> • Front leg straightens. |  |  |  |
| Swing and Contact <br> • Arms move forward and extend. <br> • Hips rotate forward. <br> • Head stays down. |  |  |  |
| Follow-through <br> • Wrists roll forward. <br> • Hands wrap around shoulder. <br> • Shoulder to chin. |  |  |  |

**Figure 4.1**  Sample recording sheet for softball.

members of the class, teachers can assess students' ability to evaluate correct and incorrect performance. If the teacher scores the cognitive assessments for accuracy, the results could be used to calculate part of the students' grades for cognitive knowledge. If the video clips are loaded onto a computer, uploaded to a Web site, or burned onto a DVD, students can do the

## Peer Evaluation Using a Video Recording

You have just created a new company designed to improve people's tennis skills. Because of your tennis expertise, people send you videos of themselves performing the skills that they want to improve. You provide feedback about their current skill level and offer suggestions about what they can do to improve their level of play. You have received videos from three people who want to improve their forehands, backhands, and serves. You do the following:

1. Watch the videos at regular speed and evaluate the skill performances (watch each person's video once). Using the critical elements presented in class as a resource, write down the critical elements that each client performs correctly and those performed incorrectly. Do this for all three skills for all three people.

2. Watch each video again. This time, you are allowed to view the performance in slow motion or even go frame by frame. Write your analysis of skills based on this second viewing. Did you draw the same conclusions, or did you detect additional cues or errors while watching at the slower speed?

3. Draw a picture (similar to the frames you might see drawn for an animated cartoon) to give each client an idea of what his or her racket head looks like during the swing for each of the three strokes.

4. Using your error correction sheet, design an improvement plan for each client for all three strokes that were submitted to you. Plan a 20-minute stroke warm-up that each client can use to improve his or her game.

5. Send your client the bill!

**Figure 4.2**  An example of peer evaluation using a video recording.

assessment as homework either at home or in a school computer facility.

Peer observation can also be used to evaluate affective behavior during game play. By listing the desired sport behaviors, students will be reminded of acceptable actions during game play and can rate and comment on their opponents' positive sport behaviors. Students value what is assessed, and this type of observation offers one way to communicate the importance of demonstrating acceptable game-play behaviors. See figure 3.1 in chapter 3 for an example of this type of assessment rubric; other examples of peer assessment can be found elsewhere in chapter 3 and in chapters 2, 6, and 8.

*Note:* Although peer evaluation can serve as a positive component of a teacher's assessment system, peer assessment results should not be part of another student's grade. If teachers want to credit a student for involvement in a peer assessment (in the affective domain), the credit should be given to the student conducting the assessment; the assessment results should not be part of the grade for the student who was observed. This latter type of evaluation is the teacher's responsibility. Skill assessments that determine a grade for an observed student should not be delegated.

## Self-Evaluation

One of the goals of secondary teaching is to help students become self-sufficient learners. According to the National Standards for Physical Education, elementary school students should develop motor skill competence as the first step toward developing a physically active lifestyle (NASPE 2004). As students grow into adulthood, they should continue to acquire new skills and improve on previously learned ones. In many cases, adult learning occurs without the benefit of formal instruction. Adults who do not have the opportunity to participate in formal classes may ultimately become their own teachers in adulthood. Thus, it is useful for students to develop self-assessment skills.

Many people who participate in physical activity do self-analysis as a form of feedback. One type of self-analysis involves knowledge-of-results feedback, which is practiced whenever basketball players watch to see if the ball went into the basket or when dancers look into the mirror to see if their movements and body positioning are correct. Kinesthetic feedback can also let people know when they are performing skills correctly. Teachers often use sensory cues to give students feedback. When teaching tennis skills, teachers instruct students to listen for that *ping!* sound (instead of a *thud!*) that means the ball has bounced off of the "sweet spot" of the racket face.

Finding ways to document self-analysis transforms the feedback into assessment. Video recording is one way to document self-assessment. If students are working at stations, a video camera can become part of the self-assessment. Students either learn to operate the equipment themselves or they can have a student aide do the recording at the station; students can then view their performances immediately after performing or at a later time. Self-assessment can also be done through the use of digital photography. Students either print the pictures by using a class computer or download them onto a Web site and complete the analysis at another time. Teachers can assess students' cognitive knowledge by having them identify performance errors, critical elements performed, and ways to improve the performance.

Here's an example. If students are provided with a list of archery errors, such as the one found in figure 4.3, they can evaluate themselves for possible form errors by looking at the

## Archery Errors

After shooting a round of six arrows and recording the placement of the arrows on the sheet provided, use the following list of archery errors to develop a list of form errors that may have caused the arrows to land as they did. Have a partner observe while you shoot the next round of six arrows in order to see if you have correctly identified any of the form errors.

### Common Errors Causing Flight to the Left

Hunching the left shoulder

Anchoring away from the face

Throwing the bow arm to the left

Sighting with the left eye

Placing the weight on the heels

Holding the arrow tightly at the nock

### Common Errors Causing Flight to the Right

Throwing the bow arm to the right

Jerking the string

Turning the head to the right

Placing the weight on the balls of the feet

Tilting the body forward

### Common Errors Causing Low Flight

Inching forward with the string fingers on release

Dropping the bow arm too soon after release

Using an understrung bow

Stretching the chin forward to meet the string

Using an anchor point that is too high

### Common Errors Causing High Flight

Throwing the bow arm after the arrow on release

Lifting the bow arm on release

Lowering the string elbow or hand before or during release

Drawing beyond the anchor point

Tilting the body away from the target with the weight on the rear foot

**Figure 4.3**   Students can use this form to evaluate their archery errors.

performance product (i.e., where their arrows land after being shot). Students should mark the grouping of their arrows on a target and list possible reasons for the arrow placement. Teachers can assess students' cognitive knowledge by asking them to diagnose their errors and record their conclusions in a journal. Students can then try to eliminate the errors and use self-evaluation to determine their level of success (i.e., improved performance) by looking at the same performance product (arrow groupings) during subsequent rounds of archery.

As a sponge activity (an activity used at the beginning of class requiring little or no explanation by the teacher) for class, students can self-record their best scores or performances for an assessment on the attendance sheet as they sign in for class. The assessment could be one of the skill assessments that contribute to each student's grade or simply one of the drills or activities learned during the previous class.

Students can also self-evaluate in terms of affective-domain behavior. Instead of having students fill out a form listing the appropriate behaviors for their opponents, teachers can have them evaluate their own behaviors. By comparing their own results with those provided by opponents, students can gain important insights about how other students perceive their affective-domain behaviors. If students write a reflective journal entry comparing the results of the two observations (by self and by peer), they will have an additional opportunity to self-assess and potentially improve their affective-domain learning. See figures 3.1 and 3.2 in chapter 3 for examples of a peer assessment in the affective domain and a self-administered assessment in the affective domain, respectively.

As with peer evaluation, students should never be required to self-assess for grading purposes. If teachers want students to provide honest appraisals of their skills and abilities, then the results of these assessments should not be used to calculate a student's grade.

# GAME PLAY AND MODIFIED GAME PLAY

When writing objectives for activities or sports, many teachers want students to be able to play a game at a recreational level upon completion of instruction. Skill tests are designed to be approximations of game-play ability. The assumption is that if a student can effectively perform a variety of skill tests, then he or she should be a competent player in an actual game. However, while skill tests allow teachers to evaluate skills in a somewhat closed environment, game play allows the teacher to look at students' abilities to *apply* these skills, in addition to other elements important for game play, such as skill selection, movement on the court, and the ability to use the skill strategically. Small-sided or modified games that teach students to use skills in an increasingly open environment are an essential part of skill development.

If teachers want to assess students' ability to perform skills, individual skill tests are probably the best way to go. On a skill test, students have the opportunity to demonstrate their ability to perform the skill, usually in a closed or controlled environment. With the setup used in a skill test protocol, the student is ensured a chance to perform the skill to the best of his or her ability. If assessing skills during game play, the setup for the skill may be less than ideal, which may result in process or form errors as the student attempts to make a play. A student should not be penalized for using poor form while making a skill attempt during game play. Another reason for assessing skill with a skill test is that some students may never have the opportunity to perform certain skills in game play. To assess these skills, an environment (e.g., a skill test) designed to elicit the skill must be created. For example, some students are reluctant to spike a ball during volleyball game play or may never get an opportunity to attempt a spike during a game because they are not set up by teammates or because another skill (e.g., a dink) is a more appropriate response. In such situations, if game play were the only setting in which the skill was assessed, the student would receive a zero regardless of his or her ability to execute it.

Despite these caveats, there are two reasons to include skill execution in a game-play assessment. First, students must know that while they are playing a game, "just any old performance" is not okay. For example, when playing volleyball, students sometimes revert to using backyard volleyball skills such as clasping the hands together and then striking the ball by means of an overhand chopping action instead of performing a set in preparation for sending the ball over the net with a spike or a dink (i.e., an offensive attack). Additionally, the person doing the evaluation needs a way to reward students who execute skills correctly and make note of those who commit form breaks. The second reason for including an assessment of skills on a game-play rubric is to recognize the play of more competent players who successfully use more difficult skills during a game. Students who have the confidence to perform spikes and dinks during game play—and who do so with correct form—are probably better players. Rewarding players for successful use of more advanced skills also encourages players to attempt to use those skills. Because a good rubric should discriminate between skill levels, it makes sense to include skills in a game-play assessment, because better players demonstrate them and usually use correct form. In the final analysis, assessments should look at students' achievements through a variety of lenses. By assessing skills via both skill assessments and game play the teacher has more information about student achievement.

In addition, game play allows teachers to look at much more than skill competence. For example, during invasion games, students can be assessed on whether they pass the ball to teammates instead of keeping the ball for themselves. Teachers can also observe students' practice of court courtesy, proper etiquette, and fair-play behaviors in competitive situations, as well as their ability to apply rules and effective court movement strategies.

The assessment of game-play performance must be progressively more difficult. By beginning with small-sided (e.g., 2v2) games and then progressing to more complex situations with more players, teachers have the opportunity to look at students' responses in increasingly difficult game situations and thus determine whether they have grasped the concepts necessary for effective game play. Too often, students know what to do in a two-on-one transitional drill but are incapable of recognizing that situation in game play. When teachers assess during small-sided games, gaps in learning become apparent, and teachers can identify which lessons to reteach. Modified games can also be used for summative assessments. In many cases, small-sided games make it easier to see what students are capable of doing and teachers can accurately assess their abilities.

When assessing game play, beginning teachers often find it easier to develop their own assessment rather than to use one from another source, since they naturally feel more familiar and therefore more competent with their own assessment. To create a game-play assessment, teachers should develop a list of skills that they consider essential for competent players; unit objectives provide an appropriate starting point for developing the list. Teachers then develop this list of skills into descriptors for a quantitative analytic rubric. They might include skills, knowledge of rules, game-play strategies, and selected affective-domain dispositions. The list should capture the important elements of the game without being so long as to make the assessment burdensome. In most cases, 12 to 15 descriptors will do the job. If a given descriptor is too long to fit on the evaluation sheet, an abbreviated form of the descriptor is written on the scoring sheet and the entire descriptor is written out on another page. If students use this rubric to evaluate peers, teachers must make sure that they understand what is meant by any abbreviated descriptors on the score sheet. Letting students use these score sheets to assess other classmates helps them better understand the assessment process and know the specific criteria the teacher is looking for during the evaluation.

Students enjoy comparing their scores to those of the teacher to see where they agree and where they differ. This system also provides a convenient way to discuss criteria so that students better understand them. Students sometimes question a teacher's judgment of their abilities. The better they understand the criteria the less likely they are to question assessment results. Since assessment should be used to enhance learning, giving students an opportunity to understand the areas in which they are being assessed is an important part of this process.

When deciding what items to include in a game-play rubric, teachers can often get useful feedback from a colleague. For one thing, sharing the descriptors with a colleague who is knowledgeable about the game or activity can help ensure validity for the rubric. Another way to ensure that a rubric assesses the important game-play elements is to pilot it during preliminary game-play days in order to see whether it discriminates or distinguishes between levels of skill. If the best players are not receiving the highest scores and the poorest players are not receiving the lowest scores, some adjustments to the descriptors are needed. When the results of the evaluation do not differentiate levels of skill, the teacher is receiving a clear signal that important components are missing.

When assessing game play for a large number of students, a teacher needs to have the assessment memorized, since it is very difficult to repeatedly look at a rubric yet still conduct an accurate assessment. When a teacher is first learning how to assess game play, a quantitative analytic rubric can be a little overwhelming, especially if the teacher is looking at 12 to 15 descriptors. For this reason, teachers who are new to doing game-play assessments should begin by concentrating on only 3 or 4 of the descriptors on a given day, because it is easier to assess a smaller number of items than to keep the entire rubric in mind. Even for teachers with large classes, it is possible to assess all students if the teacher is looking at only a few items. One possible strategy is to look at psychomotor skills on one day, cognitive abilities on another day, and affective dispositions on a third day. Novice observers might also begin to develop their game-play observational skills by looking at small-sided or transitional games. By removing some of the complexity from the game, teachers can assess students' performances accurately.

If a pencil is used to record assessments, students' scores can be changed as their game-play skills improve. An alternative is to make several copies of the recording form and use a new one for each day's assessment. When students are given the opportunity to improve scores on subsequent days, game play becomes a formative assessment. When assessment results are shared with students, they can see what they must work on in order to improve their skills—yet another way in which assessment can be used to enhance learning. When separate score sheets are used on different days, grades should *not* be determined by averaging the scores. Skills are expected to improve, and students should not be penalized for poor performance at the beginning of instruction. Rather, a student's final scores and final grade should reflect his or her level of achievement at the conclusion of the unit, which is most representative of the degree to which the student has met the unit's learning objectives.

The type of rubric selected for game play should be based on what the teacher wants to assess. Quantitative rubrics typically contain more elements, and they are probably the best choice if teachers want to separate students' use of various skills, types of knowledge, or strategies. This type of assessment is used in the initial stages of game play. Qualitative analytic rubrics contain fewer descriptors and combine several concepts into one descriptor. For example, shot execution might include both the selection of the correct skill and the form used in performing that skill. Additionally, a qualitative rubric could specify that a variety of skills is used, meaning that the student does not rely on only one or two skills for an entire game (for an example, see figure 3.5 on page 53). Holistic rubrics (e.g., figure 3.6 on page 55) are valuable for a final or summative analysis of game play, because they give students a single score that represents an overall analysis of their game-play ability. Holistic rubrics are less useful for formative evaluation of game play, because the student does not know the exact reason that he or she was rated at a given level of play.

Statistics can also serve as good indicators of game-play performance. Teachers can assess students' learning by tracking game-play statistics and noting improvement over time (when deciding which statistics to track, teachers should select those that are most relevant to what they are trying to teach). The Sport Education Instructional Model uses game-play statistics to track student learning. Having students keep statistics is also an excellent way to assess their knowledge of game play, since they must know what those statistics mean to track them. If using this approach as an assessment tool, do not assume that students have the skills to carry out the assessment. When a colleague was using Sport Education to teach basketball, the person had the students keep track of "assists." One student commented that some students were not making very many assists, which led to a conversation about just what an assist is. With this example in mind, do not assume that students know what a particular game component is; teach them.

In the interest of saving time—and because it provides rich material for developing feedback for students—many teachers prefer to evaluate live game play. Beginning assessors might prefer to make video recordings of games and evaluate the students later. One benefit of this approach is that when the teacher or assessor misses a play, the video recording makes it possible to go back and see what was missed. Video-based assessment of game play also provides a way to establish reliability. Interrater reliability is established if the teacher and a colleague assign the same scores to students involved in game play. Intrarater reliability can be calculated if a teacher watches a recording twice, with adequate time allowed between the observations.

Grading is easier when a holistic rubric is used because it in a single score. A teacher might use a qualitative analytic rubric for formative assessment, then convert the rubric into a holistic one for summative assessment. To make the conversion, the teacher would combine all of the statements on a given level (i.e., level 1) for each descriptor into a paragraph that explains the quality of performance required for that level. Following this same process for each level results in a holistic rubric. *Note:* The holistic tennis rubric presented in figure 3.6 was created in this manner from the quantitative analytic rubric shown in figure 3.5.

If teachers want to use a qualitative analytic rubric for grading, they should divide the rubric into psychomotor, cognitive, and affective descriptors. Next, each category is weighted for importance and a point value is assigned to each level of each category, then an average score is taken for each of those areas. If a teacher's grading philosophy (see the discussion in chapter 11) calls for the overall score to consist of 50 percent psychomotor, 30 percent cognitive, and 20 percent affective, then the average scores should be multiplied by these percentages, respectively, to determine the final grade.

Whatever method used to calculate a grade, the important thing to remember is that a grade should reflect the degree to which a student has achieved the learning objectives for the unit or class.

## ROLE PLAY

Role play, another type of performance-based assessment, is especially useful for assessing affective-domain behaviors but can be used for assessing other knowledge as well. It allows students to examine scenarios from a variety of perspectives. When teachers use **role-play**

**assessment** to evaluate affective-domain behavior, students are given a scenario and asked to react to it. The scenario may relate to events that have occurred in class or may concern a topic about which the teacher wishes to teach and assess. For example, a teacher might create a role play that involves discussing what to do with a low-skilled player who is unable to perform the skills necessary for the big game. This role play would be appropriate before the teacher announces who will be on which team for the class tournament. Group members might be asked to brainstorm ways to increase this person's contribution to the team. The teacher could also use a related scenario in which the lower-skilled person meets with friends after school and is upset over being assigned to play with team members who have an elitist attitude. The person is afraid of being ridiculed and needs to develop a strategy for handling the situation. The first scenario might be made more complex by having the lower-skilled player come into the locker room unannounced in the middle of the discussion. The role play would then continue with the lower-skilled person present, thus giving students an opportunity to address an even touchier situation.

When assigning roles, teachers must make sure that the student assigned to a given role cannot be associated with that role outside of the class. Middle school students, in particular, are notorious for teasing classmates, and roles should be assigned in such a way that students cannot "brand" one another and create a possible source for teasing or embarrassment. Teachers must make sure that students understand that the roles are purely for role-play purposes and are not to be continued after the exercise concludes. Following the role play, teachers can conduct a debriefing session in which students are given the opportunity to express how they felt during the scenario. The debriefing gives students a chance to consider the feelings of others, and teachers can use it to teach important lessons. Teachers can also have students write scripts for their own role-play scenarios to address a topic provided by the teacher.

Depending on how a given scenario is developed, role plays can also be used to look at cognitive learning. If cognitive or affective knowledge is assessed, then criteria for assessing them should be conveyed to students. When role plays are used to assess affective-domain topics, teachers should avoid assessing content and look instead for participation by all group members and a willingness to let others have an opportunity to speak. Checklists that give credit to students who participate can be used for evaluation.

Role-play assessments are used to document learning. Thus, when selecting role-play topics, teachers must consider the content that they are trying to assess, then develop an appropriate scenario and evaluation criteria.

# EVENT TASKS

**Event tasks** are performance tasks that can be completed within a single class period (National Association for Sport and Physical Education 2004); in physical education, they usually involve psychomotor activity. A teacher might pose a problem to a group of students and have them design a solution. For example, students are asked to combine several locomotor skills designated by the teacher into a movement combination set to music. In another example, the teacher might conduct a beginning dance choreography assessment by having students create a piece that integrates various elements of dance (e.g., level change, direction changes, and symmetrical and asymmetrical balances). Adventure education event tasks frequently present challenges in which students are required to demonstrate cooperation and problem-solving skills. Event tasks can also be used as stepping stones to more complex assessments.

Event tasks give students the opportunity to apply concepts covered in class even as they give teachers a way to check students' understanding of those concepts. Some event tasks are fairly simple, making them more appropriate for formative assessments than for summative assessments. More complex event tasks could be used as summative assessments.

Event tasks can be used to evaluate students' game-play ability. Evaluating game play is often a lengthy process because the games last so long. A teacher might use an event task where students develop a video that presents their game-play abilities within a relatively short time frame. For example, a teacher might require students to play a 6-minute doubles game of bad-minton, during which they are expected to demonstrate the ability to serve, use the overhead and underhand clear shots, play both forehand and backhand shots, and use the smash. Teachers could also require students to demonstrate knowledge of serve rotation and other rules, as well as fair-play behaviors and simple game-play strategy. Since a competitive game lasting only 6 minutes would not include all of these elements, students will need to choreograph the game to ensure that all the components are included in the video. This type of purposeful movement requires a great degree of skillfulness and knowledge, and it provides an excellent way for teachers to observe students' game-play ability in a relatively short time.

As with all performance-based assessments, students must have the criteria by which their performances will be evaluated. In addition, since the process used to complete a performance-based assessment is just as important as the product, teachers need a way to assess not only the product but also the process that students follow to complete the task. Adventure education event tasks usually conclude with a debriefing session, in which the teacher has the opportunity to ask students about the process they used to solve the problem. Reflection papers or journals could also be used to assess adventure education event tasks, evaluating the process used to solve the problem.

When creating event tasks, a teacher must begin by looking at the objective that the task will be used to assess. By fully evaluating all of the objective's components, teachers can design a suitable assessment with which to measure student learning. The type of rubric written for the task depends on the criteria specified in the objective. For example, combining locomotor skills shows the teacher that students are able to perform the skills and move smoothly between them, so those criteria would appear on the rubric. If students perform the movements to music, they are demonstrating their ability to count musical beats and perform the locomotor skills to an external rhythm. Since an event task assessment is probably formative, a quantitative or qualitative analytic rubric is appropriate. An adventure education event task conducted at the conclusion of a unit could use a holistic rubric that evaluates the level of quality for the process used by students to solve the problem.

# STUDENT PERFORMANCES

These assessments are generally conducted over the course of several days or even several weeks. Student performance assessments may be preceded by a series of previous assessments (e.g., event tasks) that lead up to this complex assessment. This type of assessment requires students to integrate skills and knowledge into a meaningful performance. In the case of dance or gymnastics routines, performing the skills to music adds another dimension of difficulty. When teaching dance or gymnastics units, teachers can instruct students on the elements of choreography so that they know how to combine dance or gymnastics elements into meaningful and engaging compositions or routines. Students are then evaluated on their ability to create the composition, their ability to perform the composition, or their ability to both create and perform, depending on the teacher's objectives.

Another example of a student performance assessment involves having students create an exercise sequence for a fitness warm-up. By specifying the purpose of the warm-up, teachers can evaluate students' knowledge of certain principles of exercise physiology, as well as their ability to exercise the particular muscles used in the activity. If aerobic dance is included in the warm-up, students will also be required to set some of their exercises to music. The focus of the assessment is to determine whether students can apply concepts learned in class to a real-life situation. Although students' performances are generally done live, teachers or students might choose to video-record the presentation for later use.

Depending on the learning objectives established for the unit, teachers often require students to create performances when teaching units on dance, gymnastics, rope jumping, and synchronized swimming. These culminating performances provide students with an opportunity to combine the various steps or skills learned in the unit into a final product. Students usually work very hard at creating these pieces and making the final product as polished as possible.

When teachers want to use student performance for the culminating event, they should divide the project into sections instead of requiring only the final product. Giving a choreography assignment on the first day of a unit without providing future instruction or guidance will be quite a daunting task for beginners. Students should not be given the entire project without some formative assessment tasks that let them demonstrate their skills as they work toward the final performance product.

As with all performance-based assessments described in this book, teachers must begin with the final objectives in mind and then develop assessments that allow students to demonstrate mastery of the final goals. A teacher might begin by showing videos of students' performances or clips of other people performing dances or routines. When students have the end product in mind, the lessons that enable them to learn these skills make more sense to them along the way. These videos can also serve as exemplars that clarify the rubric associated with the performance.

Since this type of performance-based assessment looks at a culminating performance, it is appropriate to use a holistic rubric for the final assessment. See chapter 3 for an explanation of how to create a holistic rubric. If using a holistic rubric, teachers should spend some class time breaking the rubric apart and looking at the elements contained in the descriptions. Students can generate their own analytic rubric for self-assessment while creating their performance.

Because evaluating students' performances takes practice, teachers should consider video-recording them to ensure accurate assessment of the work. Video recording also offers a way for students to assess their own work. It is impossible for a performer to envision just how a performance looks to an audience. Video-recording a performance allows students to see how the composition looks to others and to self-assess the quality of their own work. Students can also do peer assessments of other performances as formative assessments.

Teachers can add a cognitive assessment to the performance. In a dance choreography evaluation, teachers can assign students the role of dance critic and have them write a review of other students' work. If teachers want to avoid having students critique one another, students could evaluate student performances from past years using criteria established by the teacher. Such assessments provide students with an opportunity to become familiar with the guidelines that will be used to evaluate their own work later on in the unit.

# JOURNALS

Student journals provide an excellent way for teachers to measure students' knowledge and understanding of physical education concepts. Teachers should not just require journal writing to repeat information that has been presented in class. Rather, students should be required to put information into their own words while engaging in some type of interpretation or comparison. When students explain a concept in their own words, they are forced to process the information, which elevates their learning from the simple recall of knowledge to a higher level of thinking (e.g., comprehension and analysis) on Bloom's taxonomy.

When selecting topics or questions for students' journal writing, teachers must, as always, go back to the purpose of the assessment to determine the desired content. When teachers assess students' ability simply to remember information presented in class, they can use more traditional assessment methods (e.g., selected-response tests) that take less time to score. In contrast, when the questions are phrased appropriately, journal writing requires students to process information at higher levels of thinking. Prompts for journal writing should ask students to explain things in their own words or relate them to previous learning to involve their analytical skills. *Why, which,* and *how* are excellent words to use when probing student learning in this manner.

Journal writing allows students to self-evaluate their own learning and progress, provide their teachers with insight about their feelings toward participating in various sports or activities, and reveal any confusion they might have about learning the cognitive aspects of physical education. Although some teachers allow more of a freewriting format, when teachers focus student attention and narrow the topic instead of using a free-writing format, the journal responses are more relevant to instruction and provide better feedback about levels of student understanding.

A student prompt might be a question (e.g., What are some indicators that your skill in volleyball is improving?) or a request to explain a concept or strategy covered in class. (e.g., Explain what is meant by transition.)

Journals also give teachers an excellent way to gather information about the affective domain. Here are some samples:

- Did you feel successful while practicing today's activities? Please explain your answer.
- What was the hardest thing that you accomplished today? Why was it was more difficult than other tasks or activities?
- What practice strategy did you use during today's lesson? Was it successful? Why or why not?
- If you were to learn a new skill from someone in this class, who would you select as your teacher? Why this person?
- Select one thing that you would change about today's lesson. Why did you choose that event or task? If you could rewrite the script concerning that event, how would it read?

Prompts for journal entries should be complex enough to require more than a yes-or-no response. Questions that probe the student's response, requiring an explanation of the initial answer, provide teachers with more information. Frustration or feelings of alienation toward other class members or certain physical activities can be detected through journal entries. Without such insight, teachers may remain unaware of class events or dynamics that contribute to students' lack of learning or lack of enjoyment in the learning process.

If teachers want students to take journal writing seriously, they must read the journals and let students know the entries have been read. When student work is returned, students usually look through their journals to see the teacher's responses, which can be written comments, smiley faces, or even stickers. As is probably clear by now, reading journals is a time-consuming endeavor. For this reason, it is suggested that teachers do not require journals from every student in every class to be submitted simultaneously. Staggering the due dates makes assessment less of a chore for teachers.

Although teachers might check an affective journal entry for completion of the assignment, length of the entry, or coverage of certain topics, student journals should *not* be graded for content if teachers expect to see honest entries. One of the quickest ways to shut down students' openness is to require them to think or respond in a certain way (e.g., giving a zero to a student who indicates that an activity was boring). Teachers should assess journal entries for content in terms of students' *cognitive* understanding of a concept covered in class, but not for content in terms of the affective domain.

## STUDENT PROJECTS

Student projects are another excellent performance-based assessment. They require students to engage in a higher level of thinking and typically take several class sessions to complete. Student projects can evolve into meaningful end products while at the same time allowing teachers to assess learning. Students rarely have an opportunity to show their creativity, and student projects allow creative students to shine. Many times shy or quiet students are the ones who perform especially well on these assessments.

One student project evolved from a concern expressed by a teacher that students no longer know about the games that children used to play before the advent of video games. For the project, the teacher identified a number of older games and toys, such as jacks, penny boards, croquet, four square, marbles, pick-up sticks, hopscotch, darts, horseshoes, and yo-yos. Students were required to research an older game's history and rules and determine the skills, and then produce a video showing game play and explaining the rules and skills. Originally, the final project consisted of the video presentation and a written assignment on the rules and history. However, since the high school was located adjacent to an elementary school, the project evolved into an interactive activity in which, on a spring afternoon, the high school students taught their games to fourth graders (see figure 4.4). Students were assessed on their knowledge of the activity (NASPE Standard 2) and their ability to work with others (NASPE Standard 5) as they completed the project.

In another example, a folk dance project could be used to determine how well students can interpret instructions for five relatively simple folk dances and then put them to music. Students could be assessed on their ability to

**Figure 4.4**   A student project might involve having older students teach games or activities to elementary school students.

perform the steps correctly (NASPE Standard 1), read and interpret folk dance directions (NASPE Standard 2), and perform the steps to music (NASPE Standard 1). A video recording of the final project provides a permanent product in which students demonstrate their dance and music skills.

Sports skills can also be assessed through the use of a group project. For example, high school students could be assigned to make an instructional video recording for middle school students that shows correct form of the skill from a variety of angles, as well as errors, ways to correct errors, and application of the skill during game-play situations. The video could be used to evaluate both cognitive learning and psychomotor skills. The teacher could also assess students on affective-domain behavior observed as the members of the group work to complete the project.

Another way to assess students' knowledge through a student project is to have them develop a magazine. If, for example, the magazine's content addresses activity settings available in the community, students can be assessed on some elements of NASPE Standard 3. For the project, each member of the group is in charge of some type of editing (e.g., features, cover, artwork, advertising), and every student in the group is expected to contribute an article and an advertisement (the ad must address something healthy and make use of information learned in class). Students choose a title for the magazine, and all articles must reflect the title or overall theme. Teachers often find that students produce many creative results, especially given the computer skills that many of today's students possess. Students are required to reflect on their input into the magazine and also about what they learned by doing the publication.

Students should be given some class time to complete tasks that require the efforts of the whole group. Once they create a division of labor, individuals in the group can work on their own to complete their components of the project. Because several people are usually involved in a project, a teacher must have a way to assess individual contributions to the final product. One way to do so is through reflection papers in which a student describes his or her role in the group. This type of writing lets teachers find out who did each of the various tasks, as well as who provided leadership skills when the students were working as a group. These reflection papers should be turned in directly to the teacher; other members of the group should not see them. Another technique is to have each student start with a large amount of imaginary money (e.g., US$100,000) and then distribute hypothetical paychecks to members of the group. Each student must award every other member of the group a different amount of money and must justify his or her decisions.

Another way to determine individual effort is to require (as with the magazine project) individual products from each student in addition to the final group project. When a teacher does not conduct some type of assessment of each individual's contribution to the group, some group members usually receive less credit than their efforts deserved, while others receive more than they earned.

## STUDENT LOGS

Student logs are excellent ways to show the process involved in learning. Teachers can look at a behavior over time to see how students show improvement when they make an adequate effort. Skill practice or physical activity outside of class is easily documented on logs. With these logs, students can demonstrate their willingness to engage in a physically active lifestyle as suggested by NASPE's standard 3 (National Association for Sport and Physical Education 2004). Students can also use logs to document fitness activities. Many teachers use student logs as one of the artifacts included in student portfolios (see figure 4.5). For example, students might document strength training or conditioning for a fitness unit and thus address NASPE standard 4, which calls for achieving and maintaining a health-enhancing level of fitness. Other students might set a goal of participating in a bicycle race or triathlon. Logs could document training miles and demonstrate student ability to condition the body using sound training principles learned in physical education classes.

### Student Activity Log

| Date | Activity | Amount of time |
|------|----------|----------------|
| 3/15 | Tennis | 45 minutes |
| 3/17 | Jogging | 30 minutes |
| 3/18 | In-line skating | 30 minutes |
| 3/21 | Aerobic dance | 1 hour |
| 3/21 | Stretching | 20 minutes |
| 3/22 | Swimming | 45 minutes |

**Figure 4.5** This student log might be used to document out-of-class activity as part of an assessment involving NASPE Standard 3 or as an artifact for a fitness portfolio.

Logs of class participation can also be used for assessment. Students can use logs to track their skill or fitness improvement over time. Students who are initially unable to do skills presented in class—and thus fall below the normal expectations for students of their age—can use logs to demonstrate progress toward the learning objectives designed by the teacher, thereby documenting their learning process as well as the effort they have made. Such logs can function as motivational tools for students as they demonstrate evidence of improvement over time.

The scoring criteria used to assess logs depend in part on the teacher's objective. If a teacher merely wants a student to complete the log and does not intend to judge it for quality, then a checklist might be used to indicate the presence or absence of various components designated by the teacher. If, on the other hand, a teacher wants to determine a level of quality, an analytic evaluation of the designated log components can be done. If participation was one goal, then teachers would want students to demonstrate evidence of regular activity. If improvement was another goal, then the percentage of improvement would be another category to assess. Teachers must keep in mind the potential problems with assessing improvement and remember that high-performing athletes will probably show little improvement compared with someone who is just beginning. When multiple levels of talent co-exist in a class, the teacher might develop a dual assessment system. First, the teacher would establish the criteria to be reached and if these were achieved, the student would not need to demonstrate improvement. Those who were unable to reach the designated criteria could be evaluated on gain or improvement scores. The dual system can be designed to maximize students' performance regardless of their ability level at the beginning of the unit.

## CONCLUSION

When thinking about assessment, teachers must continually address two questions: What do I want students to know and be able to do, and what am I willing to accept as evidence that students have met the stated objectives? Although this book addresses many types of performance-based assessment, the authors do not recommend that teachers throw aside all of their current assessment practices and move exclusively to a performance-based approach. Assessment in physical education can be viewed as a recipe. When one uses too much of any single ingredient, the final product does not come out as expected; extra ingredients can disrupt the delicate balance of a recipe. Unfortunately, the ideal recipe for balancing the various types of traditional and performance-based assessments is still unknown. As a result, teachers must experiment until they achieve a balance through which their assessment systems are evaluating and documenting the desired student learning.

By developing a variety of assessments, teachers have many different lenses through which to observe students' learning. Only by using many lenses do teachers grasp the full extent of students' learning and achievement. Teachers also should keep in mind that many of the assessments described in this chapter can become artifacts in student portfolios. Even though assessments provide insight only into student performance for a given activity or concept, when combined with other assessments and put into a portfolio they provide a more complete picture of student learning. Chapter 6 offers much more information about portfolio development.

In many cases, performance-based assessments serve multiple evaluation purposes, depending on what the teacher requires. Adding a reflective component requires students to evaluate their own role in the process of completing the assessment, as well as their progress in learning. Cognitive components can be evaluated along with psychomotor skills. The criteria used for an evaluation explains what the teacher expects. For some assessments, multiple rubrics can be written for the same task, thus providing additional lenses through which to view student learning.

This chapter provides teachers with hints for using the assessments described in this book. Some of the suggestions presented were developed as the result of a failed assessment. Teachers who conduct an assessment that bombs are encouraged to look for the reasons that it did not work. Some suggestions given in this chapter resulted from ultimately successful assessments that were not so effective when used for the first time. Good assessments usually require several refinements to eliminate the rough edges and work out the snags. Teachers are also encouraged to start working with an assessment buddy. Having someone with whom to share and brainstorm ideas is invaluable. As an additional benefit, if people share their assessments with others, it usually takes less time to develop a really good assessments arsenal.

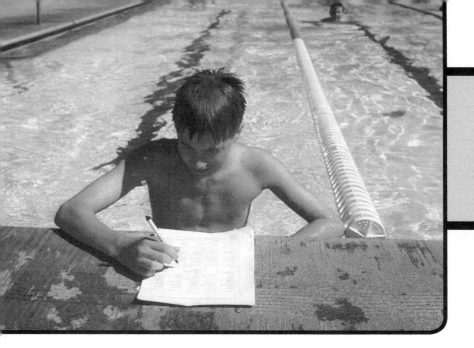

# Open-Response Questions

---

*Assessment of student learning should come from educators' keen judgments about what's worth learning, just like in the selection of content. . . . We tend to take more care as we decide what to teach than when we make decisions about how we will determine if students developed and learned (Lambert 1999, 4).*

---

In physical education, the traditional way to assess cognitive knowledge or affective dispositions are through written tests. When teachers want to assess only comprehension or knowledge, they can use tests with selected-response formats that require minimal time for students to complete and for teachers to score. When a teacher wants to determine how well students actually use their knowledge, another type of assessment is necessary. Open-response questions give teachers alternative ways to assess students' ability to use and apply knowledge in real-world situations or settings. These questions are useful for assessing knowledge, understanding, and affective dispositions in performance-based instruction, since they require students to think critically while developing solutions or responses to challenging prompts or scenarios.

Open-response questions offer two advantages over selected-response items. First, when students are prompted to respond to an unfa-

miliar situation (one that has not been directly addressed or used as an example in class), the teacher can determine whether students really understand the information that has been presented as they reprocess that information to address the open-response question. Second, when students are required to evaluate, create, synthesize, or analyze information, they use higher-level thinking skills and often force themselves to stretch their cognitive abilities. When students demonstrate creativity and insightful thinking, teachers can recognize and reward their efforts.

## OPEN-RESPONSE QUESTIONS VERSUS ESSAY QUESTIONS

Open-response questions are very different from essay questions. Whereas essay questions require a specific answer, open-response questions have multiple possible solutions. An open-response question can be answered using one of several responses. One response is not more correct than another. Several responses might be considered acceptable if the student provides an adequate justification for it. An appropriate answer to an open-response question typically begins with these words: "It depends." Table 5.1 shows how open-response questions differ from essay questions.

Consider the difference between the following two questions:

1. Explain what is meant by a person-to-person defense and a zone defense.
2. You are about to play in the regional finals of a basketball tournament. You know that your opponent has two outstanding guards who score most of the points, whereas the other three players usually take a combined total of less than 10 shots per game. Describe a potential way to defend this team and give reasons for your choice.

The essay question (number 1) simply asks students to provide two definitions, whereas the open-response question (number 2) requires students to analyze the abilities of their own team to develop a game-play strategy for taking on a particular opponent. Thus the open-response question requires students to possess knowledge of both types of defenses as well as when and how they are best used. The better a student understands basketball, the richer his or her response will be. As a result, the open-response question affords the teacher greater insight into students' understanding of basketball. This kind of in-depth analysis can carry over to game play, as students develop strategies for facing different opponents based in part on the analysis they did while answering the open-response question. Physical activities can be very complex, and when students are encouraged to think critically about various aspects of the game, a whole new dimension is added to their learning.

Essay questions measure what students know, whereas open-response questions measure both what students know and what they can do with that knowledge. Simply supplying facts, as one does to answer essay questions, is not sufficient for answering open-response questions. Students must use information from the scenario described in the question and address the situation presented while solving the problem posed. In other words, an open-response question looks at a student's ability to use material taught in class and apply it to a novel, true-to-life scenario.

**Table 5.1**  Open-Response Versus Essay Questions

| Open-response questions | Essay questions |
|---|---|
| Allow for a variety of solutions | Require a definite solution or answer |
| Reward creative and insightful thinking | May recognize creative thinking while not being able to reward it |
| Allow integration of subjects and learning from other classes | Reveal how much students have learned in class |
| Incorporation of students' personal experiences and prior learning | Focus on knowledge from class |
| Require much time to score effectively | Are usually scored fairly quickly |
| Encourage students to expand their thinking | Measure a finite body of knowledge |
| Require students to apply knowledge and information to the big picture | Measure content and factual knowledge |
| Reveal levels of student understanding and misunderstanding | May be difficult to determine level of understanding |
| Format must be learned by students and teachers | Are familiar to students and teachers |
| Have a real-world context | Do not usually give or explain context |
| Usually involves a novel task or situation | May ask about previously covered material |

# CHARACTERISTICS OF OPEN-RESPONSE QUESTIONS

Open-response questions provide a unique way to assess students' learning and attitudes. Because open-response questions can present a problem or scenario with multiple plausible correct answers, they allow teachers to look at students' learning in ways that are not possible when using traditional assessments. Despite their openness, there are certain components or key elements that must be included in a good open-response question. The following section provides an overview of open-response questions while discussing characteristics that good questions include.

## Real-World Problem or Scenario

Because one purpose of education is to prepare children for life in the adult world, students must be exposed to situations that are reflective of the adult context. In keeping with this view, establishing a realistic context is an important characteristic of open-response questions, because it helps reveal how well students understand concepts or skills as they apply them to real-world scenarios. Context can also be used to personalize a question, thus making it more meaningful and relevant to students, as well as impressing on them the fact that information learned in class will be useful to them as adults. For example, a teacher who wishes to assess knowledge about fitness concepts might write a question requiring students to develop a plan for staying fit throughout the remainder of their high school years. Thus, instead of merely listing the five components of fitness and the principles of training, students would apply this knowledge in a practical, real-world context in which they can demonstrate knowledge of the subject and explain this using their own preferences for staying active.

## Scenario or Prompt That Provides the Context for the Question

With open-response questions, students are given a prompt that provides the situation to which they will apply their knowledge. This prompt, which narrows or focuses the possible responses, varies according to the type of question used for the assessment (types of open-response questions are covered in the next section of this chapter). As discussed in chapter 2, performance-based assessments establish an audience, which helps define the context of the performance. For example, conditioning for a ski trip is quite different from preparing for a triathlon competition, and developing levels of fitness for a high school student is very different from developing a fitness plan for someone who is getting ready for retirement.

When reading passages are used as prompts, teachers typically require students to respond to the information or topic and provide facts to justify their responses. The prompt sets the stage for students' responses and piques students' interest, while focusing and thus limiting the scope of their answers.

## Alignment With a Learning Objective

A good open-response question aligns with or links to a learning objective. Open-response questions can assess learner objectives that other forms of assessment do not touch. Many of today's educational standards are written in terms of students understanding concepts and applying knowledge (see figure 1.1 on page 4 for a list of the National Standards for Physical Education), and open-response questions are designed to accomplish just that. Teachers can assess students' understanding at a conceptual level, which is what most standards and objectives are striving to attain.

For example, effective game-play strategy requires students to gain an advantage over an opponent. During instruction, a student learns to create a two-on-one situation allowing the student and a teammate to outmaneuver the opponent. This advantage can be set up in a variety of ways. The student's answer to a good open-response question on the concept would reveal to the teacher whether the student really understands how to create a mismatch rather than just knowing that such a mismatch constitutes a playing advantage.

## Use of Higher-Order-Thinking Verbs

Because open-response questions require application, analysis, synthesis, or evaluation, the verb that describes what students are required to do to respond to the question must require at least one of these higher-order or critical thinking skills. Figure 5.1 presents a list of power verbs (i.e., those that indicate action or observable performance) to use with open-response prompts (adapted from Kemp, as cited in Vickers 1990). Comparing two entities (e.g., badminton and tennis) allows students to demonstrate their ability to analyze. Since badminton and tennis are both net games that involve rackets, some of the same strategies apply to both games. However, the type of object used for play (ball or shuttlecock) greatly affects the types of shots that players use. Using a different type of higher order thinking, students might evaluate a product or game, giving reasons for or against using or playing it. Open-response questions encourage students to use critical thinking skills as they utilize knowledge gained from their physical education classes.

## More Than One Plausible Answer

Real-world problems can usually be addressed in a variety of ways, and open-response questions exemplify this characteristic in that there are many possible ways to respond to them. Teachers can encourage "out-of-the-box" thinking and allow students to use their personal experiences as they generate a response. This is not to say that just any answer is correct. Students are required to provide correct information while answering the question, and their responses must be plausible and reasonable. Because students have to justify and defend their responses and explain the logic behind them, teachers can detect incomplete learning and incorrect thinking, or misunderstandings about the topics being assessed.

## Requirement That the Solution Be Explained

When students answer an open-response question, it is not enough simply to provide an answer to the problem or question; students must also explain the reasoning they used in formulating their answer. In some cases, an answer may at first appear wrong, but when the student explains his or her reasoning the additional factors make clear that the answer works and in fact may indicate that the student has gone beyond the teacher's original intent for the question. If Dick Fosbury, the high jumper who revolutionized the event in the 1968 Olympics, had merely presented his technique for clearing a high bar

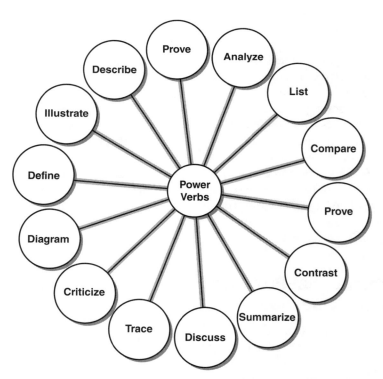

**Figure 5.1** These power verbs may be helpful when writing open-response questions.

without explaining his reasoning for why it would work and be superior to other high jump methods in use at that time, a teacher might have marked his approach incorrect.

Having students develop a stretching routine for an activity or game and explain the benefit of each exercise would reveal their knowledge of the demands or requirements of the activity and of the benefits derived from doing the stretches. Teachers could then determine whether students knew the value of the various stretches well enough to develop a stretching routine for a regulation game or activity. Students can sometimes memorize and provide a correct or plausible response to a question without really understanding the concept being measured; in the stretching example, students could respond by simply listing exercises that they had done in the past. By requiring an explanation of the process used to develop or arrive at this list, teachers can evaluate whether students know the benefits of the selected stretches. Requiring students to explain the process they used to derive an answer and justify their response gives insight into their learning and depth of understanding. Open-response questions call on students not just to display content knowledge but also to support their answers and show their reasoning.

## Possible Revelation of Hidden Student Knowledge

Open-response questions can even reveal knowledge and learning that a teacher did not think to ask about. In addition, since students come from various backgrounds, open-response questions give them the opportunity to bring prior learning while responding to the question prompt. Although information learned in class must be present in the response, when students add insight from their personal experiences they demonstrate that they possess a broad understanding of the knowledge surrounding the concept.

## Focus on Big Ideas, Important Skills, and Key Concepts

Open-response questions provide the opportunity to evaluate students' thinking about and understanding of key concepts by giving them an opportunity to see connections between concepts addressed in class. Open-response questions often explore the how and why of learning rather than focusing only on the what. As students begin seeing connections between concepts, their learning becomes more meaningful and more enduring.

## Presentation of a Situation That Is Interesting to Students

Students are subjected to many assessments while in school, many of which are of little or no interest to them. By choosing a topic that students find appealing, a teacher can increase students' interest in completing the assessment and perhaps even spark their creative energy. Open-response questions should center on subjects that engage students and at the same time provide challenges for them to meet. With this approach, students are more likely to take the assessment seriously and feel motivated to do

On one occasion, I was using an open-response question in a unit on folk dance. One student pointed out the patterns that were made as class members went around the circle using a right and left grand move. The student, who had been studying patterns in math class, noted that as the dancers went around the circle, every other person faced either in or out. From the response, I knew that the student understood his relationship with other members of the class instead of only knowing what he was to do. The student had a different way of explaining the step and what he was doing, using knowledge gained in another academic discipline. When students make this kind of connection, learning is more likely to be retained. Similar levels of understanding can be demonstrated by having students respond to questions that address game-play strategy. Too often, students know how to run a play, but when asked to analyze or explain the strategy they have little sense of where other members of the team should be positioned.

their best. For example, a teacher might establish a scenario by prompting students to envision preparing for a hiking trip in the mountains, taking the stage for a dance performance, or playing in a highly competitive tennis tournament (Wimbledon, anyone?).

### Interdisciplinary Possibilities

Interdisciplinary learning is important in today's schools. Instead of compartmentalizing knowledge, students are asked to apply it across areas. Physical education provides an excellent way to assess students' learning of concepts from the physical and social sciences in an applied setting. Open-response questions can require students to address problems through interdisciplinary lenses by applying their knowledge of sport and exercise to other content areas, thus making their learning more meaningful and important in their lives.

# TYPES OF OPEN-RESPONSE QUESTIONS

There are several formats used for open-response questions: single-dimension, scaffolded, multiple-independent-component, student-choice, and response-to-provided-information (Kentucky Department of Education 2008). As the complexity of the question increases, the teacher requires more information from the student and the student must produce a longer response. When deciding which format to use, teachers should consider the information or student knowledge that they wish to access. The following section explains the characteristics of the various types of open-response questions and provides examples of each.

### Single-Dimension Question

**Single-dimension open-response questions** are straightforward. This format is used when a teacher wants an open-response question that requires 10 to 15 minutes to answer. Single-dimension open-response questions usually ask students to draw a conclusion or take a position and support their responses with explanations, examples, and evidence. Single-dimension questions are also useful when teachers want students to explain a phenomenon or describe a procedure. Consider the following example:

Your team has been criticized by opponents for exhibiting unfair play and poor sporting behavior. When does behavior stop being a way to support the team and start being an issue of fair play? Explain the reasoning behind your response and, where possible, provide examples to clarify your answer.

### Scaffolded Question

**Scaffolded open-response questions** contain a sequence of tasks that become increasingly difficult. When writing this type of question, teachers start with the simplest task and the subsequent questions become more complex. Each successive question depends on the response given to the previous question, so that success on subsequent questions depends on whether previous parts were answered correctly. Here is an example of a scaffolded open-response question:

You see an ad for a new abdominal shaper machine. The ad states that for just US$99, you can flatten your abdominal muscles and look great for the pool.

a. What muscles should an abdominal shaper exercise?

b. Identify several exercises that would also work these muscles that do not require an apparatus.

c. Using a strip of rubber tubing, devise exercises that work the same muscles addressed by the abdominal shaper.

d. Decide whether to buy the abdominal shaper and explain your reasoning that supports your response.

### Multiple-Independent-Component Question

**Multiple-independent-component questions** give students fairly independent questions that address the same prompt. They have at least three parts. Since the components are independent, one response is not dependent upon the previous one(s), and any given question is not necessarily more complex than a previous one.

The Big Game is coming up, and you want your team to win the district league title. To do so, you want to sharpen your batting abilities.

a. Identify several drills that you might use to improve the power of your swing; explain the purpose of each drill.

b. Changing your bat might also be a way to improve the power of your swing. What effect might different bats have on batting power, and how might the bat affect the batter's swing?

c. You have popped up to the shortstop during your last eight at-bats. Identify and explain possible reasons for these pop ups and propose what you might do to correct this problem.

## Student-Choice Question

**Student-choice open-response questions** allow students to select the topic they wish to address from a list of several options. These questions are more difficult to grade because of the variation among answers. When giving students choices within an open-response question, teachers must make sure that the options

Open-response questions can address topics that are relevant to students, thus making the assessment more interesting and enjoyable for them.

are similar so that answering one is not easier than answering another. If written conceptually (e.g., focus on big picture ideas), a single scoring guide can be used to evaluate any of the student choices. Here is an example:

> You have just finished a unit on tennis and wish to learn another sport. You noticed some similarities and differences between the striking patterns found in tennis and those used for another sport. Select volleyball, badminton, pickleball, or racquetball, then compare and contrast the striking patterns for your chosen sport and tennis.

## Response-to-Provided-Information Question

As the name suggests, a **response-to-provided-information question** requires students to respond to certain information provided in the question. Readings could be used for the prompt (articles from *Strategies* or the *Journal of Physical Education, Recreation & Dance* are excellent sources) or a graph or chart. In questions that prompt students to respond to a selected reading, teachers must remember to give them enough time to read the article or passage, as well as write their response. Pictures can also be used for writing prompts, thus providing visual information for the question. Here is an example:

> Examine the accompanying pictures and descriptions of two tennis rackets. Compare the two rackets, analyze your game-play needs, and decide which racket to buy. In your answer, explain the specific advantages that the racket you selected offers for your game. Also note any benefits of the other racket and explain why you decided that the chosen racquet better suited your needs.

In this question, students are prompted to give reasons for their choice based on the information presented. The knowledge assessed here would be a self-analysis of playing ability, knowledge of the various types of striking patterns used in tennis, the mechanical advantages offered by each racket, and an explanation of game-play strategy. If students have developed an affinity for playing tennis during the tennis unit, then choosing a new racket to purchase might be a real-world situation for them. If a price tag was also included for each racket, students could also make a judgment about the decision by considering: How much will I play tennis in the future? Will I play enough to justify buying a very expensive racket?

# HOW TO WRITE OPEN-RESPONSE QUESTIONS

The following steps are useful when developing any of the types of open-response questions outlined in this chapter.

1. Identify the standard or knowledge that the teacher wishes to evaluate.
2. Determine a real-world context in which this knowledge would be needed or valued.
3. Write the prompt or scenario to be used for the question.
4. Create the task, telling students what they must do to solve the problem.
5. Write a rubric for the people who will evaluate the response (i.e., the scorers).
6. Write a rubric for students, outlining criteria that help them address the question or problem.
7. Pilot the open-response question.
8. Revise and improve.

The following sections explain these eight steps and offer suggestions for implementing them.

## Step 1: Identify the Standard or Knowledge to Evaluate

When developing open-response questions, teachers should always have a clear purpose for the assessment and identify the information they want to assess. The first step is to clearly identify the content that the question addresses. Sources for content might include

- national, state, or local standards;
- goals established for the unit; or
- several units of study, which can require students to compare or evaluate ideas, showing links or relationships between them.

When looking at their unit objectives, teachers must determine the best way to assess students' learning in pursuit of those objectives.

Teachers should target and develop areas that lend themselves to open-response questions, since they may be the most appropriate form of assessment when multiple approaches or solutions to a problem are possible or when teachers want to determine whether students can apply facts and knowledge. Open-response questions are not geared toward addressing mere basic facts and information that teachers want students to memorize. Instead, teachers should target content that requires higher-order thinking skills. For example, simply identifying the shots used in pickleball does not require higher-order thinking, and such learning can be assessed more efficiently through selected-response questions. Getting students to see the relationships between badminton and pickleball skills and the impact that those differences have on game play strategies requires more complex forms of assessment and would be appropriate content for an open-response question.

## Step 2: Determine the Real-World Context

Determining a real-world context in which the targeted learning would be used is critical for two reasons. First, an interesting context motivates students to put forth extra effort, because they can see a real purpose for answering the question. For example, devising a strategy for playing a championship game is much more appealing than simply describing an offensive or defensive strategy. Second, using a real-world context helps students see that information learned in class is important not only while in class but also in the world beyond. Students tend to learn material better when they can see its relevance and usefulness.

## Step 3: Write the Prompt or Scenario for the Question

This is the fun part of developing open-response questions. Teachers can create a scenario that has real-world implications while adding a context to the open-response question. The prompt should focus on an important problem that students will want to solve. Sufficient background information must be provided to frame the question and provide a meaningful context for it. The scenario is considered the hook that engages students by giving them something to which they can relate. Reading passages or an interesting fact or bit of information can increase the complexity of the question. The scenario should be realistic and is only limited by one's own imagination. Here are some possibilities:

- You are trying to get a summer job at a fitness facility. It is a great job that pays well and offers a free membership for employees, and several of your friends work there.

- Your classes this year have really been hard, and you have spent a lot of time studying for them. The chocolate ice cream that you eat while studying has put an extra 10 pounds (4.5 kg) on your body, and you wish to lose that extra weight.

- You have a new friend who likes to play tennis. You would like to be able to play tennis with this person, but your skills need work.

- You have always been a good athlete but have never learned to dance. You want to ask someone to the school dance but are hesitant to do so because you are unsure of your dancing skills.

When students can relate to the context, they are more likely to see how knowledge applies to their own life. Developing upper-body strength might not seem too important to some students, but when the teacher uses a prompt that states, "Your house is on fire and you are on the second floor," the context makes upper-body strength meaningful and important.

## Step 4: Create the Task for the Problem

This next step is critical, because it is here that the teacher establishes the specific task that students will be required to perform. The product that students must generate in order to respond effectively to the question must be described in detail.

The instructions given should be very clear, explaining what the final product or performance will involve. Here are some task possibilities:

- Persuade an audience
- Analyze a perspective

- Make a comparison
- Make a decision
- Create a dialogue
- Construct an interview with a person (on paper)
- Outline a plan

The list of action verbs presented in figure 5.1 is helpful as teachers decide the type of task that the question involves. Teachers must also determine whether they want students to analyze, compare, synthesize, or judge something. These higher levels of Bloom's taxonomy require more time to complete, since they require students to engage in more thought and complex reasoning. Teachers must allow adequate time if students are to answer the question to the best of their ability.

Once the task is generated in this step, it is added to the scenario developed in the preceding (third) step of the question development process. Here are the sample scenarios listed in step 3 with a specific task added to each:

- You are trying to get a summer job at a fitness facility. It is a great job that pays well and offers a free membership for employees, and several of your friends work there. *Prepare a 5-minute pitch to convince the owner that you are well qualified for the job.*

- Your classes this year have been really hard, and you have spent a lot of time studying for them. The chocolate ice cream that you eat while studying has put an extra 10 pounds (4.5 kg) on your body, and you wish to lose that extra weight. *Develop an exercise plan to burn calories and help you get in shape. Also identify eating habits that you can adopt to decrease your caloric intake.*

- You have a new friend who likes to play tennis. You would like to be able to play tennis with this person, but your skills need work. *Analyze your present skills and abilities and identify the skills you must improve to become a better player. Develop a practice sequence and schedule for improving your game.*

- You have always been a good athlete but have never learned to dance.

You want to ask someone to the school dance but are hesitant to do so because you are unsure of your dancing skills. *Analyze the steps needed to perform the dances that are currently popular. Identify the basic skills involved in doing each of these steps and realistically evaluate your ability to perform these skills when you are doing sports and other activities. Identify the dance skills that you need to practice and make a plan for improving them.*

The previously stated ideas are quite concrete, and they will enable students to understand exactly what they need to do to answer them. When describing the desired product, teachers should keep in mind what students are capable of doing, and the knowledge base that they possess. When a teacher does not give students information that is necessary to complete a question, students cannot be expected to respond to the prompt in class without the use of outside resources.

After writing the task, the teacher must determine whether it assesses the desired information. For example, requiring students to compare a striking pattern across sports is very different from having them analyze it for possible errors. Asking a colleague to read the question and give input or feedback is one way to ensure that the question addresses the information that the teacher wishes to assess. Another way is to personally complete the question prior to use with students. Some things to look for include the following (Dick, Buecker, and Wilson 1999):

- Have I clearly stated the task?
- Will students understand what they must do to complete the question?
- Do the verbs used in the question require students to perform the desired task?
- Could I select another, more appropriate verb?
- Have I given students enough time to complete their responses?
- Have I provided my students with the necessary background information to answer the question?
- Will any of the information I've provided mislead students?

The checklist provided in figure 5.2 presents useful items to consider when designing open-response questions.

Open-response questions should be broad enough that several approaches are acceptable, thus encouraging students to use their creativity while answering the question. The rubric gives students the criteria that are used to evaluate their responses, including a clear explanation of what is expected in a high-quality response. If using a scoring guide, a level of quality should also be indicated. Students must know that not just any answer is acceptable.

## Checklist for Designing Open-Response Questions

The question should do the following:

- Provide students with a real-world setting and problem
- Use power verbs, thus requiring students to demonstrate higher-level thinking skills
- Require students to explain the processes they used in responding to the question
- Require students to explain their reasoning or justify their answer
- Accept a variety of approaches and solutions for an answer
- Clearly identify what is required of students
- Provide sufficient detail for students to respond effectively to the question
- Use developmentally appropriate language
- Include a rubric for evaluation

**Figure 5.2** By addressing the items presented in this checklist, teachers can evaluate the quality of their open-response questions.

## Step 5: Write a Rubric for People Evaluating the Response

The rubric created for people who will evaluate students' answers should present all the necessary information in rich detail. For results to be reliable, scorers need to fully understand the expectations for the response. When specific information is required for part of an answer, that information should be provided to the scorer. Even if a scorer possesses a strong background in the subject, a list of acceptable response possibilities is provided. For instance, for a question concerning components of fitness, the assessor's rubric should list the elements. Similarly, if an answer requires knowledge of the critical elements of a striking pattern, then these elements should be listed in the assessor's rubric. In short, if *any* content knowledge is required for an answer, then the rubric should convey that information to the evaluator rather than assuming that he or she possesses the knowledge and will use it when evaluating the response. Furthermore, when some elements carry more importance than others, the scorer's rubric should make the weighting clear.

When writing a rubic, it is necessary to go back to step 1 and recall what the question was intended to measure. Doing so can provide a list of criteria that should be present in the answer. Here are some things to remember when writing a rubric for an open-response question:

- The verbs used in the description of the task also indicate the criteria that must be met.
- When items are to be identified, they should be listed in the rubric for the people that will score the response.
- When a comparison is asked for, the rubric should require students to present and address all sides of the issue.
- The number of levels contained in the rubric depends on the purpose of the question. At a minimum, two levels should be described: one for an acceptable answer and another for an unacceptable answer.

## Step 6: Write a Rubric for Students

Writing a rubric for students is one of the most difficult parts of creating an open-response question. As a result, some teachers try to bypass this step by giving students the question without an explanation of how it will be evaluated. The first time a question is administered, a checklist or point system performance list might be used because looking at student responses is the best way to develop meaningful descriptions for the levels in the rubric. The performance list used to evaluate a question should contain at least enough criteria to inform students of what is expected in a thorough, high-quality answer.

The rubric created for students must contain guidelines that help students respond to the question appropriately; however, the guidelines should not be so thorough that students are spared the task of developing their own thinking or approach to answer the question. Care must be taken to ensure that the scoring guide is not so transparent that students can simply follow the procedure outlined in the question to produce a high-quality answer. When writing a scoring guide for students, the criteria used should let them know teacher expectations without providing the answer or explaining the process that they should use to complete the response.

## Step 7: Pilot the Question

As with any performance-based assessment, the first administration of the question should be considered a dry run or pilot. Teachers are advised to use the question as a minor assignment or possibly with a small group of students instead of with all students in every class. Bad questions can waste both the teacher's and the students' time. Piloting the question is an excellent way to prevent this from happening.

## Step 8: Revise and Improve

With any performance-based assessment, revision and improvement are standard procedures. Every time a question is used, it probably will change slightly. Teachers should continually be on the lookout for improvements to make. Some changes may also be triggered by students' responses. Here are some questions to ask when revising a question:

- Does this question satisfy my learning objective?
- What does this question tell me about student learning?

- Does this question reflect what I want students to know and be able to do as a result of my teaching?
- Does my rubric focus students' responses on the targeted knowledge?
- Is the real-world application relevant to physical education?
- Do students have the necessary content knowledge to answer this question?
- How much time do students need to answer this question?
- Do my students have all the skills necessary to answer the question?
- Do my students have the necessary resources to answer this question?

Most teachers truly want to develop a sound assessment system, and revisions are part of the journey when developing a good open-response question.

# SUGGESTIONS FOR USING OPEN-RESPONSE QUESTIONS

Open-response questions provide teachers with a way to assess students' learning of information that is difficult to access through other types of assessment. Because open-response questioning is a relatively new form of assessment for many teachers, the following suggestions are offered to help teachers incorporate this approach into their assessment plans:

- Start slow and keep it simple.
- Use open-response questions to measure students' understanding of major concepts.
- Consider teacher's time when using open-response questions.
- Consider students' time when assigning open-response questions.
- Remember managerial considerations when using open-response questions.
- Avoid indistinct questions.
- Create questions that can be completed in a reasonable time frame.
- Pilot the question before using it for a grade.
- Be sensitive to equity issues when writing the question or designing the product.

Open-response questions can assess information that other forms of assessment do not measure. With the suggestions offered in the next section, teachers will increase their expertise for developing open-response questions, which are valuable assessment tools.

## Start Slow and Keep It Simple

With any form of assessment, some teachers have the tendency to jump in only to find out that the water is a little deeper than they expected. To start the journey of using open-response questions, teachers should begin slowly by using a single-dimension question with one class. Open-response questions can be time-consuming to evaluate, and there is no feeling worse than knowing that one has 175-plus bad questions to evaluate! With practice, question-writing skills will improve, as will the rubrics used with them. Teachers should also recognize that open-response questions are probably a new form of assessment for many students. A brief explanation of the purpose of the assessment, along with a strategy for completing it, saves both the teacher and the students a lot of time in the long run. A single-dimension question that requires 5 to 10 minutes for students to complete is a nice way to begin the journey toward using open-response questions effectively.

## Use These Questions to Measure Students' Understanding of Major Concepts

Open-response questions provide an excellent option when teachers want to determine how well students really understand major concepts and whether they can apply them to other settings. Open-response questions do require more time to write, administer, and score than do other, more traditional forms of assessment. As a result, if teachers are merely interested in knowing whether a student has acquired a certain body of knowledge, then other assessment options offer better choices. However, when teachers wish to assess more complex levels of thinking, open-response questions are a wonderful vehicle for doing so. It is not easy to measure cognitive ability in physical education, especially at higher levels of thinking. Many schools today place great emphasis on critical thinking, and open-response questions give students an opportunity to use this type of thinking in meaningful and productive ways that are relevant to physical education content. Open-response questions are excellent choices for culminating assessments that look at the big picture of what the class has covered.

## Consider Teacher's Time

Open-response questions take considerable time to write and score. Given the number of students typically enrolled in physical education classes, using open-response questions for all students simultaneously can put a huge burden on a teacher's time. Assessment should not punish a teacher; it should enhance instruction, benefiting both the teacher and the students. When an open-response question is the best way to assess students' learning, teachers might stagger when they are given to students, thus making the evaluation less of a burden. If a teacher were to receive 200 open-response question answers for grading all at once, he or she could give only a very limited amount of time to each one. When teachers space out the administration of the questions, they will have more time to devote to scoring each response, which improves the quality of feedback given to students.

For example, teachers might use an open-response question for two classes while staying with traditional assessments for the other classes (assuming all the classes taught are similar). Or, when teachers have some elective classes in their schedules (e.g., team sports, dance, advanced physical education), they might use open-response questions in one of the sections (e.g., dance class) , then in another type of class in couple of weeks (e.g., advanced physical education).

## Consider Students' Time

Teachers also must consider student time when having students write open-response questions. Some open-response assessments require considerable time to produce a good response, and, in light of the limited time available in physical education classes, teachers should make every minute count. Some single-dimension questions can be completed when students are waiting for their team to play or to present their dance or gymnastics composition. Physical education

teachers can also work with teachers from other content areas to evaluate a student response. Using this approach, each teacher grades the response in terms of his or her area of expertise. Many subject-area teachers are willing to give class time for administering an open-response question. For example, English teachers might grade a response as a writing assignment, and the physical education teacher could then evaluate it for content and understanding in physical education. Science and social studies also share content (e.g., principles of physics and biology, participating in games, and dances from other cultures) with physical education. When a question is used to address multiple content areas, students sense increased importance for the assessment, which can also improve the quality of their responses. An additional benefit of multi-area open-response questions is that they cut down on the overall number of open-response questions students are asked to write. Writing open-response questions in several classes can become tedious for students. When students are required to do fewer open-response questions, a more insightful response is likely to result, as students are able to focus intently and give a high-quality answer.

## Managerial Issues to Consideration

When administering an open-response question in physical education, teachers should make sure that students have an appropriate location in which to answer the question. When the question requires only a short response (as is the case with a single-dimension open-response question), students' lap boards or clipboards in the gymnasium are appropriate. When the question is going to require 45 minutes or more to complete, an effort should be made to move to a classroom or other area that offers seating.

Another factor to consider is time. Some children need longer than others to complete their response, and those who require more time should have it. To keep those occupied who finish sooner, teachers can set up an activity for students to engage in after they have completed their response. Assuming that a teacher would be able to monitor the activity while also supervising those who are still finishing their response, those who are finished might be given the opportunity to practice skills (e.g., through station work). Students might also begin a fitness workout after they have completed their response. Teachers do not want to decrease the importance of the question by giving activity options, but they should make provisions for those students who finish earlier than others in the class.

Some questions may lend themselves to being completed at home. If the teacher is trying to determine an affective disposition or attitude or wants to give students an opportunity to practice answering open-response questions, then a take-home question might be a viable option. When deciding whether to allow students to complete a question at home, teachers should consider the question's complexity, its purpose, and its implications for students' grades. If teachers do not want students to use outside resources, then the question should be administered in a controlled and monitored setting. When a question can be completed outside of class without jeopardizing the nature of the assessment, then a take-home format may be worth considering.

## Avoid Indistinct Questions

It is important to remember that with open-response questions, some fuzziness is to be expected. However, if a teacher has trouble writing a question or the rubric, the problem may be that the content for the question was poorly defined. When a teacher has trouble with the development of a question, he or she should go back to the original purpose or intent and identify the concepts or knowledge that the question was designed to assess. When the content is clearly articulated, the question and rubric will be more focused and measure the desired student learning.

## Consider the Time Needed to Answer the Question

Open-response questions must be broad enough to allow students to pull information from various sources; however, they should not be so large that students spend hours completing them. Aside from general variations in students' work speeds, the amount of time required to complete an open-response question depends on the purpose of the assessment, the content of the question, and the age of the student. Obviously,

when working with younger students, a teacher must take care to ensure that the question is not too demanding or overwhelming to students. With older students, the question should have sufficient breadth and depth to challenge students. A complex question will probably require between 45 and 90 minutes to complete, though this should not be considered an absolute time frame. The purpose of the assessment along with other contextual factors and considerations (e.g., content, prior knowledge, resources available, length and frequency of class) dictates the amount of time required to complete it. A way to estimate the time required to fully answer a question is to see how long it takes a colleague to answer it, then calculate that students will need about twice as much time to complete their answers.

## Pilot the Question Before Using It for a Grade

As with any written assessment, students can misinterpret the intent of a question. Words are sometimes defined differently than the teacher intended, or a critical piece of information is omitted, leaving students unable to correctly answer the question. In light of the potential for errors or misunderstanding, it is a good idea to conduct a pilot administration of an open-response question to work the bugs out before using the question to determine part of a student's grade. A poorly written open-response question will not lead to a response that indicates the level of a student's learning, and students should never be penalized because of a teacher's error. Piloting a question before using it in the grading system is simply sound pedagogy.

## Be Sensitive to Equity Issues

Please read and consider the following open-response prompt:

> Fitness is a key component of many physical education programs. Twenty years ago, teachers led exercises, and students followed without giving much thought to explaining the value of different exercises or sports to students. Today, many of these adults want to increase their levels of fitness, but they may not have

the necessary information to choose or develop an exercise program that meets their needs. Describe your current fitness levels and what would be necessary for you to become fit at the present time. Develop an exercise program for keeping fit while in college that addresses all five components of fitness.

At first glance, this question may look like an excellent way to prompt students to think about how they might apply principles of fitness after graduation; however, it raises an issue of equity. The question assumes that the student will attend college, but this is not the case for every student who graduates from high school. The assumption might raise a sensitive issue for some students and hinder them as they write their response. Going to college is not an important part of the question. The focus should be on assessing students' knowledge of fitness components and their ability to develop an exercise program for themselves in adult life.

When creating open-response questions, teachers must be aware of language that may prevent students from doing their best when generating their responses. Teachers should avoid using language that is insensitive. Gender, ethnicity, race, and fitness level are obvious areas to consider when desensitizing open-response questions. Harvey and Popham have written about test inequity and the problems caused by questions that contain hidden biases or agendas (Harvey 2003; Popham 2001, 2003).

Another equity issue can arise if teachers require students to complete an open response on a computer. Socioeconomic status enters into equity issues if a teacher assumes that all students have access to the Internet or even just to a computer at home. No student should be forced to do poorly because of external factors.

Student-choice open-response questions can serve as an excellent option when dealing with potentially sensitive or biased topics. When a teacher is trying to assess a concept, several prompts can address the desired information or content. When students are allowed to select their topic, it gives students some control over the topic and makes equity issues less of a problem.

# CONCLUSION

Open-response questions provide teachers with another alternative for assessment in the cognitive and affective domains. Students must apply facts and knowledge learned in class by using higher-level thinking skills to formulate a response to a real-world prompt. Because students can answer open-response questions in a variety of ways with one approach being as valid as another, these questions encourage students to think out of the box. Open-response questions can be challenging for students and at the same time help teachers identify areas of students' understanding and misunderstanding.

As with most performance-based assessments, open-response questions require more time to develop, administer, and score than do traditional, selected-response test questions. For this reason, teachers should carefully examine what they wish to assess to determine whether open-response questioning is the best form of assessment for the content knowledge they wish to evaluate. Although open-response questions should be broad, they should not be so vague that they become unmanageable in terms of the students' or the teacher's time. Careful attention must also be paid to the language used in an open-response question to ensure that equity factors do not negatively influence a student's response.

When teachers address the various issues and factors discussed in this chapter, they can use open-response questioning as a viable form of assessment that is enjoyable to both students and teachers. Physical education teachers are encouraged to begin using open-response questions to assess students' application of knowledge and their ability to use information in realistic situations.

# Portfolios

*Portfolios offer a dynamic, visual presentation of student abilities, strengths, and areas of needed improvement over time—a more naturalistic, authentic, and performance-based assessment of student learning (Kelly and Melograno 2004, 207).*

Widespread emphasis on performance-based, continuous, and authentic assessment as a tool for determining students' achievement of targeted goals and standards has led to the emergence of portfolios as an exciting and broadly used form of alternative assessment in middle and secondary schools. More specifically, you need only look at the latest professional literature to see that portfolio assessment is used in physical education (Wilson and Roof 1999; Kulinna et al. 1999; Melograno 2006; Kirk 1997).

A **portfolio** is "a purposeful, integrated, collection of actual exhibits and work samples showing effort, progress or achievement in one or more areas. It presents a broad, genuine picture of student learning" (Melograno 1999, 2). The portfolio is not a new form of assessment and evaluation. For years, artists, architects, journalists, photographers, and models have gathered and presented their best work in portfolios as evidence of their talent and abilities. In recent years, many educators have also realized the tremendous potential that the portfolio

process holds as a learning and assessment tool for K–12 students and for preservice teachers (Melograno 1999).

Portfolios are considered to be dynamic, living documents with changing collections of student work (Hill and Ruptic 1994). As such, a portfolio can serve not only as a body of work for evaluation but also as a process for learning and assessment (Herman, Aschbacher, and Winters 1992). Students can choose from among a variety of assessment tools when deciding what to include in their portfolios for evaluation. Through this process, the portfolio serves as a receptacle for "the collection of student work that documents students' effort, progress and achievement toward a goal or goals" (Siedentop and Tannehill 2000, 191). Moreover, students continue to learn as they engage in this process of completing a variety of learning and assessment tasks across time, selecting those that are the most representative of their effort and achievement, and reflecting on how the collected artifacts provide evidence of the student's achievement of targeted goals. Therefore, a portfolio is not only a collection of work for assessment but also a learning process through which students gain insight about themselves as performers and learners (Siedentop and Tannehill 2000).

The portfolio is an exciting and flexible tool for learning and assessment in physical education. It can be used in a variety of ways that meet the needs of the teacher, the program, and the students. Introducing students to portfolio assessment and implementing the process is demanding, requiring considerable planning, organization, and, usually, a change in teaching styles for the teacher. However, the results, though occasionally frustrating, are well worth the effort. The teacher can observe students as they become more actively involved in the learning and self-assessment process. Integrated learning and assessment tasks become more realistic and authentic for students, which often results in higher levels of student interest and motivation (Mitchell 1992). Portfolios give students the opportunity to demonstrate their achievement by displaying their progress, improvement, and learning. In a sense, then, a portfolio is a celebration of student achievement that allows students, teachers, parents, and the school as a whole to take pride in students' performances (Siedentop and Tannehill 2000).

To help physical education teachers better understand this process so that they can implement a portfolio process in their own programs, this chapter discusses the following aspects of using portfolios as tools for assessment:

- Characteristics of portfolios
- Types of portfolios
- Portfolio guidelines in performance-based assessment
- Evaluation of portfolios

# CHARACTERISTICS OF PORTFOLIOS

The portfolio has many characteristics that make it an effective learning and assessment tool for physical education. These characteristics allow teachers and students to use portfolios to enhance and support student learning. The characteristics discussed in the following sections encourage

- use of flexible and multidimensional forms of assessment;
- documentation of student progress, improvement, and goal achievement;
- active student involvement in the learning process through choice, self-evaluation, and reflection;
- provision of feedback and continuous evaluation of students' progress toward goals;
- increased motivation of students and teachers; and
- use of portfolios to spotlight students' achievements while promoting the physical education program through students' work.

## Flexible and Multidimensional

The portfolio is a flexible form of alternative assessment. It is an alternative approach because it differs so much from traditional forms of assessment, yet it may include both traditional *and* authentic pieces. The teacher must, however, establish a clear vision of the assessment's purpose and scope and communicate this information to students at the beginning of the process (Mitchell 1992). Evaluation portfolios can be **representative** or accumulative (Siedentop and Tannehill 2000); that is, student work included in a portfolio can either represent achievement for one unit of instruction or serve as a cumulative assessment of student work across a semester, academic year, or sequence of school years (e.g., grades K–5, 6–8, or 9–12). A portfolio can also serve as either a **single-dimensional** or a **multidimensional assessment**. That is, it may include either many documents focusing on the attainment of one goal or standard (e.g., a healthy level of physical fitness) or artifacts collected as evidence for the achievement of multiple standards. In addition, students may be required to provide work that represents their level of achievement not only in the psychomotor domain but also in the cognitive and affective dimensions of educational development. Here is a handy summary of these key points:

- Representative: covers learning for one unit
- Cumulative: represents learning across multiple units
- Single-dimensional: represents the attainment of one goal or standard

- Multidimensional: represents the attainment of two or more goals or standards

## Documentation of Students' Progress, Improvement, and Goal Achievement

In the portfolio assessment process, students collect their work and then choose the pieces that most accurately document their progress toward targeted goals or standards for the identified scope of the physical education program (e.g., unit, semester, year, program). Once students have chosen which of their best works to showcase in the portfolio, they submit the portfolio for evaluation. The pieces included may compare earlier performances or products with later ones in order to demonstrate improvement, progress, or growth over time, as well as achievement of targeted goals (Westfall 1998). The documentation presented in the evaluation portfolio can provide a comprehensive view of the student's learning and achievement that is both authentic and performance-based.

Teachers and schools may ask students to present **artifacts** that provide evidence that they have progressed toward or achieved state and local learner goals. In the states that have adopted the National Standards for Physical Education published by the National Association for Sport and Physical Education (NASPE; 2004), students can also be required to provide evidence that they are "physically educated persons" who have demonstrated a desirable level of achievement of the six national standards. For example, a student might include a detailed log (signed by a witness) that lists dates and describes physical activity outside of class over the course of a semester as evidence that the student is moving toward achieving NASPE standard 3: "Participates regularly in physical activity" (NASPE 2004). Another student might provide evidence for the same standard by including newspaper reports or awards that focus on his or her training for and participation in community or statewide mini-marathons.

## Individualized Learning and Assessment

When portfolios are used as a form of performance-based assessment, students are encour-aged to complete and choose the pieces of work that they will include as evidence for achievement of various goals. This process encourages students to engage in developmentally appropriate and individualized learning activities. Students work at their level of skill, knowledge, and ability—and they work on projects or tasks that are of interest to them (Kirk 1997). Indeed, because students come to class with a great variety and depth of experiences and abilities, the portfolio approach to assessment opens the door for teachers to individualize goals, expectations, learning, and assessment tasks.

Within particular activity units—and with the guidance of the teacher—students can identify individual goals that they will work to accomplish in order to address broader class goals. For example, consider NASPE standard 1: "Demonstrates competency in motor skills and movement patterns needed to perform a variety of physical activities" (National Association for Sport and Physical Education 2004). To address this standard, two students in the same class—let's call them Juan and Emily—can select two very different movement activities and provide a variety of artifacts to support their work in their chosen activities. Juan may choose to submit documents showing that he has achieved proficiency in playing tennis, while Emily's portfolio may provide evidence of her proficiency in canoeing. Both students participated in both activity units (i.e., tennis and canoeing) in class, and each made a decision about which one to address in the portfolio based on achieving the proficiency level rather than merely the competency level. In this instance, then, the portfolio assessment process encourages students to make individual choices about the activities in which they try to develop proficiency. These choices may be based on individual interest, skill, or achievement.

Even within the same activity unit, students may identify and work toward different individual goals. During a track-and-field unit in a ninth-grade physical education class, Keeshana is very interested in sprinting and jumping events, and she sets the following individual goals for herself: (1) high-jump 5 feet (about 1.5 m) using the flop technique, (2) long-jump more than 15 feet (about 4.6 m) in the class track meet, and (3) run a personal best of 14 seconds in the 100-meter dash. Li, on the other hand, is more interested in throwing events and middle-distance running, and he sets the following goals for himself: (1) throw the shot put at least 40 feet (about 12.2 m), (2) throw the discus at least 100 feet (about 30.5 m), and (3) run a personal-best time of under 2:50 in the 800-meter run in the class meet. After identifying these goals, Keeshana and Li each spend time in class working on the events in which they have some ability and interest. With their objectives clearly established, they are able to experience what it means to train and practice for these events in pursuit of personal goals. They also decide how they will record work, track progress, and show achievement. Using a portfolio in this way, students make choices about what they want to learn, how they will practice, and how they will demonstrate their learning.

Independence and choice are important considerations when trying to motivate adolescents to strive to achieve goals. Although Keeshana and Li chose different activities, their personal goals, projects, and performances can each satisfy NASPE standard 1 (National Association for Sport and Physical Education 2004).

Portfolio assessment permits students to work toward individualized goals; for example, one student can focus on running events while another focuses on throwing events.

## Responsibility and Active Learning

Student and teacher roles change when students choose activities and skills to work on and set individual achievement goals that address broad class or program goals. "In order to complete products and assemble their best work as evidence of achievement of those goals, the students must work independently and take responsibility and ownership for their own learning" (Kirk 1997, 30). Specifically, students must make decisions about learning and assessment tasks (or products) that they will complete, and in this new role they must be much more than an unengaged participant—they must be actively involved in the learning process.

The teacher, in turn, takes on the role of facilitator or guide. Initially, the teacher introduces all skill events in the track-and-field unit to the entire class. Next, students have an opportunity to try all of the events. In our track-and-field example involving Keeshana and Li, the teacher might present the skill of high jumping to a group of interested students, take them through the initial steps of performing and practicing the skill, and make recommendations regarding tasks to use for continued practice. Teachers then organize the class by establishing learning stations for instruction and practice, and students identify events in which they would like to develop proficiency. They set personal goals, then rotate to the relevant event stations in order to practice during class.

A student might also decide to seek more information about how to train and practice for his or her chosen event. Keeshana, for example, might decide to interview the high school track coach or a varsity high jumper, observe varsity high jumpers during practice, search the Web to find coaching tips from experts, or check out a video about high jumping from the library. Using the information that she gathers, Keeshana might then choose to design her own practice and training schedule for class, and during class she might ask the teacher or a peer to video-record her performance so that she can complete a self-analysis regarding her performance. She might keep a log of practice performances to help her track progress (or lack thereof), and this practice will help her review her personal goals for performance and training strategies. If documented, any or all of these individual projects could provide evidence that Keeshana could choose to include in her portfolio. With the portfolio approach, then, students have a myriad of opportunities to direct and engage actively in their own learning endeavors, which, as a result, are much more authentic.

## Self-Evaluation and Reflection

The portfolio process encourages students to evaluate and reflect on themselves as learners. They must reflect on the quality of their work or performances in order to make decisions about which pieces present the best evidence of their effort, progress, and level of achievement. They should not only select artifacts to include in the portfolio but also write convincing rationales explaining why each item was selected and how it provides evidence of progress or level of achievement in terms of targeted standards or goals. When reflecting, students must make personal judgments about the quality of their work and performances. In some cases, a student will ultimately decide not to include an artifact that he or she originally thought would provide evidence of achievement toward a certain standard; instead, he or she will determine that another artifact provides stronger evidence, perhaps even for a higher level of performance in terms of the standard (for a sample reflection form, see figure 6.3 later in this chapter).

In selecting evidence of improvement, students must compare performance artifacts that they have accumulated throughout the unit, looking at their own work with a critical eye in order to identify the best pieces and relate the artifacts to targeted standards or goals. This process gives the student—and the teacher—a clear picture of the student's improvement and level of performance. It enables students to see the big picture of their learning, rather than just the separate pieces.

## Feedback and Continuous Evaluation

The portfolio process encourages teachers to provide students with many opportunities to complete a variety of assessments throughout

> n a 1997 article (Kirk 1997), I demonstrated this concept of student self-evaluation and reflection in an example from a badminton unit in which I provided students with daily opportunities to practice their long and short serves. When I realized that students who were completing 100 percent of their serves in practice were completing a significantly lower percentage during game play, I revised this daily assessment activity. Initially, students simply recorded the number of accurate short and long serves made out of 10, but now they were asked to take their practice serves in a gamelike situation—with an opponent returning the serve. This refinement added a new dimension to the goal of the practice, because students not only had to serve the shuttle over the net and into the service court but also had to do so in such a way that the receiver could not return the serve. Working on serves in this modified game activity creates a realistic or authentic practice situation for students, who can record performance criteria data every day about their percentage of serve accuracy and trajectory, serve placement, criteria, and success. Thus this assessment activity provides data that students can use to chart their progress, analyze their performance across time, and make interventions for improvement when needed. They can then use their systematic recording, graphing, and analysis of the data as an artifact of evidence in their portfolio. Students in my badminton class demonstrated significant improvement in their serving performance when these assessment strategies were implemented.

the unit, semester, or year. Because most assessments are formative or completed throughout the unit and integrated with learning activities throughout the portfolio process period, the teacher and student are provided with ongoing feedback about learning and progress of performance through systematic documentation. This process allows students and teachers to modify learning and practice activities to better meet students' needs. As students receive feedback regarding their progress, they may seek assistance from a peer or their teacher. Teachers can also use the information produced by continuous feedback and evaluation to make changes in curriculum or instructional strategies.

## Increased Motivation for Students and Teachers

Students are more motivated to engage in assessment tasks that are integrated with learning activities, reflective of real-life situations, and infused with personal meaning. Personal and realistic tasks for students include setting personal goals for daily participation in physical activity outside of class and keeping a daily log that addresses the type of activity, records the

priate action to maintain or encourage regular participation. Moreover, students can use this process to motivate themselves, analyze their practices, and make interventions in their physical activity patterns throughout their lives.

Students can also be strongly motivated when they are given the freedom to creatively develop and participate in their own learning and assessment tasks. Teachers can also be strongly motivated by seeing their students get excited about their own learning and take responsibility for it. In the absence of this accountability, some students would not even attempt the task of being proactive about learning.

Students are also motivated by the knowledge that not every assessment completed inside or outside of class is evaluated or graded. This fact helps students try harder and attempt tasks that they might otherwise rule out due to fear of failure. It is also motivating to students when they are provided with the time and opportunity to complete multiple practice and assessment tasks, which allows them to keep trying until they have met the criteria or are satisfied with their performance.

While teaching a badminton unit to a 10th-grade class, I asked my students to create and complete a group assessment task. The task was one that they could use in their portfolios to provide evidence of their knowledge of and skill in playing badminton, as well as their ability to work cooperatively in a group in order to accomplish a goal. One group of five students chose to create an instructional video about badminton. They opened the video with a shared presentation on the history and current status of the sport. Then each student introduced a different badminton shot, presented a rationale for using the shot, identified performance cues, and gave several demonstrations of the shot. Meanwhile, other members of the group took turns directing and operating the video camera. To demonstrate their knowledge of the rules, four of the group members served as players on the court while one student served as a commentator, explaining the rules as they were demonstrated. Students took turns serving as the commentator. As I observed this group, it was obvious to me that the students were engaged and motivated to complete a high-quality project.

In addition, it is highly motivating to adolescent students to be given the opportunity (and, ultimately, the responsibility) of choosing the artifacts they will submit for evaluation. By giving students this choice, the teacher is saying to them, "You are a responsible individual, and I trust you to make good decisions about your learning."

amount of activity time, indicates whether participation was completed alone or with someone else, and identifies the reason when a student does not participate. Completing this task allows students to analyze and reflect on their activity patterns and on their reasons for participation or nonparticipation so that they can take appro-

Teachers tend to feel tremendous motivation and renewed enthusiasm for teaching when they see students develop the responsibility and initiative to perform individual portfolio tasks and complete the overall portfolio process. It is especially gratifying for teachers when students take ownership of and pride in their portfolios—when they genuinely take time to personalize their portfolios and are obviously eager to share their work. In the case of the badminton video discussed in the tip, students provided other artifacts (in addition to the video) in order to represent their work on the project; these items included written scripts, photographs of the scripts rendered in large print (for use by the actors), and pictures chronicling the entire process. When class members were asked to present their badminton portfolios to the class, the members of this group were highly excited to show their video and explain their process. These students were not always the best or most responsible students in the class, but because this was *their* project, which they were creating for *their* portfolios, they engaged in it enthusiastically. It was obvious to me that they were having fun, both in learning and in developing evidence of their learning. In fact, the project became the centerpiece of their portfolios, and for me as a teacher this was one of those light bulb moments!

### Display of Student Work

It has been said that "[a] portfolio is like a trophy case for a student's accomplishments" (Wilson and Roof 1999, 11). Just as athletic trophy cases recognize athletes' accomplishments, portfolios can be used to recognize students' work and accomplishments in the physical education program. Showcasing students' portfolios also serves as an effective way to demonstrate accountability on the part of teachers and programs. Portfolios can also be displayed to provide evidence of students' learning and achievement in terms of goals and standards at the district, state, and national levels. For example, instead of having teachers explain the physical education program to parents via lecture presentation, you could display students' portfolios around the gymnasium so that parents can view them during open houses at the school. Imagine the impressive scene when students stand with their portfolios on display—surrounded by groups of parents, teachers, administrators, and other students—as they explain the artifacts included in the portfolio and discuss how each artifact provides evidence of their achievement of targeted goals and standards. This approach

offers a powerful way to demonstrate the physical education program's accountability and measure its success.

# TYPES OF PORTFOLIOS

Portfolios can be designed for a variety of purposes, and the purpose you choose for a given portfolio assessment should determine the type of portfolio you ask students to complete (Melograno 2006). Here are several types of portfolio that can be used either alone or in combination (Burke, Fogarty, and Belgrad 1994; Kimeldorf 1994; Melograno 2000):

- Working portfolio
- Evaluation or showcase portfolio
- Thematic portfolio
- Multiyear portfolio
- Group portfolio
- Electronic portfolio

### Working Portfolio

The working portfolio is an individual student's collection of daily or weekly work, projects, assessments, and assignments. The student collects these materials from class by placing them into a file folder, box, or envelope, which can be either stored by the teacher or kept by the student. Each item is logged in or out on the portfolio register form, which is stored with the working portfolio. Periodically, the student makes decisions about which items will be eliminated and which will be retained as artifacts to provide evidence of the student's achievement of class goals in the evaluation or showcase portfolio.

### Evaluation Portfolio

The finished product submitted by the student for evaluation is referred to as an evaluation (or showcase) portfolio. It contains a limited number of artifacts chosen by the student from the working portfolio to represent his or her best work. The pieces included in the evaluation portfolio demonstrate the student's achievement of personal, class, and program goals and standards, as well as the student's growth over time. This portfolio is developed in such a way that it can be showcased or exhibited to audiences beyond the teacher (e.g., peers, other teachers, administrators, parents) in order to demonstrate the student's growth and achievement; it can also be used to demonstrate program quality.

## Thematic Portfolio

A **thematic portfolio** is used for a specific unit of study. The unit might last anywhere from 2 to 12 weeks, depending on the theme or activity involved. A variety of themes could be emphasized in a middle school or high school physical education class that uses the portfolio process for assessment. Some common themes in physical education include personal fitness, cooperation, teamwork, and self-expression through movement (Melograno 2000, 2006).

## Multiyear Portfolio

A **multiyear portfolio** focuses on showing a student's growth or achievement of goals and standards across a period of years. For instance, middle school students could demonstrate their breadth of knowledge and skill development in various physical activity units (e.g., volleyball, basketball, soccer, badminton, in-line skating, dance, golf, tennis, ultimate, gymnastics, track and field, canoeing, hiking, orienteering) over the course of their schooling from sixth grade through eighth grade. Eighth-grade students could include a reflective writing assignment in which they identify two to four activities in which they experienced the most interest, joy, or success, and these activities could then be pursued in a high school elective program. A multiyear portfolio approach could also be used effectively to help students and teachers follow growth in a student's knowledge, attitudes, physical fitness, and levels and types of participation in regular physical activities.

## Group Portfolio

Melograno (2000, 2006) suggests that the use of **group portfolios** is an effective way for students to experience their initial exposure to the portfolio process because they go through it with a group instead of alone. Students might be asked to contribute either individual or group work to the portfolio in order to help the group achieve its goals. The group portfolio process also enables teachers to evaluate students' coop-

eration and teamwork, and it offers an excellent assessment form for teachers to use in evaluating group achievement in a unit based on the Sport Education model.

## Electronic Portfolio

The ongoing development of multimedia software and high-tech hardware has enabled the development of the electronic portfolio, the use of which in physical education creates nearly endless possibilities (Mohnsen 2000). An electronic portfolio can be created with a computer and a CD-ROM (or flash drive), which enables students to easily store and transport files so that they can their work on their portfolio at school, in a computer lab, at a library, or at home. Multimedia technology also makes it possible for students to create video sequences in which they demonstrate skills, show game-play sequences, and perform dance and gymnastics routines. Other multimedia tools and activities that students can use to prepare artifacts include blogging, PowerPoint presentations, Web site creation, podcasting, and digital cameras. For instance, students could develop a school Web site where they present current evidence-based material regarding fitness and wellness topics for students, teachers, and parents. Such a Web site could serve as a rich, engaging portfolio artifact. These technological tools are now available to students, and using electronic portfolios as a means of assessment is an excellent way to integrate technology into students' learning process in physical education. Indeed, when students prepare artifacts in this manner, they demonstrate another increasingly important ability in today's world—that of using emerging technology.

# PORTFOLIO GUIDELINES IN PERFORMANCE-BASED ASSESSMENT

To make portfolio assessment a positive and enjoyable process for everyone involved, it is extremely important for teachers to clearly explain the process and guide students through it, especially the first time that students develop a portfolio. Teachers must remind themselves that using portfolios as a form of continuous performance-based assessment is a learning process for students. To be successful, teachers must plan ahead, make the necessary preparations, and attend to each of the following tasks:

1. Identify learner outcomes to be demonstrated through portfolio assessment
2. Develop and communicate portfolio guidelines to students
3. Build flexibility into the class schedule to provide class time for students to work on their portfolios
4. Provide a variety of performance-based learning and assessment opportunities for students
5. Guide students as they generate portfolio ideas
6. Provide opportunities for students to share or showcase their portfolios

## Guideline 1: Identify Learner Outcomes

The teacher must begin the portfolio process by identifying what students should know and be able to do by the conclusion of the unit, semester, year, or program. The teacher must clearly identify the objectives, goals, and standards that students are expected to meet and share these with students at the outset. These goals and standards will then guide students as they develop their portfolios. The student outcomes that are initially identified may include any of the following: very specific activity goals; sport unit goals; broad goals on the school, district, or state level; and selected NASPE standards for physical education (National Association for Sport and Physical Education 2004). The broad goals or standards can serve as the organizational format for the student portfolio. For example, if all six NASPE standards for physical education are identified as desired outcomes, then students might choose to organize their portfolios into six sections—one for each standard—and provide at least one artifact to demonstrate their level of achievement for each standard. By sharing the expected destination with students from the start, teachers can provide them with a better understanding of where they must go and what they must do to get there.

## Guideline 2: Develop and Communicate Portfolio Guidelines

Once the teacher has identified standards and decided to use portfolio-based evaluation for the students' culminating product, it is time to establish a plan and guidelines and share them with students. Even if your students have worked with portfolios before, they still need specific guidelines; and for students who do not have experience with portfolio assessment, it is crucial that you guide them carefully through the process.

The portfolio process must be designed for the setting in which it will be implemented. We have found that "if class time and space are limited, then the number and scope of tasks must be geared to the contextual limitations of the program" (Kirk 1997, 30). Once you have determined the dimensions and criteria of the portfolio, give students a handout noting this information for future reference (see, for example, figure 6.1) and carefully review the guidelines with students to make sure that all questions are answered and all students have a clear understanding of what is expected. A sample of a portfolio assignment guideline is provided in figure 6.6

We have found that it is best to provide organized storage of students' working portfolios at the physical education facility. One approach that works well is to provide a milk crate for each class and a hanging file folder or colored folder for each student in the class. You can label the crates by class and, if you like, use a different color for each class's crate. The crates can be stacked and stored in your office or in a secure storage room near the gym, where students would have easy access to their portfolio materials during each class. A supply of pencils and pens should be kept near the crates so that students can record new documents.

### Daily Storage of New Materials

Each assessment task or item should be dated or numbered and recorded in the artifact registry taped to the front of the working portfolio container (see figure 6.2). Melograno (1999) suggests that this approach provides a chronicle of when and why items are included, removed, and

---

### Recommendations or Requirements for How the Portfolio Should Be Contained and Submitted

Suggestions include file folders, three-ring binders, photo albums, hanging files, large envelopes, and CD-ROMs.

### How the Portfolio Should Be Organized

In standards-based educational programs, students may be required to include a section in their portfolio that contains a specified number of artifacts for each targeted state or program standard or for each NASPE standard (National Association for Sport and Physical Education 2004). The teacher might recommend or require that students use dividers with labeled tabs to separate the sections by goal or national standard or to color-code each section, which corresponds to the table of contents. In the final evaluation portfolio, students should be required to include a comprehensive table of contents to help organize their work and assist the evaluator in locating materials.

### How Working Portfolios Are Stored and How Students Gain Access to Them

The working portfolio is where students collect all of their work until they compile and submit their evaluation portfolio. Teachers must address the following questions regarding the storage of working portfolios: Are students responsible for keeping their own working portfolio, or does the teacher provide an accessible space for storing them? Do students have access to stored working portfolios outside of class time?

---

**Figure 6.1**   This includes tips for the teacher and student on how to construct the portfolio and for the storage of student portfolios and portfolio materials.

**Figure 6.2**   The record form helps students keep track of all documents placed into or removed from their working portfolio.

replaced as students continue to reflect on their work to date. This process makes things easier for students when the time comes to assemble their final evaluation portfolio. Without a written record, it can be difficult for students to remember when and why they originally decided, weeks ago, to include certain artifacts.

## Sample Assessment Tasks

Teachers should provide suggestions, but they should also remember to allow students room for choice if they expect students to take ownership of their portfolios. A list of possible task ideas is presented later in this chapter (see figure 6.5). When providing students with task ideas, focus on the targeted student outcomes and ask, "What tasks can students complete in order to demonstrate a level of achievement for at least one of the outcomes?"

## Written Reflections

Students should provide written reflections expressing why they included each artifact and how it shows growth, progress, and achievement (see figure 6.3). The reflection statement should provide a connection between the artifact and targeted student outcomes.

**Written Reflection Portfolio Form**

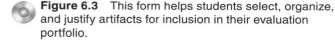

Name_____ Class_____ Semester <u>Fall/Spring</u>

| Artifact or document | Goal, standard, or objective | Reflection (why item is included) |
|---|---|---|
|  |  |  |

From J. Lund and M. Kirk, 2010, *Performance-Based Assessment for Middle and High School Physical Education, Second Edition* (Champaign, IL: Human Kinetics).

**Figure 6.3** This form helps students select, organize, and justify artifacts for inclusion in their evaluation portfolio.

## Time Lines and Progress Checkpoint Dates

The practice of establishing time lines and checkpoints helps ensure that the assessment process is continual; it also allows the teacher to give students feedback along the way. Encourage students to make early decisions about possible assessment tasks or projects that they would like to submit as part of their final portfolio. The most effective way to help students do this is to provide them with a timetable that includes scheduled checkpoints for which students compile specific parts of their portfolio and schedule conferences with you. If you like, you can even set up a portfolio station in the corner of the gym, away from the action, where you can periodically check on students' progress in developing their portfolios. While the class is engaged in practice or game activities, you can meet with students individually or in small groups at the station in order to check their progress and answer any questions.

## Provide a Rubric

As discussed in chapter 3, a rubric is a scoring guide that teachers can use to evaluate a portfolio; it can also be used by students to guide them in their construction of their final portfolio. The rubric provides students with the criteria they must meet in order to achieve each level of quality the teacher has designated. Sample rubrics can be found in chapter 3 and, later in this chapter, in figure 6.6 and table 6.1.

## Provide Models of Student Portfolios

Often students are unable to visualize either a completed portfolio or the types of items that it might include. By viewing model portfolios, students develop a better understanding of the finished product. Teachers can place model student portfolios (with the student creator's permission) on reserve in the school library or keep them on a table in a teacher's office or in the gym for students to examine. It is important, however, to remind students that they should not just copy another person's portfolio but create and personalize their own.

## Encourage Personalization

It is a good idea to suggest to students that they include their own artwork, computer graphics, choice of colors, photographs, stickers, or memorabilia in their portfolios. Adolescence is a time when students' need for independence emerges strongly, and portfolios give students a chance to be creative and individualize their work. When students are encouraged to personalize their work, they tend to be more enthusiastic and take more pride in it.

## Guideline 3: Build Flexibility Into the Class Schedule and Provide Time in Class for Students to Work on Portfolios

In order to facilitate a successful and positive portfolio process for students, the teacher must build flexibility into the class schedule, organization, and instructional format (Kirk 1997). Specifically, students must be provided with adequate time, space, equipment, materials, and learning or assessment opportunities.

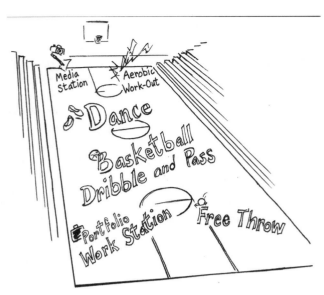

The gym should be organized into a variety of learning stations to encourage students to work—independently or in small groups—on different types and levels of portfolio projects or assessments.

Instead of leaving the gym as a large open space, teachers can organize it into separate work, practice, and play areas. They can also set up learning stations or centers, where students can

- practice and analyze skills and skill combinations,
- work in small groups to apply skills and strategies in gamelike situations (e.g., 2v2, 3v3),
- engage in strength training or aerobic exercise in a designated workout area,
- create a dance,
- complete projects,
- make video recordings of self-analysis,
- conduct research via the Web,
- complete a self-test to address fitness components and record performance data by using Fitnessgram,
- plan group projects, and
- view relevant educational videos or use other resource materials provided by the teacher.

This approach turns the gymnasium into a multipurpose learning center for physical education.

Teachers may choose to arrange class time in a variety of ways. For example, if the class is scheduled as a 90-minute block, the teacher could designate the last 20 to 30 minutes of each class (or every other class) as work time for students to address their projects, assessments, or portfolios. During this time, students could work on individual or group projects or required assessment tasks for their portfolio. Alternatively, some teachers find it more efficient to reserve one entire class during the week for students to work on portfolio tasks. In any case, the key to a successful portfolio process for students is that units of instruction must be extended for longer periods of time so that students can develop in-depth knowledge and skills and complete their portfolio projects. This is especially true for high school classes, where students should be given the opportunity to develop proficiency in at least two physical activities (National Association for Sport and Physical Education 2004). Ways to provide flexibility during class time are discussed later in this chapter.

## Guideline 4: Provide a Variety of Performance-Based Learning and Assessment Opportunities

This chapter has provided suggestions for integrating continual performance-based learning and assessment tasks into a unit of study. It is very important to provide students with continuing opportunities to complete a variety of assessment tasks through the portfolio process. Doing so provides students with a steady supply of performance artifacts that they can catalog in their working portfolio. As a result, when students later assemble their final (evaluation) portfolio, they have many artifacts from which to choose in order to demonstrate their level of achievement of the targeted goals and standards. Teachers might require that students include certain specified items, but they should also allow students to personalize their portfolios by making their own choices about other documents to include.

Possible assessments that can be completed in class or as a project for the portfolio include the following (as explained in chapter 2):

- Artwork or drawings
- Attitude surveys
- Contracts
- Criterion-referenced skill tests
- Exit slips
- Individual or group event tasks
- Individual or group projects
- Rating scales
- Reflections
- Skill-specific checklists for peer or self-assessment
- Skill-specific self-analysis
- Student logs
- Student writings
- Task sheets
- Teacher's analysis or anecdotal record
- Video recordings of student performances
- Workbooks or homework
- Written tests and quizzes

I n my badminton units, I require students to provide data regarding skill and game performance. This information is collected during daily practice activities and during game play for the class tournament. In practice, the assessment might take the form of counting the number of accurate shots made in 10 attempts as part of a daily drill, then graphing one's progress in using the overhead clear, the drop shot, and the long and short serves. Game-play data can also be easily gathered by having students design personal statistics sheets so that they can exchange them with other students and collect and calculate stats for one another. Students can create or choose a project that, in some way, demonstrates their knowledge of the rules and strategies of the game.

Figure 6.4 presents an example of a student's log for practice scores, complete with graph and self-analysis. When students complete such assessments—or the teacher completes the evaluation—the results are added to the student working portfolio to be considered later for inclusion in the evaluation portfolio.

## Guideline 5: Guide Students as They Generate Portfolio Ideas

Teachers may require students to include certain projects or tasks in their portfolio or give students their choice of tasks to complete; they may also give students prompts to help them create their own tasks. "The possibilities for student portfolio tasks are infinite, bounded only by the imagination and the creativity of the teacher and the student" (Kirk 1997, 33). Teachers must take care to ensure that tasks are aligned with the targeted unit or program goals and standards.

To modify instruction—and thereby address individual students' abilities and interests—teachers should allow students to choose, with guidance, the specific types of portfolio assessment tasks they wish to complete; the teacher must, however, check to make sure that each student is challenged at his or her ability level and encouraged to give his or her best effort. Teachers must also help students determine how many artifacts should be included. The number of artifacts depends on the quality and depth of the items chosen. One student might include a single project that provides excellent evidence that the student achieved three of the five targeted standards, whereas another student might need to provide a separate project or artifact as evidence for achievement of each standard. Figure 6.5 presents some suggested portfolio tasks that interest and motivate students and encourage them to learn actively and take responsibility for their learning.

## Guideline 6: Provide Opportunities for Students to Share Their Portfolios

When evaluation portfolios are due at the end of a grading period, semester, or year, it is a good idea to provide class time for students to present their portfolios to each other in small groups. In addition, during open houses for parents, you can set up tables in the gym and in hallways where students can display their portfolios. When students know from the start that they will be displaying or presenting their portfolio to an audience other than the physical education teacher, the stakes are higher for them, and it motivates them to provide their best work.

## Skill Practice Scores

| | Total attempts | Dates and successful attempts | | | | | | | | | |
|---|---|---|---|---|---|---|---|---|---|---|---|
| | | 9/1 | 9/2 | 9/3 | 9/4 | 9/5 | 9/8 | 9/9 | 9/10 | 9/11 | 9/12 |
| Short serve | 10 | 3 | 4 | 5 | 4 | 2 | 4 | 5 | 6 | 6 | 7 |
| Long serve | 10 | | | | | | | | | | |
| Serve return | 10 | | | | | | | | | | |
| Defensive overhand clear | 10 | | | | | | | | | | |
| Offensive overhand clear | 10 | | | | | | | | | | |
| Drop shot | 10 | | | | | | | | | | |
| Forehand or backhand drive | 10 | | | | | | | | | | |

## Graph of Short Serve Progress

| Score | | | | | | | | | | | |
|---|---|---|---|---|---|---|---|---|---|---|---|
| 10 | | | | | | | | | | | |
| 9 | | | | | | | | | | | |
| 8 | | | | | | | | | | | |
| 7 | | | | | | | | | | | * |
| 6 | | | | | | | | | * | * | |
| 5 | | | * | | | | * | | | | |
| 4 | | * | | * | | * | | | | | |
| 3 | * | | | | | | | | | | |
| 2 | | | | | * | | | | | | |
| 1 | | | | | | | | | | | |
| 0 | | | | | | | | | | | |
| | 9/1 | 9/2 | 9/3 | 9/4 | 9/5 | 9/8 | 9/9 | 9/10 | 9/11 | 9/12 |

## Student Self-Analysis and Actions Taken

From day 1 to day 3, my short serve accuracy showed steady improvement. On days 4 and day 5, my performance declined. I kept hitting the shuttle into the net or short of the service area. On day 5, I asked my partner to observe my short serve and complete a Short Serve Performance Checklist. Following the observation, we discovered that instead of dropping the shuttle from my hand and contacting it with my racket at knee level, I was hitting the shuttle out of my hand. This meant that I was contacting the shuttle at waist level or above, which is illegal. It was also making the shuttle hit the net or land short of the service area because the shuttle was traveling in a short, high trajectory.

**Figure 6.4** Sample student log for practice scores, along with graph and self-analysis.

# Suggested Portfolio Tasks

## Engage in Self-Analysis and Peer Assessment

1. The student keeps a log in which he or she records performance results (e.g., number of accurate badminton serves in 10 tries) for practice activities across the unit, along with a graph or chart of progress across time. The student can also analyze the learning and performance curve to indicate where in the curve an intervention was necessary and what that intervention strategy was.

2. After a specified number of practice or game sessions, the student completes a written self-analysis regarding skill performance, with attention paid to individual goals for improvement and possible intervention strategies.

3. The student keeps a daily journal to set goals and record successes, setbacks, and progress and then analyzes the situation to make recommendations for present and future work.

4. The student completes a series of continuous self-analyses and peer assessments of skill and playing performance across time to show student progress in a sport or activity (process and product assessments: skill checklists and rating scales, criterion-referenced tasks, task sheets, game statistics sheets, win-loss record with scores in a round robin tournament).

5. The student and a partner record video footage of each other playing a sport or performing a skill or activity. Then they complete together a written analysis of the video, evaluating each other's performance and giving feedback for improvement.

6. The student conducts a self-analysis regarding game-play performance (i.e., application of skills and strategies) based on the collection of game statistics (e.g., shooting percentage, assists, successful passes, steals, service aces, saves). The analysis should discuss how the student used the data to improve performance.

7. Using self-analysis, peer observation and assessments, and teacher feedback, the student identifies strengths and areas that need improvement. The student then selects or designs appropriate practice or training programs, implements the practice or training schedule, and records the results.

8. After having video footage taken while performing in a game or practice situation, the students views the video and completes a self-evaluation or analysis of his or her performance and makes suggestions for improvement.

## Participate and Learn

1. The student provides documentation of his or her participation in practice, informal game play, and organized competition outside of class. This documentation might include a student's descriptive log (with signatures by witnesses), score or statistics sheets (or statistics from intramural play or participation in a community-based recreational league), or statistics and articles reported in local newspaper write-ups about his or her performance.

2. In small groups, students set up, conduct, and participate in a class tournament. They must keep a record of the collaborative process they used in order to accomplish the task. The group evaluates their own work after completion.

3. The student attends a youth, high school, college, or professional sporting event and writes a report regarding some aspect of the event (e.g., displays of good and bad sporting behavior by players, coaches, or fans; the role of the officials in maintaining the necessary conditions for a fair contest; the skills and offensive and defensive strategies used by a player or team; an account of the traditions that surround the contest).

4. The student records a play-by-play or color commentary of a class tournament game. Acting as if he or she is preparing a demo to use in applying for a job, the student acts either as a radio sports announcer (and makes an audio recording) or as a television announcer (and makes a video recording) of his or her performance.

*(continued)*

**Figure 6.5** Teachers can help students choose from these portfolio tasks.

## Create

1. Guided by criteria provided by the teacher, the student creates and performs an aerobic dance or a routine in step aerobics, jump rope, gymnastics, ice skating, or swing dancing. The evidence provided for the portfolio might include a script for the routine or a video recording of it.

2. The student creates a sculpture or paints or draws a picture that represents some aspect of his or her feelings about participating in or observing a sport or physical activity.

3. The student creates and maintains a Web site about physical education for students and parents. The site presents the class schedule; current fitness information and research findings; class tournament game-play results and standings; and photographs and video recordings of class games, activities, field trips, and performances. It also includes links to other Web sites of interest.

4. The student writes an essay or poem about feelings experienced while participating in a favorite (or least favorite) physical activity.

5. The student writes a newspaper article reporting on the class tournament, or on a single game in the tournament, as if he or she is a sports reporter (must demonstrate knowledge of the game). The student then works with others in a group to put articles together and design and publish the *PE Sports Page* for students. This newspaper could also include photographs taken by one or two students who serve as photographers during class games.

6 The student writes an essay titled something like "My Big Accomplishment: Overcoming My Fear of Water in Swimming Class" (the student chooses which activity unit to address). The essay discusses what the student learned about him- or herself and about life as a result of the experience.

## Research

1. Students research the community resources available for various physical activities and develop a community-based physical activity resource guide for students and teachers in the school. In a group, the students write, design, and edit a class sport or fitness magazine that addresses topics studied in class and uses graphics or photographs to create visual appeal.

2. The student researches the latest training strategies for a particular skill or a sport by means of the Web, the library, or interviews conducted with youth, high school, or college coaches or athletes in the area. The student demonstrates how the new strategies are applied in a personal training program to improve performance.

3. The student completes a written scouting report regarding his or her next opponent in a class tournament. The student identifies the opponent's strengths and weaknesses and develops a game plan of offensive and defensive strategies to use during the game. After the game, the student evaluates the game plan's effectiveness.

4. In small groups, students research current information regarding physical activity and health by means of the Web, the library, or an interview with an exercise physiologist or fitness specialist. The students then design a newsletter addressing fitness, wellness, or physical activity and health; the newsletter includes accurate and helpful information for students, teachers, parents, and administrators. You can integrate the use of technology skills into this project by having students use publishing and graphics software.

5. The student interviews an athlete about competing with a disability or otherwise overcoming adversity to compete. The student then applies the lessons learned to personal situations in audio, video, or written form.

**Figure 6.5**   *(continued)*

# EVALUATING PORTFOLIOS

If, at the beginning of the portfolio process, you prepare a scoring guide or rubric based on the established criteria and guidelines you have given to the students, then the evaluation process is not difficult. The process of preparing rubrics or scoring guides is addressed in chapter 3. See also figure 6.6 and table 6.1, which present sample portfolio guidelines and a scoring rubric to be given to students at the start of the unit.

## Guidelines for Badminton Unit Portfolio

At the end of the 6-week unit on badminton, you must submit your badminton portfolio, which provides documents (pieces of your work) that demonstrate in authentic ways that you have achieved the following unit goals at an acceptable level. (Some suggested assessment project ideas are provided under each unit goal; you may, of course, come up with your own ideas.)

You will be able to do the following:

1. Demonstrate your knowledge of history, current status, equipment, court lines and areas, singles and doubles rules, and scoring procedures of the sport of badminton. Assessment ideas:
   - Create an informational pamphlet about the sport of badminton.
   - With a small group, create an instructional video about the sport of badminton.
   - Officiate or serve as a scorekeeper for games played during the class tournament.

2. Demonstrate the ability to identify critical learning cues; observe and analyze your own and your peers' skill performance; make recommendations for practice to help improve performance of the short serve, long serve, offensive and defensive overhead clear, underhand clear, drop shot, smash, and forehand and backhand drive. Assessment ideas:
   - Keep a journal.
   - Conduct video analysis.
   - Use a skill observation checklist and provide written feedback.
   - Create an instructional video.

3. Demonstrate the ability to effectively perform the badminton skills (shots) listed in the second objective while playing badminton in the class tournament. Assessment ideas:
   - Use peer and self-observation skill checklists.
   - Keep a record of daily class practice scores and graphs with self-analysis.
   - Keep game-play observation statistics sheets.
   - Conduct video analysis of game play.
   - Compile tournament record and results.

4. Demonstrate respect and caring for your fellow classmates by helping them improve their skill performance and game play through verbal feedback, practice suggestions, encouragement, and cooperative practice. Assessment ideas:
   - Write journal entries.
   - Provide written feedback and practice suggestions.
   - Keep a practice log.

5. Demonstrate personal improvement in skill performance and game play. Assessment ideas:
   - Keep a journal.
   - Use skill performance checklists.
   - Track daily practice scores and perhaps graph them.
   - Keep a written tournament record.
   - Conduct video analysis.

6. Demonstrate the ability to explain and use (a) the basic offensive strategy of covering court space and returning to home and (b) the defensive strategies of hitting the shuttle to open spaces and moving the opponent out of position by using a variety of shots. Assessment ideas:
   - Create an instructional video.
   - Engage in peer teaching.
   - Keep game-play statistics.

*(continued)*

**Figure 6.6** Sample guideline sheet.

- Present video sequences in which you demonstrate strategies.
- Create an audio recording in which you call a tournament game like a radio sportscaster.
- Create a video in which you cover a game like TV sportscaster.

You must provide at least one artifact as evidence of achievement for each of the unit goals. In some cases, you may need to provide more than one artifact as evidence for a particular goal. Remember also that if you include only one artifact for a goal, that artifact must provide strong evidence for your achievement in terms of that goal. Some of your artifacts may be assessments that you completed in class; other evidence might include documents (e.g., group projects, journals) that you choose to complete during the 6 weeks.

You need to collect artifacts that are developed each day in class and place them in your working portfolio. Each student has a file with his or her name printed on it. The files are placed in alphabetical order (please keep them in order) in the milk crate marked for your class. Select your best work as evidence for your evaluation portfolio.

At the front of your portfolio, you must include the completed Written Reflection Portfolio Form (see figure 6.3). List each artifact, along with the goal for which it provides evidence, and include your reflection statement, in which you explain why you included the artifact and how it provides evidence that you have achieved the goal.

If you have chosen personal or group projects, they should be identified by the beginning of the second week of the badminton unit so that you have sufficient time to complete them. Check with me before beginning such a project. *You must complete at least one small group cooperative project to be included in your portfolio.* The choice is yours, but you must keep and submit in your portfolio a record of your collaboration with the group.

You may personalize your portfolio. The form in which you present your portfolio is up to you, as long as it is well organized and includes a table of contents, a tabbed section for each unit goal, and at least one rich artifact for each goal. Feel free to use color, computer graphics, pictures, and drawings. Some of you technology wizards may even want to submit your portfolio on a CD-ROM.

**Figure 6.6** *(continued)*

**Table 6.1**  Evaluation Rubric for a Badminton Unit Portfolio

| Performance level | Organization | Presentation | Quality of content | Reflections |
|---|---|---|---|---|
| 4 Proficient | • Neatly and effectively organized<br>• Tabbed section provided for each goal<br>• Well-organized table of contents; all artifacts listed in each goal section<br>• Portfolio registry and reflection page provided after title page<br>• Artifacts all listed in registry | • Complete title page<br>• All materials neatly and creatively displayed<br>• Presentation creative and personalized | • Solid evidence of achievement of all unit goals<br>• Clear demonstration of student growth and improvement across the unit<br>• Demonstration of personal contribution to cooperative effort<br>• Wide variety of assessment projects<br>• Appropriate inclusion of graphics, pictures, or drawings<br>• Demonstration of achievement of all unit goals | • Rich explanation of why and how artifacts provide evidence of achievement of standards or unit goals |

| Performance level | Organization | Presentation | Quality of content | Reflections |
|---|---|---|---|---|
| 3 Competent | • Neatly and effectively organized<br>• Tabbed section provided for each goal<br>• Organized table of contents; all artifacts listed in each goal section<br>• Portfolio registry and reflection page provided after title page<br>• Artifacts all listed in registry | • Complete title page<br>• Most materials neatly and creatively displayed<br>• Presentation *somewhat* creative and personalized | • Evidence of achievement of *all but one* of unit goals<br>• Demonstration of student growth and improvement<br>• Demonstration of cooperative effort<br>• Variety of assessments<br>• Inclusion of graphics, pictures, or drawings<br>• Demonstration of achievement of all but one unit goal | • Clear connection between most artifacts and achievement of standards or unit goals |
| 2 Novice | • Some organizational problems<br>• Lack of thoughtful organization<br>• Incomplete or incorrect table of contents<br>• Registry and reflection page do not follow the title page<br>• Separate sections provided but no tabs | • Sloppy display of artifacts<br>• Incomplete display of artifacts<br>• Little creativity and personalization | • Artifacts missing for two or more goals<br>• Evidence of achievement for some goals<br>• Weak evidence for achievement across the unit<br>• Little evidence of cooperative group effort<br>• Little variety in assessment tasks<br>• Some graphics, pictures, drawings | • Reflections not clear or thoughtful<br>• Lack of clear connection between artifacts and achievement of goals |
| 1 Needs improvement | • Unorganized and messy<br>• Sections not clearly delineated<br>• No tabs provided<br>• No table of contents provided<br>• Artifact registry and reflection missing | • Lack of creativity, personalization<br>• Clear lack of individual effort | • Lacks evidence for most goals<br>• Weak evidence of achievement<br>• Lack of variety of assessment types (most are similar)<br>• Weak evidence of growth across the unit | • Reflections very vague or missing |

# CONCLUSION

As more states move away from traditional forms of assessment and toward standards-based educational programs, portfolios are coming into increasingly widespread use. The portfolio process offers an authentic, performance-based form of assessment for physical education that is exciting and promising. It allows students to complete projects and performances and gather and present artifacts in their portfolios in order to provide evidence that they have met program and national standards. Implementing a portfolio-based assessment process involves much planning and organization, but it is well worth the effort for both students and teachers.

The process encourages students to become self-sufficient learners and provides teachers with a way to individualize teaching and learning in order to meet the needs and interests of all students (Melograno 2006). Teachers who have implemented the portfolio process successfully indicate that students are more actively engaged and highly motivated. This process holds much promise for teachers who are willing to challenge themselves and their students.

# Developing Culminating and Progressive Assessments

*Summative assessments happen after learning is supposed to have occurred to determine if it did (Stiggins 2007).*

The preceding chapters have presented reasons for integrating new forms of assessment into your teaching, as well as discussion of various types of performance-based and authentic approaches that teachers can use to design assessments. This chapter begins our consideration of how to design the following: (a) culminating, or summative, assessments that are linked to specific unit goals and targeted broad standards and (b) formative, or progressive, assessments that are integrated with learning activities in order to help students prepare to complete their culminating performance or product. The chapter provides you with sample culminating and progressive assessments in three units: tumbling, archery, and golf. Chapters 8 and 9 then take you through the entire process of designing standards-based instructional units that include integrated formative and summative assessments; they also present two sample unit plans, one for tennis and one for soccer, along with sample assessments for each.

## CULMINATING (SUMMATIVE) ASSESSMENTS

A **culminating** or **summative assessment** is generally a final performance or product that the student completes in order to provide evidence that he or she has achieved broad standards and specific unit goals (Kentucky Department of Education 2008). Identifying these standards and unit goals is the first of five steps that teachers take when implementing the standards-based planning process, which is described in detail in chapter 8. For now, however, in order to guide you through the sample culminating assessments presented in this chapter, we will provide the relevant national standards and specific unit goals for you, which are usually identified in the first steps of planning. Teachers can use the National Standards for Physical Education (NASPE 2004) or individual state or district goals as broad and targeted goals in the planning process, which serve as the final student destination in the planning and teaching process. Teachers must also identify content-specific unit goals, which directly relate to the broad standards and goals, before developing the culminating assessment. The targeted standards and unit goals determine the destination—the culminating performance or product—and indicate to the students and the teacher how close the student has arrived to the destination.

Once you have identified standards and goals and thus know where your students are headed, design a culminating assessment to determine whether they do, in fact, arrive at the desired destination (see figure 7.1). At this

## Initial Steps in Standards-Based Physical Education Planning

1. Identify broad, targeted goals based on the National Standards for Physical Education (National Association for Sport and Physical Education 2004) and state or district goals.

2. Identify specific goals that are relevant to unit content or activity and link directly to achievement of the broad standards and goals.

3. Design a summative or culminating assessment performance or product that engages students and requires them to demonstrate their ability to apply knowledge and skills in a realistic setting.

4. Design a series of progressively complex formative assessments—for students to participate in throughout the unit—that are linked with learning activities. These assessments should provide students with feedback about their progress toward completing the culminating assessment and meeting the goals.

**Figure 7.1** These steps help teachers link the demonstration of students' learning through the culminating assessment to standards and goals.

point, it is essential to address the following question: How will the students and I know if they have achieved the unit goals and targeted standards—and at which level? Much of the answer to this question can be found in the culminating assessment in which students participate at the end of the unit. In standards-based instruction, this culminating or summative assessment should serve as a demonstration of students' learning and their achievement of goals, as well as their progress toward targeted standards. Students should demonstrate their ability to apply the knowledge and skills they have learned in the context of an authentic or realistic task or performance. The culminating performance or product then serves as the accountability measure for both the students and the teacher.

When designing the culminating assessment, teachers must consider unit goals and targeted standards; they must also think about how students can demonstrate their achievement of unit goals and their progress toward targeted standards in a true-to-life situation. This final assessment should be designed before the unit begins, and it should be tailored to the length of the unit and the available instructional time per day. This final assessment should consist of a group or individual performance, a completed product in which the student assumes a real-life role and engages a specific audience, or a student portfolio. The culminating performance, product, or portfolio—along with the corresponding scoring guides or rubrics—should be shared with students at the beginning of the unit so that they know from the outset what is expected of them. The culminating performance may take the form of a project that students work on for several weeks, or it could consist of an event task that they complete during one or two class periods. This final assessment should be authentic or realistic, should be engaging to the students, and should serve as both the ultimate learning experience and the summative assessment. It is this final performance or product that ultimately demonstrates a student's level of achievement of unit goals and standards.

Once you have established the student goals for your unit, you must then think about ways in which students can provide evidence that they have achieved those goals by demonstrating their knowledge, skills, and abilities in a culminating performance or final product. Culminating experiences should give students an opportunity to apply what they have learned in a way that is authentic in terms of the activity or a real-life application. As you design a culminating assessment for an activity unit, ask yourself the questions featured in figure 7.2. Using these guiding questions, we have developed culminating performances and sample progressive assessments for three activity units—tumbling, archery, and golf—which make up the bulk of this chapter.

In the culminating performance or product, students may take on an authentic or realistic role (e.g., athlete, coach, sportswriter or fitness writer, director, sportscaster) appropriate to the task. The performance or product might take any of various forms, as suggested by the list presented in figure 7.3.

# PROGRESSIVE LEARNING ACTIVITIES AND ASSESSMENTS

**Progressive learning activities** and formative assessments should be designed to help students achieve the broad targeted standards and specific unit goals. Therefore, progressive learning activities should relate directly to the unit goals and provide students with experiences in which they are able to learn the essential identified knowledge and skills needed to complete the culminating assessment successfully. The performance-based formative assessments should be interwoven with the learning activities throughout the unit so that students receive feedback on how they are progressing toward goals. Feedback from the students' performances on the formative assessments also provides the

---

## Guidelines for Designing Culminating Assessments

1. What is the nature of the activity or content? How are students expected to use the skills and knowledge?

2. How can my students demonstrate that they understand and can apply knowledge and skills authentically in this activity?

3. How can I design the assessment so that it is meaningful and has real-life applications for my students?

4. How can I make this culminating assessment an interesting and fun learning experience that fully engages my students?

5. Should the culminating assessment be a performance or a product? What is my rationale? Should I have students do both?

6. How can I design the culminating experience so that I am assessing all three educational domains: psychomotor, cognitive, and affective?

7. What is the culminating assessment?

8. Should it be a group or individual effort?

9. Is the culminating assessment designed so that students of all ability levels can complete the assessment successfully at their level of performance?

10. What criteria should students have to meet when completing the culminating assessment? How can I encourage students to use higher-order thinking skills, such as synthesis, evaluation, and analysis?

11. How do I evaluate student performance on the culminating assessment?

12. How much does the culminating experience contribute to the student's learning and grade?

13. Is the culminating assessment efficient? How much time will students need to complete the assessment?

**Figure 7.2** Teachers can use these guiding questions to design effective culminating assessments that authentically measure students' learning and achievement of goals.

## Possible Culminating Performances and Products

- Perform a gymnastics routine in a class meet or exhibition.
- Develop a brochure addressing the components of health-related fitness or good sporting behavior.
- Develop a multimedia presentation.
- Choreograph and perform a creative dance routine.
- Create and perform a folk or square dance.
- Develop a display that presents information about fitness centers in the community.
- Develop a newspaper in which you report on class competitions or, say, a class backpacking trip.
- Design and teach an aerobic dance routine.
- Make an educational video about a sport, form of dance, or fitness activity.
- Assume the role of a sportswriter and write a collection of columns, articles, or editorials.
- Play in a tournament.
- Develop a scripted slide show.
- Write and perform a skit.
- Develop a portfolio that demonstrates learning across the semester.
- Officiate or keep score for a game.
- Write a journal about learning experiences in sport or fitness.
- Develop a fitness or sport Web site.
- Plan, implement, and manage a class sport tournament.
- Act as a radio or TV announcer for a class game or performance.
- Keep a log or personal journal about your involvement in physical activity across a specified length of time.
- Coach a youth sport team.
- Design a personal fitness program based on analysis of fitness assessment scores and personal goals.
- Teach skills, games, or elements of dance to younger children.
- Analyze an athlete's or dancer's performance recorded on video.
- In your group, plan and implement a weekend backpacking or kayaking trip and keep a journal during the trip.

**Figure 7.3** Various types of assessment can be used in a wide variety of units as culminating assessments to measure students' achievement of standards or goals.

teacher with information about the appropriateness of instruction. These formative assessments are progressive because, as the unit progresses, they require students to learn, perform, and apply more difficult strategies, concepts, skills, and skill combinations—all of which help the student move gradually toward accomplishing the culminating performance or product. Thus these formative assessments serve as steps or gates which students ascend or pass through on their way to successfully completing the culminating or summative assessment. The formative assessments involve a variety of assessment methods. Grant Wiggins and Jay McTighe (2005) suggest that teachers think of these formative assessments in a unit of instruction not as a single test or performance task but as "collected evidence."

Because these assessments are integrated with learning and practice activities throughout the unit, this assessment approach is referred to as **continuous performance-based assessment**. The progression of instructional and assessment activities should include and extend from learning activities that begin with the initial practice of a skill in which the focus is to learn, practice, and ultimately demonstrate the critical performance elements (also referred to as learning cues). The progression of learning activities involves **extension, refinement,** and **application tasks** (Rink 2006) in which skills are performed in controlled situations that allow modeling of how the skill is performed in game-play situations (e.g., tennis, soccer) or in a performance activity (e.g., gymnastics routine).

## TUMBLING UNIT

Gymnastics and tumbling are popular with adolescents, and a tumbling unit provides students with many challenging and fun learning activities. Participation in tumbling can help students develop upper-body strength, endurance, flexibility, coordination, and balance. In addition, working with partners and in small groups gives students opportunities to develop social skills; as they learn and practice their routines, they also assist and encourage one another. Because students come in with varied levels of interest and ability, it is important to build individual choice into learning and assessment tasks.

The first step in designing the culminating assessment for the middle grades tumbling unit is to identify relevant national or state standards that students are expected to meet by participating in the unit and to fulfill in their culminating performance. The relevant National Standards for Physical Education (National Association for Sport and Physical Education 2004) for the tumbling unit are identified in figure 7.4. The

next step is to develop more specific unit goals that students are expected to meet in order to prepare for completing the culminating performance. Specific content goals for the tumbling unit are provided in figure 7.5. These goals are more specific to the activity content and provide specific behavioral and performance guidelines for the teacher and the students. They should

### Relevant National Standards for a Tumbling Unit

1. Demonstrates competency in motor skills and movement patterns needed to perform a variety of physical activities.
2. Demonstrates understanding of movement concepts, principles, strategies, and tactics as they apply to the learning and performance of physical activities.
5. Exhibits responsible personal and social behavior that respects self and others in physical activity settings.
6. Values physical activity for health, enjoyment, challenge, self-expression, and/or social interaction.

**Figure 7.4** Four of the National Standards for Physical Education are identified for student achievement through participation in this unit of instruction.

From NASPE, 2004, *Moving into the future: National standards for physical education,* 2nd ed. (Reston, VA: National Association for Sport and Physical Education).

Gymnastics can be enjoyable for all levels of ability.

## Goals for Tumbling Unit

1. Students master four or more tumbling skills at their assigned level in each of the following categories: upright balance, inverted balance, upright agility, inverted agility, forward rolls, and backward rolls (United States Gymnastics Federation 1992). For each category, students are given a list of tumbling skills at the beginning, intermediate, and advanced levels.

2. Students demonstrate the ability to analyze skills in each of the six tumbling skill categories at their performance level; they also apply the biomechanical principles learned to give feedback to peers.

3. Students are able to put skills together according to event guidelines in order to perform sequences of 3 to 10 skills.

4. Students demonstrate the ability to work positively and collaboratively in a small group to accomplish group goals.

5. Students demonstrate the ability to accurately judge peer performances of a tumbling sequence.

6. Students demonstrate the ability to work independently within a small group in order to improve skills and develop and refine skill sequences.

7. Students identify feelings they experienced while learning, refining, and performing skills and skill sequences and while helping members of their team improve during the unit.

8. Students demonstrate the ability to be creative by composing skill sequences or routines according to class guidelines.

9. Students demonstrate knowledge of principles of training by designing a personal conditioning routine to improve strength and flexibility for tumbling.

**Figure 7.5** The goals identified here for this tumbling unit were developed by the teacher to lead students toward achieving specific unit goals and the broader national standards identified in figure 7.4.

relate directly to the targeted national standards (figure 7.4). These documents are then used by the teacher to design the performance tasks for the culminating assessment.

## Culminating Assessment and Rubric

Figure 7.6 presents a culminating performance for a tumbling unit and a sequence of continuous "checkpoint" (Lambert 2007) progressive assessments that are integrated with learning activities. Figure 7.7 summarizes the culminating performance guidelines for the unit. The assessment samples (figures 7.6 and 7.7) provide general guidelines, within which students are free to make choices about the skills in each category that they will master and perform in their routines; they are also free to choose how they plan to transition from one skill to another. Students must create routines according to criteria that are authentic to the sport of tumbling, but they can choose the skills that they will perform within each category. This approach gives students the choice to perform skills within each category that are at the level of their ability:

## Culminating Performance for a Tumbling Unit

Perform a routine in the class tumbling meet. Create the routine according to the guidelines. If you would prefer not to perform in front of a live audience, you may perform your routine at another time and have it recorded on video for the judges to evaluate. Everyone is encouraged to perform in person, since doing so is more authentic in the sport of gymnastics. The class is divided into four teams of seven students each. Team scores are determined by adding the top four scores for each team on each event. Each performance will be judged on the basis of the evaluation rubric, which will be provided to you while you create and practice your routine.

**Figure 7.6** This culminating assessment requires students to create and perform routines in class meets. It serves as an example of a culminating performance that is authentic to the activity.

beginning, intermediate, or advanced. Students of all levels of ability can be very successful and enjoy the experience.

## Guidelines for the Culminating Performance of a Tumbling Unit

At the end of the tumbling unit, each student creates and performs a sequence of tumbling movements in a routine for a class meet according to the following criteria:

- The sequence must contain 10 movements.
- The sequence must include a variety of movements, with at least one skill from each of the following categories: forward rolls, backward rolls, upward agility movements, inverted agility skills, upright balances, and inverted balances.
- The sequence must contain forward, backward, and sideward movement.
- The sequence must have a definite beginning and ending.
- The sequence should be continuous—that is, free of stops (with the exception of balance skills, which must be held for at least 3 seconds)—and should feature smooth transitions from one movement to the next.
- The movements should be performed with amplitude and good form.
- You may choose to perform the sequence for the class or for only the instructor and judges.
- You may choose to perform the routine with or without music.

Before performing the tumbling routine, you must submit the routine form, which includes the names of the skills and the order and direction in which they will be performed. The form must also include a diagram of the floor pattern for the routine.

**Figure 7.7**   This list presents culminating performance guidelines.

You should develop a scoring guide or rubric and share it with students prior to the culminating performance. Students can then use the rubric to score each other's practice performances and provide feedback to one another. Table 7.1 presents a sample scoring rubric.

## Continuous Performance-Based Assessments

In order to give students continuous feedback as they progress through learning activities to prepare for the culminating performance, the teacher should integrate a series of shorter but similar—and progressive—performance assessments throughout the unit. A good time to use this assessment is when students have been introduced to a group of skills and had an opportunity to learn, practice, and master them. Following Lambert (2007), we refer to these progressive authentic assessments, which are spaced strategically throughout the unit, as *checkpoints*. A checkpoint is a designated point in the unit (e.g., 1 day every week or 2 weeks) set aside for a performance-based assessment so that the teacher can check students' progress toward the culminating experience.

For our tumbling unit, a checkpoint would involve students putting together a few chosen skills they have learned in order to create a short performance sequence. Recall that the culminating experience for this unit involves performance of a sequence of skills that meet the criteria of the assessment. Therefore, performing short sequences of skills learned along the way helps students prepare for the culminating performance and gives them feedback on their progression. The idea of using checkpoints to ensure continuous, progressive assessment in a unit of instruction is discussed in chapter 2. Figure 7.8 provides examples of progressive, formative assessments that can be used as checkpoints to enhance student learning.

The continuous performance-based assessments provided in figure 7.8 are progressive. That is, each assessment is more difficult than the preceding one, requiring analysis and refinement of new skills, and each concludes with the performance of skills in longer and more complex sequences. This series of progressive, performance-based, formative assessments prepares students for their culminating performance. As students move from one formative assessment to the next, they gain confidence and build their skill repertoire.

**Table 7.1**  Scoring Rubric for the Culminating or Summative Performance Assessment of a Tumbling Unit

| Performance level | Routine content | Transitions between skills | Quality of performance | Comments |
|---|---|---|---|---|
| Gold medal performance: A | • Contains a *variety* of at least 10 different movements.<br>• Contains *at least one skill from each category*: forward rolls, backward rolls, upward agility, inverted agility, upward balance, inverted balance.<br>• Contains movements in *forward, backward, and sideward directions*.<br>• Contains a *definite* observable *beginning and end*. | • Executes *smooth transitions with no stops* from one move to the next.<br>• Uses a *variety of ways of transitioning* from one skill to the next. | • *All movements* and transitions are *performed correctly, featuring good form and high amplitude*. | |
| Silver medal performance: B | • Contains a *variety* of at least 8 different movements.<br>• Contains *at least one skill from each of the six categories:* forward rolls, backward rolls, upward agility, inverted agility, upward balance, inverted balance.<br>• Contains movements in *forward, backward, and sideward directions*.<br>• Contains a *definite* beginning and end. | • Executes *smooth transitions with a few brief hesitations between skills*.<br>• Uses a *variety of ways of transitioning* from one skill to the next. | • *Most skills are performed without error* and *with good form and amplitude*.<br>• Errors appear in *one or two skills*. | |
| Bronze medal performance: C | • Contains at least 6 movements but repeats one skill.<br>• Contains *skills from at least five of the six skill* categories: forward rolls, backward rolls, upward agility, inverted agility, upward balance, inverted balance.<br>• Contains *movements in two directions only*.<br>• Contains a definite beginning *or* ending. | • Sequence is continuous, but *occasional hesitations* cause transitions to lack fluidity.<br>• Includes *some repetition of ways of transitioning* from one skill to the next. | • Errors appear in *two or more skills*.<br>• *Form breaks* appear in more than two skills.<br>• Performance occasionally lacks in amplitude. | |

| Performance level | Routine content | Transitions between skills | Quality of performance | Comments |
|---|---|---|---|---|
| Novice level performance: D | • Contains fewer than 6 movements and/or repeats more than one movement.<br>• *Contains skills from fewer than five of the skill categories.*<br>• Contains movements *in two directions only.*<br>• Contains a definite beginning but does not hold the ending. | • Sequence is not continuous; includes *frequent stops and breaks between skills.*<br>• Includes *frequent repetition of ways of transitioning* from one skill to the next. | • *Major errors appear in some skills.*<br>• *Minor errors appear in most skills.*<br>• Includes many skill-form breaks and a *total lack of amplitude throughout the routine.* | |

This rubric incorporates the performance criteria presented in the guidelines given to students at the beginning of the semester.

## Continuous Performance-Based Assessment for a Tumbling Unit

Students complete the following assessments when skills or skill categories are introduced and during skills practice sessions.

1. For each skill, use a check sheet that includes critical performance elements of the skills for students to use in self-assessments, peer observations, or teacher observations. (A sample is included in figure 7.8a on the CD.)

2. Use a teacher observation, class skill-performance checklist, or rating scale. The teacher may include all skills in the category checklist or rating scale. These may be skills that students learned and practiced during a 1- or 2-week period. When students are ready to perform a skill for evaluation, they inform the instructor. This skill demonstration gives both the student and the teacher information about the number of skills the student is mastering and where assistance and more practice is needed. (A sample is provided in figure 7.8b on the CD.)

3. The teacher or a partner makes a video recording of the student performing targeted skills. Students view their own skill performance and compare it with a correct performance video, conduct analysis of the two, and write a paragraph comparing their personal performance with the model performance. In the analysis, students identify areas and strategies for improvement.

4. After a new skill or category of skills is introduced and demonstrated, students practice the skill with partners or in small groups. During practice, students work on analyzing the critical performance elements of the skill. Students write the answers to the following analytical questions:

• Describe the preparatory position.

• How is momentum developed, transferred, and controlled during the skill performance?

• Describe how momentum is controlled and absorbed as the skill ends.

• Describe the ending position.

• How can the performer move smoothly from the completion of this skill into another skill movement?

Following the analysis phase of this learning and assessment activity, students can be asked to share their conclusions with other groups or the entire class for evaluation and comparison.

As skill categories are introduced and practiced, students develop and perform short sequences of skills, and these assessments enable students to develop their tumbling abilities, develop competency and confidence in creating and performing increasingly challenging skill sequences, and receive

*(continued)*

**Figure 7.8** Students complete this series of progressive assessments during the unit in order to receive continuous feedback on their progress and prepare for their culminating performance.

feedback along the way. The teacher may also include specific skill combinations, in which students practice beginning and ending differently so that they develop a variety of transitions from which they can later choose as they create and perform their sequences. Because this assessment strategy helps students progress toward their culminating performance by taking small steps each day, it helps them be confident and well prepared when the big day arrives. The following formative assessment sequence presents the progression of a sample checkpoint assessment.

5. Design and perform a sequence that includes a forward roll variation. The sequence must begin and end with two different balance skills. It should be smooth and continuous and feature graceful transitions between skills. Balance skills must be held for at least 3 seconds. Challenge yourself to include skills that you really have to work at to learn. You will perform the sequence in front of the teacher when you are ready for evaluation.

6. Design and perform a sequence that includes a balance skill at the beginning and end, as well as a backward roll variation and an upright agility skill. Make sure that you move smoothly from one skill to the next. Be sure to hold the balance skills for at least 3 seconds in order to show control, then move into the next skill with a smooth transition.

7. Design and perform a sequence that begins and ends with a balance skill (either upright or invented) and contains a forward roll variation, a backward roll variation, and an upright agility skill. Make sure that one skill flows smoothly into the next and that you show balance skills for at least 3 seconds.

8. Design and perform a sequence that contains six skills. The sequence should include at least one skill from each of the tumbling skill categories: forward roll, backward roll, upright balance, inverted balance, upright agility, and inverted agility. Your sequence should include at least two changes of direction, and you should make smooth transitions between skills. Perform your sequence for your partner and use the feedback to polish your performance. When you are ready, you will perform the routine for me for evaluation. (See figure 7.8c on the CD for an example.)

**Figure 7.8** *(continued)*

**Handstand Forward Roll Observation Checklist**

Performer _____ Evaluator _____ Date _____

**Instructions**

1. Stand to the side of your partner as he or she performs the handstand forward roll.
2. Observe as your partner performs the skill five times.
3. After each observation, check each of the performance cues that you observed.
4. Focus on only one part of the skill during each observation.

**Preparation**

_____ Stretch arms/shoulders overhead.
_____ Step into a lunge position.
_____ Stretch the body.

**Handstand Execution**

_____ Use teeter-totter action (as hands go down, back leg goes up).
_____ Place hands on floor shoulder-width apart.
_____ Keep shoulder angle extended.
_____ Push off strongly and lift with support foot.
_____ Bring legs together.
_____ Position head between arms.
_____ Keep body tight and aligned over hands.
_____ Maintain balance for two counts.

**Forward Roll Execution**

_____ Shift hips and legs forward beyond the hands to initiate an off-balance position.
_____ Tuck head.
_____ Bend arms for soft landing.
_____ Round the shoulders and back.
_____ Tuck hips and knees.
_____ Execute a smooth roll-out to feet.
_____ Stretch body with arms extended overhead.

Write feedback statements to help your partner improve his or her performance.

_____
_____
_____
_____
_____
_____
_____

**Figure 7.8a** Teachers can use checklists such as this one in their observation and assessment of tumbling skills.

**Forward Rolling Skills Checklist**

Performer _____ Class _____ Date _____

**Forward Rolling Skills**

_____ Rocker
_____ Tip-up
_____ Look-back
_____ Tip-over
_____ Rock-up to feet
_____ Squat forward roll

**Perform at Least Six of the Following Skills**

_____ Forward roll to a knee scale
_____ Forward roll to a V-seat
_____ Forward roll walkout
_____ Forward roll to a lunge
_____ Forward straddle roll
_____ Forward pike roll
_____ Forward roll to a scale
_____ Forward roll from a scale
_____ Forward roll jump
_____ Jump, then forward roll
_____ Two continuous forward rolls

**Figure 7.8b** Checklist for forward rolling skills.

Students develop the ability to perform skills from the six categories and move from one skill to the next by means of a smooth transition—all of which are requirements for the culminating performance. When it comes time for students to design and perform their culminating tumbling sequence, they are experienced and prepared as a result of their participation in continuous, progressive assessments during the unit.

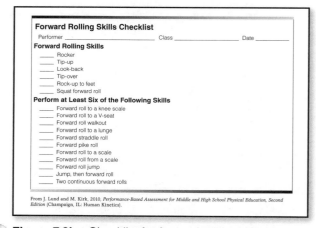

**Culminating Tumbling Sequence Performance**

Balance skill _____
Transition_____
Forward roll variation_____
Transition_____
Backward roll variation _____
Transition_____
Upright balance _____

Draw a diagram of your floor pattern in the square below. Mark the beginning and the end of your sequence with an X.

**Peer Evaluator Feedback**

Things you did really well:

_____
_____
_____
_____
_____

Things you can improve:

_____
_____
_____
_____
_____

From J. Lund and M. Kirk, 2010, *Performance-Based Assessment for Middle and High School Physical Education, Second Edition* (Champaign, IL: Human Kinetics).

**Figure 7.8c**    Peer evaluation form for performance of culminating tumbling sequence.

Archery is an excellent sport for adolescents because it is challenging and fun and can develop into a lifetime activity.

# TARGET ARCHERY UNIT

This section provides examples of both culminating assessments and continuous, progressive assessments that can be used by you and your students as checkpoints to determine and monitor student progress in a target archery unit. Target archery is a recreational activity that students may choose to participate in for a lifetime of enjoyment, challenge, and social interaction. The following goals, standards, and authentic assessments help students develop the skills, knowledge, and competence that are necessary for participation. *Archery: Steps to Success* (Haywood and Lewis 2006) was used as a resource in the development of the learning and assessment tasks provided in this sample. The culminating product in this unit is a student-developed evaluation portfolio. Please note that many of the suggested artifacts from which students may select are performance assessments that students will participate in throughout the unit; they are integrated with learning activities. Some of these assessments can be designated as checkpoints so that you and a student can check how the student is progressing toward achieving

the culminating experience and the unit goals.

As in the tumbling unit, you must begin your development of the culminating assessment by identifying broad goals and standards, as well as specific unit goals and objectives. Before you design assessments to determine how your students will demonstrate and apply the knowledge and skills they learn, you must identify what students should know, feel, and be able to do, both during and upon completion of the unit. Figure 7.9 presents four broad national standards (National Association for Sport and Physical Education 2004) that students could accomplish by participating in the archery unit and achieving the unit goals. Figure 7.10 presents the specific goals for the unit. We used the unit goals to design both the culminating and progressive assessments for the unit.

## Culminating Assessment and Rubric

Once you have identified the broad standards and specific goals that students should strive to achieve, the next step is to design the culminating performance or product that students must complete at the conclusion of the archery unit. Our sample culminating experience for a target archery unit is a product—specifically, a portfolio (see chapter 6 for a fuller discussion of portfolios as assessment tools in physical education). We call this final assessment an archery

### Relevant National Standards for a Target Archery Unit

1. Demonstrates competency in motor skills and movement patterns needed to perform a variety of physical activities.
2. Demonstrates understanding of movement concepts, principles, strategies, and tactics as they apply to the learning and performance of physical activities.
3. Participates regularly in physical activity.
6. Values physical activity for health, enjoyment, challenge, self-expression, and/or social interaction.

**Figure 7.9** Four national physical education standards are identified for students to achieve by participating in this unit of instruction.

From NASPE, 2004, *Moving into the future: National standards for physical education,* 2nd ed. (Reston, VA: National Association for Sport and Physical Education).

"sportfolio." This portfolio, or archery sportfolio, not only serves as a summative student product but also requires students to participate in and collect artifacts from continuous formative assessments throughout the unit.

This form of culminating assessment helps students attach meaning to and see the value of their participation in continuous performance-based assessments throughout the unit. As a result, they take those assessments more seriously, and their efforts in compiling a working portfolio and putting together the final evaluation portfolio constitute not only an assessment process but also a learning process. The following section provides a sample set of portfolio guidelines and a sample rubric (see figures 7.11 and 7.12), which provide students with specific criteria (based on unit goals) that they must follow. You should give students a copy of the guidelines and rubric or scoring guide and explain them at the beginning of the unit.

The portfolio guidelines offer suggestions for artifacts that students might include as evidence of their achievement of broad and specific unit goals; this list includes progressive performance-based assessments that you might use as formative assessments throughout the unit. These sample progressive assessments give students feedback about their progress and help them

### Goals for a Target Archery Unit

1. Students demonstrate knowledge of the following: names and functions of parts of the bow, arrow, and safety equipment; information necessary to purchase appropriate equipment; and how to repair and properly store equipment.
2. Students identify and rationalize safety rules and apply them before, during, and after a round of target archery.
3. Students identify and demonstrate the critical performance cues for each part of the shooting process: stance, grip, nock, draw, anchor, aim, release, and follow-through.
4. Students identify and demonstrate the cues for aiming at a target using the point-of-aim method or using a bow sight.
5. Students diagnose possible errors in the shooting process by identifying arrow groupings in the target, then make adjustments in their own shooting technique and help peers make adjustments to improve shooting accuracy and scores.
6. Students demonstrate improvement across the unit in shooting performance scores while participating in individual and team class shooting rounds at various distances.
7. Students articulate their feelings about their skill development and participation in the sport of target archery, and they develop a plan for how they can continue to participate in the sport, if desired.

**Figure 7.10** The goals identified here for the target archery unit were developed by the teacher to lead students toward achieving specific unit goals, as well as the broader-based national standards identified in figure 7.9.

complete the culminating product assessment (i.e., the archery sportfolio).

## Continuous Performance-Based Assessments

This section provides you with sample performance-based assessments that are continuous and progressive and that are linked with learning and practice activities throughout the archery unit in order to help students develop knowledge and skill and receive feedback (see figure 7.13). Students are encouraged to select artifacts from these formative assessments to include in their portfolio; specifically, they are advised to choose those that offer the best evidence of their achievement of unit goals and portfolio criteria.

### Guidelines for a Target Archery Unit Portfolio

For this unit, you will complete and submit an archery sportfolio, in which you provide evidence of your knowledge, skill improvement, and skill performance level. In order to collect documents for evidence during the unit, you must participate in assessments that are integrated with learning and practice activities, complete individual projects throughout the unit, and file results from all of these activities in your working portfolio folder. Be sure to record your artifacts in your record log. Later, you will make judgments about which artifacts show your improvement and constitute your best work as you determine which to include in your evaluation sportfolio. You should organize your portfolio based on your artifacts, all of which should provide evidence of the following:

- Your knowledge of target archery equipment, purchasing information, repair, and storage
- Safety rules that must be followed when shooting in a group (in class or outside of class), alone, or with a friend
- How to aim at a target with and without a bow sight
- Knowledge of critical elements of the shooting stance and process: stance, grip, nock, draw, anchor, aim, release, and follow-through
- Ability to identify errors and corrections that you can make in the critical elements of the shooting process
- Evidence of your competence in the shooting process

Your evaluation sportfolio will be submitted on the final day of the archery unit. Your portfolio will be evaluated based on the portfolio scoring guide or rubric, which can be found on the second page of this handout.

**Figure 7.11** These guidelines include specific performance criteria that students must follow when developing their portfolio for the target archery unit. Students should receive the guidelines at the beginning of the unit.

### Levels of Organization, Presentation, and Content Level

#### Outstanding: A
- Portfolio is very well organized and neatly presented.
- Sections are based on unit goals and clearly marked.
- Table of contents lists each artifact in proper order under the correct unit goal.
- All materials are neatly and creatively displayed.
- Complete title page is provided.

*(continued)*

**Figure 7.12** This rubric for a target archery unit incorporates the criteria from the portfolio guidelines and is used to evaluate students' portfolios.

- Portfolio registry and reflection page are provided after the title page.
- Artifacts provide solid evidence of achievement of unit goals.
- Artifacts clearly demonstrate the student's improvement across the unit.
- Reflections provide a rich and clear explanation of each artifact and why it is included as evidence.

## Very Good: B

- Portfolio is organized and neat.
- Sections are based on unit goals but are not marked clearly.
- Table of contents is included.
- Complete title page is provided.
- Portfolio registry is provided with reflection.
- Documents provide evidence of achievement of most goals.
- Documents provide evidence of improvement in some areas.
- Reflections lack depth and explanation.

## Needs Improvement: C

- Portfolio is unorganized and sloppy.
- Artifacts are not divided into sections based on unit goals.
- Table of contents is not included or is unorganized.
- Title page is missing.
- Portfolio registry is missing or incomplete.
- Documents provide little or weak evidence of some unit goals.
- Reflections lack depth of explanation.
- Little or no evidence of improvement is provided.

**Figure 7.12**  *(continued)*

## Series of Continuous or Formative Performance-Based Assessments for a Target Archery Unit

1. Partner or teacher completes and signs a shooting process checklist and rating scales while the student shoots an end of arrows. This assessment should be completed every other day during the first week of shooting practice.

2. Make a video recording of each student shooting an end of arrows. Next, students should view their own shooting segments and complete the shooting process checklist, then view a model performance. Each student writes a self-analysis of his or her performance that identifies strengths and weaknesses and proposes recommendations for improving in weak areas of the shooting process.

3. Present evidence of student participation, practice, and progress in target shooting from the beginning to the end of the archery unit. Possible choices for assessments that students could use as artifacts for their portfolio include the following:

- Dated scorecards for various shooting distances
- Graph of progress at various shooting distances
- Arrow grouping charts that show improvement in accuracy
- Arrow grouping charts across consecutive shooting events for each shooting distance, along with written analysis of shooting errors that may have caused each grouping, proposed remedies for identified problems, and later grouping charts showing improvement (refer to the sample in figure 7.13a on the CD-ROM)

*(continued)*

**Figure 7.13**  Students complete this series of progressive assessments during the unit in order to prepare them for their culminating product—the archery sportfolio.

4. Present scorecards from rounds shot at various distances during class practice to demonstrate improvement in shooting ability (students may show improvement by graphing scores across time for each distance). Refer to the sample in figure 7.13b on the CD-ROM.

5. Present scorecards from practice outside of school or from formal student participation in competitive contests inside or outside of class.

6. In groups, students plan and implement a class tournament. Duties for groups include tournament planning, officiating, awards preparation, handling of media, and special events.

7. Students participate in repairing class archery equipment during and at the end of the unit.

8. Students develop a resource guide for target archery by gathering information from books, the Web, or experts in the community. The guide could be used by the next class in target archery.

9. Students develop a plan for continuing to participate in target archery outside of school.

10. Students develop a plan for securing their personal equipment—what it will cost and how they will raise the money.

11. Students identify facilities or space where they can participate in target archery.

12. Students develop a proposal to start a target archery club at school or in the community so that they can participate in target archery activities with friends or family members.

13. Students write an essay in which they describe why they would or would not pursue involvement in target archery beyond this class.

**Figure 7.13** *(continued)*

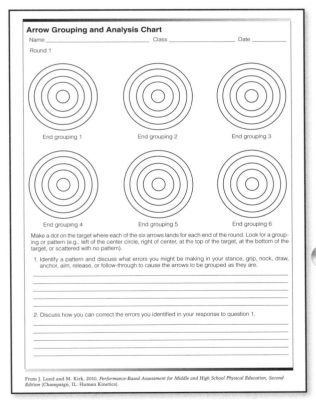

From J. Lund and M. Kirk, 2010, *Performance-Based Assessment for Middle and High School Physical Education, Second Edition* (Champaign, IL: Human Kinetics).

**Figure 7.13a** Students use this assessment chart to record where each arrow lands in each end during a round of shooting, which allows them to identify any grouping or pattern that can be linked to a particular shooting error.

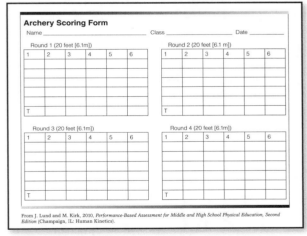

From J. Lund and M. Kirk, 2010, *Performance-Based Assessment for Middle and High School Physical Education, Second Edition* (Champaign, IL: Human Kinetics).

**Figure 7.13b** Archery scoring forms and performance graph.

By participating in continuous, progressive, performance-based assessments that link to broad standards and specific unit goals, students accumulate many assessment documents for inclusion in their working portfolio. These documents then provide a rich resource to students as they make decisions about how to document their achievement of broad and unit goals and how to complete the evaluation portfolio as a culminating assessment.

# GOLF UNIT

Golf is a very popular lifetime sport and a healthy form of physical activity. When students participate in an in-depth instructional unit about golf—in which assessments are continuous, progressive, authentic, and linked to learning activities—they gain knowledge, skill, competence, and experience that may ultimately encourage them to participate in golf for a lifetime. It is important to remember that the more progressive and authentic you make the golf unit's learning and assessment activities, the more students will gain competence, confidence, experience, knowledge, and skills that are rooted in a genuine experience of the sport. A student could stand on a mat and hit golf balls into the curtains for weeks, but that practice alone would not prepare them to play a round of golf. They also need practice and performance assessment in a variety of realistic golf situations. For example, they can hit from uphill and downhill sites, from different distances and at different targets, from different lies, and with different clubs. Through this type of experience and feedback, students develop competence and confidence in their abilities and decisions and thus are more likely to participate in golf throughout their lives. *Golf: Steps to Success* (Owens and Bunker 2005) was consulted as a resource in developing these learning and assessment tasks.

As with the tumbling and target archery units, we identify here the broad physical education goals we want students to accomplish and the national standards we think students can achieve by participating in the in-depth golf instructional unit. We also identify specific goals for the golf unit in order to give teachers direction for planning and to give students goals to work toward. To accomplish these standards and goals, the unit must be of sufficient length and depth. Merely introducing students to skills, rules, and knowledge does not guarantee that they will develop to the point at which they are able and willing to apply them in a realistic setting (in this case, playing a round of golf). To help students develop competence and confidence in their ability as players, we must provide students with appropriate learning and assessment experiences in which they test their skills and knowledge. They can do so when they learn a progression of skills, from simple to complex, and when they practice in a variety of environmental settings—which is really the essence of golf. Figures 7.14 and 7.15 present the standards, selected from the National Standards

Golf is a very popular lifetime sport.

---

## Relevant National Standards for a Golf Unit

1. Demonstrates competency in motor skills and movement patterns needed to perform a variety of physical activities.

2. Demonstrates understanding of movement concepts, principles, strategies, and tactics as they apply to the learning and performance of physical activities.

3. Participates regularly in physical activity.

5. Exhibits responsible personal and social behavior that respects self and others in physical activity settings.

6. Values physical activity for health, enjoyment, challenge, self-expression, and/or social interaction.

**Figure 7.14** Five of the National Standards for Physical Education are identified as possible targets for students to achieve by participating in this instructional unit.

From NASPE, 2004, *Moving into the future: National standards for physical education,* 2nd ed. (Reston, VA: National Association for Sport and Physical Education).

## Goals for a Golf Unit

1. Students are able to grip the golf club by using either the interlocking or the overlapping grip.
2. Students are able to correctly address the ball and assume the correct stance for a full swing.
3. Students are able to identify and demonstrate the process and performance cues for the full swing with a wood while hitting balls from a tee.
4. Students are able to analyze his or her full swing performance, as well as that of a peer, through observation and offer corrective feedback for improvement.
5. Students are able to define and appropriately use identified golf terms.
6. Students are able to name and identify the areas of a golf hole and course.
7. Students are able to identify errors in swings and ball flight (e.g., hook, slice, topping, mulligan) and determine how to correct the swing in order to avoid these errors.
8. Students are able to identify and demonstrate the performance cues when hitting either a chip shot or a pitch shot from a mat or from the grass.
9. Students are able to identify and make necessary adjustments to the stance, and the selection of the club in relation to the lie of the ball and the distance of the ball from the pin, when hitting an approach stroke or a shot from the fairway, the rough, or a sand trap.
10. Students are able to implement correct grip, stance, preparation, swing, and follow-through for putting.
11. Students are able to play three rounds of nine holes each on a par-3 golf course.
12. Students are able to identify and apply correct procedures, rules of play, and rules of etiquette when playing on a golf course.
13. Students are able to keep track of his or her shot progress, golf skill, and knowledge development, during both practice and play.
14. Students are able to keep track of practice in which he or she participates outside of class over the course of the unit.
15. Students are able to articulate his or her feelings about playing golf as a leisure activity.

**Figure 7.15**   The goals identified here for the golf unit were developed by the teacher to lead students toward achieving specific unit goals and broader-based national standards identified in figure 7.14.

for Physical Education (National Association for Sport and Physical Education 2004), and the specific goals for a unit on golf. We used these standards and goals as guides in developing the culminating and progressive performance-based formative assessments presented here for golf (see figure 7.16).

## Culminating Assessment and Rubric

After identifying the standards and unit goals, we developed the unit's culminating assessment. The goals made it clear that we would need to use a performance-based culminating assessment in which students were asked to apply skills and knowledge in an authentic situation. If the unit were taught over a period of weeks

in a high school with block scheduling, then the culminating assessment described in figure 7.16 would be appropriate.

## Continuous Formative Performance-Based Assessments

To prepare for playing three rounds of golf during their culminating or summative assessment, students must participate in a series of progressive learning, practice, and assessment activities throughout the course of the unit. Figure 7.17 suggests some learning and assessment activities that can serve as continuous or formative assessments and checkpoints. These assessments and learning activities gradually prepare students to complete the culminating assessment and achieve unit goals.

## Culminating or Summative Assessment for a Golf Unit

During the last 2 weeks of this unit, you participate in a field trip with the class to play three rounds of nine holes of golf at the par-3 course near the school. To save time, each round has a shotgun start. For each round, you submit a scorecard that notes the score for each hole and the total score; for formal verification, one member of your foursome signs the card. For each hole, you also complete the log sheet that will be provided to you. On the log sheet, you record and describe each shot that you take for each hole; for each shot, you give the approximate distance from the hole, the club you used, and a description of the results. The log sheet also includes a diagram of each hole on which you diagram each shot for that hole. Completing the log sheet for each hole helps you recall, reflect, analyze, and make corrections in your game play.

The three rounds of golf for this assessment will be spaced apart from each other by 3 to 5 days. Following each round, use your log-sheet reflection and analysis to seek assistance or to modify your practice activities in order to improve your play in the next round. You must also submit a comparison (a written narrative of one to three paragraphs) of the three rounds. If your score does not improve, you should write a narrative describing any improvements that you observed in your play regardless of your scores.

During the third round, you will participate in a scramble tournament. In this format, everyone in a foursome hits his or her next stroke from the spot of the group's best lie after the previous shot.

During each of your three rounds, the teacher observes you playing at least one hole. During this observation, the teacher evaluates how well you know and demonstrate playing etiquette and rules of the game.

**Figure 7.16** This authentic, or real-to-life, culminating assessment can be used to evaluate students' learning and achievement of goals and standards.

## CONCLUSION

This chapter addresses how you can link assessments to targeted standards and goals in physical education. These initial steps in integrating meaningful, standards-based assessment into the planning process for units of instruction in middle school and high school help you ensure that students learn and achieve important goals in physical education. The first step in the assessment planning process in standards-based education is to identify both targeted broad standards and student goals specific to the unit activity. We recommend that you first select the broad standards and goals from the National Standards for Physical Education (National Association for Sport and Physical Education 2004) and from your state and local school district goals. Next, develop specific content-related unit goals that link directly to the broader goals. Once you have identified what students should know, value, and be able to do, you are then able to design the final or culminating assessment performance or product by means of which students demonstrate their achievement of those targeted standards and goals.

We have provided sample standards, goals, and assessments for units in three individual sports and taken you through the process by identifying broad standards and specific unit goals and linking them to a culminating assessment. We have also provided samples of a sequence of continuous, formative, performance-based assessments, which students complete throughout the unit in order to prepare for the culminating assessment. The assessment tasks provided in this chapter are samples that you can use as models for developing your own assessment tasks for other individual, dual, and group sports and activities. Chapters 8 and 9 take you through the entire unit planning process for a standards-based physical education program.

The message we hope you take away from this chapter is one of accountability! When you expect students to learn and achieve broad standards and specific goals in your classes, you must plan for that to occur. Give students goals to reach, then plan how they can achieve them and how they—and you—will know when they have done so. Hold yourself *and* your students accountable for learning.

## Continuous Formative Performance-Based Assessments for a Golf Unit

1. Use the checklist provided by the teacher to have partners observe and assess each other's full swing while hitting balls in an outdoor environment. Students use feedback from their partners and the teacher during subsequent practice to improve stroke performance. This assessment should be used frequently during practice to improve stroke performance for the full swing with woods and long swings (e.g., drives) to irons with shorter swings (like chipping and pitching) (see figure 7.17a on the CD-ROM).

2. Make video recordings of students as they hit golf balls outside. Students use the video to observe their own swing and compare it with video of a model swing. They also assess their swing using a checklist or rating scale provided for them.

3. Students hit plastic practice balls with various clubs into designated target areas marked in the gym or on the field. This activity helps students learn how to adjust their stance and line up to the ball; it also helps them select the appropriate club for the lie, distance, and situation. To assess their performance, students can record the number of balls landing within 10 yards of the designated target.

4. Students hit real balls in a school field or at a community driving range. This activity and assessment are similar to the one completed at school with plastic practice balls. Students attempt to hit a specific number of balls (15 to 25) to designated targets set at various distances. Students record the number of balls landing within 10 to 20 yards of the flag. This exercise should be completed a number of times to graph progress across practice trials and so that students can determine the percentage of balls landing within the designated area around the flag. Students can graph their progress (or lack thereof). As a student hits balls, a partner can use a target form to chart where the balls are landing in relation to the flag. The student and the teacher can then analyze the chart, determine whether the student is developing consistency in his or her swings or is having directional problems (e.g., topping the ball, slicing, hooking), and develop a plan to eliminate any recurring errors (see figure 7.17b on the CD-ROM).

5. Working in groups of five, students design a golf hole in the field adjacent to the gym. Each hole must have a tee area, a fairway (straight or dogleg), a rough, a water hazard or sand trap, and a green. The teacher must make available materials with which to create designated hole areas (e.g., rope to mark off the rough and the hazards). Each hole must be at least 100 yards long, and each group must create a diagram of its hole and indicate the designated par for the scorecard. All students will have the opportunity to play each group's hole and evaluate the design. In addition, each group evaluates another group's performance on the hole and gives that group feedback about how well it followed the rules of etiquette and the rules of the game.

6. Students view a golf tournament by means of a video recording that includes no audio. Their job is to make an audio recording of commentary typical of what they would hear from a sports announcer for three consecutive holes. Through their analysis and commentary, the students demonstrate knowledge of the rules of golf and understanding of the strategies players use in playing different holes (e.g., choice of club; how to address the ball's lie; how to handle wind; environmental aspects such as bunkers, water, trees).

7. On a field trip, students play three holes of golf and write reflections about how well they played and how well they knew and applied the rules. They repeat this assessment three times before the culminating assessment.

**Figure 7.17** The series of progressive learning and assessment activities presented here enables students to prepare themselves to succeed in the culminating assessment.

## Analysis Checklist for Full Swing in Golf

Performer _____  Evaluator _____

Observe the performer swing many times, each time focusing on only one specific part of the swing.

| | Dates of evaluation | | | | | | |
|---|---|---|---|---|---|---|---|
| **Stance** | | | | | | | |
| Weight balanced | | | | | | | |
| Knees relaxed or bent | | | | | | | |
| Feet shoulder-width apart | | | | | | | |
| **Grip** | | | | | | | |
| Vs of both hands | | | | | | | |
| Two knuckles showing | | | | | | | |
| Thumb positions | | | | | | | |
| Grip firm, not tight | | | | | | | |
| **Backswing** | | | | | | | |
| Waggle or forward press | | | | | | | |
| Club head pulled back along ground | | | | | | | |
| Left arm straight | | | | | | | |
| Head down and steady | | | | | | | |
| Eyes on ball | | | | | | | |
| Hips rotate away from ball (coil) | | | | | | | |
| Right leg straight | | | | | | | |
| Club parallel with crown at top of swing | | | | | | | |
| **Swing and contact** | | | | | | | |
| Uncoil | | | | | | | |
| Lead with left hip | | | | | | | |
| Eyes on ball | | | | | | | |
| Head down | | | | | | | |
| Wrists firm at contact | | | | | | | |
| Swing through the ball | | | | | | | |
| **Follow-through** | | | | | | | |
| Clubhead follows the ball | | | | | | | |
| Proper rotation toward the target | | | | | | | |
| Left leg straight | | | | | | | |

From J. Lund and M. Kirk, 2010, *Performance-Based Assessment for Middle and High School Physical Education, Second Edition* (Champaign, IL: Human Kinetics).

 **Figure 7.17a** Checklist for golf swing.

## Golf Target Accuracy Form

Name _____
Recorder _____
Date _____

Please place a dot where each ball lands in the target area near the pin.
After you hit 20 balls, add up your accuracy score and enter here.

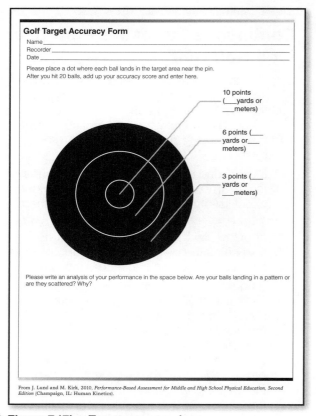

10 points (____yards or ____meters)

6 points (____ yards or____ meters)

3 points (____ yards or ____meters)

Please write an analysis of your performance in the space below. Are your balls landing in a pattern or are they scattered? Why?

From J. Lund and M. Kirk, 2010, *Performance-Based Assessment for Middle and High School Physical Education, Second Edition* (Champaign, IL: Human Kinetics).

**Figure 7.17b** Target accuracy form.

8

# Planning for Continuous Performance-Based Assessment

*Rather than merely assessing an isolated skill such as the forehand or backhand drive in tennis, teachers need to focus also on holistic assessment in which the overall quality of the game, tennis in this case, is judged (Hensley 1997, 22).*

This textbook focuses on helping students improve their learning and achievement in physical education through standards-based instruction and continuous performance-based assessment of students' progress toward the established exit standards or expectations for student learning. To successfully implement performance-based assessments continuously throughout a unit of instruction, the teacher must begin with the standards-based planning process. When continuous assessment is not planned by teachers before the implementation of the unit of instruction, it usually does not occur or the attempt at assessment is at best piecemeal. This chapter takes you through a standards-based planning process for a high school tennis unit in which assessment plays a continuous and integral part. This example illustrates the fact that the progression of learning

and assessment tasks and activities can be integrated throughout the learning process. We take you through the planning process step-by-step, from identifying unit objectives and national and program standards to designing scoring guides and learning and assessment tasks.

In guiding you through the planning process for this unit of instruction, we use a planning model that takes as its foundation the "design-down, deliver-up" (Hopple 2005) or "backward or reverse curriculum mapping planning process" (Lambert 2007; Wiggins and McTighe 2005; Kentucky Department of Education 1993, 2008). We can graphically represent the standards-based, backward-mapping planning model by using the analogy of a staircase (figure 8.1). In this model, targeted standards are placed at the top of the staircase, and the unit plan is designed down the staircase from there, then instruction is delivered *up* from the bottom of the staircase. Each step identifies what students need in order to get to the next step, and ultimately reach the top, where they demonstrate their achievement of targeted standards.

In the **five-step, standards-based planning process**, the teacher first determines the unit's major focus by identifying three parts: (a) the central organizer, (b) the targeted national and program standards, as well as the unit goals that relate to the standards or program goals, and (c) essential questions that students should be able to answer during and at the completion of the unit (Wiggins and McTighe 2005). Once the unit's major focus and essential questions are stated, the teacher develops the culminating performance or product assessment and evaluation rubric—that is, the final (or summative) assessment for the unit. In this culminating assess-

ment, students should be expected to apply and demonstrate knowledge, understandings, and skills that they have learned in an authentic assessment task. The final performance or product should relate directly to the unit goals and objectives, as well as to the overall program and national standards. When the unit's major focus has been chosen and the culminating assessment and evaluation rubric has been developed, the teacher has established students' destination for the unit.

The next step is to ask this question: What do students need to know, understand, and be able to do in order to get to the targeted destination for this unit? The teacher answers this question by identifying the essential knowledge, skills, and abilities that students must learn, and apply in order to successfully complete the culminating performance or product to

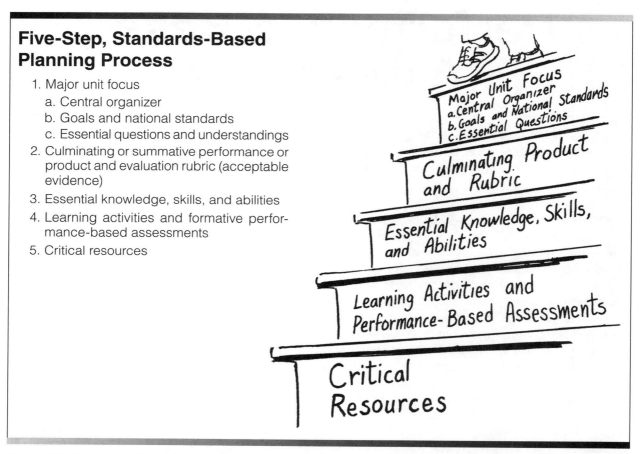

### Five-Step, Standards-Based Planning Process

1. Major unit focus
   a. Central organizer
   b. Goals and national standards
   c. Essential questions and understandings
2. Culminating or summative performance or product and evaluation rubric (acceptable evidence)
3. Essential knowledge, skills, and abilities
4. Learning activities and formative performance-based assessments
5. Critical resources

**Figure 8.1**    Here is the five-step planning process, which begins at the top of the stairs and proceeds downward (Kentucky Department of Education 1993). Instruction is then delivered *up*, leading students from the bottom step to the top.

Based on *Transformations: Kentucky's Curriculum Framework,* Vol. II (Frankfort: Kentucky Department of Education, 1993, 53–60).

demonstrate their achievement of the targeted goals and standards. The next step the teacher must complete in the unit planning process is to identify the route that students must travel in order to reach the destination by carefully creating (4) progressive instructional activities and formative assessments that students engage in and to learn the necessary knowledge, skills, abilities, and demonstrators to be able to reach the destination. In the final step, teachers must (5) identify the critical resources needed for the learning and assessment activities.

This process is referred to as a **curriculum backward planning map** (Kentucky Department of Education 1993, 2008; Wiggins and McTighe 2005) because the teacher first establishes the destination (i.e., where students should be and what they should know and be able to do by the end of the unit), then determines how the students will get to the destination (by means of learning activities), and, finally, decides how the students and teacher will assess progress as students move toward the destination (through progressive assessments and culminating performance).

# MAJOR UNIT FOCUS

The major focus of the unit should serve as the starting and ending point of the planning process. It includes three interrelated aspects: the central organizer, the targeted broad standards and specific unit goals, and the essential questions. These elements of the major unit focus identify for the teacher and the student what the student should know and be able to do within this unit in order to accomplish the broader targeted standards. The central organizer statement focuses unit content on a particular theme, concept, problem, skill, or issue that relates to the targeted standards and goals. The central organizer should both captivate and motivate students. To explore and understand the central organizer, students must be able to ask and eventually answer the essential questions that the teacher generates for the unit. The unit's major focus (and its main answer) derives from the question, "What should students know and be able to do as a result of participating in this unit of instruction?" The following sections discuss the three parts of the major focus in more detail

and provide examples geared to the beginning tennis unit.

## Central Organizer

To establish a unit's major focus, start by identifying the **central organizer**. The organizer can involve a theme, concept, set of content, skill, issue, problem, or question that is relevant to students—or some combination thereof. For instance, for a sixth-grade unit, you might select the skill of striking with an implement as the central organizer. The unit might then focus on skill patterns of striking with various implements (e.g., rackets, sticks, clubs) and how these skills are used in a variety of games and sports. In another example, a high school physical educator might identify the following problem as the central organizer for a backpacking class: How can we safely enjoy the wilderness while making the least impact on it? The central organizer for our sample instructional unit on tennis is illustrated in figure 8.2.

## Tennis Unit Central Organizer

### Concept and Theme

Tennis is a sport that you can enjoy playing with others for a lifetime. If you learn the knowledge, skills, and strategies that allow you to play tennis successfully and confidently early in life, then you are more likely to enjoy playing tennis for physical activity and socialization throughout your life, and well into your senior years. In order to develop the necessary skills and tactical and strategic ability to enjoy and be successful at playing tennis, it is important to practice the skills and strategies often—and in effective ways.

### Content and Skills

Success in recreational tennis hinges on your ability to perform and apply the basic strokes, rules, scoring procedures, rules of etiquette, and tactics and strategies (for both singles and doubles tennis) during game play.

**Figure 8.2** The central organizer for an instructional unit identifies a theme, problem, question, content, or skill (or some combination thereof) around which the unit can be developed.

## Targeted Standards and Goals

The next step in the planning process is to identify targeted standards, specific unit goals, and objectives that relate to the organizer. There are many resources available to help teachers in this process. Here are a few:

- National Standards for Physical Education (National Association for Sport and Physical Education 2004)
- State outcomes, standards, or goals
- District or school goals
- Individual students' needs, abilities, and interests

The National Association for Sport and Physical Education (NASPE) developed and published *Moving Into the Future: National Standards for Physical Education* (2004) to help school districts, administrators, and teachers identify outcomes that students should achieve as a result of participating in a high-quality physical education program from kindergarten through grade 12. These six national standards are listed in chapter 1 on page 4. To provide further assistance to teachers in curriculum planning, the standards document lists student expectations and sample performance outcomes by grade level—K–2, 3–5, 6–8, and 9–12—for each standard.

For the sample 10th-grade unit of instruction presented in this chapter for beginning tennis, the teacher began by consulting the student expectations for grades 9 through 12, as well as the sample performance outcomes, for each of the national standards in order to identify appropriate targeted goals and unit content goals related to the unit's central organizer. The targeted standards identified by the teacher are presented in figure 8.3.

The number of unit goals should be determined by several factors:

- Students' developmental level and ability
- The nature of the content
- The length of the unit
- The amount of time students spend in physical education
- The equipment and facilities available

The teacher determines what is reasonable to expect students to accomplish. Remember: There is no set number! It is important to keep in mind that longer units (more time) are needed if students are expected to develop the knowledge, understanding, abilities, and skills needed for successful participation in sport and other physical activities. High school teachers tend to teach multiple short units, which often do not challenge students, rather than fewer but more in-depth units. With the targeted national and program standards in mind, the teacher identifies specific tennis unit goals that students should achieve throughout or by the end of the unit (see figure 8.4).

The standards, goals, and outcomes identified in figure 8.4 serve as a destination to which students travel during the tennis unit. They identify what each student should know, understand, and be able to do throughout and at the conclusion of the tennis unit. They also serve as a guide for the teacher as he or she identifies learning activities and assessments in which students participate to help them reach their destination.

---

### Relevant National Standards for a Tennis Unit

1. Demonstrates competency in motor skills and movement patterns needed to perform a variety of physical activities.
2. Demonstrates understanding of movement concepts, principles, strategies, and tactics as they apply to the learning and performance of physical activities.
3. Participates regularly in physical activity.
5. Exhibits responsible personal and social behavior that respects self and others in physical activity settings.
6. Values physical activity for health, enjoyment, challenge, self-expression, and/or social interaction.

**Figure 8.3** Five of the six National Standards for Physical Education were identified as broad goals for students to achieve through their participation in the tennis unit.

From NASPE, 2004, *Moving into the future: National standards for physical education,* 2nd ed. (Reston, VA: National Association for Sport and Physical Education).

## Goals for a Tennis Unit

1. Student demonstrates knowledge of and ability to perform the critical performance elements using the following forehand and backhand skills: ground strokes, volleys, and lobs. Student also serves properly and effectively. Student works to improve skills through effective practice strategies, analyzing partners' play and giving them feedback, and self-evaluation.

2. Student applies and demonstrates the rules of tennis and the rules of etiquette and fair play while participating in class activities and in the class tennis tournament.

3. Student applies and demonstrates the offensive strategies of covering court space and the defensive strategy of hitting to open space or to opponents' weaknesses while playing in the class tennis tournament.

4. Student demonstrates improvement in performance of the forehand and backhand drive, volley, lob, and smash, as well as the overhand serve and appropriate combinations of these skills, over the course of the unit through participation in progressive practice activities.

5. Student successfully applies appropriate tactics and strategies and demonstrates the following skills: forehand and backhand drive, volley, and lob, as well as the overhand serve, while participating in the class singles and doubles tournaments.

6. Student demonstrates the ability to participate in the game of tennis outside the school setting in order to show participation in a physically active lifestyle.

7. Student experiences personal satisfaction and enjoyment while pursuing personal goals during his or her participation in tennis in both competitive and recreational settings.

8. Student recognizes that playing tennis can provide a positive social environment for activities with others.

**Figure 8.4**   This list presents specific unit goals directly linked to the targeted broad (national) standards.

## Essential Questions

The third component of the unit plan's major focus involves the **essential questions** that organize the several targeted standards and focus the unit of study. Here, the teacher identifies questions that students should be able to answer throughout and by the end of the unit in order to achieve the unit goals and move toward accomplishing the targeted standards. These questions help both the teacher and the students narrow the focus of learning; they divide the central organizer into logical, sequential parts for instruction. The questions should require students to think, analyze, gain understanding, and apply knowledge acquired during the unit, and they should be acutely relevant to students.

Many subject areas lend themselves to the development of essential questions, yet a considerable number of teachers seem to think that this is not the case in skill areas such as physical education. Wiggins and McTighe (2005), however, suggest that posing important questions is essential to skill mastery and to "fluent and flexible performance." They propose that essential questions for skill areas should be "framed around the four categories of big ideas for effective skill learning": (1) key concepts, (2) purpose and value, (3) strategies and tactics, and (4) context of use. The following example is provided by Wiggins & McTighe (2005, 113): "for any sports that involve the skill of swinging with a long-handed object, such as in baseball, golf, and tennis, *key concepts* include power, torque, and control."

The number of questions should be limited to between five and seven so that they can be fully answered by students during the course of the unit. It is very important that all of the goals are addressed with the questions. Because the essential questions help guide learning and assessment, they should be shared with students and posted in the gym. In fact, the questions could be developed with students' input. Figure 8.5 presents essential questions identified for our tennis unit.

---

### Essential Questions for a Tennis Unit

1. What are the benefits of playing tennis throughout a lifetime?

2. What skills are necessary in order to play tennis successfully? What critical performance elements and cues do you use to successfully perform these skills?

3. What major movement concepts and mechanical principles apply to the performance of tennis skills? How do they apply, and in what situations?

4. What rules of the game must one know and be able to apply in order to successfully participate in a tennis match?

5. What social skills, rules of etiquette, and sportsmanship are necessary to develop to successfully play and enjoy tennis?

6. What offensive and defensive tactics and strategies should you use while playing singles tennis in order to outplay your opponent? How about doubles tennis?

7. How can you continue to expand and improve your tennis skills and playing ability beyond this particular class? What effective practice and learning strategies can you identify?

**Figure 8.5** These are the questions, generated by the teacher (and sometimes by students), that students should be able to answer in order to accomplish the tennis unit's goals and standards.

## CULMINATING (SUMMATIVE) ASSESSMENT AND EVALUATION RUBRIC

Once the elements of the major focus have been identified and the teachers knows where the students are headed (the unit destination), then the teacher must design a culminating or summative assessment to determine whether students arrive there. Therefore the following question must be addressed: How will the teacher and the students know if they have achieved the unit goals and targeted standards and at what level? The culminating unit experience in which students participate at the end of the unit can provide much information for the final assessment of student learning. This culminating performance or product serves as the final and summative assessment for the unit. In standards-based instruction, the summative assessment should be a demonstration and application of students' learning, their achievement of unit goals, and their progress toward targeted standards. Students should richly demonstrate their application of the knowledge and skills they have learned in an authentic or realistic, and engaging, task or performance. This culminating performance or product serves as the accountability measure for both the students and the teacher.

When teachers design a culminating experience, they must consider unit goals and targeted standards. They must also think of how students can demonstrate their achievement of unit goals and thus their progress toward achieving the targeted standards in a true-to-life situation. This final assessment should be designed before implementing the unit, and the design should take into consideration the length of the unit and the available time. The culminating assessment should consist of a group or individual student performance, a completed product or project in which the student assumes a real-life role with a specific, identified audience, or a student portfolio. The culminating performance, product, or portfolio and the corresponding scoring guides (or rubrics) should be shared with students at the beginning of the unit, so that they know from the outset what is expected of them. The culminating performance might take the form of a project that students work on for several weeks, or it could be an event task that they complete during one or two class periods. This final assessment should be authentic or realistic, and it should be one that engages students. The culminating experience is the ultimate learning experience as well as the summative assessment. It is this final, performance, product, or portfolio that ultimately demonstrates students' level of achievement of unit goals and standards. It is through completing this culminating experience that students take their final step to the top of the curriculum planning staircase—and how they see clearly just what they have learned and achieved by participating in the unit. This is powerful motivation to the students.

In a culminating performance or product, a student may take the role of an athlete, coach, sportswriter or fitness writer, director, sports announcer, or other performer, as appropriate in light of the task. The experience should richly engage students, and it will probably be multidimensional. The task should be designed to allow students to show their learning in different ways so that all students can succeed at their level of ability. For our beginning tennis unit, the multifaceted culminating performance or product is identified in figure 8.6.

The culminating performance and products allow students to take a real-life role in authentic tasks in order to demonstrate and apply what they have learned during the tennis unit. Allowing students to choose which assessments to complete enables them to work at a level that is compatible with their ability and learning style. The teacher must be prepared to allow students sufficient class time to complete the culminating performance and products and to serve as a facilitator and assist students when necessary.

Once the design of the culminating performance or product is completed, the teacher must design a rubric or a scoring guide that is used by students to help their performance and that is used by the teacher to evaluate students'

---

## Culminating Performance and Product for a Tennis Unit

### Performance

You will demonstrate and apply the basic strokes of tennis, knowledge of the rules and etiquette of the game, and offensive and defensive strategies appropriately while playing in the class singles and doubles tournament. You will also serve in some capacity as a tournament official in order to help the tournament run smoothly.

### Portfolio

Your portfolio should include evidence that you have achieved unit goals. It must include the following artifacts:

1. Answers to the essential questions for the unit, including performance cues for each of the tennis strokes.

2. A reflective journal regarding your daily class goals, practice activities, and practice performance and assessment results. It should also include a list of your short- and long-term personal goals, a discussion of whether or not you have reached these goals, and what strategies you have used to pursue them.

3. Graphs that represent your practice progress for each stroke over the course of the unit.

4. A summary of your performance statistics for each tournament match, as well as a summary of totals and averages for the entire tournament. In addition, write a reflection about your performance during the tournament.

5. A log detailing practice and playing episodes outside of class, including where you played, who you played with, how well you played, and any other relevant information.

6. Documents of your choice. Please check with me before developing your own documentation.

### Project

In a group of five, prepare for and produce a video that promotes tennis as a valuable, accessible, and enjoyable physical activity for a lifetime. The video should also be instructional and address the essential questions of our tennis unit. It should be edited and should be of high quality so that it can be used with classes and community recreation programs, placed in the community library, and posted on the school's physical education Web site in order to promote the sport and help people get started.

**Figure 8.6**  In our sample tennis unit, students can choose from three culminating options.

performances and products. More information about developing rubrics can be found in chapter 3. For this tennis unit, the rubric for the game-play culminating performance is provided in table 8.1, the rubric for the portfolio culminating assessment is provided in table 8.2, and the rubric for the project culminating assessment is provided in table 8.3.

 **Table 8.1**   Rubric for Performance Culminating Assessment (Game Play)

| Performance level | Performance criteria | | | |
|---|---|---|---|---|
| | Skill performance | Application of strategy | Court movement | Application of rules and etiquette |
| Proficient: 4 | Consistently selects and performs appropriate strokes. Consistently performs correct forehand stroke cues. Consistently performs correct backhand cues. Consistently performs overhead serve correctly. | Consistently and correctly applies appropriate offensive strategy. Consistently and correctly applies appropriate defensive strategy. Consistently demonstrates good ball placement. | Consistently anticipates ball placement and moves to the ball. Returns to "home" when appropriate after stroke. | Consistently applies rules correctly. Demonstrates correct scoring during set, game, tiebreaker. Consistently applies and follows the rules of game etiquette and fair play. Consistently demonstrates good sporting behavior. |
| Competent: 3 | Selects and performs appropriate strokes most of the time. Performs correct forehand stroke cues most of the time. Performs correct backhand cues most of the time. Performs overhead serve correctly most of the time. | Frequently applies appropriate offensive strategy. Frequently applies appropriate defensive strategy. Consistently demonstrates good ball placement. | Frequently anticipates ball placement and moves to the ball. Returns to "home" when appropriate after stroke. | Consistently applies rules correctly. Demonstrates correct scoring during set, game, tiebreaker. Consistently applies and follows the rules of game etiquette and fair play. Consistently demonstrates good sporting behavior. |
| Recreational: 2 | Selects and performs appropriate strokes at least half the time. Performs correct forehand stroke cues at least half the time. Performs correct backhand cues at least half the time. Performs overhead serve correctly at least half the time. | Sometimes applies appropriate offensive strategy. Sometimes applies appropriate defensive strategy. Sometimes demonstrates good ball placement. | Sometimes anticipates ball placement and moves to the ball. Sometimes returns to "home" when appropriate after stroke. | Applies rules correctly. Demonstrates correct scoring during set, game, tiebreaker. Applies and follows the rules of game etiquette and fair play most of the time. Demonstrates good sporting behavior most of the time. |
| Novice: 1 | Is inconsistent in selection and performance of appropriate forehand and backhand strokes. Is inconsistent in performing the overhead serve correctly. | Does not appear to understand or is not able to apply offensive and defensive strategies during game play. Does not intentionally place the ball. | Frequently remains in the same place on the court. Does not move to the ball until it is too late. Does not move well on the court. | Applies rules correctly most of the time. Does not demonstrate correct knowledge of scoring during set, game, tiebreaker. Frequently breaks the rules of game etiquette and fair play. Sometimes displays poor sporting behavior. |

**Table 8.2**  Rubric for Portfolio Culminating Assessment

| | Performance criteria | | | |
|---|---|---|---|---|
| **Performance level** | **Portfolio presentation and organization** | **Evidence of achievement of unit goals** | **Inclusion of all required artifacts** | **Artifact quality** |
| Proficient: 4 | Portfolio is neatly organized. | Artifacts and reflections clearly demonstrate that the student has achieved all unit goals. | Portfolio contains all five required artifacts, as well as additional artifacts. | All artifacts are of good quality and meet the stated criteria. Artifacts provide evidence that the student has achieved all unit goals. |
| Competent: 3 | Portfolio is neatly organized. | Artifacts and reflections clearly demonstrate that the student has achieved most unit goals. | Portfolio contains all five required artifacts. | All artifacts are of good quality and meet the stated criteria. Artifacts provide evidence that the student has achieved most unit goals. |
| Novice: 2 | Portfolio is somewhat organized. | Artifacts and reflections do not clearly demonstrate that the student has achieved most unit goals. | Portfolio contains four of the five required artifacts. | Some artifacts are of good quality and meet the stated criteria. Artifacts provide evidence that the student has achieved some unit goals. |
| Needs improvement: 1 | Portfolio is messy or unorganized or both. | Artifacts and reflections clearly demonstrate that the student has achieved few unit goals. | Portfolio contains fewer than four required artifacts. Portfolio lacks the reflective journal. | Artifacts are not of good quality and do not meet the stated criteria. Artifacts do not provide evidence that the student has achieved some unit goals. |

**Table 8.3**  Rubric for Project Culminating Assessment

| **Performance level** | **Performance criteria** | | |
|---|---|---|---|
| | **Group effort** | **Video content** | **Video quality** |
| Proficient: 4 | Everyone in the group had an assignment in producing the video. All group members completed their assignments. Group members worked well together. They were positive, shared constructive feedback, and helped each other when needed. | The video is instructional and addresses all of the unit's essential questions. Skill and rules demonstrations are appropriate, accurate, and easily digested. The script text is appropriate and accurate. | Video length is appropriate. The video recording is of good quality. Video is edited to eliminate unnecessary footage. All transitions are smooth. Sound editing is of high quality. |
| Competent: 3 | Everyone in the group had an assignment in producing the video. All group members completed their assignments. Group members worked well together. They were positive, shared constructive feedback, and helped each other when needed. | The video is instructional and addresses all or most of the unit's essential questions. Skill and rules demonstrations are mostly appropriate, accurate, and easily digested. The script text is appropriate and accurate. | Video length is appropriate. The video recording is of good quality. Some unnecessary footage was not eliminated. Most transitions are smooth. Sound editing is good. |

*(continued)*

Table 8.3 *(continued)*

| Performance level | Performance criteria | | |
|---|---|---|---|
| | **Group effort** | **Video content** | **Video quality** |
| Novice: 2 | Everyone in the group had an assignment in producing the video. Most group members completed their assignments. Group members worked separately rather than collaboratively. | The video is instructional and addresses some of the unit's essential questions. Skill and rules demonstrations are sometimes not appropriate, accurate, and easily understood by the audience. | Video is too long or too short. The video recording is not always of good quality. Some unnecessary footage was not eliminated. Some transitions are not smooth. Sound editing is good. |
| Needs improvement: 1 | Everyone in the group had an assignment in producing the video. More than one group member did not complete his or her assignment. Group members did not work well together. | The video is somewhat instructional. Many of the unit's essential questions are not addressed. Skill and rules demonstrations are not appropriate or accurate. | Video is too long or too short. The video recording is not always of good quality. Much unnecessary footage was not eliminated. Most transitions are not smooth. Sound editing needs improvement. |

## ESSENTIAL KNOWLEDGE, SKILLS, AND ABILITIES

Once the teacher has written the culminating performance or product, the next step in the standards-based, five-step planning model is to clearly identify the knowledge, skills, abilities, and demonstrators that students must learn in order to successfully complete the culminating performance or product. At this point, the teacher must ask the following question: "What do my students need to know, understand, and be able to do to successfully in order to complete the final assessment, demonstrate that they have reached the unit goals, and establish their progress toward the targeted standards?"

In our sample tennis unit, the teacher performed a task analysis to clearly identify what students must know, understand, and apply about tennis in order to successfully play in the class tournament and continue to play tennis beyond the physical education class. The essential knowledge for the tennis unit is presented in figure 8.7. In addition, through analysis of the game of tennis, the teacher identified skills and abilities that students must learn and apply in order to succeed. It is unlikely that physical education teachers can complete this task without referring to helpful resources, and in this

case the book *Tennis: Steps to Success* (Brown 2004) was a very useful resource. We strongly recommend that teachers consult experts and other resources when completing this step and the next one. The essential skills, abilities, and demonstrators identified by the teacher for the tennis unit are presented in figure 8.8.

The heart of the standards-based, five-step planning process (i.e., the staircase planning model) lies, then, in identifying essential skills, abilities, and demonstrators and in developing the instructional, learning, and assessment tasks. These items represent the stairs that students climb in order to reach targeted standards and goals and achieve a higher level of performance.

Once the teacher has identified the essential knowledge, skills, and abilities, he or she then uses this information to develop a progression or sequence of integrated instructional and assessment activities. Students participate in this sequence of learning and assessment activities to learn, practice, improve, and apply the knowledge and skills they will need in order to accomplish the culminating assessments. These learning and assessment activities help students move to the next step in their climb toward achieving the targeted goals and standards.

## Essential Knowledge for a Tennis Unit

- Names, functions, and locations of lines and areas in the singles and doubles tennis courts
- Rules and procedures for playing singles and doubles tennis
- Scoring systems used in tennis: traditional, no-ad, and tiebreaker
- Rules of etiquette
- Singles strategies for ground stroke, serve, volley, and lob
- Doubles play strategies: up-and-back, side-by-side
- Critical performance elements and learning cues for forehand drive, backhand drive, forehand volley, backhand volley, serve, and lob
- How to perform appropriate combinations of the identified skills
- How to place the ball in the opponent's court in various situations
- Principles of biomechanics that apply to efficient and effective skill performance (e.g., leverage, summation of forces, balance, ball spin)
- Benefits that can be derived from playing tennis regularly

**Figure 8.7** When designing a unit, the teacher identifies essential knowledge that students must possess in order to answer essential questions, complete the culminating assessments, and achieve targeted goals and standards.

## Essential Skills and Abilities for a Tennis Unit

1. Beginning in and always returning to the ready position (i.e., "home")
2. The Eastern forehand and backhand grips and the continental grip for the serve
3. Court footwork (ready position, home court, shuffle steps, crossover, split stop)
4. Forehand drive and backhand drive
   - Reverse pivot to create space between player and ball
   - Moving forward, backward, to the side to return the ball
   - Placement of ball by hitting deep to opponent's baseline, both crosscourt and down the line, or shallow to the forecourt
   - Receiving and returning an opponent's serve with a forehand or backhand
   - Placing the ball in open space on the court—moving the opponent out of position or balance
5. Forehand and backhand volleys
   - Hitting an approach stroke to safely go to the net
   - Hitting a volley to the opponent's court and away from the opponent.
   - Moving to the right or left to return a shot with a volley
   - Placing the volley to the outside baseline corners and the outside service corners
   - Hitting a passing shot and an approach stroke
6. Overhand serve
   - The punch serve
   - Consistent toss
   - Flat serve (Eastern forehand grip)
   - Spin serve (continental grip)
   - Placement of serve within opponent's service court on first or second attempt
   - Hitting a hard, fast second serve
   - Hitting serves into the back corners of the opponent's service court

*(continued)*

**Figure 8.8** The skills and abilities identified here are essential for students to learn and apply in order to complete the culminating assessment and reach unit goals and standards.

7. The lob: forehand and backhand
- Offensive lob (low, deep trajectory)
- Defensive lob (high, deep trajectory)
- Moving to hit forehand and backhand lobs
- How to effectively return a lob shot from an opponent
- Using the lob at the correct time
- Accurate placement of the lob

8. Stroke combinations
- Serve, serve-receive, return
- Approach, net position, return, volley
- Volley, lob
- Forehand and backhand; crosscourt and down the line
- Sustained rally with partner

9. Court strategies (singles and doubles)
- Returning to home base and ready position
- Making opponent move to get to the ball
- Up-and-back
- Side-by-side

**Figure 8.8** *(continued)*

# PROGRESSIVE LEARNING ACTIVITIES AND FORMATIVE ASSESSMENTS

In this section of the planning process, the teacher identifies and designs activities that engage students with the content in ways that encourage cognitive and psychomotor learning. These learning and practice activities should eventually lead students to achieve the broad targeted standards and more specific unit goals. This achievement will be demonstrated in each student's level of performance on the culminating assessment; therefore, learning activities should relate directly to unit goals. They should provide students with experiences that allow them to learn the identified essential knowledge and skills necessary to do the culminating performance or complete the culminating product successfully. In other words, students need the right experiences in order to demonstrate achievement of targeted standards. You can integrate a variety of performance-based assessments with learning and practice activities throughout the unit so that students receive feedback on their progress. This process also provides information about the appropriateness of the instruction to the teacher.

Because the assessments are integrated with the learning and practice activities throughout the unit, this practice is referred to as continuous assessment. The progression of instructional and assessment activities should include and extend from the initial practice of a skill, in which the focus is to learn and ultimately demonstrate the critical performance elements (also referred to as learning cues). The progression of learning activities involves the extension, refinement, and application tasks (Rink 2006) in which skills are performed in controlled situations that model the ways in which they are performed in game-play situations (e.g., a tennis match) or performance activities (e.g., gymnastics). Here are a few examples of extension tasks:

- Moving forward to hit a forehand drive across the net to the opponent
- Returning an opponent's hit with a backhand drive (crosscourt or down the sideline) to a strategically desirable area of the court

- Putting skills together in combinations that are required in game-play situations (e.g., hitting a good approach stroke to move the opponent out of position so that the player can move to the net and volley the next return to put the opponent at a disadvantage)

Each activity should help students develop their ability to select and perform strategically correct skills and skill combinations in a variety of situations that they are likely to encounter during game play or activity performance. Both learning and assessment activities are designed to systematically move students toward mastery of the unit goal—in this case, playing the game of tennis. The assessments, which are integrated with the learning tasks, should provide continuous feedback to students about their progress. They should also allow the teacher to make informed decisions about subsequent instruction and learning tasks. Table 8.4 presents a progression of learning activities and **integrated assessment tasks** for the unit of instruction on beginning tennis for a high school tennis unit of instruction.

**Table 8.4**    Learning Activities and Continuous Performance-Based Assessment for a Tennis Unit

| Forehand drive (FHD) | |
|---|---|
| **Instructional and learning activities** | **Assessment tasks** |
| 1. Observe as the teacher performs the FHD on the court by returning a ball to a hitter across the net 5 times (following instruction in which critical performance cues are identified and students perform cues without a ball while mirroring the teacher). | 1. Use the FHD checklist handed out in class to identify cues performed by the teacher. (This helps students become familiar with the checklist and the observation of cues.) |
| 2. Standing 15 feet (4.6 meters) from the fence, drop and hit the ball with the FHD to the fence 15 times. | 2. Peer observation assessment: Partner observes performance while focusing on the Cues Performance Evaluation (CPE) and uses the FHD checklist or shares the checklist with partner. |
| 3. Partner-tossed FHD on court: From baseline area, student hits partner-tossed ball with FHD so that the ball lands in the singles court 8 of 10 times. Repeat for 4 days as a warm-up. | 3. (a) Repeat peer observation using FHD checklist. (b) Use practice record form to note number of accurate hits and chart progress. |
| 4. Partner-hit FHD on court: Same as item 3 except partner increases speed of hits so that hitter must react to the ball more quickly. Criteria: 8 of 10 times; complete 4 times. | 4. (a) Use practice record form to note number of accurate hits and chart progress. (b) Use peer observation to check performance cues during at least one trial. (c) Conduct self-evaluation based on data from previous assessments and write a paragraph describing FHD progress and strategies for improvement. |
| 5. Partner-tossed FHD with movement to ball: With performer at center baseline, partner tosses ball to right and left of center so that performer must shuffle or cross over to hit ball. Criteria: 8 of 10 times; complete 4 times. Then increase speed of hits and use same criteria. | 5. Use practice record form to note successful hits and chart progress. |
| 6. Performer-tossed or performer-hit FHD with forward and backward movement: With performer at center baseline, partner tosses or hits ball so that performer must shuffle back behind baseline to hit the ball or run forward to hit the ball. Criteria: 8 out of 10 times; complete 4 times. | 6. Use practice record form to note successful hits and chart progress. |

*(continued)*

Table 8.4 *(continued)*

| Forehand drive (FHD) | |
|---|---|
| **Instructional and learning activities** | **Assessment tasks** |
| 7. Reverse pivot to hit FHD: With hitter at center baseline, partner tosses or hits ball close to hitter, who must use reverse pivot to hit FHD so that ball lands in opponent's singles court. Criteria: 8 out of 10 times; complete 4 times. | 7. Use practice record form to note successful hits and chart progress. |
| 8. Placing the ball by hitting FHD crosscourt: From center baseline, return a partner-tossed or partner-hit ball so that it lands along the opponent's opposite sideline near the baseline. Criteria: 7 out of 10 times; complete 5 times. | 8. (a) Use practice record form to record successful hits and chart progress. (b) Complete hit chart. Mark a dot on the court chart in the area where each hit lands. (c) Conduct self-observation via video; use the FHD skill checklist. |
| 9. Placing the ball by hitting FHD down the sideline: From center baseline, return a tossed or hit ball so that it lands along the opponent's sideline near the baseline. Criteria: 7 out of 10 times; complete 5 times. | 9. (a) Use the practice record form to note successful hits. (b) Complete a hit chart; mark a dot on the area of the court in which each ball lands. (c) Conduct self-assessment via video; use FHD skill checklist. |
| 10. Placing the ball by hitting deep to the baseline: From center baseline, apply topspin to return a tossed or hit ball so that it travels low and lands near opponent's baseline. Criteria: 7 out of 10 times; complete 5 times. | 10. (a) Use practice record form to note successful hits. (b) Complete hit trajectory chart. |
| 11. Placing the ball by hitting into the forecourt: From center baseline, return a tossed or hit ball so that it travels low and lands in the forecourt. Criteria: 7 out of 10 times; complete 5 times. | 11. (a) Use practice record form to note successful hits and chart progress. (b) Complete hit trajectory chart. |
| 12. FHD rally with partner: Use the FHD to hit the ball back and forth with a partner. Move as needed to hit the ball back. Hit the ball crosscourt to a right-handed hitter and down the line to a left-handed hitter. | 12. (a) Count the number of times you and partner hit back and forth for 4 or more shots; record your longest rally. (b) Have teacher or peer conduct observation using rally rubric and FHD checklist. |
| Backhand drive (BHD) | |
| **Instructional and learning activities** | **Assessment tasks** |
| 1. Observe as the teacher performs the BHD on the court by returning a ball to a hitter across the net (following instruction in which critical performance cues are identified and students performed cues without a ball while mirroring the teacher). | 1. Use the BHD checklist to identify cues performed by the teacher. (This helps students become familiar with the checklist and the observation of cues.) |
| 2. Standing 15 feet (4.6 meters) from the fence, drop and hit the ball with the BHD to the fence 15 times while focusing on the performance of the CPE. | 2. Peer observation assessment: Partner observes performance and uses BHD checklist/shares the checklist with a peer. |
| 3. Partner-tossed BHD on court: From baseline area, student hits partner-tossed ball with BHD so that the ball lands in the singles court 8 out of 10 times. Repeat for 4 days as a warm-up. | 3. (a) Repeat peer observation using BHD checklist. (b) Use the practice record form to note the number of accurate hits each time and chart progress. |

| Backhand drive (BHD) | |
|---|---|
| **Instructional and learning activities** | **Assessment tasks** |
| 4. Partner-hit BHD on court: Same as item 3 but partner increases speed of hits so that hitter must react to the ball more quickly. Criteria: 8 out of 10 times; complete 4 times. | 4. (a) Use the practice record form to note the number of accurate hits each time and chart progress. (b) Use peer observation to check performance cues during at least one trial. (c) Conduct self-evaluation of BHD progress based on data from previous assessments and write a paragraph describing BHD progress and strategies for improvement. |
| 5. Partner-tossed BHD with movement to ball: With performer at center baseline, partner tosses ball to right and left of center so that performer must shuffle or cross over to hit ball. Criteria: 8 out of 10 times; complete 4 times. Then increase speed of hits and use same criteria. | 5. Use the practice record form to note successful hits and chart progress. |
| 6. Partner-tossed or partner-hit BHD with forward and backward movement: With performer at center baseline, partner tosses or hits ball so that performer must shuffle back behind baseline to hit the ball or run forward to hit the ball. Criteria: 8 out of 10 times; complete 4 times. | 6. Use the practice record form to note successful hits and chart progress. |
| 7. Reverse pivot to hit BHD: With hitter at center baseline, partner tosses or hits ball close to hitter, who must use reverse pivot to hit BHD so that ball lands in opponent's singles court. Criteria: 8 out of 10 times; complete 4 times. | 7. Use the practice record form to note successful hits and chart progress. |
| 8. Placing the ball by hitting the BHD crosscourt: From center baseline, return a partner-tossed or partner-hit ball so that it lands along opponent's opposite sideline near the baseline. Criteria: 7 out of 10 times; complete 5 times. | 8. (a) Use the practice record form to note successful hits and chart progress. (b) Complete a hit trajectory chart. (c) Conduct a self-observation via video; use the BHD skill checklist. |
| 9. Placing the ball by hitting the BHD down the sideline: From center baseline, return a tossed or hit ball so that it lands along the opponent's sideline near the baseline. Criteria: 7 out of 10 times; complete 5 times. | 9. (a) Use the practice record form to note successful hits. (b) Complete a hit trajectory chart; mark a dot on the area of the court in which each ball lands. (c) Conduct a self-assessment video; use the FHD skill checklist. |
| 10. Placing the ball by hitting deep to the baseline: From center baseline, apply topspin to hit a tossed or hit ball so that it travels low and lands near opponent's baseline. Criteria: 7 out of 10 times; complete 5 times. | 10. (a) Use the practice record form to note successful hits. (b) Complete a hit trajectory chart. |
| 11. Placing the ball by hitting it into the forecourt: From center baseline, hit a tossed or hit ball so that it travels low and lands in the forecourt. Criteria: 7 out of 10 times; complete 5 times. | 11. (a) Use the practice record form to note successful hits. (b) Complete a hit trajectory chart. |
| 12. FHD and BHD rally with partner: Use the FHD and BHD to hit the ball back and forth with a partner. Move as needed to hit the ball back. | 12. (a) Count the number of times you rally for 4 shots or more. (b) Have teacher or peer conduct observation using rally rubric and FHD checklist. |

*(continued)*

Table 8.4 *(continued)*

| Serving and receiving | |
|---|---|
| **Instructional and learning activities** | **Assessment tasks** |
| 1. Observe as the teacher performs the punch serve on the court 5 times (following instruction in which the critical performance cues are identified and students perform cues without a ball while mirroring the teacher 8 times). | 1. (a) Teacher observes and provides feedback. (b) Teacher questions students for understanding of the cues. |
| 2. Toss practice: While standing behind the baseline, allow the ball to drop to the court inside the baseline in the direction of service court 20 times. Criteria: 10 of 20 attempts land in the target area. | 2. Partner observes toss and gives feedback. |
| 3. Overhand throw into the service court: Standing behind the service line, use an overhand action to throw the ball to the opposite service court (5 times to each court). Criterion: 8 of 10 times. Move back to the baseline and repeat. Criteria: 8 of 10 times. | 3. Record number of throws that land in correct service court. Repeat for partner. |
| 4. Serve to the fence. Using the punch serve, face the fence, stand inside baseline, and serve the ball to the fence. The ball should land on the fence between 3 and 4 feet (roughly a meter) from the ground. Perform 15 times. | 4. (a) Use skill practice and progress record (SPPR) to record number of accurate serves out of 15. (b) Partner observes and uses serve checklist form to assess serve. |
| 5. Serving on the court: Standing behind the service line, hit 5 good serves diagonally to opponent's service court (hit 5 to each service court). | 5. Student uses SPPR to record the number of accurate serves for each trial of 10. |
| 6. From a spot halfway between the service line and baseline, serve 5 times diagonally to each service court. If 70 percent of serves are good, move back to baseline and complete item 7; if not, repeat step 6 until you reach the criterion. | 6. Student uses SPPR to record the number of successful serves for each trial of 10. |
| 7. Serving from the baseline: From behind the baseline, stand in the appropriate area and stance and punch-serve 5 times diagonally to each of opponent's service courts. Repeat 5 times. If not at 70 percent, continue to practice each day. | 7. (a) Conduct peer observation using the checklist to evaluate serve form. Provide feedback to performer; focus on missing or weak cues. (b) Have partner take video of performer serving. Performer views video performance with instructor for feedback, then completes written self-evaluation. (c) Student uses the SPPR to record the number of successful serves for each trial. |
| 8. Placing the serve: Divide each service court into quarters (e.g., with chalk, tape, or cones). Serve the ball so that it lands deep in the back right or left corner 3 out of 10 times. Then serve to the front outside corners 3 out of 10 times. Repeat the process 4 times. | 8. Student uses the SPPR to record performances. |
| 9. Presentation of tips for receiving serve with FHD and BHD: Provide demonstration. | 9. Question students for understanding of things to do when receiving serve. |

| Serving and receiving | |
|---|---|
| **Instructional and learning activities** | **Assessment tasks** |
| 10. Serve and return practice: Working with two partners, serve from the baseline, alternating between right and left service courts. Receivers, positioned with one in each service area, return the serves. Serve 10 times to each court, then rotate positions. | 10. Student uses SPPR to record number of successful serves and aces. When receiving, student records the number of successful returns to server's singles court. |
| 11. Modified game of serve and return: With partner, play a game using only serve and return. Scoring: successful serve or return earns 1 point. Play to 15 points. | |

| Rules, etiquette, scoring, history, status, equipment | |
|---|---|
| **Instructional and learning activities** | **Assessment tasks** |
| 1. Teachers present areas and lines of the singles and doubles tennis courts. Students receive court handout and do self-test for homework. | 1. (a) Draw and label a complete tennis court. (b) Complete a written or oral quiz. |
| 2. Scoring for game, set, match: (a) traditional, (b) no-ad, (c) tiebreaker. Students receive handout and play demonstration games using each scoring system. | 2. (a) Complete scoring self-test. (b) Complete written quiz. |
| 3. Students play games with traditional scoring, no-ad scoring, and tiebreaker scoring. | 3. Instructor observes to give feedback of scoring. |
| 4. Introduce singles and doubles rules. Have students demonstrate the game in which rules are applied. Students receive handout. | 4. Complete rules self-test. |
| 5. Introduce unwritten rules (etiquette), honor system, rules of fair play. Students receive handout. | 5. (a) Demonstrate application of knowledge during modified games as teacher observes. (b) Play "You Be the Judge!": While viewing tennis videos, stop after a play and have students identify the next call and next procedure. |
| 6. Students use the Internet to find information regarding history, current status, selection of proper equipment, conditioning, and common tennis injuries and treatment. | 6. Each student is assigned a topic on which he or she writes a report to share with other students through a presentation or handout. |

| Forehand and backhand volleys and playing the net | |
|---|---|
| **Instructional and learning activities** | **Assessment tasks** |
| 1. Identify critical performance cues of the forehand volley (FHV). Teacher demonstrates on court. Students receive copy of FHV checklist to follow. | 1. Question students regarding cues to check for understanding. |
| 2. Students perform FHV without ball (mirroring teacher). Attempt 10 times while focusing on the critical performance cues. | 2. Teacher conducts observation and gives individual and group feedback (verbal and visual). |
| 3. Repeat items 1 and 2 for the backhand volley (BHV). Students receive copy of BHV checklist. | 3. Check for understanding through questions, teacher observation, and feedback. |

*(continued)*

Table 8.4 *(continued)*

| Forehand and backhand volleys and playing the net | |
|---|---|
| **Instructional and learning activities** | **Assessment tasks** |
| 4. Reacting to the ball: Standing 3 feet (about 1 meter) from center net, have partner toss ball to FH side. Reach out and catch the ball (using a blocking action typical of a volley). Do this 10 times. Repeat for the BHV. | 4. Peer gives feedback. |
| 5. Volley with back to the fence: Standing with heel of back foot against the fence, have partner toss ball to FH side. Volley the ball back to the partner with emphasis on short backswing and moving forward to hit the ball. Do this 10 times. Repeat for BHV. | 5. Perform peer observation and provide verbal feedback. |
| 6. Partner toss to FH: With hitter 3 feet (1 meter) from center net and partner near the service line across the net, have partner toss balls to FH side for hitter to return with FHV so that the ball lands anywhere in the opponent's singles court. Do this 10 times and complete 4 rounds. Gradually increase the speed with which the ball is tossed. Criteria: 8 of 10 times. | 6. (a) Perform peer observation using FH volley checklist and give feedback to performer. (b) Student uses SPPR to record number of successful FHVs. |
| 7. Partner toss to BHV: With hitter 3 feet (1 meter) from center net and partner near the service line across the net, have partner toss balls to BH side for hitter to return with BHV so that the ball lands anywhere in the opponent's singles court. Do this 10 times and complete 4 rounds. Gradually increase the speed with which the ball is tossed. Criteria: 8 of 10 times. | 7. (a) Perform peer observation using BH volley checklist and give feedback to performer. (b) Student uses SPPR to record number of successful BHVs. |
| 8. Partner toss to FHV and BHV: With hitter 3 feet (1 meter) from center net and partner at service court line, have partner toss unpredictably to FHV or BHV. Do total of 10 times to each side. | 8. Provide peer feedback using SPPR to record number of successful FHVs and BHVs. |
| 9. Partner hit to FHV and BHV: Partner, at baseline, hits balls to performer's FH and BH side unpredictably. Performer returns the ball with FHV or BHV to opponent's singles court. Partner mixes hits up so that performer must move to contact the ball. Do total of 10 times to each side. | 9. Students use SPPR to record number of successful FHVs and BHVs. |
| 10. Getting to the net: Introduce the sequence of approach stroke, run to net, split stop, ready position. Emphasize importance of going to net only after hitting strong approach stroke that puts opponent out of position or off balance. Teacher demonstrates on court a number of times until students understand the idea. | 10. (a) Check students for understanding through questioning. (b) Students complete exit slips. |
| 11. Hitting an approach stroke: Students rally from baseline; when opponent is moved out of position or caught off balance, player should run to net, use split stop, assume ready position, and return ball with FHV or BHV to opponent's court. Do 10 times on each side. | 11. Students use SPPR to record results. |

| Instructional and learning activities | Assessment tasks |
|---|---|
| 12. Hitting volleys at target areas: With hitter at net position, partner hits ground stroke to FH 10 times, then to BH 10 times. Hitter attempts to volley the ball first to the service court's outside corner, then to baseline outside corner, using the down-the-line or crosscourt shot. Do 10 times on FH side and 10 times on BH side. Criterion: Hit target 3 out of 10 times. | 12. Students use SPPR to mark areas of court where ball lands for each hit. |
| 13. Defending against the volley by hitting passing shots: With partner at the net, hit FH drive at him or her. Partner returns volley to FH or BH baseline corner, and you return a passing shot down the line to opponent's back corner baseline. Do 10 times each. | 13. Students use SPPR to record number of successful passing shots. |

| Offensive and defensive lobs | |
|---|---|
| **Instructional and learning activities** | **Assessment tasks** |
| 1. Introduce critical performance cues for the FH lob (FHL). Demonstrate on court and point out difference between offensive and defensive lobs (cues and placement). Students receive FHL and backhand lob (BHL) checklist. Review it with them. | 1. Question students regarding the critical performance cues for FH and BH lobs, as well as differences between offensive and defensive lobs. |
| 2. Students perform FHL without a ball, mirroring the instructor, 10 times. Repeat with BHL 10 times. | 2. Teacher observes and gives group and individual feedback (verbal and visual). |
| 3. Self-dropped ball for hitting FHLs and BHLs: Standing behind the baseline, drop the ball to FH side and hit a defensive lob to opponent's baseline area 10 times. Repeat with BHL 10 times. Criteria: 7 of 10 times; repeat 3 times. | 3. (a) Conduct peer observation using FHL and BHL checklist. Provide feedback. (b) Student records score on SPPR. |
| 4. Self-dropped ball for hitting FHLs and BHLs to target areas: Standing behind baseline, drop ball to FH side and hit offensive lobs to opponent's FH and BH baseline corners. Complete 10 times. Repeat for BHL 10 times. Repeat 4 times for each. Criteria: 6 of 10 times. | 4. (a) Conduct peer observation using FHL and BHL checklist. (b) Student records score on SPPR. |
| 5. Volley and lob with partner: With partner at net, stand at baseline, hit FH or BH drive to partner. Partner volleys to either FH or BH side. Return with offensive lob to opponent's FH or BH baseline area. Partner runs back to attempt return with defensive lob. Do 10 times to each side. | 5. Student records score on SPPR. |

*(continued)*

**Table 8.4** *(continued)*

| Playing the game of tennis: tournament and league play | |
|---|---|
| **Instructional and learning activities** | **Assessment tasks** |
| 1. Students view video of U.S. Open, Wimbledon, French Open, or NCAA tournament match or attend a varsity high school or community tennis tournament match. | 1. Using the game analysis form, analyze or assume the role of a sportswriter and write an article about the match. Include an interview of a player. |
| 2. Students are taken on a class field trip to observe league play, play on the indoor courts at the facility, and receive a lesson from the club professional. | 2. (a) Write a reaction paper to the field trip experience. (b) Take a tour of your neighborhood to locate tennis courts which you could use to play tennis with family members or friends. |
| 3. Students participate in the class round robin tournament as players (singles or doubles) and as tournament officials (i.e., tournament committee member, tournament director, official scorer, statistician, line judge, umpire, ball person, awards committee member, or athletic training staff). | 3. (a) Keep a record of your tournament matches and individual play stats. Use this information, to evaluate and analyze your individual or doubles performance and make decisions about what and how to practice. (b) As a member of the tournament committee, research and report to the committee on the duties for your assigned position. Write a reflection about your participation as an official in tournament. |

## Developing a Schedule

After identifying and developing learning and assessment activities, the teacher must create a timetable for implementing them. We recommend that this timetable be developed through the use of a block plan (see table 8.5), in which the teacher maps out the progression of learning and assessment activities for each day and week. The teacher identifies the order of the activities and the duration of each one and places them on the calendar. Thus specific learning and assessment activities are scheduled for each day; the schedule also helps teachers later, as they develop lesson plans for each class meeting. When developing the block plan, teachers should keep in mind that the schedule should be flexible, because students may need more time than planned to learn skills, practice strategies, and complete activities. Assessment forms for the learning and assessment activities are provided on the CD-ROM that accompanies this text.

## Depth Versus Breadth

It is important that teachers plan units of sufficient duration so that students have ample time to learn, practice, and apply skills and strategies that are necessary to successfully play or participate in the sport or activity. Traditionally, physical education teachers have taught units

that last only 2 to 3 weeks; as a result, students have had time only to review skills that they have not previously mastered. Rarely have they been introduced to more advanced skills and strategies, and thus they continue to play a game or participate in an activity for which they lack the skills and strategies needed to be successful. In contrast with this history, units should extend over a sufficient period of time—6 to 12 weeks, depending on the activity—so that students are given the necessary learning and practice opportunities to master the knowledge, skills, and strategies to become proficient or at least competent in the game or activity (Siedentop and Tannehill 2000). Students do not learn skills and strategies and how to apply them after one or two class periods. In order to learn and be successful participants, students must practice skills and strategies many times and in a variety of situations, all of which ultimately lead to gamelike applications. If the teacher takes time to plan learning and assessment activities that are developmentally appropriate, progressive, challenging, interesting, authentic, and fun, then students become enthusiastic and highly motivated to participate because they see that they are making progress toward unit goals. The teacher no longer hears the proverbial student whines of "Do we have to do more drills?" and "When are we going to play the game?"

**Table 8.5**  Block Plan for a Tennis Unit

| | Week 1 | | | | | | | | |
| Day 1 | | Day 2 | | Day 3 | | Day 4 | | Day 5 | |
| Learning activity | Assessment | Learning activity | Assessment | Learning activity | Assessment | Learning activity | Assessment | Learning activity | Assessment |
|---|---|---|---|---|---|---|---|---|---|
| FHD 1 | FHD 1 | Review FHD | | Review | | Review FHD | | Review and refine FHD. | |
| FHD 2 | FHD 2 | FHD 4 | 4a, b | FHD 4 | 4a, b, c | FHD 6 | 6 | FHD 5 | 5 |
| FHD 3 | FHD 3 | FHD 5 | 5 | FHD 5 | | FHD 7 | 7 | FHD 6 | 6 |
| FHD 4 | FHD 4 a, b, c | Introduce BHD | | FHD 6 | 6 | Review BHD | | FHD 7 | 7 |
| | | BHD 1 | 1 | Review BHD | | BHD 3 | 3 | Review and refine BHD. | |
| | | BHD 2 | 2 | BHD 1 | 2 | BHD 4 | 4a, b, c | BHD 4 | 4a, b, c |
| | | BHD 3 | 3 | BHD 2 | | BHD 5 | 5 | BHD 5 | |
| | | Quiz on tennis court markings | BHD 4 | BHD 3 | 3a, b | | | BHD 6 | 6 |
| | | | | BHD 4a, b, c | | | | BHD 7 | 7 |
| | | | | Exit slip on FHD cues | Exit slip on BHD cues | | | | |
| Introduce game of tennis 1 | | | | | | | | | |
| Tennis court markings 1a | | | | | | | | | |

(continued)

Table 8.5  (continued)

| Week 2 | | | | | | | |
|---|---|---|---|---|---|---|---|
| **Day 6** | | **Day 7** | | **Day 8** | | **Day 9** | **Day 10** |
| Learning activity | Assessment | Learning activity | Assessment | Learning activity | Assessment | Checkpoint assessment | Checkpoint assessment |
| Introduce the serve. | | Review the serve. | | **Review and refine serve.** | | Teacher evaluates student performance on FHD. | Teacher evaluates student performance on BHD. |
| Serve/receive (S/R) 1 | 1a, b | S/R 1 | 1a | S/R 7 | 7a, b, c | FHD 5 and 6 | Use BHD skill checklist. |
| S/R 2 | 2 | S/R 2 | 2 | S/R 9 | 9 | Use FHD skill checklist. | Students submit records of performance and self-evaluation on the BHD. |
| S/R 3 | 3 | S/R 4 | 4a, b | S/R 10 | 10 | Students submit records of performance and self-evaluation on the FHD. | Review and refine serving and receiving. |
| S/R 4 | 4a | S/R 6 | 6 | **Introduce placing the ball-FHD.** | | Review serving and receiving. | S/R 7 7 |
| S/R 5 | 5 | S/R 7 | 7a | FHD 8 | 8a, b | S/R 7 7a, b, c | S/R 10 10 |
| **Review and refine FHD and BHD.** | | **Review and refine FHD and BHD.** | | FHD 9 | 9a, b | S/R 10 10 | |
| FHD 6 | 6 | FHD 5 | 5 | **Review moving to hit the ball-BHD.** | | | |
| FHD 7 | 7 | FHD 6 | 6 | BHD 5 | 5 | | |
| BHD 5 | 5 | FHD 7 | 7 | BHD 6 | 6 | | |
| BHD 6 | 6 | BHD 6 | 6 | BHD 7 | 7 | | |
| | | BHD 7 | 7 | | | | |

| | | | Week 3 | | | | | | |
|---|---|---|---|---|---|---|---|---|---|
| **Day 11** | | **Day 12** | | **Day 13** | | **Day 14** | | **Day 15** | |
| Learning activity | Assessment | Learning activity | Assessment | Learning activity | Assessment | Learning activity | Assessment | Learning activity | Assessment |
| **Introduce tennis rules (singles).** | | Placing the serve | | Introduce FH and BH volleys. | | **Review placing the ball.** | | **Review and extend volley.** | |
| Tennis (T) 4 | 4 | S/R 8 | 8 | FHV 1 | 1 | FHD and BHD 8 | 8a, b | FHV and BHV 9 | 9 |
| **Review placing the ball (FHD).** | | Modified game | | FHV 2 | 2 | FHD and BHD 9 | 9a, b | **Introduce the approach stroke.** | |
| FHD 8 | 8a, b | S/R 11 | | FHV 3 | 3 | **Review FH and BH volleys.** | | FHV and BHV 10 | 10a, b |
| FHD 9 | 9a, b | **Tennis rules (singles) quiz** | | FHV and BHV 4 | 4 | FHV and BHV 6 | 6a, b | FHV and BHV 11 | 11 |
| **Introduce placing the ball (BHD).** | | **Introduce tennis doubles rules and rules of etiquette.** | | FHV and BHV 5 | 5 | FHV and BHV 7 | 7a, b | Modified game | |
| BHD 8 | 8a, b | T 4, 5 | | FHV 6 | 6a, b | FHV and BHV 8 | 8 | S/R 11 | |
| BHD 9 | 9a, b | | | BHV 7 | 7a, b | **Review and practice serve.** | | **Quiz on tennis rules** | |
| | | | | Review placing the ball. | | S/R 8 | 8 | | |
| | | | | FHD and BHD 8a, b, c and 9a, b, c | | Tennis rules | 5a, b | | |

*(continued)*

Table 8.5 (continued)

| | | Week 4 | | | | | | | |
|---|---|---|---|---|---|---|---|---|---|
| Day 16 | | Day 17 | | Day 18 | | Day 19 | | Day 20 | |
| Learning activity | Assessment | Learning activity | Assessment | Learning activity | Assessment | Checkpoint assessment | Assessment | Learning activity | Assessment |
| **Review and refine serving.** | | FHD and BHD rally | | **Review approach and volley.** | | Teacher observes and evaluates student performance on serve and receiving. | | **Introduce offensive and defensive lobs.** | |
| S/R 10 | 10 | FHD and BHD 12 | 12a, b | FHV and BHV 12 | 12 | Use skill observation checklist. | | FHL 1 | 1 |
| **Review and refine placing the ball.** | | **Introduce scoring in tennis.** | | FHV and BHV 11 | 11 | Practice approach, volley, and passing shots. | | BHL 1 | 1 |
| FHD 8 and BHD 8 | 8a, b, c | T 2 | 2a | Hitting passing shots | | FHV and BHV 12 12 | | FHL and BHL 2 | 2 |
| FHD 9 and BHD 9 | 9a, b, c | **Play games using various scoring systems.** | | FHV and BHV 13 | 13 | FHV and BHV 11 11 | | FHL and BHL 3 | 3a, b |
| FHD 10 and BHD 10 | 10a, b | Practice serving. | | **Play games with tiebreaker scoring.** | | FHV and BHV 13 13 | | FHL and BHL 4 | 4a, b |
| FHD 11 and BHD 11 | 11a, b | S/R 8 | 8 | | | Assignment T6 due | | **Playing the game of tennis.** | |
| Review and refine approach and volley. | | S/R 10 | 10 | **Quiz on tennis scoring systems** | | Assignment 6 due | | Assignment 1 | |
| FHV and BHV 9 | 9 | | | | | | | | |
| FHV and BHV 11 | 11 | Assignment: T 6 | | | | | | | |

| Week 5 | | | | | | | | | |
| --- | --- | --- | --- | --- | --- | --- | --- | --- | --- |
| Day 21 | | Day 22 | | Day 23 | | Day 24 | | Day 25 | |
| Learning activity | Assessment | Learning activity | Assessment | Learning activity | Assessment | Learning activity | Assessment | Learning activity | Assessment |
| Practice FHV and BHV. | | Practice skills as needed. | | Playing the game of tennis. | | Playing the game of tennis. | | Playing the game of tennis. | |
| FHV and BHV | 12 | Field trip to indoor tennis club. | 2a, b | | | Doubles partners practice skills as needed. | 3a | Doubles partners practice skills as needed. | |
| FHV and BHV | 11 | Checkpoint assessment: | | | | Select tournament committees and assign committee duties. | | Play set of doubles tennis. | |
| Review FHL and BHL. | | Teacher evaluates FHV and BHV using skill observation check sheet. | | | | Committees work together to plan doubles/singles class tournament. | | Committees work on planning class tournament. | |
| FHL and BHL 3a, b | 3 | Students submit practice performance record for FHV and BHV. | | | | | | Assessment 3a, b | |
| FHL and BHL 4a, b | 4 | | | | | | | | |
| FHL and BHL 5 | 5 | Playing the game of tennis. | | | | | | Assessment 2a, b due | |
| Play a set of tennis doubles. | | Assignment 1 due | | | | | | | |

(continued)

Table 8.5 (continued)

| | | Week 6 | | | | | | | |
|---|---|---|---|---|---|---|---|---|---|
| Day 26 | | Day 27 | | Day 28 | | Day 29 | | Day 30 | |
| Learning activity | Assessment | Learning activity | Assessment | Learning activity | Assessment | Learning activity | Assessment | Learning activity | Assessment |
| Committees organize and conduct class tennis tournament. | | Committee organizes and conducts tennis tournament. | | Same as day 27 | | Same as day 27 | | Same as day 27 | |
| Class doubles and singles tournament begins. | | Class doubles and singles tournament continues. | | | | | | Class tournament completed | |
| Assessment 3a, b | | Assessment 3a, b | | | | | | Winners receive awards. | |
| Students not playing take stats. | | Students not playing take stats. | | | | | | Students submit assessment 3a, b on Monday. | |
| Teacher evaluates students during game play using the game-play rubric. | | Teacher evaluates students during game play using the game-play rubric. | | | | | | | |
| Assessment 2a, b (playing the game of tennis) due | | | | | | | | | |

# CRITICAL RESOURCES

Finally, the teacher must identify, secure, and schedule the necessary resources to enable students to engage in the planned activities and educational experiences. Critical resources can include many items. Here are a few examples:

- Adequate facilities
- Sufficient equipment for all students
- Arrangements for off-campus community facility or outsourcing (e.g., having outside groups or instructors with necessary expertise and equipment, which the teacher might not have, in order to deliver the content for the unit)
- Invitations for guest experts to teach, lecture, or demonstrate
- Print or multimedia materials to support learning and assessment
- Technology to support the learning process
- Reference materials to assist the teacher in planning and teaching

Critical resources should be secured and scheduled before the beginning of the unit to avoid the disruption that occurs when a needed resource turns out to be unavailable. See figure 8.9 for the critical resources needed in the sample tennis unit.

# PLANNING LESSONS FROM THE UNIT PLAN

Once you have developed a detailed unit plan and block plan, the next step is to plan individual daily lessons. Lesson planning is much easier once you have developed a detailed unit plan to serve as a road map for guiding students toward achievement of targeted standards and unit goals. Lesson plans are the vehicles by means of which you implement the unit plan and move students along the mapped route to their destination. Lesson plans can be designed in many formats, but they all must include certain components in order to be effective (see figure 8.10 for a sample lesson plan):

- Identification of targeted standards, unit goals, and specific lesson objectives directly related to the standards and unit goals
- Statement of what students accomplished in previous lesson(s)

## Critical Resources for a Tennis Unit

### Equipment
- 26 tennis rackets, depending on how many students are in the class
- 3 balls per student

### Facility
6 high school tennis courts and one-half of the gym for class on bad weather, depending on how many students there are or how many courts are available days.

### Book
*Tennis: Steps to Success, Third Edition* by Jim Brown (Champaign, IL: Human Kinetics, 2004).

### Field Trip Arrangements
Community tennis courts and indoor racket club (tennis professionals work with students for one class period at each site)

### Tennis-Related Web Sites
www.tennisone.com
www.successfuldoubles.com
www.professionaltennisinstruction.com

**Figure 8.9**  In this section of planning, the teacher identifies all materials, equipment, facilities, and community resources that are essential to helping students accomplish the unit's identified goals.

- Identification of learning activities and statement of how students will be organized in order to maximize practice and learning opportunities
- Identification of assessments that will give feedback to students and the teacher in order to determine whether students have achieved lesson objectives
- Reflection on the lesson and next steps

## Targeted Standards, Unit Goals, and Lesson Objectives

When writing lesson objectives, the teacher must first identify which targeted standards and unit goals this lesson will serve. Lesson objectives are then written in behavioral terms, and they should include the task or behavior that students should demonstrate, the situation in which students will perform the task, and the **criteria** that must be met for the student to accomplish the lesson objective. If you include the task, situation, and criteria in each lesson objective, the lesson objective itself may serve as a lesson assessment. For example:

*From the baseline area, the student will use a forehand drive to return a ball, hit by his or her partner, to the opponent's baseline area 7 out of 10 times.*

## Identifying What Students Learned in Previous Lessons

This component should simply be a statement indicating what students have or have not learned in previous lessons. The teacher should base the lesson plan on where students are in the learning process.

## Instructional and Learning Activities

Instructional and learning activities are chosen from those identified in the unit block plan and may be modified based on students' level of success in previous lessons. Lesson planning must also take into account the amount of time available for the class, the class space, and the availability of equipment. Activities for instruction, learning, and practice should include both a review of content from previous lesson(s) and new content that builds on the previous content.

When the teacher identifies new instructional and learning content and activities in this section, he or she should also identify how students will be organized in the available space and with the available equipment in order to maximize students' opportunities to practice and learn the content. In most cases, activities will be more efficient if you organize students in pairs, small practice groups, and small-sided teams (e.g., 2v2, 3v3, 4v4) rather than lines and large-group games.

Instructional and learning or practice activities should relate directly to lesson objectives. Activities should be arranged progressively so that students continue to learn knowledge and skills that ultimately enable them to demon-

strate the lesson objectives by the end of the class period. If students have difficulty achieving objectives and mastering content, then the teacher will need to adjust the lesson plan during the class period.

## Learning Assessments

Although assessments are separated from instructional and learning activities in this discussion, they should generally be embedded in learning activities so that students and the teacher get timely feedback about students' learning and performance. To emphasize this point, as we developed the sample unit plan for tennis, we included the assessment activities with the learning activities. With this approach, the teacher simply looks at the learning and assessment activities included in the unit plan to find appropriate assessment activities embedded in the progressive learning activities (the block plan identifies the progressive activities planned for each day of the unit).

## Lesson Reflection

The final section of the lesson plan is completed through observation of students' behavior during and at the conclusion of the lesson. The teacher observes students while they practice and complete assessment activities and also looks at assessment forms to determine whether students were successful and whether lesson objectives have been achieved.

As part of the reflection, the teacher may identify organizational, managerial, instructional, and contextual changes that should be made in order to improve the lesson. The reflection also includes recommendations for the next lesson, and the teacher may identify students who are having problems so that he or she can focus on helping them in the next lesson. In short, sound reflections are critical to good teaching.

It is crucial in the standards-based planning process to maintain a close relationship between the unit plan and the lesson plans that deliver the unit plan to students. Figure 8.10 presents a lesson plan developed from the sample tennis unit. This sample lesson plan establishes a clear relationship between standards, unit plan, and lesson plan, and it includes all of the lesson plan components discussed here.

Teacher _____ Class _____ Date _____

Number of students_____ Class time _____ Day of unit _____

## Targeted Standards

1. Demonstrates competency in motor skills and movement patterns needed to perform a variety of physical activities.

## Unit Goals

1. The student demonstrates knowledge of and the ability to perform the critical performance elements using the overhand serve, forehand drive stroke, and backhand drive stroke.
2. The student works to improve skills through participation in practice strategies, analyzing, and giving feedback to self and to partner.

## Lesson Objectives

1. The student will serve the ball from the baseline to opponent's service court (3 of 5 times to each court).
2. The student will receive serves, at a slow speed, from an opponent from behind both service lines, using a forehand and backhand drive as appropriate (return 50% of serves from both the right and left court).
3. The student will be able to move to the ball (forward, to the side) and away from the ball (reverse pivot) and return the ball with a backhand drive (8 out of 10 times).

## What Students Learned and Practiced in Previous Lessons

Students have been introduced to and have practiced the forehand and backhand drive strokes and the punch serve on the court.

| Content, instruction, and learning activity | Organization | Assessment |
|---|---|---|
| Review and refine the punch serve. Reinforce with demonstration and review of performance cues:<br>• Forward-and-back stance.<br>• Racket back between shoulder blades.<br>• Elbow points up.<br>• Lift hand, toss ball.<br>• Extend arm and racket.<br>• Contact ball at highest point, in front of forward foot.<br>• Follow through. | Students spread out behind the baseline of three courts. Teacher demonstrates. Students demonstrate and call out cues without a ball. | Teacher observes and checks for understanding. Teacher asks students to repeat cues while performing the serve without a ball and observes performance. |
| **Serving activity 7: Serving from baseline to opponent's court.** From behind baseline, stand in appropriate area, with correct stance. Serve diagonally to each of the opponent's courts. Repeat 5 times on each side; 7 out of 10 land in service court area. | Four students per court: 2 serving and 2 retrieving and returning balls to server. | **7a:** Peer observation: Give feedback to server on performance cues.<br>**7c:** Student records the number of good serves to each court on the SPPR form. |

*(continued)*

**Figure 8.10** Sample lesson plan for the tennis unit of instruction. This lesson was developed from the eighth day of the unit block plan.

| Content, instruction, and learning activity | Organization | Assessment |
|---|---|---|
| **Serving activity 9: Receiving the serve.** Teacher provides tips on how to receive the serve to the forehand and backhand sides, then demonstrates on the court.<br>• Ready position, racket in middle.<br>• Stand in middle and well behind the service court line.<br>• Watch the server and the ball.<br>• Move quickly into forehand or backhand position behind and before the ball hits the court.<br>• Get the racket back quickly.<br>• Return ball to opponent's court and return to home position, ready for the next hit. | Students spread out behind sideline on court for demonstration. | Teacher checks for understanding by asking the students to repeat the receiving tips. |
| **Serve and return practice 9.** In groups of 4, servers on one side serve alternating between serving to right and left courts. One receiver behind each service court returns serve to server 10 times to each court. Rotate positions. | Four students per court (2 per side). One side is servers, the other side is receivers. Servers alternate turns at serving. | Using the SPPR, students record number of successful serves and aces. When receiving, students record number of successful service returns. |
| **Review and practice backhand drive.** Teacher models and leads students through the performance of the backhand drive without ball. Students yell out the performance cues while performing:<br>• Ready position.<br>• Pivot, step.<br>• Step across and forward toward ball.<br>• Racket across and back.<br>• Shift weight forward.<br>• Swing, lead with racket head.<br>• Swing through the ball.<br>• Follow through.<br>• Back to home and ready position. | Students spread out behind baseline of three courts. Teacher demonstrates. Students demonstrate and call out cues without a ball. | Teacher observes and checks for understanding by asking students to repeat cues while performing the serve without a ball. |

**Figure 8.10** *(continued)*

| Content, instruction, and learning activity | Organization | Assessment |
|---|---|---|
| **5. Partner toss, backhand drive, move to ball.** Performer at baseline tosses ball to right and left of center so that performer must shuffle or cross over to hit ball 8 of 10 times. Complete 2 times, then increase speed of ball and complete 2 times. Same criteria. | Four students per court: 2 tossers, 2 hitters; 1 set on each half of court. | Each student records number of successful hits on Practice Record Form. |
| **6. Performer toss, hit, backhand drive, move.** Forward and backward. Tosser tosses ball over net to backhand side so that performer must shuffle back to behind the baseline to hit the ball 7 of 10 times. Repeat two times. Repeat with tosser tossing the ball so that the performer has to move forward to hit the backhand drive 7 of 10 times. Repeat 2 times. | Same as previous. | Each student records number of successful hits on Practice Record Form. |
| Review and check for understanding. Ask students to demonstrate, without the ball, performance cues for these skills:<br>• Punch serve<br>• Moving to hit a backhand drive<br>Ask students to repeat the strategies for returning serves. | | |

## Lesson Reflection

Students did well on the service drills today. Many are ready to move from the punch serve to the full overhand serve. Many students had some difficulty with moving to the right (and left) to hit the backhand drive. The biggest problem seems to be getting the racket back quickly so that they can get a full swing. I will review and practice the backhand and moving to the side to hit the ball at the beginning of the next class. Also, next class I will introduce placing the ball by hitting cross-court and down the line with the forehand drive.

Jimmy, Karen, Jerome, and Keesha either need to be split into different groups or need to be on the middle court so that I can frequently be near them. They were off task many times when I looked their way today.

**Figure 8.10** *(continued)*

## CONCLUSION

Planning is absolutely essential if you want to successfully implement continuous performance-based assessment and integrate assessment tasks with learning activities. When teachers do not plan, they often find that the unit comes to an end before they have addressed student assessment, and this is why we tend to see more summative assessment than formative assessment in middle and secondary physical education programs. To accomplish the necessary planning for continuous performance-based assessment, we recommend that teachers follow the standards-based, five-step planning model presented in this chapter. We have taken you through the planning process and provided you with a sample unit plan for beginning tennis for 10th graders. You could implement this unit plan in your classes or use it as a model for developing other activity unit plans in which continuous performance-based assessment is an integral part of student learning experiences.

In this model of curriculum development, you design from the top of the stairs, where targeted standards and goals are identified as the students' destination, down to the learning and assessment activities that help students get there. You then deliver instruction upward, from the learning and assessment activities at the bottom of the steps to the targeted standards and goals at the top. During the unit, you continue to help students move up the steps as they work to develop the necessary knowledge and skills to reach the culminating experience. At that point, they demonstrate their achievement of those targeted standards. When students begin at the bottom of the steps and participate in learning and assessment activities that provide them with feedback about their learning, they have an opportunity to gradually move up the steps and achieve the targeted goals and standards at the top of the stairs.

# Implementing Continuous Performance-Based Assessment

This section of the book provides additional examples of performance-based assessment. It also discusses ways to implement an effective grading system, which frequently poses one of the biggest challenges for teachers. The book concludes, in chapter 12, with a variety of hints and suggestions to help you begin incorporating performance-based assessment into your physical education curriculum.

# Continuous Performance-Based Assessment in Team Sports

*Understanding is revealed in performance. Understanding is revealed as transferability of core ideas, knowledge, and skill, on challenging tasks in a variety of contexts. Thus assessment for understanding must be grounded in authentic performance-based tasks (Wiggins & McTighe 2005, 153).*

As indicated in chapter 8, teachers must plan concertedly if they wish to effectively assess students' performance continually throughout a unit of instruction so that students can be aware of their progress and the teacher can take an informed approach to future instruction. This chapter provides you with a sample unit plan for a team sport—specifically, middle school soccer (for sixth graders). We prepared and wrote this unit using the five-step, standards-based planning model presented in chapter 8. For this soccer unit plan, we provide the following:

- Unit major focus
- Central organizer
- Targeted standards and goals
- Essential questions
- Culminating assessment and rubric
- Essential knowledge, skills, and abilities
- Learning activities and continuous performance-based assessments
- Critical resources
- Discussion of how to use the student soccer portfolio

The presentation of this unit sample is geared to show you the continuous nature of performance-based assessment and the ways in which assessment can be integrated throughout a unit and integrated with learning activities through systematic planning. This planning process also ensures alignment between learning activities, assessments, unit goals, and overall program goals. When instruction is thus aligned, the learning activities, content, and assessments should help students learn what they need to know and be able to do in order to achieve unit and program goals. The program goals identified for this unit are taken from those recommended in *Moving Into the Future: National Standards for Physical Education* (National Association for Sport and Physical Education 2004) for the sixth-grade level. Starting with these national standards helps the teacher identify appropriate goals and content for the middle grades. For each standard, the appropriate content and benchmarks are identified. In addition, *Soccer: Steps to Success* (Luxbacher 2005) was used as a resource in developing this instructional unit.

# MAJOR UNIT FOCUS

The major focus of the unit identifies a central organizer, targeted goals and standards, and essential questions that relate to the central organizer. These three items identify for the teacher and students what the unit is about, what students are to accomplish both broadly and specifically, why this unit is important to the students, and what questions they need to answer.

## Central Organizer

The central organizer is designed to catch students' attention, draw them into the content, and get them excited about learning and participating. It may involve a problem, theme, skill or set of skills, concept, issue, type of content, or question that is relevant to students. The teacher should share the central organizer with students and post it in a prominent place in the gym so that they are constantly reminded of it during the unit. To engage students even more intensively, a teacher might even ask students themselves to identify and write the central organizer for a unit. The central organizer for the soccer unit is presented in figure 9.1; it focuses the unit for students in a way that is relevant to their lives.

## Targeted Standards and Goals

To identify the broad goals that sixth graders should achieve through participating in the

soccer unit, we turned to the sixth-grade section of *Moving Into the Future: National Standards for Physical Education* (National Association for Sport and Physical Education 2004). Under each standard, we looked at recommended content and benchmarks for sixth graders, then selected those standards that we believed students could achieve by participating in the soccer unit. The relevant standards that we selected to guide our planning are reproduced in figure 9.2.

Teachers also identify more specific goals based on the particular unit and the local school context. These goals should relate directly to the broad goals or standards and to the central organizer. Figure 9.3 presents the specific unit goals we identified for the soccer unit, as well as the national standard(s) to which each goal relates.

## Essential Questions

The essential questions help students focus on and address the central organizer. They should be stated as if students were asking the questions themselves. As with the central organizer, share the essential questions with students by posting

---

### Central Organizer for a Soccer Unit

Soccer can be an enjoyable group activity in which to participate and make friends, whether it be in my school, my neighborhood, or my community. Being physically active by playing soccer regularly, I help to maintain and improve my heart strength and muscular endurance. To enjoy participating in soccer, I must be able to perform basic skills and strategies fairly well and know and follow the rules of the game. I do not necessarily have to be highly skilled to enjoy playing the game, but I do need to demonstrate reasonable competence in the skills and strategies. Therefore, I must practice them both alone and with others in order to improve. Learning skills and strategies takes time, many trials, and effort, but it can also be a lot of fun. Practicing these skills regularly can help fulfill the recommended daily requirement for physical activity.

**Figure 9.1** This central organizer establishes the theme around which the middle school soccer unit is designed.

## Relevant National Standards for a Soccer Unit

1. Demonstrates competency in motor skills and movement patterns needed to perform a variety of physical activities.

2. Demonstrates understanding of movement concepts, principles, strategies, and tactics as they apply to the learning and the performance of physical activities.

3. Participates regularly in physical activity.

5. Exhibits responsible personal and social behavior that respects self and others in physical activity settings.

6. Values physical activity for health, enjoyment, challenge, self-expression, or social interaction.

**Figure 9.2** The physical education standards, demonstrators, and benchmarks identified for this soccer unit are taken directly from the National Standards for Physical Education.

From NASPE, 2004, *Moving into the future: National standards for physical education,* 2nd ed. (Reston, VA: National Association for Sport and Physical Education).

them in the gym or providing them as a handout. These questions help guide students' learning and achievement of unit goals and standards. Figure 9.4 provides essential questions for the middle school soccer unit.

Soccer can be an enjoyable group activity.

## Goals for a Soccer Unit

1. In five-on-five modified soccer games, students demonstrate competence in performing the following basic skills: dribbling against an opponent; passing to a teammate against defenders; receiving and controlling the ball with the foot, thigh, and chest; shooting at the goal; and using the front and side tackles to take the ball away from an opponent. This goal relates to the first national standard for physical education (National Association for Sport and Physical Education 2004).

2. In five-on-five, modified soccer games, students demonstrate knowledge of and ability to use the basic, offensive off-the-ball strategy of creating space for a pass and the on-the-ball strategies of passing into open spaces, leading the passer, and, when in possession of the ball, putting one's body between the ball and the opponent. This goal relates to the second national standard for physical education (National Association for Sport and Physical Education 2004).

3. In five-on-five, modified soccer games, students demonstrate knowledge of and the ability to apply the basic defensive strategies of marking an opponent closely and moving to block the opponent's passing lanes. This goal relates to the second national standard for physical education (National Association for Sport and Physical Education 2004).

4. Students demonstrate effective practice strategies and the ability to work both independently and with a partner in order to complete assigned tasks. This goal relates to the second national standard for physical education (National Association for Sport and Physical Education 2004).

5. Students demonstrate the ability to work cooperatively in a group in order to accomplish assigned tasks and thus organize and conduct a successful five-on-five, modified soccer tournament within the class. This goal relates to the fifth national standard for physical education (National Association for Sport and Physical Education 2004).

*(continued)*

**Figure 9.3** Here are the specific goals that students are expected to achieve during the soccer unit; each unit goal is linked to one of the national standards for physical education (National Association for Sport and Physical Education 2004).

6. Students demonstrate the ability to find necessary information in order to solve problems that arise while they carry out assigned duties while organizing and conducting the class soccer tournament. This goal relates to the sixth national standards for physical education (National Association for Sport and Physical Education 2004).

7. Students practice soccer skills and play games outside of school and keep a log to provide evidence of their participation. This goal relates to the second, third, and seventh national standards for physical education (National Association for Sport and Physical Education 2004).

8. Students can analyze performance of skills by themselves and by other students and give feedback and suggestions for improvement. This goal relates to the first, second, and fifth national standards for physical education (National Association for Sport and Physical Education 2004).

9. Students can identify the benefits of participating in soccer and consider whether they are likely to continue participating in it into their adult years. This goal relates to the first and fifth national standards for physical education (National Association for Sport and Physical Education 2004).

10. Students can identify facilities and programs in their communities where they can participate in soccer if they so desire. This goal relates to the third national standard for physical education (National Association for Sport and Physical Education 2004).

11. Students can demonstrate their knowledge of the rules of soccer when participating in a five-on-five class tournament, and they can demonstrate the ability to modify rules of the game in order to make the game more developmentally appropriate and fun. This goal relates to the first, second, and sixth national standards for physical education (National Association for Sport and Physical Education 2004).

12. Students can demonstrate knowledge of how to improve soccer skill performance by designing a personal practice plan for themselves and their team. This goal relates to the first and second national standards for physical education (National Association for Sport and Physical Education 2004).

**Figure 9.3** *(continued)*

## Essential Questions for a Soccer Unit

1. Why and how can participating in soccer help me reach my daily recommended requirement for physical activity and stay active for life?
2. What offensive and defensive skills should I learn and become competent at performing in order to be successful and have fun playing soccer?
3. What offensive and defensive strategies do I need to learn and use in order to gain an advantage against my opponent in a soccer game?
4. What do I need to do in order to be a contributing member of a team and help the team reach its goals?
5. What rules of soccer are important to know and follow in order to make the game fun, safe, and fair for all?
6. What opportunities are available to me at school and in my community to help me continue to participate in soccer for fun, socializing, and exercise? How can I work this participation into my schedule?

**Figure 9.4** Students should be able to answer these questions at the end of the soccer unit. Developing essential questions during planning helps you focus on instruction and assessment.

# CULMINATING (SUMMATIVE) ASSESSMENT AND EVALUATION RUBRIC

This section provides a variety of authentic, performance-based assessment types, from which you can select one or possibly two to use as culminating assessments (see figures 9.5 and 9.6). In addition, all of the sample culminating performances and products could be modified for use in other team sport units of instruction.

# ESSENTIAL KNOWLEDGE, SKILLS, AND ABILITIES

Here, we identify the skills that students must learn in order to complete the culminating (summative) performance and achieve the unit goals and standards. This forecasting is accomplished through a task analysis of the selected sport or activity for the unit.

## Essential Knowledge

This section answers this question: "What knowledge must my students possess and apply in order to complete the culminating performance?" Figure 9.7 presents the knowledge that students need to know and apply for our sample soccer unit. The essential knowledge and skills serve as the teacher's guide for developing learning and assessment activities.

## Essential Skills and Abilities

Figure 9.8 presents the skills that students must be able to execute in the culminating performance in order to achieve the targeted unit goals and standards. Most culminating performances for a team sport require that students demonstrate the ability to perform skills in a game or modified game situation.

# PROGRESSIVE LEARNING ACTIVITIES AND FORMATIVE ASSESSMENTS

The learning and assessment activities that are listed for this unit in table 9.1 constitute a progression designed to help students learn, apply, and perform the necessary knowledge, skills, and strategies in increasingly complex situations. The progression provides students with experiences that prepare them to play in a soccer game and achieve the unit goals. For each learning or practice activity, the table presents a performance-based assessment that gives the students and the teacher information about students' performance and progress. For this unit, we have prepared a student assessment portfolio booklet, titled "Keeping Track of My Soccer Performance" (see figure 9.10 on page 196 [thumbnail] and full size on the CD-ROM), that gives students the learning activities and corresponding assessment forms and directions.

# CRITICAL RESOURCES

When identifying critical resources for your soccer unit, consider first those elements that are absolutely necessary (e.g., equipment and facilities) and then other elements that enhance student learning (e.g., textbooks, articles, appropriate Web sites, community facilities, speakers). The critical resources for our soccer unit are presented in figure 9.9. As you create your list of critical resources, consider each of the earlier steps in the planning process and how any potential resources might fit into that plan. The types of resources you focus on may differ from unit to unit, depending on your major unit focus.

# HOW TO USE THE STUDENT SOCCER PORTFOLIO

For each assessment, the student or a partner records performance results in an assessment booklet so that the student and the teacher can track progress during the unit. We recommend that the teacher provide an area where students can store their booklets so they won't get lost. Using a prepared assessment booklet gives you an effective way to introduce students to the concept of the sportfolio (Marmo 1994) as a culminating project before you require them to keep and submit a portfolio for assessment in a sport activity unit. Remember, a sportfolio is a portfolio that students complete as they participate in a unit of sport instruction. For our sample soccer unit, we designed the sportfolio so that assessments are integrated with learning and practice activities and are arranged in a progression from simple to more complex.

## Culminating Performance and Product for a Soccer Unit

### Student Project

Demonstrate improvement in skill performance and game-playing ability throughout the class's five-on-five, modified soccer tournament. Improvement should be documented through the collection, summary, analysis, and graphing of individual game statistics for assists, scores, steals, blocked shots, and effective passes. You must also prepare a final written report, in which you discuss your progress, areas of strength, and areas in which improvement is needed. Using the information in the report, develop a practice plan for how to improve your soccer skills for game play.

### Student Journal

Keep a personal journal about learning to play soccer. For each day of class, write an entry that includes a summary of practice activities in which you participated, new skills that you learned, and your reaction to your performance in the practice activities and modified game. Was participating in class practice and games enjoyable to you? Why or why not? Also include a daily log of any practice or soccer games in which you participated outside of class (in the evening or on the weekend).

### Student Self-Assessment

At the end of the soccer unit, write a summary of your own assessment of your soccer skill and game-play performance. Include a discussion of your strengths and areas in which you think you need to improve. Compare your soccer performance at the end of the unit with your performance when the unit began. Include a section in which you discuss why you would or would not choose to participate in soccer on a regular basis for physical activity outside of class. If you plan to continue to participate, discuss your plan for doing so.

### Group Event Task

In groups of four to six, design a modified soccer game that you could play in class or at home with siblings, friends, or neighbors. Give your game a name and list the needed equipment. Include a diagram specifying the dimensions of the playing area, and write a sentence or two stating the main objective of the game. List and clearly explain the rules; include the following information: how to start the game, number and positions of players, how to restart when the ball goes out of bounds, fouls and penalties, scoring, and length of game.

Make sure that your game is inclusive. Everyone on the team should have an opportunity to be actively involved in the game. Discuss modifications that you could make so that students of all abilities, including any students with a disability, can join in as contributing participants and enjoy the game. Once you have designed your game, try it out. Play the game with your group to see if it works as you planned. Evaluate the game and make any necessary modifications.

Complete the following:

- Write all the information requested on the form provided and hand in the form at the end of class.
- During the next class meeting, teach the game to the rest of the class and officiate the ensuing games to make sure students are playing correctly.
- Reevaluate the game after the other members of your class have played the game.

### Portfolio Assessment—Soccer Sportfolio

See figure 9.10 (thumbnail) near the end of this chapter and full size on the CD-ROM.

### Group Project

During the soccer unit, you are assigned to a team, and each team participates in a five-on-five, double-elimination, round robin tournament with a championship round. Everyone signs up for one of the four tournament committees:

*(continued)*

**Figure 9.5** Here are several culminating assessments that could be used in a soccer unit.

- Tournament Organization and Rules Committee
- Awards and Souvenirs Committee
- Media, News, and Sports Information Committee
- Officials' Committee (scorekeepers, statisticians, and officials)

The tournament is organized and conducted by the members of the class through the cooperation of the tournament committees. The guidelines and recording sheets for each committee can be found in your Keeping Track of My Soccer Performance sportfolio booklet (see page 196). You will be given time in class to meet with and work with your fellow committee members. You may have to do some research in order to do your job well. Each committee is evaluated on the basis of how well it carries out its assigned duties and how well its part of the tournament is conducted.

**Figure 9.5** *(continued)*

# Culminating or Summative Performance Rubric for Group Event Task: Design a Modified Soccer Game

## Level 3: Professional

### Game Creativity

- Game is simple and involves the use of soccer skills.
- Game is fun and practical.
- Game name is related to the game.
- Play area diagram is clear and contains appropriate dimensions.
- Game description states very clear game objectives.
- Rules are simple, clearly written, fair, and appropriate.
- Rules cover required items.
- Game provides appropriate and active inclusion strategies.
- Game form is complete and demonstrates considerable group effort.

### Teamwork

- Group worked cooperatively to accomplish the task.
- All members participated, contributed equally, and were fully included in the project.
- Group members gave each other compliments and encouraged each other.

### Game Presentation and Evaluation

- Group played the game and made necessary adjustments along the way.
- Group provided clear and concise directions to the class when teaching the game.
- Each group member officiated and helped clarify rules and procedures.
- Class members were able to quickly grasp the objectives and the rules of the game.
- Class members were able to play the game well and had fun while doing so.
- Group sought input from class members while evaluating the game and made appropriate modifications to improve the game.

## Level 2: Varsity

### Game Creativity

- Game is a bit too complicated for the class.
- Game incorporates some soccer skills.

*(continued)*

**Figure 9.6** This rubric can be used with the group event task shown in figure 9.5.

- Game is fun and practical.
- Game name is somewhat related to the game.
- Game objectives are stated.
- Rules are written at various levels: somewhat complicated, fair, and appropriate.
- Rules cover most of the required areas.
- Game provides inclusion strategies that are, for the most part, appropriate.
- Game form has been completed and demonstrates group effort.

### Teamwork

- Group worked cooperatively to accomplish the task.
- Most members participated, contributed, and were included in the project.
- Group members encouraged each other.

### Game Presentation and Evaluation

- Group played the game and made some adjustments along the way.
- Group provided directions to the class when teaching the game.
- Each group member officiated and helped clarify rules and procedures.
- Class members had some difficulty grasping the objectives and rules of the game.
- Class members were eventually able to play the game well and had fun while doing so.
- The group evaluated the game and suggested modifications to make the game better.

## Level 1: Junior Varsity

### Game Creativity

- Game is too complicated or restrictive for the class.
- Game incorporates minimal soccer skills.
- Game is not practical.
- Game name is not related to the game.
- Game objectives are not stated or are not clear.
- Rules are not fair or appropriate.
- More rules are required in order to make the game fair.
- Inclusion strategies are not provided or are inappropriate.
- Game form is incomplete and demonstrates little group effort.

### Teamwork

- Group did not work cooperatively to accomplish the task.
- Most members did not participate, contribute, or get included in the project.
- Group members did not encourage each other or were even argumentative.

### Game Presentation and Evaluation

- Group played the game but did not make adjustments along the way.
- Group provided unclear directions to the class when teaching the game.
- Not all group members officiated or helped clarify rules and procedures.
- Class members had difficulty grasping the objectives and the rules of the game.
- Class members had difficulty playing the game well.
- Group did not evaluate the game or suggest modifications to make the game better.

**Figure 9.6**  *(continued)*

## Essential Content Knowledge for a Soccer Unit

1. Basic rules of soccer and modified soccer
   - Kickoff
   - Fouls: direct and indirect free kicks
   - Restarts: throw-in, corner kick, goal kick, penalty kick
   - Positions: goalkeeper, fullback (sweeper), forward (striker, wing), midfielder (stopper)
   - Field markings, lines, areas
   - Length of game
   - Substitution
   - Scoring
2. Critical performance elements
   - Dribbling with the inside, outside, and instep of the foot
   - Passing, kicking, and shooting with the inside, outside, and instep of the foot
   - Trapping a moving ball with the foot, thigh, and chest
   - Tackling: front tackle and side tackle (poke tackle)
   - Punting
   - Catching or deflecting the ball when playing goalkeeper: ground ball, line drive, ball kicked overhead
   - Throw-in
3. Basic offensive strategies
   - Off-the-ball movement to create open passing lanes
   - Off-the-ball movement to spread the defense
   - Leading the receiver with the pass
   - Moving into open spaces
4. Basic defensive strategies
   - Marking the offensive player with and without the ball
   - Blocking passing lanes and moving into passing lanes to intercept passes
5. Elements of good sporting behavior
6. Working cooperatively as a member of a group to accomplish a goal

**Figure 9.7**   The necessary content knowledge serves as a guide for developing learning and assessment activities to help students achieve unit goals and standards.

## Essential Skills and Abilities for a Soccer Unit

- Dribbling the ball and maintaining control with the inside and outside of the foot while moving at various speeds, distances, and pathways, both alone and against an opponent
- Placing the body between the ball and defender in order to shield the ball while dribbling or maintaining possession of the ball
- Passing the ball to a stationary or moving teammate with a defender nearby (using the inside, outside, or instep of the foot)
- Shooting the ball with the foot from a dribble or pass at the goal from various angles and distances against a defender so that the ball has a chance to score
- Trapping or stopping the ball on the ground or in the air to gain control of it with the foot, thigh, or chest
- Closely marking an opponent who is in possession of the ball and using a front or side tackle to gain possession
- From the sideline, performing a legal throw-in to a teammate so that he or she gains possession of the ball
- As a goalkeeper, catching or deflecting a ball kicked on the ground or into the air by an opponent and then either throwing or punting the ball to clear it away from the goal area
- Performing a legal throw-in from the sideline to a team member on the field so that he or she can gain possession of the ball
- Performing a stationary kick for distance and for accuracy: free kick, goal kick, corner kick

**Figure 9.8**   Middle school students must develop these skills and abilities and be able to apply them in a game situation in order to achieve unit goals and standards.

Students are able to follow the class activities and complete the assessments as they go along, and in some cases they receive feedback about their progress as they complete the tasks. In other cases, the teacher may have to look at student responses and provide written feedback about performance.

**Table 9.1**  Continuous Performance-Based Assessments for a Soccer Unit

| Soccer: dribbling, passing, shooting, defending | |
|---|---|
| **Activity** | **Corresponding assessment from figure 9.10 (student sportfolio) on the CD-ROM** |
| 1. Each student dribbles in a straight line across the width of the gym or field at varying speeds while keeping control of the ball (5 times). | |
| 2. Students repeat activity 1 while a partner observes and uses an assessment checklist to look for critical elements. The partners switch roles after one has completed the task. | Peer Observation Assessment<br>Use the partner assessment form for activity 2 in the student sportfolio. |
| 3. Each student dribbles a ball around in the general space and maintains possession of the ball while changing direction quickly and using different pathways to avoid running into others. Conduct peer and self-assessment using a checklist or scoring guide. Switch roles and repeat. | Use the peer and self-assessment rubric for activity 3 in the student sportfolio. |
| 4. Students dribble against an opponent in a small area, trying to maintain possession of the ball and dodging and feinting as needed. Initially, the opponent moves with the dribbler but does not attempt to get the ball; defender increases pressure and eventually attempts to get possession of the ball. Switch roles and repeat. | Use the peer assessment and self-assessment forms for activity 4 in the student sportfolio. |
| 5. Student passes the ball with the inside of the foot to a large stationary target (e.g., the wall) and varies the distance of the pass. | Use the self-assessment form for activity 5 in the student sportfolio. |
| 6. Student passes the ball to a partner who is stationary. Partner moves to the ball and gains control of the ball. Students complete designated number of repetitions, usually around 10 times each, then switch roles. | Students use the self-assessment and peer assessment forms for activity 6 in the student sportfolio. |
| 7. From a stationary position, student (passer) passes the ball to a partner (receiver) who is moving. The receiver gains control of the pass. Students complete this activity 10 times each. | Use the self-assessment form for activity 7 in the student sportfolio. |
| 8. While dribbling the ball, student (passer) passes to a partner (receiver) who is moving. The passer gains control of the ball, dribbles it, and passes back to the partner. | Use the self-assessment form for activity 8 in the student sportfolio. |
| 9. The student works with a partner and against an opponent to dribble and pass in a restricted space (2v1). Students rotate positions periodically. | Group Assessment.<br>Use the assessment form for activity 9 in the student sportfolio to identify strategies that worked best when passing against an opponent and when trying to intercept a pass. Students compare answers with other groups in class. |

| Soccer: dribbling, passing, shooting, defending | |
|---|---|
| **Activity** | **Corresponding assessment from figure 9.10 (student sportfolio) on the CD-ROM** |
| 10. Students play 2v2 keep-away in a restricted area. | Use the peer assessment form for activity 10 in the student sportfolio to report performance statistics: percentage of successful passes and number of intercepted passes and successful tackles. |
| 11. Student shoots the ball at a target (varying the distance and angle) and records the percentage of shots made. | Use the self-assessment form for activity 11 in the student sportfolio. |
| 12. With a partner (passer), the student (shooter) shoots a ball at a target (goal) from a pass. The shooter records the percentage of shots made. Students switch roles, and the student records the percentage of successful assists. | Use the self-assessment form for activity 12 in the student sportfolio. |
| 13. With a partner, student passes and shoots at a defended target (2v1) and records the percentage of assists and goals made. | Use the self-assessment form for activity 13 in the student sportfolio. |
| 14. Students play in a 3v3 modified soccer game. | Group Assessment. Use the assessment form for activity 14 in the student sportfolio to work with team members in answering questions about the effectiveness of strategies used in the modified game. Then plan and conduct a team practice to help improve the team's and each player's performance. |
| 15. Students participate in a 3v3 soccer game and complete an assessment about improving fitness level by playing soccer (students take their pulse and calculate target heart rate). | Use the self-assessment form for activity 15 in the student sportfolio. |
| 16. Students plan, implement, and participate in a 5v5 modified soccer tournament. All students serve on one of the following tournament committees: Tournament Committee; Rules Committee; Awards and Souvenirs Committee; Media, News, and Sports Information Committee; Officials' Committee. | Committee members produce a portfolio product by completing the appropriate assessment form for activity 16a in the student sportfolio. During the tournament, every student uses the self-assessment form for activity 16b in the student sportfolio to keep a record of his or her performance. |
| 17. Students work in groups of 3 to help coach a third-grade soccer team. Each group member teaches a specific skill to the third graders by identifying performance cues, giving a good demonstration, and identifying three learning or practice activities for the third graders to participate in. | Use the assessment form for activity 17 in the student sportfolio. |
| 18. Students complete two assessments (either as homework or at a portfolio workstation in the gym) about soccer as a lifetime physical activity. | Use the individual assessment form for activity 18 in the student sportfolio. |
| 19. Students complete a final self-assessment (either as homework or at a portfolio workstation in the gym). | Use the self-assessment form for activity 19 in the student sportfolio. |

## Critical Resources for a Soccer Unit

### Equipment

- One soccer ball per student
- Cones and hot spots
- Four modified soccer goals (i.e., smaller so they are developmentally appropriate)

### Facility

- Outdoor field divided into four small fields
- One gym court for bad weather days

### Books

*Soccer: Steps to Success, Third Edition* by Joseph A. Luxbacher (Champaign, IL: Human Kinetics, 2005)

### Community Resources

Speakers: soccer coaches and players from a local college or high school program.

### Field Trip

Local soccer facility.

**Figure 9.9** The teacher must plan ahead to ensure access to the materials, equipment, space, facilities, and community resources that are critical to student learning.

---

**Keeping Track of My Soccer Performance**

Sixth-Grade Physical Education
River Ridge Middle School
Name _____
Date _____
Teacher _____

During the learning and practice activities for our soccer unit, you will be asked to track your progress as you master the soccer skills of dribbling, passing, trapping, shooting, tackling, and defending and apply these skills and basic offensive and defensive strategies in modified game situations. You will accomplish this task by completing each assessment task found in this booklet, either during or upon completion of each learning or practice task. Doing so will enable you to track your progress throughout the unit, which will help you identify skills that you need to work on, both in physical education class and outside of class. This booklet will go with you to seventh-grade physical education, so that you can continue to follow your progress in soccer skill and game play.

At the beginning of each class period, as you enter the gym, you will pick up your booklet and a pencil. Keep the booklet with you as you move around the gym, and always make sure that it is in a safe place so that no one will step on it or trip over it. The best place to keep it is probably close to a wall. At the end of class, you will leave the booklet and pencil in the box on the table by the door as you exit the gym, unless you have a homework assignment and need to take the booklet home with you.

To get better at any skill or sport, you must practice, practice, practice! We may not have enough time for you to practice skills as many times as you need to in order to get better. Therefore, it is important for you to remember ways of practicing skills that help you progress from one level of performance to the next. In the first section of your soccer portfolio, you will record the ways in which you practice skills, as well as the times when you practice at home, during lunch, and on the weekends.

**Activity 1: My Practice Record**

| Skills | Practice Activity | Where | Date | Results |
|---|---|---|---|---|
| | | | | |
| | | | | |
| | | | | |

**Activity 2: Partner Assessment Form**

Directions: As your partner dribbles the ball across the floor and back, make sure that you are in a good position to observe clearly and correctly evaluate his or her performance of the dribble.

Make sure that you record the results in your partner's booklet. In completing this assessment, use the following checklist. Place a check mark in the space in front of each performance element that you observed your partner consistently demonstrate.

Remember, this assessment will not be used as a grade for your partner. It is intended to help your partner improve his or her performance. You are the teacher or the coach.

**Checklist: Dribbling the Ball for Speed**

Date Completed _____ Name of Evaluator _____
Comments _____
_____ Maintains upright body position _____
_____ Keeps head up, looks downfield _____
_____ Looks at the ball _____

From J. Lund and M. Kirk, 2010, *Performance-Based Assessment for Middle and High School Physical Education, Second Edition* (Champaign, IL: Human Kinetics).

**Figure 9.10** The soccer sportfolio, which is given to each student at the beginning of the unit, contains guidelines and forms for completing individual, partner, and group continuous assessments throughout the unit. Students use the sportfolio to track their progress throughout the unit.

---

The learning activities for the sixth-grade soccer unit are provided in figure 9.10. For each learning activity, we refer you to the corresponding performance-based assessment in the student soccer sportfolio booklet. We keep the student soccer sportfolios for each class in a separate box or crate that is stored near the door in the gym, along with a box of clipboards and a box of pencils. Our students pick up their sportfolios when they enter the gym. As needed, time is provided at the beginning of class for students to go back and complete a task that they were unable to finish during the previous class; students may also choose to repeat an activity and assessment to see if they can improve their score. Students then move on to the next learning activity and assessment. As they complete an activity, they complete the corresponding assessment in their soccer sportfolio booklet. When giving directions and demonstrations

to students for each learning activity, we refer them to the page number of the corresponding assessment form and directions. At the end of the class, students return their soccer sportfolios, clipboards, and pencils to the appropriate box as they exit the gym.

## CONCLUSION

This chapter provides a unit plan for middle school soccer. The plan was developed using the five-step, standards-based planning model, which means that the unit was designed downward from the targeted goals and standards to the appropriate content and learning and assessment activities. These activities were designed to enhance students' learning and help them move up the steps to the top where their ultimate goal rests—the achievement of the targeted standards and goals. This unit provides an excellent example of how teachers can incorporate continuous performance-based assessment into the teaching of an activity or sport unit. The most valuable asset of this chapter is a unique assessment tool that is integrated with the learning activities in the student sportfolio booklet. Each student is given a copy of the soccer sportfolio to use each day in class in order to complete assessments along with the learning and practice activities. This portfolio enables the student and teacher to track the student's progress and achievement along the way and at the end of the unit. The teacher can choose to make copies of the sport-folios as evidence of student achievement so that students can keep their own work.

This approach has been used quite successfully by Mary Kirk. We encourage you to either try it for yourself or use it as a guide and model for designing your own unit plan for another sport or activity. It offers a variety of performance-based assessments that you can use as models. Most important, it demonstrates that you can incorporate continuous performance-based assessment into your program in a fun and engaging way.

# 10

# Assessing Fitness and Physical Activity Participation

*The most important benefits of authentic assessment are enhancing student motivation and learning. When you emphasize self-assessment, self-responsibility, and goal-setting, you motivate students to improve their performance. Most important, however, you teach students how to learn the processes of self-analysis and self-direction—something they can take with them when they leave your program (American Alliance for Health, Physical Education, Recreation and Dance 1999, 52).*

Most teachers have seen, experienced, or heard of scenarios in which physical education teachers used fitness testing in inappropriate ways (some would say "traditional ways") in order to assess and grade students. In many cases, some students in these physical education classes had negative experiences that caused them to avoid further fitness and physical activities. In one familiar scenario, students are tested on a variety of fitness components (not always health-related components) at the beginning and again at the end of a grading period or semester, and their grades are determined by their performance on the fitness tests. Students who score higher on the test components receive higher grades, and those who perform less well receive lower grades. Between testing periods, students receive no or little instruction and participate in few physical activities that would improve their performance in the posttest. I have even observed a situation in which students were assessed for their fitness level at the beginning and end of the grading period (the only times they participated in this activity) based on how quickly they could climb to the ceiling on the vertical rope!

In another familiar scenario, well-meaning teachers administer fitness assessments focused on the health-related components of fitness, but students receive little or no explanation of what the test is measuring or why a given test component is important to overall fitness. Following the testing, either the scores are not shared with or explained to students, or the students' individual scores are compared with national performance norms and students simply receive a percentile score indicating where they rank for their age and gender in their class and nationally. Between testing sessions, these students rarely participate in specific goal-oriented class instruction and activities focused on improving their performance on the fitness components to be assessed. As a result, most students' scores for the posttest vary little from their pretest scores. Even so, individual student fitness scores are quite often used by the instructor as the major component of a student's grade. These practices often leave students with a lack of knowledge regarding why fitness assessment is important, what individual test items measure and why, what their individual scores mean, and what activities or exercises they should participate in if they want to improve their scores. Moreover, particularly low-performing students, who need this information and encouragement the most, develop negative attitudes toward participation in fitness and physical activity.

## NEW STRATEGIES AND RECOMMENDATIONS FOR FITNESS EDUCATION AND ASSESSMENT

In the last several years, through the efforts of many concerned professionals and professional organizations such as the National Association for Sport and Physical Education (NASPE), the American Alliance for Health, Physical Education, Recreation and Dance (AAHPERD), the President's Council on Physical Fitness and Sports (PCPFS), and the Cooper Institute, a set of best practices, recommendations, guidelines, and materials in physical fitness assessment, curriculum, and instruction have been identified and prepared for K–12 physical education teachers. These guidelines and materials describe appropriate and effective use of fitness assessment, curriculum, and content goals. As a result, teachers now have access to clear recommendations and guidelines for preparing and administering physical fitness assessment with an emphasis on student learning and understanding, individual goal setting based on initial individual performance scores and health and fitness target scores, strategies for helping and motivating students to improve their scores, and comparing students' scores with their own achievements rather than with the scores of others.

This chapter discusses and integrates these assessment materials, guidelines, recommendations, motivational strategies, and resources available to teachers to make fitness assessment an educational and positive experience for students. Instead of thinking of fitness assessment, we urge teachers to broaden their thinking to envision fitness *education*, in which fitness testing is just one of several important components that help students achieve NASPE's physical education standard 3 ("Participates regularly in physical activity") and standard 4 ("Achieves and maintains a health-enhancing level of physical fitness") (2004).

## INTEGRATING FITNESS EDUCATION AND ASSESSMENT INTO THE PHYSICAL EDUCATION CURRICULUM

Teachers can choose from many options for fully integrating fitness education, fitness development, and regular participation in physical activity into the middle and high school curriculums—and for assessing whether students are achieving national standards, as well as course and program goals. Some teachers and program coordinators choose to incorporate a semester-length physical fitness course or unit into the physical education curriculum. Such a unit may focus on knowledge of health-related physical fitness components, principles of conditioning and exercise, and participation in activities to develop or improve student fitness levels. In other programs, fitness content knowledge and concepts may be distributed across multiple units and applied to the activity focus of each specific unit. We advocate a combination of these curriculum approaches, in which an introductory fitness course helps students learn health-related, developmentally appropriate fitness content and concepts, which are reinforced across all activity units as appropriate.

Rink (2009) recommends that fitness education content should be included in the physical education curriculum at each grade level from sixth through twelfth. She provides sample school program goals, as well as a scope and sequence (organized by NASPE's National Standards for Physical Education [2004]) of specific objectives to help students meet those goals for both middle school and high school physical education. As we have discussed in earlier chapters, identifying clear goals and objectives based on national standards is the first step in planning and having good assessment practice. Rink's book provides an excellent resource for curriculum planning in middle and high school physical education—especially for fitness education.

# RESOURCES FOR FITNESS EDUCATION CURRICULUM, INSTRUCTION, AND ASSESSMENT

A wealth of good resources is available to teachers looking to enhance their fitness education curriculum, content, instruction, and assessment strategies. Some provide excellent guidance for curriculum development in which fitness education content is effectively integrated into middle and secondary physical education programs. They identify essential fitness education and lifetime physical activity concepts and content that should be integrated into the curriculum in order to achieve the National Standards for Physical Education (National Association for Sport and Physical Education 2004). They also provide effective strategies for instruction of content and concepts, specific learning activities, and assessment strategies that help teachers motivate students and teach them to take responsibility for themselves. Many of these resources are presented in the following discussion.

## Physical Best Program

Many outstanding resources are available to help teachers plan and implement the integration of fitness content, concepts, and assessment into their physical education curriculum. The Physical Best program provides the most comprehensive information about incorporating individual student goal-setting strategies into the fitness education curriculum. We recommend *Physical Education for Lifelong Fitness: The Physical Best Teacher's Guide* (National Association for Sport and Physical Education 2005) and the *Physical Best Activity Guide: Secondary Level* (AAHPERD 2005), which provide recommended pedagogical strategies and content for fitness education, including motivational strategies, principles of conditioning and health-related fitness, assessment strategies and learning activities for health-related fitness concepts, and activities for teaching this content.

NASPE also conducts annual Physical Best certification workshops both nationally and regionally. Workshop participants are trained in Physical Best content materials and strategies and can earn program certification. For more information, go to the NASPE Web site at www. aahperd.org/Naspe/.

## Fitnessgram and Activitygram Assessment Program

The Cooper Institute developed the *Fitnessgram/ Activitygram Test Administration Manual* (2007) and test kit for teachers to use in assessing the health-related fitness performance of their students. The Fitnessgram test uses criterion-referenced standards to compare and evaluate student performance. Users are provided with an assessment module that includes equipment and written and video instructions and examples of test administrations for each test item. The following health-related fitness components are addressed:

**Aerobic Capacity**
- The PACER test
- 1-mile (1.6 km) run
- Walk test

**Body Composition**
- Skinfold measurements
- Body mass index
- Bioelectrical impedance analysis (with portable unit)

**Abdominal Strength and Endurance**
- Curl-up

**Trunk Extensor Strength and Flexibility**
- Trunk lift

### Upper-Body Strength and Endurance
- 90-degree push-up
- Modified push-up
- Flexed-arm hang

### Flexibility
- Back-saver sit-and-reach
- Shoulder stretch

The Fitnessgram/Activitygram program includes software that students and teachers can use to enter students' test results and generate various class and individual reports, as well as individual student Fitnessgrams. A Fitnessgram provides an individual student (and, if desired, his or her parents) with a one-page report that includes the student's scores on each of the health-related fitness test items and indicates how the student's score on each item compares with scores in the Healthy Fitness Zone (HFZ) or the Needs Improvement Zone (NIZ) for the student's age and gender. The HFZ provides criterion-based reference scores for each test component. If a student's score falls within the HFZ for a particular component, then the student has achieved sufficient fitness for this component to provide health benefits. If the student's score falls within the NIZ, then the student should set a goal to improve performance in that component in order to gain health benefits. The student is also provided with feedback suggesting ways to improve the score for each test item. The parent report explains the Fitnessgram tests and the Healthy Fitness Zone criteria that students are encouraged to achieve. Teachers can print a number of reports that provide feedback on student progress and use them to track progress or lack thereof for specific fitness components and thus identify individual students' needs. This assessment data can also help teachers make decisions about the design of future curriculum and instruction. A sample Fitnessgram for students is presented in Figure 10.1.

The Activitygram helps students and teachers assess students' levels of participation in physical activity both in school and beyond. The program manual provides teachers with resource materials for teaching concepts related to physical activity guidelines and intensity based on the physical activity pyramid. Students can use the Activitygram software to get a clear picture of their current activity level by logging what type of activity they engaged in during each hour of a 3-day period. A printed Activitygram report then compares their activity data with the recommended goals for physical activity at their age; the report also provides a time-and-intensity profile and an activity profile with explanatory messages and recommendations for increasing the level and intensity of physical activity as appropriate. A sample Activitygram form is presented in Figure 10.2.

Both the Fitnessgram and Activitygram programs offer excellent assessment tools that teachers can use to help students achieve NASPE's national standards 3 and 4. The complete Fitnessgram (which includes the Activitygram) test kit, as well as the test manual and materials and test management software on CD-ROM, can be ordered from the Fitnessgram Web site at www.fitnessgram.net.

## Test and Awards Programs from the President's Council on Physical Fitness and Sports

The President's Challenge Physical Activity and Fitness Awards Program, developed and promoted by the President's Council on Physical Fitness and Sports (PCPFS 2007), also provides a comprehensive fitness education and assessment program as a helpful resource for teachers. It focuses on two programs: the Active Lifestyle program and the Physical Fitness and Health Fitness tests. The Active Lifestyle program emphasizes the importance of participating regularly in physical activity and provides incentives for participants to be active by tracking activity, setting personal goals for regular participation, and taking part in an awards program. Individual schools can participate in the Active Lifestyle Model Schools Award Program. The Physical Fitness program provides the test produced by the President's Council on Physical Fitness and Sports to assess the health-related components of fitness: cardiorespiratory endurance, flexibility, muscular strength and endurance, and body composition. Participating schools can also obtain Fitness File, a free software package that helps you track and manage student testing data. Students can win one of three awards—the Presidential Physical Fitness Award, the National Physical Fitness Award, and the Participant

# FITNESSGRAM®

**Felicia Fitness**
Grade: 6   Age: 13

Your scores on 4 of 6 test items were in or above the Healthy Fitness Zone. Scoring in the Healthy Fitness Zone will help you look and feel better. Keep up the good work!

**Instructor: Sally Smith**

| | Date | Height | Weight |
|---|---|---|---|
| Current: | 11/14/04 | 5' 1" | 105 lbs |

## AEROBIC CAPACITY

| | Needs Improvement | Healthy Fitness Zone |
|---|---|---|

**The PACER**
Current: ████████████ 34

**VO2Max**
VO2max is based on your aerobic test item score. It indicates your ability to perform activity such as running, cycling, or strenuous activities and sports at a high level. Healthy Fitness Zone begins at 36.
Current: ████████████ 44

## MUSCLE STRENGTH, ENDURANCE, & FLEXIBILITY

**(Abdominal) Curl-Up**
Current: ████████ 23

**(Trunk Extension) Trunk Lift**
Current: ███ 8

**(Upper Body) Push-Up**
Current: ███ 5

**(Flexibility) Back-Saver Sit and Reach  R, L**
Current: ██████████ 11.00, 10.00

## BODY COMPOSITION

**Percent Body Fat**

| Healthy Fitness Zone | Needs Improvement |
|---|---|
| Very Low | |

Current: ██████████ 25.74

*Being too lean or too heavy may be a sign of (or lead to) health problems.*

## ACTIVITY

On how many of the past 7 days did you participate in physical activity for a total of 30-60 minutes, or more, over the course of the day?

On how many of the past 7 days did you do exercises to strengthen or tone your muscles?

On how many of the past 7 days did you do exercises to loosen up or relax your muscles?

---

## MESSAGES

Your aerobic capacity score is in the Healthy Fitness Zone. To maintain fitness, you should be active most days of the week. Try to play active games, sports, or other activities you enjoy a total of 60 minutes each day.

Felicia, your body composition is in the Healthy Fitness Zone. To maintain this level, it is important to do physical activity most days. You should also eat a healthy diet.

Your abdominal strength is in the Healthy Fitness Zone. To maintain your fitness, do curl-ups or other abdominal exercises 3 to 5 days each week.

Your flexibility is in the Healthy Fitness Zone. Maintain your fitness by stretching slowly 3 or 4 days each week, holding the stretch 20-30 seconds.

You can improve your trunk extension by doing repeated trunk lifts in a slow, controlled manner. Do these exercises 3 to 5 days each week.

To improve your upper-body strength, do modified push-ups, push-ups, and climbing activities. Do these exercises  2 to 3 days each week.

**Healthy Fitness Zone** for 13 year-old girls
The PACER = 23 - 51 laps
Curl-Up = 18 - 32 repetitions
Trunk Lift = 9 - 12 inches
Push-Up = 7 - 15 repetitions
Back-Saver Sit and Reach =
  At least 10 inches on R & L
Percent Body Fat = 13.00 - 32.00  %

**Number of Days**

To be healthy and fit it is important to do some physical activity almost every day. Aerobic exercise is good for your heart and body composition. Strength and flexibility exercises are good for your muscles and joints.

©2005 The Cooper Institute

**Figure 10.1**   Sample Fitnessgram report.

Reprinted, by permission, from Cooper Institute, 2007, *FITNESSGRAM/ACTIVITYGRAM test administration manual*, 4th ed. (Champaign, IL: Human Kinetics), 64.

# ACTIVITYGRAM®

## MINUTES OF ACTIVITY

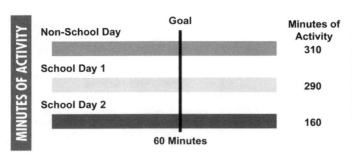

| | Minutes of Activity |
|---|---|
| Non-School Day | 310 |
| School Day 1 | 290 |
| School Day 2 | 160 |

Goal — 60 Minutes

**MESSAGES • MESSAGES • MESSAGES**

The chart shows the number of minutes that you reported doing moderate (medium) or vigorous (hard) activity on each day. Congratulations, your log indicates that you are doing at least 60 minutes of activity on most every day. This will help to promote good fitness and wellness. For fun and variety, try some new activities that you have never done before.

## TIME PROFILE

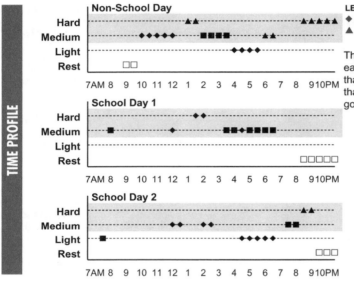

**LEGEND:**
◆ Most of the time (20 minutes)   ■ All of the time (30 minutes)
▲ Some of the time (10 minutes)   ☐ TV/Computer Time

The time profile shows the activity level you reported for each 30 minute period of the day. Your results show that you were active both during and after school and that you were also active on the weekend. Keep up the good work.

## ACTIVITY PROFILE

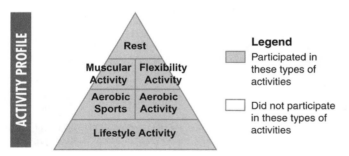

**Legend**
▨ Participated in these types of activities

☐ Did not participate in these types of activities

The activity pyramid reveals the different types of activity that you reported doing over a few days. Your results indicate that you participated in regular lifestyle activity as well as some activity from the other levels. This is great! The variety in your program should help you stay active.

Your results indicate that you spend an average of 1 hours per day watching TV or working on the computer. While some time on these activities is okay, you should try to limit the total time to less than 2 hours.

ACTIVITYGRAM provides information about your normal levels of physical activity. The ACTIVITYGRAM report shows what types of activity you do and how often you do them. It includes the information that you previously entered for two or three days during one week.

**Figure 10.2**   Sample Activitygram report.

Reprinted, by permission, from Cooper Institute, 2007, *FITNESSGRAM/ACTIVITYGRAM test administration manual*, 4th ed. (Champaign, IL: Human Kinetics), 78.

Physical Fitness Award—by achieving the relevant qualifying score as compared with normative data charts for their age and gender; they receive a patch and a certificate for the level they achieve. Most educational materials are available on the PCPFS Web site at www.fitness.gov, which can be accessed by teachers and students; teachers can also order materials and awards there.

## Fitness for Life

*Fitness for Life* (Corbin and Lindsey 2007) is an excellent high school textbook that teachers can use when teaching an introductory fitness class. The text focuses on reasons that physical activity is important, health-related components of fitness, methods of self-assessment, strategies and activities to improve one's fitness level in each component, principles of training, wellness concepts (including nutrition and stress reduction), goal setting, and personal fitness planning. The text includes a variety of performance-based formative and summative assessment ideas, and Corbin and Lindsey have integrated the use of Fitnessgram into the latest edition of the textbook. To enhance learning in class, teachers can also order a series of educational DVDs focused on topics covered in the textbook (visit the Web site at www.fitnessforlife.org).

# USING PEDOMETERS TO ASSESS PHYSICAL ACTIVITY PARTICIPATION LEVELS

In recent years, the electronic pedometer, a small device that counts the number of steps taken by the wearer, has emerged as a high-tech tool to motivate students and track their physical activity over a specified period of time. This use of the pedometer is based on a recommendation endorsed by the U.S. surgeon general (U.S. Department of Health and Human Services 1996) that "individuals minimally strive to accumulate 30 minutes or more of moderate intensity activity (like a brisk walk) on most if not all days of the week" (President's Council on Physical Fitness and Sports 2007). Pedometers are affordable (US$10 to US$30 per unit), and the data they collect tend to correlate closely with data collected by means of more sophisticated and expensive tools (accelerometers) used in research.

A universal activity goal of 10,000 steps per day has been identified (President's Council on Physical Fitness and Sports 2007), although research is needed to determine realistic goals by age level. Rowlands, Eston, and Ingledew (1999) determined in their research that the 10,000-step goal may be too low for children of ages 8 to 10, as the subject in their study averaged between 12,000 and 16,000 steps per day. Another study, this one focused on 600 U.S. adolescents (Wilde 2002), suggests that the 10,000-step goal may also be too low for that age group; participants in that study averaged 11,000 to 12,000 steps per day. Collectively, research indicates that 3,100 to 4,000 pedometer steps may be equivalent to 30 minutes of moderate-intensity walking. With all this in mind, it is recommended that, instead of using a universal goal (e.g., 10,000 steps) that is widely accepted but lacks scientific evidence, individuals would be better served if they "personalize step goals [after] having considered baseline values, specific health goals, and sustainability of the goal in everyday living" (Tudor-Locke 2002).

Many teachers have used pedometers to motivate students to increase their daily physical activity and track their data in order to support self-assessment with an eye toward personal goals. This approach provides one way to assess students in relation to NASPE's standard 3 ("Participates regularly in physical activity"; National Association for Sport and Physical Education 2005). The teacher explains to students how to use the pedometer, what it is measuring and how, why regular physical activity is an important part of a healthy lifestyle, and what goals are recommended for physical activity. Students then establish a baseline of physical activity for a few days, set a realistic goal to increase their participation (i.e., the number of steps per day), begin a physical activity program (a walking program) for an extended period (e.g., the length of the unit or semester), and keep a log of their steps per day so that they can assess their progress toward established goals. In *Pedometer Power*, Pangrazi, Beighle, and Sidman (2007) provide ideas for learning activities using pedometers to track physical activity, which could be incorporated by teachers into individual lessons and assessments.

The difficulty in using this form of assessment lies in the fact that it may not be financially feasible for the physical education program to provide a pedometer for each student over a sustained period of time. Teachers may need to secure a set of pedometers for one class and spread the use of the pedometers across classes during the year, or assign a pedometer to two partners who share the use. Given this barrier, it may be more realistic to introduce students to ways in which the pedometer can be used to motivate oneself, set participation goals, and track increased physical activity; this approach may encourage students to secure their own pedometer in order to continue the program. We suggest that teachers secure grants, seek funds from the school PTA, or find other ways to secure funds to purchase an adequate number of pedometers so that each of their students have one to use for the unit. The use of pedometers can be a very useful tool to motivate students to set goals, increase their physical activity, and measure their level of participation.

## SAMPLE AUTHENTIC ASSESSMENT STRATEGIES FOR FITNESS AND PHYSICAL ACTIVITY PARTICIPATION

This section provides sample assessment strategies and culminating and formative assessments that relate to targeted standards and unit goals for (a) a middle school unit on physical fitness and physical activity participation and (b) a semester-long unit or class on lifetime physical fitness for high school students. We do not provide a sample of a complete unit plan due to the wide variety of possible contents and organizational structures for instructional units on fitness.

### Assessments for a Seventh-Grade Fitness Unit

The fitness unit content presented here is taught across the length of a semester and interspersed with other activity units along the way. Students are introduced to the concepts and guidelines for a healthy and active lifestyle, the concepts

of health-related components of fitness, ways of assessing individual levels of performance for each health-related fitness component, principles of training (frequency, intensity, time, type, and progression), and activities to improve performance on each component. Appropriate targeted national standards (National Association for Sport and Physical Education 2004) are provided for the unit in figure 10.3, and specific unit goals related to the selected national standards are provided in figure 10.4. These standards and unit goals served as the basis for the culminating assessments presented in figures 10.5 and 10.8.

After identifying targeted national or state standards and related specific goals, the teacher must design a culminating or summative assessment to determine whether students have achieved the unit goals and therefore the standards. The standards and unit goals ask the question "What should students know and be able to do?" The culminating assessment should answer this question for both student and teacher. The culminating assessment can involve a performance or a product or both. It should be engaging to the student and realistic or authentic in terms of the unit content and the student's life. At the beginning of the unit, the teacher should share with students the unit goals and how he or she will determine whether students have reached those goals. Students should receive very specific information about the culminating assessment and how their per-

---

### Relevant NASPE Standards for Seventh-Grade Fitness Unit

3. Participates regularly in physical activity.

4. Achieves and maintains a health-enhancing level of physical fitness.

6. Values physical activity for health, enjoyment, challenge, self-expression, and/or social interaction.

**Figure 10.3** Three of the National Standards for Physical Education were targeted for the seventh-grade fitness unit.

From NASPE, 2004, *Moving into the future: National standards for physical education,* 2nd ed. (Reston, VA: National Association for Sport and Physical Education).

formance or product will be evaluated. This means that, *before the unit begins*, the teacher must very specifically identify the culminating assessment and required criteria for each level of performance and provide guidelines to help students complete the assessment. Figures 10.5 and 10.8 provide two sample culminating assessments for the seventh-grade fitness unit. You could choose one of the assessments or use both of them, depending on the time available and the particular unit you have planned.

Figure 10.5 presents an authentic, performance-based, culminating assessment that involves both a product and a performance; it is integrated with learning activities. Students are required to participate in at least 60 minutes of physical activity on most days of the week for the length of the semester. They may count their time in physical education class, but they must also participate outside of school. They must keep a record of the number of minutes and the number of days per week, the type of activity, where they participated in the activity, and with whom they participated. They must also keep a short daily activity journal and provide a summary journal at the end of the semester. Figure 10.5 provides the directions and specific criteria for students. A sample log form that students could use to record data is provided in figure 10.6, and a scoring guide or rubric for the culminating assessment (based on the criteria identified in figure 10.5) is provided in figure 10.7.

To help students stay current with activity entries and avoid misplacing their log or journal, you could keep these materials in a class folder and give students access to them during class. Another helpful strategy is to periodically collect the student assessments to check that students are keeping up, to give them feedback and encouragement, and to remind them that they may count only those minutes in which they are actually engaged in activity in class—not the full class time.

A second authentic, performance-based, culminating assessment for the seventh-grade fitness unit is provided in figure 10.8. This summative assessment focuses on students' use of their fitness test scores and of Fitnessgram to set personal fitness goals. It can be used to determine whether students are achieving the standards and unit goals identified in figures 10.3 and 10.4—in particular, national standard 4 ("Achieves and maintains a health-enhancing level of physical fitness") and unit goals 4, 5, 6, and 7. This is both a formative and a culminating assessment, and it is integrated with learning activities and activity participation in physical activities outside of the physical education class throughout the semester and across other

## Goals for Seventh-Grade Fitness Unit

1. Students will understand the importance of regular participation in physical activity.
2. Students will identify the guidelines for participation in regular physical activity.
3. Students will participate in physical activity in activities of their choice, both in class and outside of school, for at least 60 minutes per day on most days of the week.
4. Students will identify and explain each of the health-related components of physical fitness: cardiorespiratory endurance, flexibility, muscular strength and endurance, and body composition.
5. Students will explain and demonstrate how to measure their personal fitness level for each of the health-related components of fitness.
6. Based on their individual scores for the health-related components of fitness as measured by the Fitnessgram assessments, students will identify realistic personal goals for each component in relation to the Healthy Fitness Zone.
7. Through participation in appropriate training activities, students will achieve the personal fitness goals they identified at the beginning of the semester.

**Figure 10.4** Unit goals were established to help students achieve the three national standards identified for the unit.

## Personal Physical Activity Participation Log or Journal

Complete a daily or weekly log (as assigned), in which you record the number of minutes you participated in physical activity both during and outside of school. Include the following:

- Number of minutes per day (including weekends) for each activity (okay to rest 1 day per week)
- The type of activity in which you participated (e.g., walking, tennis, bike riding) and the intensity level of the activity
- Where you participated in the activity
- The person(s) with whom you participated (if anyone)
- Description of how it felt to participate in the activity (including any obstacles you had to overcome)
- Reason(s) for any missed days

At the end of your log or journal, discuss why participating in regular physical activity (at least 60 minutes per day on most days of the week) is important to a healthy lifestyle, why you were asked to complete this assignment, whether you were able to meet participation guidelines, what things motivated you to participate, and what obstacles hindered your participation. What activities did you enjoy most? Least? How did this assignment make you feel about being physically active? Do you think that your activity participation helped you reach your Fitnessgram goals and improve your physical fitness levels? Do you think this experience will help you continue to be physically active in the future?

Please use the form provided to you to complete this assignment (see figure 10.6). You will turn in your log or journal on the Monday of the last week of the semester. Please review the scoring guide or rubric to see how your work will be evaluated.

**Figure 10.5** Here are the guidelines and criteria for the seventh-grade fitness unit's culminating assessment, which involves both a performance and a product assessment.

**Personal Physical Activity Participation Log or Journal Form**

Name_____ Semester_____ Class_____

| Day and date | Minutes | Type of physical activity | Intensity level (low, medium, or high) | Location | Alone or with others | Journal entry |
|---|---|---|---|---|---|---|
| **Week #** | | | | | | |
| | | | | | | |
| | | | | | | |
| | | | | | | |
| | | | | | | |
| | | | | | | |
| **Week #** | | | | | | |
| | | | | | | |
| | | | | | | |
| | | | | | | |
| | | | | | | |
| | | | | | | |

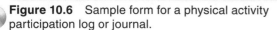
From J. Lund and M. Kirk, 2010, *Performance-Based Assessment for Middle and High School Physical Education, Second Edition* (Champaign, IL: Human Kinetics).

**Figure 10.6** Sample form for a physical activity participation log or journal.

instructional units. This approach helps students understand that fitness is not just a unit in a physical education class but is integrated with a wide range of activities.

In this integrated unit, students initially learn about the importance of health-related components of fitness (cardiorespiratory endurance, muscular strength and endurance, flexibility, and body composition), what each component is, and how to measure individual levels for each component with the Fitnessgram test. To help students understand these concepts through active engagement, the teacher uses various Physical Best activities (American Alliance for Health, Physical Education, Recreation and Dance 2005). Students then use the Fitnessgram software to enter their own scores on a school computer and print out a copy of their personal Fitnessgram to determine how their individual scores compare with the criteria of the Healthy Fitness Zone. Next, students are introduced to the strategy of setting realistic personal fitness

## Scoring Rubric for the Personal Physical Activity Participation Log or Journal

Name_____ Semester_____ Class _____

| Performance level | Participation level | Log completion | Quality of journal reflection |
|---|---|---|---|
| Level 4 | • Met the goal of 60 minutes or more of activity per day on at least 6 days per week.<br>• Gradually increased activity time and reached the goal by the end of the 12-week period.<br>• Activities involved a balance of moderate- and high-intensity levels.<br>• Participated in physical activity outside of school.<br>• Participated in activity on at least one weekend day. | • Completed all areas required on the log form for at least 6 days per week and for 12 weeks total by the end of the semester.<br>• Demonstrated an understanding of how to overcome personal obstacles to regular participation in physical activity. | • Reflectively answered all questions for the journal.<br>• In-depth journal entries went beyond the required questions.<br>• Demonstrated a clear understanding of the personal benefits of regular participation in physical activity. |
| Level 3 | • Met the goal of 60 minutes of activity per day on at least 5 days per week.<br>• Most activity was of at least moderate intensity.<br>• Participated in some activity outside of school. | • Completed all areas required on the log form for at least 5 days per week and for 12 weeks total.<br>• Demonstrated an understanding of how to overcome personal obstacles to regular participation in physical activity. | • Thoroughly completed all questions in the journal entries.<br>• Journal entries went beyond the required questions.<br>• Demonstrated understanding of the personal benefits of regular participation in physical activity. |
| Level 2 | • Generally participated in less than 30 to 60 minutes of activity on at least 4 days per week.<br>• Intensity levels for activities were low to moderate.<br>• Participated in some activity each week outside of physical education class. | • Completed most areas required on the log form for at least 5 days per week and for 12 weeks total.<br>• Demonstrated a recognition of personal obstacles to regular physical activity but did not develop strategies to overcome them. | • Completed most questions in the journal entries.<br>• Expanded entries somewhat beyond what the prompts required.<br>• Demonstrated general understanding of the benefits of physical activity. |

*(continued)*

**Figure 10.7** Scoring rubric for the culminating assessment of the seventh-grade fitness unit.

| Performance level | Participation level | Log completion | Quality of journal reflection |
|---|---|---|---|
| Level 1 | • Participated in at least 30 minutes of activity per day on 2 to 4 days per week.<br>• Intensity levels of activities were low to moderate.<br>• Activity participation was limited to physical education class.<br>• Little effort was given to participation. | • Completed some areas required on the log form.<br>• Did not record activity for the required number of weeks.<br>• Did not recognize personal obstacles to regular participation in physical activity (or recognized them but did not develop strategies to overcome them). | • Did not address (or did not adequately answer) all questions.<br>• Did not go beyond the questions in journal.<br>• Showed poor understanding of personal benefits of regular participation in physical activity. |

**Figure 10.7**   *(continued)*

goals to motivate themselves and measure their own improvement. Students use their Fitness-gram scores to establish goals for each health-related fitness component, then write each goal, in quantifiable terms, on the goal-setting form provided for them (see figure 10.9). The teacher checks each student's goals to make sure that they are realistic for that particular student and, when necessary, helps students make modifications.

Students then participate again in various Physical Best activities (American Alliance for Health, Physical Education, Recreation and Dance 2005) in order to learn about the FITT principles (frequency, intensity, time, type), the principle of progression, and ways of applying these principles to improve and maintain health fitness levels. During a 20-minute fitness activity at the beginning of each class, students are introduced to exercises and activities to help them improve their fitness and meet their fitness goals. Students may choose other activities that are more appealing to them as long as those activities will help them achieve their goals.

Following the initial introduction of the lifetime fitness unit, each class period continues to begin with a 20-minute fitness development period even as the teacher integrates other activity units (e.g., ultimate Frisbee, dance, track and field) throughout the semester. Every 3 weeks,

students are given an opportunity to retake the Fitnessgram test and compare their scores with their goals to determine whether they are making progress toward their goals. Students complete their final fitness assessment during the final week of the semester, then complete the final parts of the culminating assessment and submit the product to the teacher. The teacher can evaluate each student's performance on this final assessment by using the rubric or scoring guide presented in figure 10.10.

## Culminating Assessment for a Lifetime Fitness and Physical Activity Unit or Class in High School

Many high school physical education programs are incorporating into their curriculums a semester-long unit or class on lifetime physical fitness and physical activity. In these units, students learn and apply a depth and breadth of knowledge about physical fitness and conditioning, including the benefits of and guidelines for regular physical activity, the components of health-related fitness, and the major principles of physical training (frequency, time, duration, specificity, progression, and overload). In this type of program, students are taught content

## Setting Personal Fitness Goals and Working to Achieve Goals

At the beginning of the semester, you will learn about and be tested on the following health-related components of fitness by means of the Fitnessgram test indicated for each component:

**Cardiorespiratory endurance**

- 1-mile (1.6-kilometer) run-or-walk test

**Muscular strength and endurance**

- Abdominal strength and endurance (curl-up)
- Trunk extensor strength and flexibility (trunk lift)
- Upper-body strength and endurance (90-degree push-up, modified push-up, or flexed-arm hang)

**Flexibility**

- Back-saver sit-and-reach
- Shoulder stretch

**Body composition**

- Skinfold measurements or body mass index

Following the completion of the Fitnessgram tests, you will enter your scores via computer in the gym or media center, then generate and print your own personal Fitnessgram (see figure 10.1). Read your Fitnessgram carefully.

Use the goal-setting form provided for you to write realistic goals for each of the component tests; write goals that you think you can reach by the end of the semester. Remember that your immediate goal is to achieve a performance score for each component test that falls within the Healthy Fitness Zone. If your score on a component is already within this zone, you may want to concentrate on other components for which your score has not reached the zone. Even if all of your scores already fall within the Healthy Fitness Zone, you can still set goals to improve your scores. Once you have finished setting and writing down your goals on the form, show them and your Fitnessgram to me so that I can make sure that your goals are realistic and achievable.

Once your goals are approved, you will then begin to work toward them by engaging in physical activity both during and outside of physical education class. Each day, 20 minutes of class time will be devoted to flexibility and muscular strength and endurance activities. During the rest of the class period, you will participate in activities designed to increase your skill performance in various activity units; using those skills in 2v2, 3v3, and 4v4 modified games; and other small-group activities that are aerobic in nature and thus help you improve your cardiorespiratory endurance. At the conclusion of each class period, you will participate in cool-down and stretching activities. In order to reach your goals, you may need to participate in additional fitness development activities at home.

Every 3 weeks, you will have the opportunity to work with a partner to retest yourself on each fitness component in order to determine whether you are improving your Fitnessgram test scores and making progress toward your goals. At these times, you may need to adjust your goals a bit or increase your training activities. At the end of the semester, you will be tested again and will receive a Fitnessgram to determine how well you have progressed toward reaching your goals.

To complete this project, you will need to submit the following items:

- Fitnessgram goal-setting form
- Activity participation log
- Modified goals (if completed)
- All Fitnessgrams (the initial one, those completed every 3 weeks, and the final one)
- Final: My Physical Fitness Journal (including a weekly entry and a final summary of your fitness program)

Remember that you are not being evaluated on your fitness test scores but on your participation in the process and on your submitted projects.

**Figure 10.8** Analyzing fitness test scores and setting fitness performance goals: a culminating assessment for a seventh-grade fitness unit.

**Fitness Goals Contract**

To improve my personal fitness level, I have set the following fitness goals with the help of my teacher. In order to achieve improved physical fitness, I will participate in class activities and other activities outside of class as outlined in this plan. I believe that these goals are reasonable and achievable.

| Fitness component test item | Score date ___ | My goal | Activities to improve physical fitness | Follow-up score date ___ | Follow-up score date ___ | Follow-up score date ___ |
|---|---|---|---|---|---|---|
| Aerobic fitness 1-mile (1.6-km) walk/run | | | | | | |
| Body composition Percent body fat Body mass index | | | | | | |
| Flexibility and muscular strength and endurance Curl-up | | | | | | |
| Trunk lift | | | | | | |
| Push-ups Modified pull-ups Pull-ups Flexed-arm hang | | | | | | |
| Back-saver sit-and-reach Shoulder stretch | | | | | | |

Student _____ Date _____ Class _____
Teacher _____

From J. Lund and M. Kirk, 2010, *Performance-Based Assessment for Middle and High School Physical Education, Second Edition* (Champaign, IL: Human Kinetics). Reprinted, by permission, from NASPE, 2004, *Physical education for lifelong fitness: Physical best teacher's guide*, 2nd ed. (Champaign, IL: Human Kinetics).

**Figure 10.9** Sample fitness goal-setting form.
Reprinted, by permission, from NASPE, 2004, *Physical education for lifelong fitness: Physical best teacher's guide*, 2nd ed. (Champaign, IL: Human Kinetics).

either at the beginning of the unit or semester or during various lessons spread strategically throughout the unit or semester. Depending upon the approach used by the teacher, students are either required to apply the information by participating in activities structured and led by the teacher or given the flexibility to participate in activities of their own choosing.

Students usually participate in a fitness testing program and are asked to set goals to achieve by the end of the unit or semester. In the teacher-designed programs, students might participate in a warm-up routine for 5 to 10 minutes each day before taking part in an aerobic or cardiorespiratory development activity for 20 to 30 minutes (e.g., an aerobic dance routine or a step aerobics routine led by the teacher or by a video instructor, a circuit training routine, an aerobic game activity such as basketball or ultimate Frisbee, or a walking or jogging program). On alternating days in class, students participate in a strength training program designed by the teacher.

In the more flexible model, students are asked to design their own fitness program or plan, follow the plan in order to participate in fitness and physical activities each day, track their progress, and make modifications when needed. This type of class structure resembles the adult fitness club model, giving students choices and thus motivating them, promoting responsibility for oneself, and preparing students to engage in a physically active lifestyle beyond high school. In this model, students participate in self-designed activities or choose the activities in which they will participate during class. For instance, rather than participating in a teacher-led aerobic dance class and circuit training program, a student might design his or her plan to include a 30-minute lap-swimming workout 3 days a week for cardiorespiratory fitness and body composition, as well as a strength training program using free weights or Nautilus equipment 2 days a week for muscular strength and endurance. Students in this "design your own" type of program are still held accountable for regular participation and for reaching realistic fitness goals, and giving adolescents the independence to make choices is usually much more motivating to them than participating in a one-plan-fits-all program.

Sample targeted national standards (National Association for Sport and Physical Education 2004) for this high school unit are presented in figure 10.11, and the unit goals are presented in figure 10.12. These standards and unit goals were used to develop the culminating assessment (presented in figure 10.13).

The culminating assessment for the sample high school fitness (figure 10.13) is geared for use in a more flexible unit or class, in which students design their own personal fitness program and participate in activities that they have designed within the structure of the class. This is truly an authentic, performance-based assessment, because students are asked to apply what they have learned by designing a fitness program and are then held accountable for participating in that program and achieving self-determined goals. In order to complete this culminating assessment, students must demonstrate self-direction and self-motivation. Although this is a summative or culminating assessment, parts of it are completed throughout the semester, and documentation is submitted to the teacher at the end of the semester as the culminating assessment. Forms and guidelines for each section of the culminating assessment are provided in figures 10.14, 10.15, 10.16, 10.17, and 10.18. A scoring rubric for the culminating assessment is provided in table 10.1 on pages 219-220.

# Scoring Rubric: Personal Goal-Setting and Physical Fitness Improvement Program Participation

Name_____ Semester_____ Class _____

| Performance level | Fitnessgram | Fitness activity participation and completion of activity log | Personal fitness goals | My physical fitness journal |
|---|---|---|---|---|
| Level 4 | • Completed fitness test items and recorded and entered scores correctly each time as required.<br>• Generated a personal Fitnessgram each time as required. | • Participated vigorously and regularly in class fitness activities.<br>• Regularly completed other appropriate fitness development activities outside of class.<br>• Thoroughly completed personal fitness activity log. | • Set realistic personal goals for fitness improvement based on Fitnessgram results and made modifications when indicated.<br>• Completed the goal-setting process each time as required. | • Completed a reflective personal fitness journal.<br>• Demonstrated a realistic understanding of fitness principles and how to improve.<br>• Demonstrated growth. |
| Level 3 | • Completed fitness test items and recorded and entered scores correctly most times as required.<br>• Generated a personal Fitnessgram each time as required. | • Participated regularly in class fitness development activities.<br>• Usually completed other appropriate fitness activities outside of class as required.<br>• Completed personal fitness activity log. | • Set mostly realistic personal goals for fitness improvement based on Fitnessgram results and made modifications when indicated.<br>• Completed the goal-setting process each time as required. | • Completed a somewhat reflective personal fitness journal.<br>• Demonstrated knowledge of fitness principles and how to improve. |

*(continued)*

**Figure 10.10**  Scoring guide or rubric for the culminating assessment of the seventh-grade fitness unit: setting fitness goals and working to achieve those goals.

| Performance level | Fitnessgram | Fitness activity participation and completion of activity log | Personal fitness goals | My physical fitness journal |
|---|---|---|---|---|
| Level 2 | • Missed at least one test or Fitnessgram. | • Usually participated in class fitness development activities.<br>• Completed some other fitness development activities outside of class (some activities were not appropriate).<br>• Mostly completed the personal fitness activity log (some areas left incomplete). | • Set or modified personal fitness goals based on Fitnessgram results.<br>• Completed the goal-setting process all but one time as required. | • Journal demonstrates little reflection on the personal fitness development process or understanding of fitness principles.<br>• Showed some growth. |
| Level 1 | • Missed more than one test or Fitnessgram. | • Lacked effort or did not participate much of the time in class fitness activities.<br>• Did not complete outside activities, or activities were not appropriate for improving the student's fitness level.<br>• Left personal fitness log incomplete or did not submit a log. | • Set unrealistic goals and did not make suggested modifications.<br>• Did not complete follow-up as required.<br>• Showed little effort in setting goals and in working to try to achieve them. | • Student did not submit a journal, or the journal demonstrates little reflection on the personal fitness development process or understanding of fitness principles.<br>• Demonstrates lack of motivation and growth. |

**Figure 10.10**   *(continued)*

## Relevant National Standards
## for a High School Lifetime Physical Fitness Unit

2. Demonstrates understanding of movement concepts, principles, strategies, and tactics as they apply to the learning and performance of physical activities.

3. Participates regularly in physical activity.

4. Achieves and maintains a health-enhancing level of physical fitness.

6. Values physical activity for health, enjoyment, challenge, self-expression, and/or social interaction.

**Figure 10.11** Four of the National Standards for Physical Education were targeted for the high school fitness unit.

From NASPE, 2004, *Moving Into the Future: National Standards for Physical Education,* 2nd ed. (Reston, VA: National Association for Sport and Physical Education).

## Goals for a High School Lifetime Fitness Unit

1. Students will identify, demonstrate, and apply knowledge of the benefits of regular participation in physical activity, health-related components of fitness, and training principles.

2. Students will demonstrate an understanding of the physical activity pyramid, cardiovascular fitness, and the Activitygram.

3. Students will use a pedometer and an activity log to track their participation in cardiovascular physical activity outside of class.

4. Students will demonstrate the ability to administer the identified Fitnessgram test items and record and interpret personal scores.

5. Students will demonstrate the ability to set realistic fitness goals for each of the components of health-related fitness based on their Fitnessgram scores.

6. Students will demonstrate knowledge of the principles of training—progression, overload, FITT, warm-up, and cool-down—when designing a personal fitness program.

7. Students will participate in a self-designed personal fitness program for the length of the semester, tracking progress at identified intervals and adjusting personal goals or program activities as needed, both during and outside of class.

8. Students will achieve personal fitness goals through participation in their personally designed exercise program and participation in activity outside of physical education class.

**Figure 10.12** Unit goals for the culminating assessment of the high school unit were established to help students achieve the four national standards identified in figure 10.11.

## Assessment Project: Personal Fitness Program Design and Implementation

1. Based on your personal scores for each of the health-related components of fitness on the initial Fitnessgram test, you will identify appropriate personal fitness goals that you set for yourself in order to improve or maintain your scores by the end of the semester. Keep in mind that you should use the Healthy Fitness Zone in the Fitnessgram score table to help you in setting your goals. Remember, too, that our class goal is for everyone to score in the Healthy Fitness Zone on all or most fitness components by the end of the semester. You will share your goals with your instructor for feedback to ensure that they are appropriate and achievable during the course of the semester; with this in mind, you may be asked to make modifications in your fitness goals. In completing this part of the assessment, please use the personal fitness goals form provided to you (figure 10.14).

2. After you have finalized your personal fitness goals, you will design your own personal fitness program (PFP). When designing your fitness program, you will appropriately apply the following for each fitness component: the FITT principles and the training principles of progression, cross-training, specificity, and overload. You will design and submit your PFP using the Personal Fitness Program Form, which will be provided to you. In your PFP, you must incorporate the following items:

- Warm-up and cool-down routine that incorporates specific exercises to help you develop overall flexibility, as well as flexibility in specific areas (figure 10.15)
- Specific workout activities to develop muscular strength and endurance (figure 10.16)
- Specific activities to increase cardiorespiratory endurance (figure 10.17)
- Fun activities to increase your physical activity participation outside of class (figure 10.18)

3. You will participate in this program each day during class and, if desired and appropriate, outside of class as well. Your program should address flexibility, muscular strength and endurance, cardiovascular endurance, and body composition. You will determine what activities you will participate in for each of the health-related fitness components during the 90-minute class and beyond class.

4. After each 3-week period, you will reassess your performance on each health-related fitness component included in the Fitnessgram. Based on your performance on the reassessment and the goals you initially set for yourself, you will determine, in consultation with your instructor, whether you need to adjust your goals or program activities or whether if you feel that you are making sufficient progress to continue on with your program as is. You will complete the Program Progress Form and submit it to your instructor.

5. Each day during the course of the semester, you will keep a workout log and journal in which you record information about your workout during class for each health-related fitness component and write a reflection about that day. You will use a spiral notebook as your personal fitness journal. In your journal, please include discussions of what was motivating about the activities or program, which activities you liked best and least, which social interactions you had during your workouts, whether or not they were motivating, what obstacles hindered you from staying on schedule and completing your program, and what adjustments you made to your program or workouts to encourage you to participate.

6. At the end of the semester, you will take the Fitnessgram test again and compare your results with the individual goals that you set for yourself at the beginning of the semester (and may have adjusted during the semester) and analyze the results. You will then write a final reflection regarding your goals and your final performance scores, as well as the effectiveness of your program and your participation in the program. You will also set new goals and determine what your next steps will be in order to continue improving on or maintaining your current levels of fitness. This part of your assessment should be completed in your personal fitness journal.

Please follow the guidelines provided and use the appropriate forms for each part of this culminating assessment.

**Figure 10.13** Design and implementation of a personal fitness program: a culminating performance-based assessment project for a semester-long lifetime physical fitness unit or class in high school.

# CONCLUSION

This chapter has introduced you to suggested best practices, guidelines, and resource materials for fitness curriculum and assessment. We have also provided three samples of authentic, performance-based, culminating assessments—two for a seventh-grade unit and one for a high school unit. For each culminating assessment, we have included targeted national standards (National Association for Sport and Physical Education 2004) and unit goals that relate directly to the national standards, as well as integrated formative assessments and scoring rubrics. More sample assessments and ideas are available on the accompanying CD-ROM. We hope this chapter serves as a catalyst for teachers to develop engaging and appropriate fitness education activities and assessments that motivate their students to be physically active and fit for a lifetime.

### Personal Fitness Scores and Goal Setting Form

Name_____ Date_____

**Initial and Periodic Fitnessgram Test Scores and Personal Fitness Goals**

| Health-related fitness component and test item initial score | In Healthy Fitness Zone | Test 1 scores | Test 2 scores | Test 3 scores | Final test scores | Personal goals | Goal met or exceeded |
|---|---|---|---|---|---|---|---|
| **Flexibility** Back-saver sit-and-reach R_____ L_____ | | R____ L____ | R____ L____ | R____ L____ | R____ L____ | R____ L____ | |
| **Flexibility** Shoulder stretch R_____ L_____ | | R____ L____ | R____ L____ | R____ L____ | R____ L____ | R____ L____ | |
| **Flexibility and strength** Trunk extensor _____ | | _____ | _____ | _____ | _____ | _____ | |
| **Muscular strength and endurance** Curl-up _____ | | _____ | _____ | _____ | _____ | _____ | |
| **Muscular strength and endurance** Upper-body curl-up _____ | | _____ | _____ | _____ | _____ | _____ | |
| **Muscular strength and endurance** Modified or regular pull-up _____ | | _____ | _____ | _____ | _____ | _____ | |
| **Muscular strength and endurance** Abdominal curl _____ | | _____ | _____ | _____ | _____ | _____ | |
| **Cardiorespiratory endurance** PACER test, 1-mile (1.6-km) run-or-walk test _____ | | _____ | _____ | _____ | _____ | _____ | |
| **Body composition** Percent body fat Triceps _____ Calf _____ Body mass index _____ | | _____ _____ | _____ _____ | _____ _____ | _____ _____ | _____ _____ | |

From J. Lund and M. Kirk, 2010, *Performance-Based Assessment for Middle and High School Physical Education, Second Edition* (Champaign, IL: Human Kinetics).

 **Figure 10.14**   Sample goal-setting form.

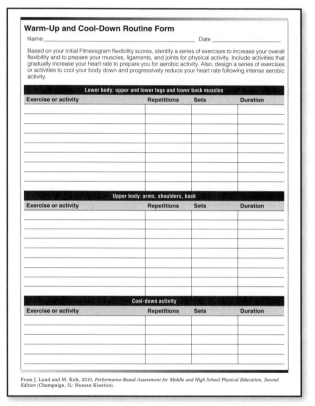

### Warm-Up and Cool-Down Routine Form

Name_____ Date_____

Based on your initial Fitnessgram flexibility scores, identify a series of exercises to increase your overall flexibility and to prepare your muscles, ligaments, and joints for physical activity. Include activities that gradually increase your heart rate to prepare you for aerobic activity. Also, design a series of exercises or activities to cool your body down and progressively reduce your heart rate following intense aerobic activity.

| Lower body: upper and lower legs and lower back muscles | | | |
|---|---|---|---|
| Exercise or activity | Repetitions | Sets | Duration |
| | | | |
| | | | |
| | | | |
| | | | |
| | | | |
| | | | |

| Upper body: arms, shoulders, back | | | |
|---|---|---|---|
| Exercise or activity | Repetitions | Sets | Duration |
| | | | |
| | | | |
| | | | |
| | | | |
| | | | |
| | | | |

| Cool-down activity | | | |
|---|---|---|---|
| Exercise or activity | Repetitions | Sets | Duration |
| | | | |
| | | | |
| | | | |
| | | | |

From J. Lund and M. Kirk, 2010, *Performance-Based Assessment for Middle and High School Physical Education, Second Edition* (Champaign, IL: Human Kinetics).

**Figure 10.15**   Personal warm-up and cool-down program form.

## Muscular Strength and Endurance Development Program

Name _____ Date _____

Identify the type of strength development activities or exercises you will participate in to increase or maintain your muscular strength and endurance and reach your goals for those areas. Make sure that you incorporate the training principles of specificity, type, progression, overload, and frequency into your plan.

**Lower and upper leg muscles**

| Machine, exercise, or action | Muscles involved | Sets | Reps | Progression | Frequency |
|---|---|---|---|---|---|
| | | | | | |
| | | | | | |
| | | | | | |
| | | | | | |
| | | | | | |
| | | | | | |

**Trunk, abdominals, lower back**

| Machine, exercise, or action | Muscles involved | Sets | Reps | Progression | Frequency |
|---|---|---|---|---|---|
| | | | | | |
| | | | | | |
| | | | | | |
| | | | | | |
| | | | | | |
| | | | | | |

From J. Lund and M. Kirk, 2010, *Performance-Based Assessment for Middle and High School Physical Education, Second Edition* (Champaign, IL: Human Kinetics).

**Figure 10.16** Muscular strength and endurance program form.

---

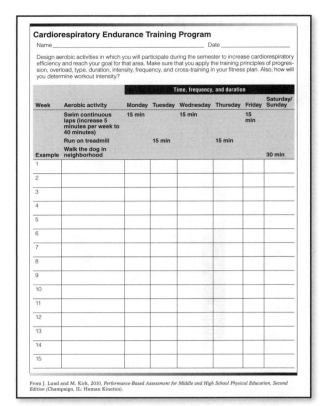

## Cardiorespiratory Endurance Training Program

Name _____ Date _____

Design aerobic activities in which you will participate during the semester to increase cardiorespiratory efficiency and reach your goal for that area. Make sure that you apply the training principles of progression, overload, type, duration, intensity, frequency, and cross-training in your fitness plan. Also, how will you determine workout intensity?

| Week | Aerobic activity | Monday | Tuesday | Wednesday | Thursday | Friday | Saturday/ Sunday |
|---|---|---|---|---|---|---|---|
| Example | Swim continuous laps (increase 5 minutes per week to 40 minutes) | 15 min | | 15 min | | 15 min | |
| | Run on treadmill | | 15 min | | 15 min | | |
| | Walk the dog in neighborhood | | | | | | 30 min |
| 1 | | | | | | | |
| 2 | | | | | | | |
| 3 | | | | | | | |
| 4 | | | | | | | |
| 5 | | | | | | | |
| 6 | | | | | | | |
| 7 | | | | | | | |
| 8 | | | | | | | |
| 9 | | | | | | | |
| 10 | | | | | | | |
| 11 | | | | | | | |
| 12 | | | | | | | |
| 13 | | | | | | | |
| 14 | | | | | | | |
| 15 | | | | | | | |

From J. Lund and M. Kirk, 2010, *Performance-Based Assessment for Middle and High School Physical Education, Second Edition* (Champaign, IL: Human Kinetics).

**Figure 10.17** Sample cardiorespiratory endurance training program form.

---

## Training Participation Log for Personal Fitness Program

Name _____ Date _____

Record the activity (strength, flexibility, aerobic, fun) in which you participate and include the time, intensity, number of stations, and type of activity for each day of the semester. Place a check mark in the space if your participation activity matched your written program. For any day that you miss, please indicate this and give a reason. Also indicate days on which you participated in the Fitnessgram test.

| Week | Monday | Tuesday | Wednesday | Thursday | Friday | Saturday/ Sunday |
|---|---|---|---|---|---|---|
| 1 | | | | | | |
| 2 | | | | | | |
| 3 | | | | | | |
| 4 | | | | | | |
| 5 | | | | | | |
| 6 | | | | | | |
| 7 | | | | | | |
| 8 | | | | | | |
| 9 | | | | | | |
| 10 | | | | | | |
| 11 | | | | | | |
| 12 | | | | | | |
| 13 | | | | | | |
| 14 | | | | | | |
| 15 | | | | | | |

From J. Lund and M. Kirk, 2010, *Performance-Based Assessment for Middle and High School Physical Education, Second Edition* (Champaign, IL: Human Kinetics).

**Figure 10.18** Sample personal fitness program training participation log form.

**Table 10.1** Assessment Rubric for Personal Fitness Program

| Performance level | Fitness goals | Fitness tests | Performance Criteria | | | | | Final analysis and reflection |
| | | | Warm-up and cool-down routine | Strength training program | Aerobic training program | Fitness participation log | Fitness journal | |
|---|---|---|---|---|---|---|---|---|
| **Level 4** | • Goals are based on FG test scores<br>• Goals are appropriate<br>• All goals relate to the HFZ<br>• Included goals for each HRF component | • Completed and recorded all tests<br>• Completed and recorded three retests | • Completed all areas<br>• Activities were very appropriate<br>• Exercises were progressive | • Completed all areas<br>• Activities were very appropriate<br>• Exercises were progressive | • Completed all areas<br>• Activities were very appropriate<br>• Exercises were progressive | • Fully completed for each day<br>• Followed original fitness plan and modified when appropriate | • Very thorough and thoughtful reflection included for each day | • Very analytical and thorough<br>• Demonstrated and learned much from the program<br>• Reached or exceeded all goals |
| **Level 3** | • Goals are based on FG test scores<br>• Most goals are appropriate<br>• Goals relate to the HFZ<br>• Included goals for each HRF component | • Completed and recorded all tests<br>• Completed and recorded three retests | • Completed all areas<br>• Activities were mostly appropriate<br>• Exercises were progressive | • Completed all areas<br>• Activities were mostly appropriate<br>• Exercises were progressive | • Completed all areas<br>• Activities were mostly appropriate<br>• Exercises were progressive | • Completed for at least four days per week<br>• Followed original fitness plan and modified when appropriate | • Mostly thorough and thoughtful reflection included for most days | • Somewhat analytical and thorough<br>• Seemed to have learned much from the program<br>• Reached or exceeded most goals |

*(continued)*

Table 10.1 (continued)

| Performance level | | Performance Criteria | | | | | | | |
| --- | --- | --- | --- | --- | --- | --- | --- | --- |
| | Fitness goals | Fitness tests | Warm-up and cool-down routine | Strength training program | Aerobic training program | Fitness participation log | Fitness journal | Final analysis and reflection |
| **Level 2** | • Some goals are based on FG test scores<br>• Some goals are inappropriate<br>• Goals relate to the HFZ<br>• Included goals for most HRF components | • Completed and recorded most tests<br>• Completed and recorded one or two retests | • Some areas missing<br>• Some activities were not appropriate<br>• Exercises were progressive | • Some areas missing<br>• Some activities were not appropriate<br>• Exercises were progressive | • Some areas missing<br>• Some activities were not appropriate<br>• Exercises were progressive | • Completed for at least three days per work<br>• Mostly followed original fitness plan and modified when appropriate | • Included for each day<br>• Reflections not very thoughtful or thorough | • Not analytical or thorough<br>• Learned some things from the program<br>• Reached most goals |
| **Level 1** | • Missing scores and retests<br>• Goals were not completed or were inappropriate | • Completed and recorded some tests<br>• Completed and recorded zero or one retests<br>• Did not record test scores | • Some areas missing<br>• Some activities were not appropriate or progressive | • Some areas missing<br>• Some activities were not appropriate or progressive | • Some areas missing<br>• Some activities were not appropriate or progressive | • Missed many days<br>• Did not make modifications<br>• Did not complete or submit | • Did not include each day<br>• Not appropriate<br>• Did not complete | • Very poor reflections<br>• Not much learned<br>• None or few goals reached<br>• Did not complete or participate |

# 11

# Effective Grading in Physical Education

*For most teachers, the giving of a single grade is always a hard and sometimes ugly compromise—all the more so as classes become more heterogeneous through mainstreaming and detracking. Without agreed-upon program goals, assessment procedures, and performance standards, there is little the individual teacher can do beyond muddling through, even though it means continued unfairness and well-meaning dishonesty in reports (Wiggins 1998b, 287–88).*

Calculating student grades is a challenging endeavor. Most people feel that the primary purpose of a grade is to communicate to parents, administrators, college officials, and students themselves how well the student has performed during the grading period (Guskey and Bailey 2001). Reducing the achievement of a student to a single grade can be daunting. When discussing grading practices with teachers, teaching philosophies tend to enter into the comments. Many teachers want to encourage students to like physical education and they feel that a low grade will turn students away from pursuing activities in the future. On the other hand, many teachers use grades as a way to encourage students to dress out for class, often failing students who decline to do so. Because many physical education teachers

have used dressing out and behavior as a basis for the entire grade, parents may interpret low grades in physical education as a reflection of those problems. As a high school physical education teacher, I (Jackie) remember many parents responding to lower grades with questions such as "Isn't he behaving himself?" or "Isn't she dressing out for class?"

There are many issues connected with grading in physical education. This chapter addresses them and offers potential solutions.

## PURPOSES OF GRADING AND GRADE REPORTING

Grading and grade reporting can serve several purposes, not all of which are used at all times. The most important purpose is to report the achievement of a student to others. A grade is a way to communicate with parents about how much a student has achieved during the grading period and during the year. Performance during the year is also used to determine whether secondary students earn credit toward graduation requirements, and employers use grades to indicate the competence of potential employees. Grade point average (GPA) is a strong predictor of student success in higher education and is frequently one of the factors used to determine whether a student is admitted to a college or university.

Students use grades as indicators of their level of achievement. Grades give teachers a way to communicate with students about whether they are meeting expectations in class or whether change is necessary. Students sometimes perceive that they either are or are not meeting expectations in a class, and the grade either confirms or refutes this perception.

A third purpose of grading is to provide an incentive for students and encourage them to learn. Some teachers view grades as a way to motivate students and reward students who dress for class and participate in an appropriate manner. Cotten and Cotten (1985) refer to grades as the ultimate weapon for student compliance. When teachers use the grade as an incentive to act appropriately, they are trying to reward effort and student compliance with the rules.

Grades can also be used to "sort" students. Students receiving high grades are often eligible for more demanding classes—advanced or elective high school physical education classes are sometimes restricted to students performing at a certain grade in a required physical education class. Some schools also offer special programs in which students can work as a teacher aide or teach others through outreach programs (e.g., serving as elementary school tutors), but students with low grades are often ineligible for these programs.

Some programs use grades as indicators of program effectiveness, when completing accreditation reports or year-end summaries. For example, grades can be used to evaluate the impact of implementing a new teaching method or approach, as changes in student GPAs are used as indicators of the effectiveness of the change.

# DEVELOPING A MEANINGFUL GRADING SYSTEM

If the primary purpose of grading is to communicate student achievement to others, then the grade should represent what the student has learned. Unfortunately, in many cases, there is lack of consistency about what the grade represents. This inconsistency can vary greatly with some teachers using product criteria to represent achievement, others using behavior to represent achievement, and still others using improvement or progress to determine the grade. When teachers fail to clearly define what the grade represents, this variation can even be seen in grades assigned to different students by the same teacher.

According to Guskey (1996a), grades should indicate the proportion of targets that students

recently had a conversation about grading with a beginning teacher. He had just finished calculating grades for his students, and I asked him about the criteria he had used. One of his students, who received a B, had been quite unfit at the beginning of the quarter and was unable to do more than three sit-ups. At the end of the grading period, she could do 15 sit-ups, and the B was a reward for her improvement. Another student, a troublemaker, also received a B, even though he was very fit and skilled. The teacher had penalized the student for behavior infractions to let him know that if he wanted an A he would need to be a model citizen in class as well as demonstrate skillfulness. A third student, who also received a B, had tried very hard in class and not been a behavior problem but had failed to dressed for class on three or four occasions. All of these students received the same grade, but each received it for a different reason. This lack of consistency makes a grade meaningless if the purpose of the grade is to communicate student achievement to others.

have mastered. Since grades are designed to report student accomplishments to others (e.g., parents, administrators, potential employers, college officials), they should be based on student achievement. Grade reports, if done correctly, represent a summary of students' major strengths and weaknesses. Because people are accustomed to receiving letter grades, they are deemed user-friendly because others understand (or think they do) what the grade represents. Despite the problems with grading, it is likely that letter grades will continue to be the way that grades are reported.

In this era of standards and standards-based curriculums, many teachers and researchers advocate for the use of a standards-based grade reporting system (Marzano 2006; Scriffiny 2008), in which a student receives a score or grade on each of the standards that the class addresses, which links the grade directly with student achievement. In many of these grading systems, progress is often reported in terms of whether the student has demonstrated an expected level of performance (e.g., proficient or advanced) or has failed to satisfy the grade-level expectations (e.g., partially proficient or below expectations) based on the standards written for the content area in the state or district.

Regardless of the grade reporting system used, if a grading format is to be effective and meaningful, teachers should formulate a grading plan before beginning instruction. Instead of merely summing all assessments that contributed to a grade during a marking period, teachers must decide in advance what they will use as a basis for the grade. After determining what types of knowledge students will need to achieve the targeted outcomes of the course, teachers design assessments to measure mastery for the covered content. Additional assessments (i.e., formative ones) may be used to provide feedback about performance, but they will not necessarily contribute to a student's final grade.

Just as it takes all of the pieces of a puzzle to make a complete picture, each assessment should represent part of the total assessment picture. When all the pieces are in place and fit together, teachers have a picture of student achievement and mastery of content that accurately portrays the extent of student learning. To assemble a complete picture, assessments must be planned before starting a marking period to ensure that they align with the teacher's vision of student achievement. Some teachers fail to do this, which results in a shotgun approach to grading. Just as one would not begin painting a wall by flicking a brush loaded with paint at the wall, student assessment should not be done in a haphazard manner in which one hopes everything will eventually be covered. "Building assessment to improve performance . . . requires that grades and reports reflect our values and provide apt feedback" (Wiggins 1998a, 288).

# PROBLEMS WITH TRADITIONAL GRADING PRACTICES

When teachers try to factor managerial concerns, effort, improvement, attitudes and behaviors, and a host of other variables into a grade, the meaning of the grade becomes distorted and confusing (Wiggins 1998a). Because a grade should represent achievement, process and progress factors should not be part of a grade. The next section provides a rationale for this position.

## Grading on Managerial Concerns

Some physical education teachers use attendance and student participation habits to calculate grades. In these classes, students who attend, "dress out" for class, participate on a regular basis, and don't cause discipline problems end up with high grades. The teacher thus lowers learning expectations in exchange for student compliance with the teacher's managerial system. For example, teachers feel that students must be dressed appropriately to participate, so that behavior is rewarded. When attendance and dressing out are used to calculate grades, teachers have measurable factors and tangible items to use for determining grades without expending energy to measure actual student learning.

Teachers who grade on managerial concerns must realize that this method of decreasing subjectivity also decreases the validity of the grade. When a grade represents whether a student has dressed for activity, arrived on time for class, and acted in an appropriate manner, it does not inform others about what the student has learned. These managerial concerns should be addressed through class rules and school policies and handled administratively rather than as part of the grade.

Unfortunately, the practice of grading on the basis of managerial concerns has become a traditional way of calculating physical education grades. The tradition is passed from one generation of teachers to the next because teachers tend to grade their students as they themselves were graded or because veteran teachers socialize student teachers and beginning teachers and pull these new teachers into the system. In some physical education programs, teachers are forced to follow departmental grading policies that are based on managerial components.

Teachers who use managerial concerns rationalize that students have to be present to learn and that dressing out is necessary for health and safety reasons. However, when teachers hold students accountable only for showing up on time and in proper uniform, the importance of physical education is significantly diminished. While it is true that students must be present to learn, students should not automatically be given participation points for attendance. Instead of using this practice, if a teacher had a series of skill assessments that contributed to part of the student's grade, using a mastery approach (i.e., students could have multiple attempts to meet the established criterion scores) for learning, then being in class would provide extra time to practice the assessment and additional opportunities to successfully reach the criterion score. The assessment rewards students who are there, while at the same time providing the teacher with information about students' progress toward learning objectives.

## Effort

Physical education teachers often tell their students to give 100 percent effort. The implication is that students should work as hard as possible to improve their skills. However, while 100 percent effort is a noble goal, defining this level of participation and exertion is a difficult if not impossible task. If one were to ask 10 physical education teachers to define effort, each would probably give a different response.

Problems arise when students perceive that they are giving 100 percent effort but the teacher perceives that they are not. Low-fit students who carry extra weight often fall victim to this problem. Given the extra weight they carry, they may be working as hard as or harder than their lean counterparts in terms of cardiovascular rate, but in terms of observable work they may appear to be slacking off. Unless teachers use heart rate monitors to measure output, measuring effort is just not possible. Also, consider the skilled athletes whose movements are so efficient that they could be performing well above others in the class but exerting little effort to do so. In fact, skilled performance is often demonstrated in seemingly effortless performance.

Instead of basing a percentage of the grade on effort, the best approach for evaluating effort is to set goals that *require* effort on the part of the students. Students who complete the assessment booklet or packet (as shown in chapter 9 for soccer) are demonstrating effort. Their levels of achievement indicate the effort they put into doing the assessment. Teachers might also use a "sponge," or instant activity, available to students as they enter class. These activities require little or no explanation, and students can start participating whenever they enter class, then record the results on a chart at the end of a specified period of time. Teachers can

Effort is very difficult to judge or measure.

individualize these instant activities, creating different levels of difficulty for low-, medium-, and high-skilled students. Teachers can either allow students to select their personal level of challenge for the activity or designate a level on which the student should work. Thus, students are challenged to work at an appropriate level of difficulty while simultaneously developing and improving skill, and eventually they are able to perform various activities at an enjoyable level of participation. Some students with lower initial skill will require longer periods of time to reach these goals, hence putting forth greater effort.

Aggressive students may be perceived as putting forth greater effort. For example, in watching a volleyball game, one might observe aggressive players trying to play the ball every time it comes to their side of the court. In some instances, however, aggressive players actually lack the desired psychomotor skills and attempt to camouflage this lack of skill through aggressive play. Additionally, although they play aggressively, they may not be meeting goals for cooperation during game play. Similarly, nonaggressive students are not necessarily trying less hard; they may simply not have an opportunity to play the ball because of interference by their aggressive classmates.

Because of the problems surrounding effort, teachers should avoid using it as a grading category and instead let it manifest itself when students work hard to reach criterion levels of performance. When teachers establish criteria for student performance, all students have the opportunity to demonstrate effort while learning.

## Including Behavior in a Grade

Reviewing content standards 5 and 6 from the National Association for Sport and Physical Education (NASPE) provides some useful ideas for assessing the students in the affective domain (2004). Specifically, students should do the following:

- Demonstrate responsibility to the teacher and other classmates, whether working individually or in groups
- Willingly accept the challenges and learning opportunities presented, whether participating voluntarily in familiar activities or learning new ones

Teachers should hold students accountable for good behavior only if the objective is written in clear, measurable, defensible terms so that students understand what they must do to satisfy the criteria. Defining fair play and appropriate student behavior toward others can be a difficult task. However, if this conduct is included in the program's goals, teachers should incorporate them in the class objectives, designate appropriate behaviors for them, and hold students accountable for meeting them. For example, a teacher might address appropriate student behavior through goals such as the following: Students will respect the efforts of others. Students will accept calls made by officials. All team members will collect or distribute their own equipment.

However, some teachers do include behavior in their grading scheme without defining their expectations. Students who behave badly in class usually cannot get a good grade (Guskey 1996a; Guskey and Bailey 2001). Although poor attitude and behavior are frustrating, they should not be used to calculate grades unless they affect student performance and directly cause a student not to meet instructional goals. Teachers who use behavior as a factor in a grade may do so in an attempt to get even with a student who causes problems for the teacher. In this case, the grade becomes a way of leveraging good behavior and getting even with students who create disruptions in class. Lowering goals and expectations in return for student compliance diminishes the content of physical education. This problem is exemplified when teachers roll out the ball and allow students to play, day after day, without requiring them to learn new skills or information. This is an environment where no new learning occurs, because no teacher instruction is being given, and it is simply an unacceptable practice that has no place in education.

Teachers need to deal directly with poor behavior by talking with the student to explain their expectations regarding behavior, making phone calls to the student's home, or by referring difficult cases to administrators. Some schools give two grades—the second being a separate evaluation for behavior—instead of factoring behavior into the achievement-based grade. O'Sullivan and Henninger (2000) created a Physical Education Behavior Profile for grading student behavior. In a ninth-grade class taught using a Sport Education Instructional Model, they assessed attitudes and observed behavior by including the following categories: displays teamwork at all times, respects the rights of others, shows prompt attention to teacher instruction, demonstrates a positive attitude, and dresses for active participation. Don Hellison also uses a behavior checklist to support his Teaching Personal and Social Responsibility Instructional Model (Hellison 2003).

Whenever attitude is factored into a grade, teacher bias may determine the final outcome. When a student makes a poor impression early in the grading period, the teacher's opinion toward him or her probably doesn't change despite what the student does. Such a judgment is clearly unfair to the student, and the grade in such a case would be impossible to justify. When grades are based on clear goals and expectations, a student cannot cop out on a low grade by saying, "The teacher just doesn't like me." Teachers should deal with inadequate behavior by using managerial strategies and avoid using it as a factor in grading.

## Improvement

In an effort to motivate lower-skilled and lower-fit individuals, some teachers attempt to grade on improvement. Grading on improvement poses a host of problems. When a teacher genuinely grades on improvement, at least two assessments are required: one before beginning the unit of study and one at the conclusion. Administering an assessment that can demonstrate improvement requires that instructional time be allocated so that an accurate measurement can be made. Many teachers object to doing assessments because they feel that they take too much time to administer; grading on improvement doubles the amount of time required for assessment because the assessment needs to be administered on at least two different occasions. The second issue is that when learning a new skill, the novice experiences the greatest learning gains or improvement. When a teacher grades on improvement, students who improve the most should have the greatest gains and therefore receive the highest grades. Thus a student who has greater initial skill may make less improvement and thus end up with a lower grade than less skilled classmates who show greater improvement.

The differences in improvement scores opens the door to a third problem—undependable gain scores that result from what is commonly known as sandbagging. In this phenomenon, students intentionally perform poorly during initial testing and then make miraculous gains as the unit concludes. The sandbagger receives a high grade because of the huge improvement from the initial assessment.

The fourth problem associated with the practice of grading on improvement is that students might improve and still not meet unit objectives for reasonable skill achievement. The teacher's goal of helping students become skillful participants remains unfulfilled.

When a teacher is truly committed to helping students achieve competence, he or she should not use the practice of grading on improvement. When teachers clearly state criteria for performance, they stabilize the otherwise moving target that results from grading on improvement. When teachers inform students about goals on the first day of a unit and then follow through with appropriate instruction, students should have adequate opportunity to reach the goals, assuming that the teacher is a competent educator and that adequate time is allowed for learning. Some units might require up to nine weeks of instruction and practice to allow students to achieve competence. Most students enjoy these extended units, because they can attain higher levels of skill. When students are successful in developing competence, their enjoyment of participation in the activity increases, as does the likelihood that they will continue participating in it beyond graduation (Rink 2000).

## GRADE FORMATS IN PHYSICAL EDUCATION

When schools first began reporting student achievement to parents, narratives were used to explain student progress when it was not possible to report to parents in person. As class sizes increased, the need arose to report grades differently. Developing a grade reporting system that is acceptable to both parents and teachers is difficult, because these two groups often attach different purposes to the grading process. In many instances, the grade reporting systems used represents a compromise between what parents want to know and what teachers wish to tell them. Although narratives and checklists are sometimes used at the elementary level, letter grades are the most commonly used form of grading at the secondary level (Hensley et al. 1987). Because letter grades are so commonly used, both parents and teachers are familiar with them, so they are seen as an acceptable compromise. Unfortunately, the disparity of how grades are calculated diminishes the information that the letter grade provides. The following section discusses several different ways to report student progress.

## Narratives

Narratives are written descriptions of student achievement. Teachers can cover a variety of topics in a narrative, including achievement, behavior, effort, and improvement. Although narratives provide a lot of information, parents do not always grasp the implications of a narrative if the narrative does not include information about the level of performance that is expected for the child. Also, being creative while writing narratives for an entire class is difficult. After the first five or six, many of the comments made about different students tend to sound alike. Narratives are also the most time-consuming of any reporting form to complete (Guskey 1996a), and, considering the number of students a secondary physical education instructor teaches, creating narratives for each of them would be nearly impossible. In an effort to address this issue, software has been developed that contains a bank of comments from which teachers select those that are appropriate, which the computer then combines into a narrative. These computer-generated narratives lose impact if students compare their narratives with other students' narratives or their own from previous marking periods.

## Checklists

Checklists contain a list of topics or skills that are considered to be the content of the class. For each characteristic, teachers can indicate with a scoring system whether a student has obtained proficiency. Because of the detail that checklists offer, they are useful for diagnosis and prescription. Unfortunately, parents tend not to understand checklists. Although they report student progress, they rarely report whether the

progress is appropriate. Parents read a narrative or checklist and then ask, "So what?" Parents want to know what their student has achieved, how their child compares with others in the class, and what the child should be doing. In other words, they want to know, "Is my child above or below grade-level expectations or on target?" To address this issue, some school districts have added extra categories to report cards so that parents can interpret the information provided by a checklist.

## Letter Grades

Although letter grades really do not address the problems identified with other grading formats, people are more accustomed to them and therefore less critical of their shortcomings. Parents usually have experience in interpreting student achievement through a letter grade. Grading with a letter, symbol, or meaningful word (e.g., outstanding, satisfactory, pass, fail) involves a process of abstracting a great deal of information into a single sign for communication. Of all the grading forms used, letter grades are probably the most easily misinterpreted (Guskey 1996a). The problem with letter grades is not the symbol but rather the lack of stable and clear reference points when using these symbols (Wiggins 1998a). Some schools assign a word to the letter grade to help clarify the meaning of the symbol (e.g., A= Excellent; B= Good; C= Satisfactory [Guskey & Bailey 2001]).

Although the move from a grading system based on participation and dressing for class to a system based on measurable student achievement is positive, parents need to be educated about what the grade really represents. When teachers give parents and students rubrics and explain where students are in reference to them, some of the mystery surrounding grades fades away.

## Standards-Based Reporting Systems

Today schools use standards to denote what students should be learning in various subject areas. In an attempt to align learning and then report students' progress toward meeting standards, some districts or even individual teachers have begun to report learning in terms of content-area standards (Scriffiny 2008). With standards-based grading, teachers give an assessment and then identify the standards addressed with the assessment. When the report card is aligned with standards, then teachers, parents, and students can readily see students' progress toward meeting the standards.

With most content standards, benchmarks are written to help define what the learning should be for the respective grade levels. Said another way, the benchmark statements help unpack the standard. For example, when reading the NASPE content standards (2004), one sees sample performance outcomes associated with the content standards for each grade-level grouping. For example, standard 1 has 9 sample performance outcomes for the K–2 level and 10 for the 3–5 level. If a teacher or school district were to list learning for each of those performance outcomes or benchmark statements for every standard, the result would be a very lengthy—and cumbersome—reporting system. To avoid this problem, teachers often list the content standard. Confusion can arise because the same content standard appears for every grade level, and if parents are not educated about this fact they may fail to realize that the expectations for the various grade levels are progressively difficult.

Another problem can occur if a teacher marks the student's progress toward the standard at the beginning of the school year at a lower level (e.g., developing), which is actually appropriate for the content covered to date in the class, and parents interpret the low score as an indication that the student is underperforming. Whereas this type of reporting system is beneficial for teachers as they measure student learning in terms of standards, a lot of parent education must accompany the use of a standards-based report card.

## Mastery Grading Reporting Systems

With a mastery learning approach to education, students are allowed multiple chances to learn the content. On any given topic, some students will learn more quickly than others. When time is used as a constant (everyone is allotted the same amount of time), the degree of proficiency on the content can vary. One way to report this variation in learning is through a letter-based (e.g., A-through-F) grade reporting system. With mastery learning, all students are expected to master the content, and the teacher realizes that it will take some students longer than others to do so. When an assessment is given, students have multiple chances to demonstrate an acceptable level of competence on the assessment. When they master the topic, they are allowed to move on to new learning.

With a mastery learning approach to education, students are not allowed to get by with an unsatisfactory score (e.g., a D or F) and move on. Instead, they are required to continue learning until they achieve a specified

n an attempt to dispel some of the mystery that often surrounds representing student achievement in a single symbol, the Cincinnati Academy of Physical Education (CAPE) provided results of evaluations for several different areas on its report cards. Students were evaluated in each of three areas: cognitive understanding, affective sensations, and motor performance. In the cognitive understanding category, students were given a score, and their performance was rated as superior, good, average, fair, or poor in each of the follow subcategories: rules, strategies, written assignments, knowledge test, and oral test. Although students did not receive an overall score for the affective sensations category, student performance in the subcategories of attitude, group play/interaction, safety, and confidence were rated superior, good, average, fair, or poor. Motor performance had no subcategories, but space was provided for instructors to list various skills for the units taught, and students were given a score and rated them as superior, good, average, fair, or poor in their performance of the skills. Because the three main components were broken down into subcategories, students and parents had a much clearer understanding of student performance versus all of this information being combined into a single letter grade.

level of competency. Continued instruction does not mean that the material is simply retaught; rather, either students are provided with corrective activities or the materials are presented using a different approach to help students fill gaps in their knowledge. Similarly, students who master the materials more quickly are given enrichment activities that allow them to continue practicing and extend their competence.

Several different assessments are used to document student mastery of content. Since students are not allowed to move ahead until they have achieved competence, all skills needed for success at the next level are mastered. When learning is progressive, all students have an equal chance for success since they have the necessary skills or building blocks to move on to new learning. With this reporting system, there are only two levels: mastery and nonmastery. This grading system cannot be used to sort students into different levels of performance, but it does honor the notion that all children are capable of learning.

A grade should reflect a student's achievement for the grading period; however, capturing the work of 6 or 9 weeks in a single letter or category is difficult. The main purpose of a grade is to communicate to others (the student, parents, administrators, employers, college officials) the student's level of mastery of programmatic goals. Because teachers should inform students of their goals for the class and keep students informed of their progress on a regular basis, it is important for a program to have well-articulated goals so that others know what the grade means. Students are more likely to be motivated when they understand what they must do to be successful. These goals can be sent home at the beginning of a semester and again with the report card so that parents know what students have achieved and what the grade represents.

# EFFECTIVE GRADING IN PHYSICAL EDUCATION

When physical education was in its infancy, the emphasis was on improving health by making people physically fit. As various sports grew in popularity, other aspects of physical activity became more important. In 1910, Clark Hetherington, one of the early leaders in physical education, proposed that physical education should

**Figure 11.1** Hetherington's four areas of physical education.

address four different areas of concern: organic, psychomotor, intellectual, and character-related (Siedentop 2001; see figure 11.1). Today these four areas continue to be the basis of many physical education program objectives. When one reads the NASPE content standards (2004), Hetherington's four areas are not only visible but also play a prominent role throughout the document. Hetherington used the term *psychomotor* to denote achievement with regard to motor skills, *intellectual* to mean the knowledge components important to physical education, *organic* for the fitness components, and *character* for those aspects of learning associated with the affective domain (e.g., leadership, positive sporting behavior, teamwork, respect, and caring for others). Having defined physical education in a manner that is still in use 100 years later, Hetherington's insight and vision are admirable.

Although Hetherington's four areas are still considered important in physical education, they are emphasized to different extents in various programs. Some physical education curriculums are moving toward an emphasis on the development of fitness, with little concern about the development of sports skills. Other programs have shifted to a sport and activity emphasis based on the assumption that fitness is embedded in the various sports and activities when students participate in them on a regular basis. Adventure education programs promote development and learning in the affective domain, and activities are selected to promote the growth of character. Some programs combine activities from several curricular models, thus encouraging student achievement in all four of Hetherington's components.

The purpose of this book is not to argue in favor of any one curriculum but rather to show how performance assessments can evaluate student performance in physical education. The items and areas used to calculate grades in physical education are dependent upon the goals and objectives of a given program. If teachers are promoting a fitness curriculum, then this component should receive the greatest emphasis in the grading scheme. If increasing students' ability to play various sports or perform a range of physical activities (e.g., dance, swimming, gymnastics) is the main programmatic goal, then the psychomotor area should receive the greatest emphasis. Regardless of the curriculum selected, grades should be based on predetermined criteria rather than on a class ranking or percentile of a normative score.

To illustrate one way of determining student grades, let us assume that the physical educa-tion program's philosophy is to develop skillful movers and that 60 percent of each student's grade comes from demonstrating competence in this area. Because this philosophy involves a cognitive component, 25 percent of the grade is based upon competence for that component. The grading plan used in the example also values achievement in the affective domain, and 15 percent of the grade is based upon affective components.

After deciding where to place emphasis for creating the grade, teachers must select units of study that address the programmatic goals. In this example, the teacher decides that team handball and pickleball will be taught during a 9-week grading period because these two units complement each other and will allow students to attain several program objectives along with addressing several NASPE standards. Next, the teacher writes unit goals and develops assess-ments that determine whether students have achieved the stated goals. When this process is completed, the teacher goes back to the original percentages determined for programmatic goals to ensure that the unit's percentages match those set for the program. Teachers can leave the numbers as percentages or, if they find it easier, convert the percentages into points, as illustrated in the example (see figure 11.2). Some grading software is designed to calculate grades from percentages without converting individual test scores to points, thus making the conversion to points unnecessary.

The teacher decides to assign 150 points to pickleball and 250 points to team hand-ball because team handball covers 30 days of the 45-day grading period. Both units involve skills, but since team hand-ball is taught for a longer period of time, the majority of the 240 points allotted to the psychomotor domain comes from team handball. Several appropriate rubrics

Some programs base a student's grade on the results of fitness testing; however, for several reasons, NASPE does not support this practice. First, many factors other than physical activity can influence scores on a fitness test, including but not limited to heredity, maturation, chrono-logical age, and other factors beyond the control of the student or teacher (Welk and Meredith 2008). Additionally, because improvement on fitness can be a slow process (each individual must start at his or her own level) and many programs do not provide sufficient time for students to become physically fit, stu-dents can be inappropriately penalized for factors related to the administration of the program. Last, the standard that addresses physical fitness is only one of six standards. As such, it is inap-propriate to base a student's grade purely on fitness results.

| Unit Goals | Percentage of Grade | Points |
|---|---|---|
| Psychomotor skill | 60 | 240 |
| Knowledge | 25 | 100 |
| Affective | 15 | 60 |
| Total | 100 | 400 |

Team handball = 250 points

Pickleball = 150 points

## Psychomotor

### Team Handball

| | |
|---|---|
| 60 points | Game-play assessments (4 at 15 points each) |
| 30 points | Team handball practice log |
| 20 points | Shooting test |
| 20 points | Passing test |
| 10 points | Goalkeeping test |
| 10 points | Dribbling test |

### Pickleball

| | |
|---|---|
| 45 points | Game-play assessments (3 at 15 points each) |
| 15 points | Serve test |
| 15 points | Volley test |
| 15 points | Continuous rally test |

## Knowledge

### Team Handball

| | |
|---|---|
| 25 points | Student project choice (write newspaper article, record a game broadcast, write broadcast script, analyze a video of game play) |
| 20 points | Game-play assessment (2 at 10 points each) |
| 15 points | Game-play officiating (3 at 5 points each) |

### Pickleball

| | |
|---|---|
| 20 points | Game-play assessment (2 at 10 points each) |
| 10 points | Scouting the competition and strategy analysis (2 at 5 points each) |
| 10 points | Written test |

## Affective

### Team Handball

| | |
|---|---|
| 20 points | Journal |
| 10 points | Peer assessment (2 at 5 points each) |
| 10 points | Teacher assessment (2 at 5 points each) |

### Pickleball

| | |
|---|---|
| 10 points | Sponge activity self-assessment (2 at 5 points each) |
| 10 points | Exit slips (2 at 5 points each) |

## Grading Scale

A 360–400 points

B 320–359 points

C 280–319 points

D 240–279 points

F 239 and below

**Figure 11.2** This figure illustrates a plan for grading student achievement.

for assessing game play are provided in chapter 3. Teachers must decide how to assign points to the various descriptors for game play using the rubric (see table 11.1). Similar decisions about the distribution of points are made about the cognitive and affective domain areas as the teacher divides all of the 400 points between the two units. The important thing to remember here is that the teacher must continually go back to program goals when deciding how to weight the assessments.

With performance-based assessments, the grade is determined by the rubric. When point systems are used, the points for the various

**Table 11.1**  Sample Game-Play Rubric

|  | Rookie | Novice | Player | Pro prospect |
|---|---|---|---|---|
| Fielding (15 percent) | (1–9 points) Stands upright and does not assume a ready position when playing the field. Gets distracted or fails to pay attention to what is going on in the game. | (10 points) Assumes a ready position when the batter steps up to the plate. Can move and catch pop flies and handle ground balls hit with moderate speed. | (15 points) Is able to move to catch pop flies within 10 feet (3 m) in any direction. Usually makes the correct choice about whether to catch the ball in the air or play it on the hop. Handles most ground balls and throws to the appropriate base. | (15 points) Can catch a fly ball on the run while moving in any direction. When playing deep fly balls, looks over the shoulder to track the ball. Handles ground balls and line drives that are hit hard. Throws quickly to the appropriate base to get the out. |
| Throwing and catching skills (15 percent) | (1-9 points) Throws are weak with incorrect form. Pushes the ball rather than throwing it. Attempts to catch the ball with one hand. Is inaccurate when trying to pitch the ball. | (10 points) Able to throw accurately from one base to the next. Holds the glove correctly when catching overhead balls or those below the waist. Can pitch the ball with some accuracy. | (15 points) Able to throw accurately when playing the infield. Can throw the ball to the relay person when playing an outfield position. Catches most fly balls and can field ground balls. Able to pitch and throw strikes. | (15 points) Can time a jump and catch balls that are seemingly over the player's head. Can field a ground ball and play the hop. Can throw accurately from an outfield position to the infield. Able to throw strikes with good force, making the ball difficult to hit. Lots of strike outs when this player pitches. |
| Batting (15 percent) | (1–9 points) Chops or lunges at the ball while hitting. Lets many good pitches go by or consistently swings at bad pitches. May rest the bat on the shoulder when up to bat. | (10 points) Uses good form when swinging at the ball. Can hit the ball when it is in the middle of the strike zone. Usually uses good judgment at the plate. | (15 points) Makes good decisions when swinging at the ball, resulting in few strikeouts. Can purposefully hit the ball on the ground or in the air, depending on the base runners and the number of outs. | (15 points) Can place the ball when up to bat. Is able to pull the ball. Can hit balls on the edge of the strike zone. Waits to swing, resulting in powerful hits. Can place the ball to advance the runner when needed. |

| | Rookie | Novice | Player | Pro prospect |
|---|---|---|---|---|
| Defense (10 percent) | (1–7 points) Stands in the same position regardless of number of players on base, number of outs, or quality and type of batter. | (8 points) Adjusts position when playing a base according to the game situation (runners, outs, pitch count). Attempts to back up the play. | (10 points) Moves to position self to back up the play or function as a relay person for deeply hit balls. | (10 points) Directs people to adjust their fielding positions depending on the game play situation. |
| Offense (5 percent) | (1–3 points) Runs to the next base when told. Runs the bases aggressively and frequently is put out on the play because of bad decisions. | (4 points) Knows when to run to avoid a force-out. Is somewhat cautious in deciding whether to advance on a hit. | (5 points) Makes good decisions when running the bases and is usually safe. Knows own ability and rarely overreaches this capacity. | (5 points) Takes the abilities of others into account when running the bases. Is aggressive when the situation calls for it but makes decisions for the good of the team rather than personal glory. |
| Knowledge of rules (20 percent) | (1–10 points) Knows some basic rules but makes bad decisions due to lack of knowledge. Struggles with the difference between a force-out and a tag-out. | (15 points) Has a working knowledge of the game regarding hitting, base running, fly-outs, and force-outs. Occasionally gets confused but has enough knowledge to play the game effectively. | (20 points) Knows more complex rules, such as what to do with an infield fly when runners are on base. Can answer most questions when asked and understands how to interpret rules and apply them to most situations. | (20 points) Uses rules to gain offensive and defensive advantages. Can answer questions when others appear confused about the situation. Is able to apply rules. Can officiate a game accurately. |
| Good sporting behavior (20 percent) | (1–10 points) Argues with the umpire. Gets angry when a call goes against self or a teammate. Makes inappropriate remarks to distract opponents. Fails to offer support when a teammate makes a mistake. Tries to play the position of another player if that player is weak. | (15 points) Accepts the calls of the umpire without argument. Encourages other members of the team. Wants to play for enjoyment of the game rather than for personal glory. | (20 points) Encourages the play of others. Plays own position even if the player in the next position is weak or known for making mistakes. Wants teammates to be successful and enjoy the game. Others enjoy having this person on their team. | (20 points) Encourages others when good plays are made, both on own team and on opposing team. Demonstrates leadership skills while making efforts to ensure that everyone is successful. Gets personal enjoyment from the success of others. |

assessment pieces are designated on the scoring guide. Analytic rubrics pose a problem for grading: The teacher must devise a system for converting the various components into grades. To convert an analytic rubric to a holistic one

for final grading purposes, the teacher can write a paragraph describing the level of performance for each letter grade (for an example, see the holistic rubric presented in figure 3.6). The teacher then simply matches student performance with the paragraph that best describes it. If certain qualities must be present for an A-level performance, then these qualities must be indicated in the rubric. Some components, though important, may not be considered essential for performance. If the less important components are at a lower level than indicated on the holistic rubric, but the key elements are present at the upper level, the student should receive the higher grade. Using this method, student performance is evaluated from a holistic and big-picture perspective, which is often more accurate than when many individual elements are assessed separately and added together to determine the final grade.

It is very important to decide the total points or percentages at the beginning of the marking period and determine which assessments will contribute to the grade. Once this has been done, teachers should not add additional assessments as the unit proceeds, because doing so can undercut the impact of major assessments. Here is an example of what *not* to do. In this scenario, the teacher required students to choreograph a dance and record the performance on video. The assessment was assigned 100 points and required a major portion of the time spent in physical education class during that grading period. After the 100 points were assigned, the teacher began to give quizzes and homework

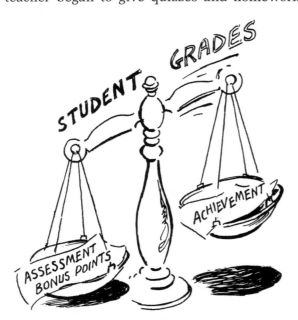

Giving out bonus points can disrupt the balance of a sound grading system that is based on student achievement.

assignments to keep students on task and motivated as the unit progressed. These quizzes and homework assignments required minimal effort and perhaps an hour of student time. By the end of the grading period, 100 points of homework and quizzes were included in the grade, making them worth as much as the project that took 4 to 5 weeks to complete. Thus, relatively insignificant work had as much impact on students' grades as did the major choreography assignment. When teachers decide in advance what factors to use to calculate student grades and then resist the temptation to pad the grade with additional points, the grading system remains true to the unit and program objectives.

# CHALLENGES IN USING EFFECTIVE GRADING PRACTICES

Physical educators face many potential problems related to grading. When these factors are known in advance, they can be avoided, thus resulting in a fair and equitable system for grading. Teachers can assign fair and defensible grades when they address issues related to validity and reliability, select assessments that evaluate students themselves without being influenced by the skill of a partner or team, and adjust the curriculum to accommodate a wide range of skills. The following section gives suggestions for addressing common problems associated with grading students.

## Validity and Reliability

Grades should represent the degree to which a student meets the program's goals. When grades are based on measures other than achievement, the grade is not a valid indicator of the goals. Teachers must articulate to students, parents, and administrators the method they will use to determine grades, and must avoid using managerial factors that supersede or override student achievement (e.g., lowering a student's grade by a full letter due to an incidence of not dressing out). Additionally, if a grade is based on invalid assessments, then the grade itself becomes invalid. Teachers must identify what they will accept as evidence that a student has met instructional goals; these assessments must measure learning. When teachers use valid, reliable assessments and base grades on the degree to which students meet instructional goals, then grades accurately represent student achievement.

## Dependence on Other Students

When designing assessments that contribute to a grade or other type of high-stakes accountability (e.g., a program evaluation), teachers must make sure that a given student's grade is not influenced by the skills of other students. For instance, during a volleyball game, a student must receive a pass to demonstrate a spike, but if the setup is poorly executed then the student has no opportunity to demonstrate his or her spiking ability. When an assessment requires a response from another student (e.g., a tennis rally, game play, a double-Dutch routine), the teacher needs to make sure that students providing the setup (i.e., the support for the skill) have enough ability to do so correctly. To provide consistency in this situation, teachers might consider providing the prior response themselves, using a student aide with good skills, or organizing game play with several different partners on several different days (i.e., providing multiple evaluation opportunities) so that they can accurately evaluate the student's competence and achievement.

## Student Skill Levels and Experience

Setting criteria for an activity or unit in a class that includes very high-skilled and very low-skilled students is difficult. Students with experience in the sport or activity should score higher on the assessments. When the standards are set too high the lower-skilled students may feel as though this level of achievement is unobtainable. When standards are set too low the higher-skilled students remain unchallenged; they may have been able to perform at the required level of achievement before instruction for the unit began.

One solution to this problem is simply to not teach familiar units or activities in which some students may already have competence. Given that many students are required to enroll in only a limited number of physical education classes, teaching unfamiliar activities seems educationally prudent, since most teachers want students to gain competence in several sport areas. However, trying to select activities in which *no* student has experience is also difficult. If the department has more than one physical education instructor, teachers could elect to offer different activities and require students to sign up for an activity in which they had not previously participated.

In a class where students bring a wide range of skill and ability, skilled players might be assessed on a basic skill level that contributes to their grade. Upon passing this evaluation, these students can be given additional activities and drills that provide them with challenges for their psychomotor abilities. Station work can also allow every student, regardless of ability, to improve his or her skills, as long as several levels of challenge are provided and students are allowed to self-select the level on which they wish to participate. These extra levels do not need to be required for a grade, but they do challenge students and provide ways for students to improve their skills.

Sport Education curriculums offer yet another solution to this dilemma. Because students have the opportunity to play a variety of sport roles during an activity, higher-skilled students might assume some other aspect of the game that they had not previously experienced. For example, students who have a lot of playing experience could benefit from serving as a coach or referee, thus experiencing the game through another lens. With dance or gymnastics, students with prior experience could choreograph dance pieces or floor exercise routines. Additionally, experienced gymnasts could demonstrate characteristics found in NASPE standard 5 ("Exhibits responsible personal and social behavior that respects self and others in physical activity settings") by spotting classmates and helping those who are less skilled learn new skills.

Another way to address the problem of wide ranges in skill or ability level is to select a variety of units within a grading period. A dance unit might be coupled with a volleyball unit, or an individual sport might be paired with a team sport. If one activity requires strength and power, teachers should pair it with another activity that requires other, equally valued traits, such as balance or rhythm. This approach provides students with a balanced curriculum and ensures that the grade is not determined by any single motor skill characteristic.

When addressing the issue of a wide variation in skill level within a class, revisiting the unit objectives should reveal goals in areas other than the psychomotor domain. Because psychomotor skill is only one of the areas on which a grade is usually determined, lower-skilled students can emphasize other areas, such as knowledge, homework, teamwork, and affective attitudes that can contribute to the final grade. When considering the total grade, all students undoubtedly have at least one area in which they can succeed, even though the bar is set high for psychomotor skill. Since the final grade reflects the total picture of how well students have met program goals, each student can excel in at least one area.

# GRADING PRACTICES FOR STUDENTS WITH SPECIAL NEEDS

This section addresses two populations: students with disabilities and students who do not have speaking skills in English (who are often referred to as ESL [English as a second language] or ELL [English language learner] students). Although the latter situation is less of a problem for physical education teachers than for classroom teachers, the language barrier still raises important issues that need to be addressed.

Most teachers have faced a dilemma when grading students with disabilities. If these students are graded on the progress that they make during the semester while other students are graded on achievement, then teachers are giving grades based on two different sets of criteria. When grading students with an Individualized Educational Plan (IEP), that document should be used as the basis for the grade. The IEP should outline the type and quality of work that the student is expected to do to document learning and achievement. Since grades are designed to communicate the degree of achievement, a narrative should accompany this grade to let parents know what the student accomplished during the semester and to establish expectations for the future. In schools where an adaptive physical education teacher delivers instruction to students with special needs, this teacher should be consulted when assigning the grade. Although a narrative requires extra work by the teacher, it is necessary to ensure good communication with parents. A copy of the narrative should be placed in the student's cumulative file so that his or her progress on the IEP can be noted.

Assessments used to determine the grade can also be modified for students with special needs. Several good physical education texts (Burton and Miller 1998; Horvat, Block, and Kelly 2007; Lieberman and Houston-Wilson 2002) provide insight into appropriate modifications for these students. An excellent resource for assessing fitness is the *Brockport Physical Fitness Test Manual* (Winnick and Short 1999). Participating in IEP meetings also provides physical education teachers with a way to communicate learning to parents and to classroom teachers and plan instruction that is most beneficial to the student. When grading students with special needs, one must go back to the purposes of grading and design a system that is consistent with legal guidelines.

For students who have special needs but do not have an IEP, the teacher should write appropriate instructional goals and then base grades on the degree to which these goals are met. These goals should be shared with parents and others who are central to the child's education to clarify what the grade is meant to represent.

When assessing students with ESL issues, several of the assessments used in this book can assess learning despite language barriers. For students who can communicate verbally but struggle with written assessments, interviews or role plays might be used. Game play can be a way to determine whether students know the rules associated with various games, instead of relying on selected-response tests to measure a student's knowledge. With ESL students, teachers need to determine how students' knowledge and skills can be accurately assessed and then use those assessments to measure students' learning. Policies need to be established so that the grade assigned to an ESL student is both fair and representative of the student's achievement.

# HINTS AND SUGGESTIONS FOR MORE EFFECTIVE GRADING PRACTICES

Developing a sound, defensible grading system is imperative for the beginning teacher. The system should be based on program goals, should be fair and consistent for all students, and should document students' learning and achievement. Here are some ideas for enhancing grading practices in physical education (see figure 11.3).

## Use Learning as a Basis for Grades

Some physical education teachers try to motivate students by giving high grades for minimal effort because they want students to like physical education. This approach is actually counterproductive because when only minimal effort is required, then students, parents, administrators, and others tend to lose respect for the subject. Meaningful learning is intrinsically motivating (Herman, Aschbacher, and Winters

---

## Hints and Suggestions for Highly Effective Grading Practices

### Achievement

- Use learning as a basis for grades.
- Set the bar at an appropriate level of achievement.
- Look at achievement through a variety of lenses.

### Fairness

- Show the assessment plan early in the instructional unit.
- Keep the grading system balanced.
- Allow students multiple opportunities for success.
- Allow extra practice time for less skilled students.
- Minimize subjectivity on assessments that lead to a grade.
- Do not give low grades to motivate students to try harder.
- Avoid averaging scores to arrive at a student grade.

### Teaching

- Use assessment for multiple purposes rather than just to give grades.
- Give extra credit for extra learning, not just for doing extra work.

**Figure 11.3** These suggestions are the result of several years of trial and error and are offered to help you develop highly effective grading practices.

---

1992). Csikszentmihalyi (2000) talks about the importance of flow in people's lives. When people experience an optimal level of challenge and when this level of challenge brings success, they tend to continue participating and in fact can lose all track of time. Several readers of this book have probably experienced this sensation while participating in physical activity. It is like a car firing on all cylinders. Everything is working together. Every member of the team is in sync. If dancing with the Radio City Rockettes, every dancer is contributing to an aesthetic picture. When people have to work hard to be successful in an endeavor, they appreciate the achievement more. They must, however, know what they are required to learn and do. The key is to define success in terms that students clearly understand, so that they know what is expected to achieve the desired outcome. Teachers then simply need to provide the vehicle for reaching these targets and outcomes. Assessments shouldn't be watered down so that students with minimal achievement receive high grades.

## Set the Bar at an Appropriate Level of Achievement

Students usually meet the teacher's expectations, but they don't often exceed them unless they are motivated by something other than a grade. When determining criteria for assessments, teachers should set the standards high—but not so high that students will be unable to reach them.

Setting the criteria for an assessment when it is used for the first time is difficult. Goals and objectives for the unit should determine where the bar of achievement will be placed. If the teacher's objective is for students to have adequate skill to engage in game play at a recreational level, then the bar for achievement should be set at that level. To do this, teachers must determine what skills are involved and the level of expertise necessary for performing each of them. Teachers can then select the assessments they will use to evaluate these skills.

Criteria for assessments should be based on the level of expertise demonstrated by individuals who play or perform at the level that the teacher wants students to achieve. By observing recreational play and noting what players at that level are capable of doing, a teacher can develop a sense of where to place expectations for assessments. Another approach is to see what athletes (junior varsity or varsity) are capable of doing on certain assessments and then make appropriate adjustments. A third option is for the teacher to do a self-administered assessment provided that the teacher has a reasonable amount of skill in the selected sport or activity.

When a teacher merely sets the bar at the level at which students are currently performing, they never become motivated to go beyond that level (Wiggins 1998a). Goals should be set at a level that ensures student success during game play (or during the culminating activity for the unit). Because physical education classes are designed to teach students new things, teachers should be cognizant of students' current abilities and require them to improve, either by learning additional skills or by becoming more proficient at performing the skills that they already can perform.

## Look at Achievement Through a Variety of Lenses

Assessments should provide teachers with several lenses for evaluating students. When qualitative researchers want to confirm their observations, they use several types of data on the same topic or subjects in an attempt to gain a clearer picture of what they are studying. This method is also somewhat analogous to a detective trying to solve a case—the more clues that point to the same conclusion, the stronger the argument. Similarly, when several indicators lead to the same conclusion about a student's grade, the teacher becomes more certain that the degree of student learning and achievement has been correctly identified. Many critics of the current approach to school accountability associated with the No Child Left Behind legislation argue that a single test or test format cannot adequately measure student learning (Popham 2001; Bracey 2008).

Physical education is based on an array of skills, knowledge, and attitudinal dispositions, all of which contribute to a physically educated person. This scope should be considered when determining student grades. A grade should never be based on a single assessment or factor. When a teacher bases grades on several types of assessment from the psychomotor, cognitive, and affective domains, then the assigned grades—for each student, regardless of skill or

fitness level—should accurately reflect his or her level of learning.

## Show the Assessment Plan Early in the Instructional Unit

Some students have difficulty achieving psychomotor goals. By showing the assessments early in the unit, clearly stating the criteria for each, and giving several chances to master the material, students should have ample opportunity to achieve goals. Informing students of criteria in advance gives them reasonable and realistic opportunities to master the material, assuming that instruction supports the necessary learning. When students know how they will be evaluated (i.e., know the criteria and assessments that will be used), they can self-assess or peer-assess during the instructional process. Instruction tends to be more focused as well, because teachers set their sights on their terminal expectations for student learning and thus act as coaches helping students reach the designated goals.

## Keep the Grading System Balanced

Figure 11.4 shows a sample grading plan that is not unlike many of those typically used in a high school physical education program. At first glance, it looks as though students are graded on four different areas. Students must achieve a certain level of skill in the psychomotor domain, perform well on written tests, and show positive direction and leadership. Closer examination of the grading system reveals that dressing for class overrides each of these areas, thus destroying the balance of the grading scheme. Regardless of performance in any of the areas, students fail the class if they don't dress out for class. If dressing for class determines the student grade, and if the grade represents the degree to which a student has met class objectives, then the objective of this class must be to have students dress for class. This is not the message that most physical education teachers want to convey about their programs, but a grading system such as this one inadvertently does just that.

When looking at the F grade descriptions, only dress cuts, absences, and nonparticipation are listed. Thus, even though skill, knowledge, and leadership seem to be identified as grad-

# Grading System

## Four Areas of Evaluation

1. Attendance and participation
2. Cooperation and attitude
3. Skill improvement
4. Learning achievement

### A Grade

- 90 percent to 100 percent on written tests
- 90 percent to 100 percent on skill tests
- Demonstrated leadership and positive direction
- Dressed and participated all but 2 days of the grading period

### B Grade

- 80 percent to 89 percent on written tests
- 80 percent to 89 percent on skill tests
- Demonstrated leadership and positive direction
- Dressed and participated all but 4 days of the grading period

### C Grade

- 70 percent to 79 percent on written tests
- 70 percent to 79 percent on skill tests
- Demonstrated leadership and positive direction
- Dressed and participated all but 7 days of a grading period

### D Grade

- 60 percent to 69 percent on written tests
- 60 percent to 69 percent on skill tests
- Demonstrated leadership and positive direction
- Dressed and participated all but 10 days of the grading period

### F Grade

- Five or more dress cuts
- Eleven days absent
- Five unexcused nonparticipation days
- Combination of any of the above

An accumulation of five dress cuts in one 9-week period constitutes failure for that 9-week period!

Excused absence days may be made up for class credit within 5 school days following the day of absence. Unexcused absences, expulsions, suspensions, truancy, and dress cuts cannot be made up.

Despite receiving passing grades for the first, second, and third items, you can still fail for the 9 weeks because of excessive absenteeism, nonparticipation, or dress cuts.

**Figure 11.4**   Although this sample grading system appears to assess cognitive, affective, and psychomotor learning, the focus on dressing out and participation can actually override student achievement.

ing considerations, they can be overridden by failure to dress for class. Additionally, three of the four categories listed for evaluation (cooperation and attitude, skill improvement, and learning achievement) are not clearly defined on the grade explanation sheet, even though those qualities might be demonstrated with a variety of behaviors. Thus, due to lack of clarity, this grading plan is very subjective and is heavily influenced by managerial components.

The stated grading plan should be the one used. One category, such as dressing for class or attendance, should *not* override other areas. Poor attendance undoubtedly decreases levels of performance and achievement on psychomotor, cognitive, and affective domains, but it should not be used as a sole determinant of a grade. Note the lack of specificity in this grading plan as compared with the one presented in figure 11.2. Teachers should clearly state what areas they will base grades on, and not allow one area to disrupt the balance in a grading format.

## Allow Students Multiple Opportunities for Success

Grades should be indicators of the degree to which students have achieved the teacher's objectives for the course. Although it is difficult (if not impossible) to collapse student work into a single letter grade, current grading policies often require teachers to do just that. To further complicate the process, some teachers use assessment results from a single day to influence a student's grade. Imagine a student who has worked hard during a 6-week volleyball unit but then bombs the one-shot assessment on the day it was administered, and thus ends up with scores that are not truly indicative of his or her achievement.

Because assessments have a dual purpose—providing feedback while assessing performance—doing multiple administrations of assessments makes sense from both a pedagogical perspective and an evaluative one. Giving students multiple opportunities to reach assessment criteria also provides an incentive for practicing and improving their skills, as well as decreasing stress for students who experience test anxiety. As a result, grades are more representative of students' actual achievements. Students also learn an important life lesson when they have multiple chances to do an assessment— that hard work pays off. Additionally, classmates tend to act as coaches and help their friends reach the criteria in a cooperative work environment.

## Allow Extra Practice Time for Lesser-Skilled Students

When lesser-skilled students don't have enough time in class, extra practice time outside of the regular class is necessary. This practice could be done prior to the formal start of the class, during the class when the student is not playing a game or doing an organized activity, before or after school, or even during a lunch break. Adequate practice time for lower-skilled student *must* be built into the program.

Students can also do practice drills or assessments as homework. If needed, teachers can let students check out equipment for use in practice outside of the school day. Lower-skilled students also benefit from multiple opportunities to reach the criteria for an assessment, because stress is reduced when they know that they have more than one chance for success. When students achieve the criterion score, the grade is recorded. Teachers should not hesitate to use achievement to determine student grades even with lower-skilled students. When they have clear and specific targets and adequate opportunity to meet these targets, students of all skill levels can experience success.

## Use Assessments for Multiple Purposes Rather Than Only to Give Grades

The primary purpose of assessment should be to give feedback to teachers and students; therefore, determining grades should be a *secondary* reason for doing assessment. With this in mind, not all assessments need to contribute to a grade. A student teacher once said that she was not allowed to administer skill tests in her classes because the school district did not allow physical education teachers to give grades based on psychomotor skills. It did not occur to the student teacher that skill tests could be used to provide feedback and increase students' learning even if they do not contribute to a grade.

Additionally, students should not be graded while they are trying to learn something. Although students may be performing the assessment that will eventually be used to determine their grade, initial attempts should not be recorded as part of the grade, unless the teacher is using improvement as a factor.

Intermediate and formative assessments provide teachers and students with feedback, but they do not have to contribute to the student's final, report-card grade.

## Avoid Averaging Scores to Arrive at a Student Grade

With performance-based assessment, a student's initial skill level is not important; only the final level of performance is important (Guskey and Bailey 2001). A student with minimal experience in an activity could perform so poorly in the initial part of a unit that even if he or she achieved mastery by end of the unit, the low initial grades would drag the final grade down (see figure 11.5). Because a grade represents the degree to which the student has achieved mastery of the teacher's goals, an averaged grade does not accurately reflect the extent of his or her achievement. Thus, when students are given multiple opportunities to complete assessments, the new grade should be used, rather than an average of the new and old scores.

When a teacher wants to show the assessment scores that did not contribute to a grade, grading program software is available that can show a student profile of scores on various assignments and assessments. Even though some assessments do not contribute to a grade, they can be useful for demonstrating improvement and progress.

Parents enjoy getting grade reports from teachers because they can see what their child is doing in class in terms of the activities occurring during instruction. The example presented in figure 11.6 shows student skill assessments, quiz scores, and homework. All assignments and assessments are shown, even though not all contributes to a

| Student name | Test 1 | Test 2 | Test 3 | Test 4 | Average |
|---|---|---|---|---|---|
| Jose | 25 | 50 | 75 | 100 | 62.5 |
| Susan | 100 | 75 | 50 | 25 | 62.5 |
| Brendan | 0 | 50 | 100 | 100 | 62.5 |

**Figure 11.5** Even though each of these students has the same average score, individual performance and the student learning that the score represents was vastly different over the four tests.

Riverside High School    Tuesday, September 29
Progress Report for Jackson, Susan L.
ID: 12047
Ms. King    Physical Education 101
Room #: Gymnasium    Section #: 01
Final average: 91.2
Final grade: A

| Name | Score | Max | Grade |
|---|---|---|---|
| SKL 1 | 6 | 10 | None |
| SKL 2 | 7 | 10 | None |
| SKL 3 | 8 | 10 | B |
| Quiz 1 | 9 | 10 | A |
| SKL 4 | 10 | 10 | A |
| SKL 5 | 14 | 15 | A |
| SKL 6 | 13 | 15 | None |
| SKL 7 | 18 | 20 | A |
| HW 1 | 17 | 18 | A |
| Fit 1 | 14 | 15 | A |

*Note: SKL* denotes skill, *HW* denotes homework, and *Fit* denotes fitness test.

**Figure 11.6** Grading software can help streamline record keeping and inform both students and parents about achievement during a grading period.

grade. Computerized grade reporting systems often allow teachers to customize the printout to fit their particular class needs.

## Avoid Giving Lower Grades to Motivate Students to Try Harder

During the early part of a grading unit or semester, students are sometimes given a grade lower than they deserve in an attempt to motivate them to work harder. This practice may cause a student to become discouraged and therefore put forth *less* effort than he or she previously expended. When grades are based on clearly stated goals and standards, teachers should reward students with precisely what they have earned. A grade is a representation of the degree to which a student has mastered the teacher's goals. It should not be manipulated in this manner in an attempt to increase a student's motivation.

## Use of Zeros When Calculating Grades

For most students, a zero is not an adequate reflection of their work. Zero grades are typically used to punish students who act irresponsibly by failing to turn in assignments, cheating on tests, or the like. A zero on a significant assignment will likely doom that student to failure because it is virtually impossible to make up the lost points during a grading period. Guskey and Bailey (2001) recommend that irresponsibility be punished with an incomplete grade and a requirement that the student attend after-school or Saturday school classes to make up missed work. Marzano (2006) and Popham (2005) advocate using an absolute grading system in which various grades are awarded (e.g., A = 4, B = 3) for assignments rather than points or percentages. All assessments are converted to this scale, and some weighting for importance is calculated into the equation. Receiving a score of zero on an assessment that uses an absolute grading scale is much less damaging to a final grade than is a zero assigned in a grading system where a single assessment carries a point value of 100 or more. If grades are to represent students' achievement of instructional goals, then the practice of awarding zeros as penalties for irresponsible behavior

is not appropriate. Teachers must address this issue when developing a grading system so that their grading is fair and equitable.

## Grading Borderline Students

Despite a teacher's best intentions, there are times at the end of a grading period when a student is on the borderline between two grades and the teacher has no rationale for tipping the grade in either direction. Since most cutoff scores are arbitrary (e.g., some teachers use 93 percent as the lowest A while others go all the way to 90 percent), teachers need to have a policy for deciding what to do in such cases. The best plan is to seek additional information about the student's performance, for example by using additional assessments and giving the student more opportunities to demonstrate learning. A mastery learning approach is beneficial in these instances, since it gives students multiple opportunities to achieve success on skill assessments. Teachers should not wait until the end of a grading period to complete all assessments because there will be no opportunity for students with borderline grades to do additional assessments of learning. Teachers need to have a plan to resolve this issue before being faced with assigning a grade that inaccurately represents a student's achievement.

## Grading on a Curve

Some teachers use the phrase "grading on the curve" to describe the practice of decreasing grade expectations from what was initially posted. This usage of the phrase is inappropriate. When teachers grade on a curve, a certain percentage of students are assigned each grade, from A through F (e.g., 10 percent As, 25 percent Bs, and so on). Grades are based on ranking the students in the class rather than on the students' achievement of learning goals. This approach lets students know how they finished when compared with others in the class, but they know nothing about the quality of their performance. An A indicates that a student was one of the best in class, but the student might still lack necessary skills for competent performance. Grading on a curve discourages students from helping one another achieve and learn, since every student is in competition with his or her classmates for the highest grades.

Basing grades on the rank order of students can camouflage results and feedback. It is much more informative to tell runners that they ran 100 meters in 11.6 seconds than it is to say that they placed third in the race. Future improvement is far easier to achieve when the level of current performance is clearly identified. When grades represent specific achievement, those students with a substandard performance know exactly what they must do to improve. Effective grading practices should point out to students their strengths and the areas in which they need to improve.

## Minimize Subjectivity on Assessments Leading to a Grade

Students must know the grading criteria, understanding in advance what the teacher expects and how they will be graded. The less mystery surrounding the teacher's goals and the grading system, the more likely that students are able to hit their achievement targets. When targets are clear, students can peer-assess and self-evaluate. This moves the sole responsibility for the student's achievement away from the teacher making the student responsible as well.

Additional detail should be included with grade reports when necessary. For example, teachers might indicate to parents which assessments were used for calculating a grade or report on a student's work habits without incorporating them into the final grade. A grade report, an explanation of program goals, and a rubric would provide additional information about how the grade was determined and clarify for parents what the grade represents. This practice would eliminate some of the confusion that often arises when a mere letter grade is used to represent several weeks of achievement. When *any* grading practice or policy has the potential to lead to miscommunication with parents or students, the teacher should include explanations or documents that clarify the process.

## Give Extra Credit for Extra Learning, Not Just Extra Work

The final grade that a teacher gives a student should be a reflection of the degree to which the student has achieved the teacher's goals. When a teacher gives extra credit, it should be for additional learning, not just more work on the same topic or area. When extra credit is given for additional work (rather than for learning), it distorts the weighting of course percentages discussed earlier in this chapter. Sometimes, at the end of a grading period, when students discover that their grades are lower than what they wanted, teachers allow students to do extra credit assignments. The problem is that this work is usually meaningless in terms of student knowledge and course content. Remembering that a grade should reflect the degree of student achievement of the teacher's goals, the practice of letting a student boost a grade at the end of a grading period goes contrary to that philosophy and therefore should not be used. Students should not be allowed to gain extra credit points unless those points are given as a reward for tackling a task that is more difficult than expected of others in the class and that leads to learning and achievement beyond the scope of the regular class.

# CONCLUSION

Guskey (1996a) reports that when parents design report cards, they look very different than when teachers design them. With this in mind, a survey might be conducted allowing parents and students to indicate what information they consider important to know about student achievement. Because they are the primary consumers of student grades, their needs must be considered when planning the reporting system.

Grades should not be used as weapons (Cotten and Cotten 1985). Teachers have far more success when they think of a grade as a reward for student achievement—one that must be earned. Basing grades on specific, clear, and defensible targets gives students the greatest opportunity for success.

Incorporating effort, improvement, attitude, and aptitude into a grade greatly increases the subjectivity of the grading system, as well as the mystery of what is necessary for success. Confusion and miscommunication decrease when the grading system is focused on student achievement and when the grade truly represents the extent to which a student achieved the goals for the class. When teachers explicitly define achievement in understandable terms, they enhance their program's credibility and let parents know how they can help their child achieve higher levels of learning.

When calculating student grades, the best policy is to use the objectives, weight them appropriately, and then decide which assess-ments indicate students' achievement. All of these decisions should be made at the beginning of the grading period or school year. When the grading method is determined before the instructional unit begins, both teachers and students know the guidelines, and there are no surprises when instruction concludes.

# 12

# Acquiring Assessment Savvy

*The task of the excellent teacher is to stimulate "apparently ordinary" people to unusual effort. The tough problem is not identifying winners: it is in making winners out of ordinary people (K. Patricia Cross).*

The switch to a performance-based assessment format should begin with the addition of a few new assessments; more changes can follow over time. To begin climbing the planning staircase, teachers should first step back and decide what they want their students to learn. When teachers look at final outcomes first, they can determine a path needed to reach them. Some curricular goals are left solely to the discretion of the teacher, while others are established by state or district educational standards. Although teachers may not have full control over the final product or program outcomes, they usually do have input into the process used to deliver instruction and about the assessments used to measure students' learning. This chapter provides teachers with strategies for developing a viable, coherent, and comprehensive assessment approach that has the potential to enhance instructional effectiveness.

## PLANNING THE ASSESSMENT PROCESS

Teachers should begin the instructional process by deciding where they are headed. After determining what they want students to know and be able to do as the result of instruction, teachers must generate assessments to measure these elements. In much the same way that a block plan is created to outline different types of learning, teachers should also plan the types of assessments they will use to measure students' learning throughout a unit. Assessments should always serve a definite purpose. Too often, beginning teachers know that they should assess but don't consider the student learning that they want to measure. This approach can result in an assessment that requires a lot of time to implement but provides little useful information about whether or what students have learned.

By systematically planning assessments, however, teachers can gather the information they need to plan instruction, as well as documentation of their teaching effectiveness. Formative assessments can be implemented into the instructional process on a regular basis. Making an assessment planning chart will help teachers decide which assessments to use for measuring learning at the conclusion of the unit. Figure 12.1 identifies assessments that will be used for a field hockey unit. By developing an overview of the instructional process, teachers can carefully consider the various assessments that they will use during the unit and also identify which assessments will eventually contribute to student grades.

| Domain | Skill, knowledge, or disposition | Assessments | When to assess |
| --- | --- | --- | --- |
| Psychomotor | Dribbling | Skill test, peer and self-assessments, teacher observation through checklists and anecdotal notes | Game play, drills, end of unit, culminating performance |
| | Tackling (block, jab) | Skill test, peer and self-assessments, teacher observation through checklists and anecdotal notes | Game play, drills, end of unit, culminating performance |
| | Shooting (quick hit) | Skill test, peer and self-assessments, teacher observation through checklists and anecdotal notes | Game play, drills, end of unit, culminating performance |
| | Fielding | Skill test, peer and self-assessments, teacher observation through checklists and anecdotal notes | Game play, drills, end of unit, culminating performance |
| | Passing (push pass) | Skill test, peer and self-assessments, teacher observation through checklists and anecdotal notes | Game play, drills, end of unit, culminating performance |
| | Drives (hitting) | Skill test, peer and self-assessments, teacher observation through checklists and anecdotal notes | Game play, drills, end of unit, culminating performance |
| | Dodge | Skill test, peer and self-assessments, teacher observation through checklists and anecdotal notes | Game play, drills, end of unit, culminating performance |
| Affective | Fair play | Exit slips, student logs, surveys, peer and self-assessments, teacher observation through checklists and anecdotal notes | Game play and group activities throughout the unit |
| | Teamwork | Exit slips, student logs, surveys, peer and self-assessments, teacher observation through checklists and anecdotal notes | Game play and group activities throughout the unit |
| | Participation | Exit slips, student logs, surveys, peer and self-assessments, teacher observation through checklists and anecdotal notes | Game play and group activities throughout the unit |

*(continued)*

**Figure 12.1**   Example of an assessment planning chart for a field hockey unit.

Reprinted, by permission, from Darren Clay.

| Domain | Skill, knowledge, or disposition | Assessments | When to assess |
|---|---|---|---|
| | Effort | Exit slips, student logs, surveys, peer and self-assessments, teacher observation through checklists and anecdotal notes | Game play and group activities throughout the unit |
| | Etiquette | Exit slips, student logs, surveys, peer and self-assessments, teacher observation through checklists and anecdotal notes | Game play and group activities throughout the unit |
| Cognitive | Rules | Selected-response test (written), exit slips, journal, group project | Pretest and posttest, game play, culminating product |
| | History | Brochure, poster, selected-response test (written), exit slips, journal, group project | Pretest and posttest, game play, culminating product |
| | Tactics (defense and offense) | Video, selected-response test (written), exit slips, journal, group project | Pretest and posttest, game play, culminating product |
| | Terminology | Dictionary pamphlet, essay assessment, exit slips, journal, group project | Pretest and posttest, game play, culminating product |
| | Positioning (court movement) | Record of statistics, selected-response test (written), exit slips, journal, group project | Pretest and posttest, game play, culminating product |
| | Safety procedures and equipment | Selected-response test (written), exit slips, journal, group project | Pretest and posttest, game play, culminating product |
| | Scoring | Official scorebook design, selected-response test (written), exit slips, journal, group project | Pretest and posttest, game play, culminating product |

**Figure 12.1** *(continued)*

# LUND AND KIRK'S TIPS FOR ACQUIRING ASSESSMENT SAVVY

The prospect of switching to a performance-based assessment format can be a little scary, but when one considers the benefits, such thoughts soon disappear. After teachers make the decision to use performance-based assessments, the question that many ask is, "Where do I begin?" We have been through the process of creating assessments many times, and the purpose of this last chapter is to give some final suggestions and hints—dos and don'ts, if you will—to help teach-

ers begin the transition to using performance-based assessments in physical education. The suggestions and hints are designed to help make this transition more efficient and meaningful for teachers students, parents, and administrators. So here you have it: Lund and Kirk's Tips for Acquiring Assessment Savvy (see figure 12.2 for a summary version).

## 1. Think Big, Start Small

When teachers switch to performance-based assessments, they should not throw out all of their old assessments immediately. By looking at the various assessments used, teachers can determine which ones need to be tossed

## Lund and Kirk's 35 Tips for Acquiring Assessment Savvy

1. Think big, start small.
2. Teach for depth, not breadth.
3. Become a facilitator of learning.
4. Write down instructional goals so that you clearly state what you want.
5. Make learning and assessment as authentic as possible.
6. Remember that learning and assessment should be inseparable.
7. Align instruction with assessment.
8. Design assessments so that novice levels of learning can be detected.
9. Measure affective-domain dispositions if you want students to acquire them.
10. Differentiate performance tasks to meet the needs of diverse students.
11. Use a variety of assessments to measure all aspects of student learning.
12. Give students choices about assessment.
13. Keep differentiated assignments equivalent to each other.
14. Write the prompt so that students have enough information to succeed.
15. Give students multiple opportunities to achieve mastery.
16. Develop assessment routines.
17. Present assessments early in the unit.
18. Use assessment continuously.
19. Use assessments for multiple purposes.
20. Establish checkpoints for assessments.
21. Avoid bottlenecks at assessment stations.
22. Keep assessment from being a burden.
23. Be prepared to revise assessments.
24. Use assessments to showcase students' learning and promote the physical education program.
25. Teach students to benefit from assessments.
26. Allow adequate time for students to complete performance assessments.
27. Weight more difficult assessments more heavily to give proper credit for extra effort.
28. Give students the opportunity to improve or correct performance.
29. Have students take assessments seriously.
30. Develop a system for assessing every student, even in large classes.
31. Avoid activities that are culturally biased.
32. Don't trust your memory when grading students.
33. Make sure the pieces fit.
34. Share your ideas with colleagues.
35. Be part of the solution, not part of the problem.

**Figure 12.2** By addressing these elements, you can begin your journey to improve student assessment practices.

immediately, which ones will be changed at some future date, and which ones are the keepers. If teachers add performance-based assessments a few at a time, the task of changing the assessment format becomes doable rather than formidable. In some instances, performance-based assessments are not even the best alternative. When testing knowledge of factual information, for example, traditional testing formats offer the most efficient way to measure learning. On the other hand, when teachers are trying to get students to apply their learning, performance-based assessments are better choices. Teachers must look at the information they are trying to measure when determining whether to keep or toss an assessment. If the current assessment does not measure the desired

student outcome, then it should be changed or replaced. The key to this suggestion is to have a plan and implement it in stages. Purposeful change that is implemented gradually makes the switch to performance-based assessments easier. Just as a builder wouldn't start without a plan, teachers need to set intermediate and long-term goals for change and then meet them.

## 2. Teach for Depth, Not Breadth

With performance-based assessment, teachers must offer units of sufficient length to allow students to develop skill. There is no point in doing assessments if learning is not occurring. Units that last 1 to 2 weeks do not allow students enough time to develop the necessary skills

Think big, start small. When moving toward a performance-based assessment system, first consider which of your current assessment practices can still be used, then change others a few at a time.

for a meaningful experience. Most skills and activities are very complex and require much practice before the participant experiences success and feels competent at doing them. In addition, because performance-based assessments usually require several days to complete, short units don't provide the time necessary for students to really get engaged in the assessment. Personal experience has taught the authors that students enjoy longer units that give them the necessary time to develop enough skill to participate in an activity on at least a recreational level. When students are successful at an activity, they don't get bored—provided that active instruction continues throughout the unit. Teaching units for longer periods of time does not mean that teachers present 5 days of lessons and then allow students to play games for the next 5 weeks with no additional instruction. Every lesson taught during in-depth units must be educational and must challenge students to learn something new. Assessments are motivational for students because they provide concrete goals that students can strive to achieve, as well as feedback about their accomplishments. Performance-based assessments require students to thoroughly understand the activity and unit in which they are engaged. This type of understanding is made possible only through in-depth coverage of the activity or unit.

## 3. Become a Facilitator of Learning

One of the features of performance-based assessments is that teachers serve as facilitators of learning rather than as the sole source of information. When students take ownership of their learning, they tend to become more engaged and interested. This is not to say that teaching should cease when using performance-based assessments, but rather acknowledge that students can learn from sources other than the teacher and that assessments can help teachers facilitate this process. When using performance-based assessments, teachers are encouraged to step away from the front of the classroom and see what is happening from the back. When teachers learn to become facilitators and encourage genuine learning, an exciting phenomenon happens in the gymnasium: Other forms of learning begin to occur, and the results are impressive when teachers coach students to learn and help them reach the outcomes or goals of the physical education program.

## 4. Write Down Instructional Goals So That You Clearly State What You Want

Teachers should begin to plan for assessment by asking themselves, "What should my students be able to do as the result of instruction?" This question helps focus the unit and points teachers toward the knowledge they should assess, as well as the type of assessments they should use to determine student learning. Unfortunately, some teachers know what they want to teach but they never put it in writing. Writing out the intended goals forces teachers to clearly define what they want students to learn. Teachers usually form a general idea about what they want students to accomplish, but until they actually write the goals down and develop assessments to measure them, they haven't clearly articulated the content or goals for the unit. After committing the goals to paper, teachers should create a list of the key understandings that students should gain by the conclusion of the unit; they should also develop a list of essential questions that address these understandings. When teachers make formal written plans, their instruction becomes much more deliberate, and their assessments target the desired learning.

## 5. Make Learning and Assessment as Authentic as Possible

Sometimes students question the relevance of an assignment or assessment. To help avoid this type of student question, teachers should ask themselves, "Is this important?" before they decide what to assess. If a teacher adds a degree of authenticity to the assessment, students can readily see the purpose and value of what the teacher is asking them to do. If questions of relevance do arise, the teacher has a thoughtful response to address student concerns and questions. When creating performance-based assessments, teachers should look for ways to make them as realistic as possible. The news media (newspapers, television programs, and other forms) provides an excellent source for ideas. Teachers should also look to those people associated with sport and determine what they do and what knowledge base they must have to do their jobs well. When this knowledge base is compatible with what a teacher is covering in physical education, and if it can be used to measure learning, then a new assessment may just have been born. Performance-based assessments provide great ways for teachers to let students know that information presented in class is important beyond class and in the world at large. Knowing that something is important can serve as an excellent motivator for students of all skill levels, from beginner to advanced. As the meaningfulness of the task increases, so do motivation, interest, and the amount of time that students are willing to spend while completing it. When assessments engage students, students are less likely to view them as onerous chores and more likely to be receptive to completing them.

## 6. Remember That Learning and Assessment Should Be Inseparable

Effective formative performance-based assessments provide students with feedback about their performance, making them fantastic teaching and learning tools. Assessments that fail to provide feedback to students are not effective and should be adjusted. The ultimate goal of assessment should be to intertwine assessment and learning so that they are seamless and it is impossible to determine where one ends and the other begins.

Assessment does not have to be an enemy of instruction; rather, it should be seen as an integral part of the learning process. It points out strengths and weaknesses and provides feedback to both teachers and students. When teachers design assessments, they should ask themselves, "How can I create assessments that help students perform better than they think they can, or better than even I think they can?" An assessment can provide challenges to learning and move students beyond their own expectations. When teachers design assessments with this goal in mind, students have greater opportunities to learn.

## 7. Align Instruction With Assessment

Assess what you teach, and teach what you assess. This sounds rather simple, but all too often it just doesn't happen. Remember the class where the teacher lectured about all kinds of topics and the test covered the book that the instructor never mentioned? Assessments should provide students with the opportunity to demonstrate what they have learned, but that doesn't happen if the teacher uses the wrong evaluation tool. Sometimes a teacher hears about a new assessment at a conference or reads about it in a journal or on the Internet—and decides to use it. Assessments must be selected carefully so that they evaluate what the teacher is teaching. Often they must be contextualized to fit the teaching environment. If the teacher's goal is for students to have adequate skill and information to play a game at a recreational level, then this is the outcome that should be assessed. If the goal is for students to play a game with a reasonable level of skill, then a skill test measuring students' performance of the skill in a closed environment may be an intermediary step in the process, but it will not directly assess game-play ability. Similarly, if a teacher wants students to perform or choreograph dances, then assessments must measure this ability as well as the requisite knowledge. Because physical education is performance oriented, performance-based assessments provide logical and appropriate ways to measure learning. With a little planning, physical education teachers can achieve excellent instructional alignment and genuinely measure what they want students to achieve.

## 8. Design Assessments So That Novice Levels of Learning Can Be Detected

Assessment should be about finding out what students can do—not what they cannot do. Again, the main purpose of assessment should be to provide feedback to students to help them improve their performance. All students have some content knowledge, and they shouldn't be punished for what they don't have. This is analogous to the pull-up test—every child has some upper-body strength, but not every child can demonstrate it on that particular test. Assessments should be sensitive enough to detect lower levels of achievement even as well as measuring higher levels of performance. Assessments should provide an opportunity for students at all levels of ability to demonstrate their achievement and learning and allow teachers to make valid decisions about whether students have learned. Designing such assessments is a challenging task, but as teachers begin to understand the various components involved in the assessment process, they can do it.

## 9. Measure Affective-Domain Dispositions if You Want Students to Acquire Them

There is a saying that students will perceive something as valuable if it is assessed. Dispositions such as cooperation, fair play, caring, perseverance, resourcefulness, and responsibility are highly desirable traits for adults to possess—and they can be measured by means of performance-based assessments. If these behaviors are taught to students and are addressed in assessments, then students are more likely to develop them. Since behaviors do not develop spontaneously, teachers need to assume the onus of teaching desired dispositions to students. For example, highly able students haven't always learned the art of persistence because the tasks come so easy for them. Performance-based assessments can be structured so that highly skilled athletes must work to achieve the highest levels of performance and thus learn valuable work habits. Cooperation and fair play are also

valuable attributes that can be assessed during game play with rubrics that delineate observable behaviors associated with the trait thus defining the attribute. By measuring affective-domain traits, teachers send a message to students that these elements are important to participation in sport and activity.

## 10. Differentiate Performance Tasks to Meet the Needs of Diverse Students

Even though students come to physical education with diverse talents, skills, and learning profiles, many teachers require them to all do the same assessments. When students are given choices about assessment, they can personalize both their learning and their performance. Instruction is most successful when teachers teach one step above a student's current level of performance. Every student has a current level of performance—low, medium, or high—and teachers must find ways to help all students learn regardless of initial ability. The work should not be so easy that students are bored or so challenging that students give up. Either state causes the brain to shut down, and students therefore fail to learn (Callahan 1997; Csikszentmihalyi 1997). Performance assessments can be structured in such a way that they are challenging to each student and that each student is capable of some degree of success.

## 11. Use a Variety of Assessments to Measure All Aspects of Student Learning

Teachers should add variety to their assessment vocabularies. Some students do poorly on one type of assessment despite possessing good content knowledge. When a variety of assessments are offered, students can choose an assessment format that embraces their strengths while still measuring their achievement. Some states use specific testing formats (e.g., open-response questions, on-demand tasks) to assess student learning. In these states, teachers must give students opportunities to practice the testing format prior to completing the statewide assessment formats. When students are unfamiliar with a testing format, they may have the desired content knowledge but may be unable to demonstrate it. The testing format mandated by a state should not be the only assessment format used in a physical education program. Performance-based assessments—such as fictitious interviews with famous people, play-by-play commentaries, and critiques or written summaries of performances—give students opportunities to demonstrate their many talents that might otherwise go unnoticed. Remember also that assessments should not be chosen because they are cute or fun but because they allow students to demonstrate their competence in a given area. Using a variety of assessments helps to ensure that students are assessed on their content knowledge and abilities and that the assessment format does not interfere with students demonstrating what they have learned.

## 12. Give Students Choices About Assessment

Adults can usually choose what they want to learn, but students rarely have that luxury. Students are often required to do exactly what a teacher decides they should do. Giving students choices about the type of assessment to complete allows them to take ownership in their learning and assessment process, thus providing them with additional motivation to achieve. Brain research tells us that student choice enhances motivation (Jensen 1998). Students won't have to ask, "Why are we doing this?" because they are the ones who select the task or assessment. Too often, the answer to "Why am I doing this?" is "For the grade," or "Because the teacher wants me to do it"—neither of which, at least to some, is very motivating. Too often in traditional assessment formats, students learn something only for the test, and then it's over. Learning is more meaningful and longer lasting when teachers let students use information and take some ownership in the learning process.

## 13. Keep Differentiated Assignments Equivalent to Each Other

When allowing differentiation or choice in assessments, teachers must make sure that the various options are equivalent, requiring equal time and effort to complete and measuring the same content knowledge (Tomlinson 1999). When differentiated assessments are of equal difficulty, each one should be chosen by some students. For example, announcing a fictitious game and writing a newspaper article summarizing the game are both ways to assess knowledge of rules and strategies. Students who enjoy speaking more than writing would probably select the former assessment. However, designing a poster for the cover of a game program might appeal to an artistic student, but would have little to do with assessing the previously identified content knowledge. If every student chooses the same option, then teachers should reexamine the assignment, because one option may require less work than the others. In other cases, certain differentiated assignments are more fun to complete but have little to do with assessing instructional goals. For this reason, teachers should look at the learning goals set for the unit and make sure that all assessments measure the degree to which students achieve them.

## 14. Write the Prompt so That Students Have Enough Information to Succeed

Teachers should be explicit in the directions they give to students so that students know exactly what is expected of them. Tasks should be clearly written and contain sufficient detail that students can produce the desired results and behaviors that the teacher wishes to assess. The rubric is often a critical addition because it helps define desired performance and identifies for students what teachers will look for in the final product or performance. Students can be more successful when they understand what the assessment requires before they begin to work on it.

## 15. Give Students Multiple Opportunities to Achieve Mastery

A mastery learning approach gives the message that teachers care about what students learn. Many teachers who are coaches give students multiple opportunities to achieve excellence because they know that doing so is important to students' confidence and future performance. With a mastery learning approach, teachers assume the role of a coach, encouraging all students to learn, rather than giving up on a child after a failed attempt on a skill assessment.

## 16. Develop Assessment Routines

When teachers establish assessment routines or protocols in a class, students know what to do during an assessment. Time is saved because the protocol doesn't need to be explained and practiced. For example, at the beginning of the school day, one teacher sets pencils and assessment sheets next to the numbers that students stand on while she takes attendance. When the time comes to do the assessments, students report to their assigned attendance number and do the assessment. At the conclusion of the assessment, the paper is handed to the teacher. Minimal management time is required to administer the assessment.

Assessing students requires time and planning. However, if students are accustomed to doing assessments and learn the routines and protocols, then the time spent actually doing assessments decreases dramatically. For example, in a Sport Education unit, a teacher could have the statistician hand out assessments and the equipment manager distribute pencils. Some teachers make available a supply of clipboards with pencils attached, and students know to pick up a clipboard for the last part of every lesson to complete the assessment. Other teachers use color-coded folders, labeled with students' names and numbers, in which students write journal entries. Whatever type of assessment is used, students should learn a protocol for completing that assessment so that the teacher doesn't need to spend valuable instructional time distributing papers and explaining to students what they should do.

## 17. Present Assessments Early in the Unit

When students know how they will be assessed, they can practice during downtime (e.g., before class when others are dressing or during game play when their team is not playing). This is true whether teachers use traditional or performance-based assessments. When students know how they will be assessed, the assessment has an impact throughout the unit, as students know what they will be expected to do on the day that skill tests are conducted. Also, when students are familiar with the assessment protocol, the time needed for explanation is decreased and the assessment can be administered much more quickly. Giving students a chance to prepare for an assessment is worthwhile from both instructional and managerial considerations.

## 18. Use Assessment Continuously

Too many teachers do assessments only when they must determine student grades. The main purpose of assessment should be to provide feedback to students. If students are going to improve, they need a continuous flow of information regarding their performance throughout the unit. To accomplish this, assessment should be a continuous, ongoing process. Teachers must continually move students toward the culminating performance or accomplishment that will demonstrate both learning and competence. Final or culminating assessments can and should be graded. However, given the paperwork connected with recording grades for the number of students that secondary teachers have on their rosters, assessments that lead up to this final assessment might not be included in the calculation of students' final grades.

When some type of assessment is given every day, either on its own or integrated with learning activities, students receive continuous feedback about how their learning is progressing. Teachers can also use this information to shape subsequent lessons. When students are unable to perform a given assessment, this alerts the teacher that they are not ready to move on

recently required students to submit artifacts for a portfolio on sport. Because I was rushed, I did not include a rubric. Although I was very specific about what should be included when I explained the list of required components, my students turned in work that was minimal and disappointing to me. For the next portfolio assignment, I included a rubric that specified levels of acceptable and unacceptable performance. The results were vastly different from the products turned in for the first assessment. When I clearly specified my expectations with a rubric, the students' work improved dramatically.

to the next skill. When assessment is done continuously, it can play multiple roles rather than merely contributing to a grade.

## 19. Use Assessments for Multiple Purposes

Assessments can serve multiple purposes if rubrics are written around the appropriate characteristics. This enables teachers to make efficient use of class time while still providing the required information about student achievement. A jump rope routine, for example, can demonstrate psychomotor performance; cognitive understanding of choreography and jumping techniques; cooperation with others; and the ability to count rhythms, perform steps, and jump to the beat. Thus the teacher can assess many programmatic goals using a single assessment.

## 20. Establish Checkpoints for Assessments

Teachers usually use different drills on different days. If, instead, the teacher used the same drill or similar ones on successive days, then students can note improvement over time. This kind of repetitive drill, or checkpoint, gives feedback to both students and teachers because it is done on multiple occasions. At the completion of a checkpoint drill, the teacher might ask students whether their performance reached the criterion set by the teacher or whether their performance improved from a previous day or previous practice attempt. When students are given three or four chances on such checkpoint activities and assessments each day, they should see improvement during a single class. Checkpoint drills can also be incorporated into assessments later on in the unit, thus transforming instruction into assessment.

## 21. Avoid Bottlenecks at Assessment Stations

There are several strategies to use to avoid bottlenecks or wait time when assessing students. When class size is large, peer assessments and self-evaluations present a way to integrate assessment with learning and practice tasks. While students are using peer and self assessment to provide feedback, the teacher can be assessing students using other formats. When

using the Personalized System of Instruction (PSI), teachers develop learning progressions that include concrete goals that allows each student to progress and learn at his or her own pace (Metzler 2005). The table tennis progression shown in figure 12.3 is a very simplified example of a PSI progression. Students self-evaluate or peer-assess on the tasks throughout the progression but are not allowed to move to the next level of learning until performing the final task of a given level for the teacher. The final task of each level should represent an application of knowledge or require students to combine several skills previously mastered in the progression. In the example shown, the teacher is required to assess one skill or drill out of seven. Because students move through this progression at different rates, teacher evaluations of students are generally spread out, and students are not required to wait for their turn to be assessed by the teacher.

## 22. Keep Assessment From Being a Burden

Although performance-based assessments make wonderful additions to the learning process, they are time consuming to create, administer, and evaluate. Teachers who rely exclusively on performance-based assessment may come to dread the whole assessment process. To keep assessment from becoming a burden, teachers should try a variety of approaches. First of all, major assessments that require a lot of time to grade can be spread out; teachers should not simultaneously give all of their students an assessment that requires significant time to grade. If teachers determine that a performance-based assessment is an appropriate measure of learning, they might require it in one or two classes while having students in other classes complete other types of assessment that measure similar learning. With a rotation of performance-based assessments through the various classes, every student would eventually have an opportunity to do a performance-based assessment, but teachers would not be burdened with assessing all of their students at once on this type of assessment. Using portfolios as an example, if teachers taught three different sport or activity units during a semester, each class could be expected to do one portfolio during the semester and use other

# Table Tennis Skill Assessment

## Level I

1. Six returns of serve using a forehand push shot
   - Must be consecutive
   - Can be placed anywhere on the table
2. Six returns of serve using a backhand push shot
   - Must be consecutive
   - Can be placed anywhere on the table
3. Six *consecutive* returns of serve using a forehand pick shot
   - Can be placed anywhere on the table
4. Six *consecutive* returns of serve using a backhand pick shot
   - Can be placed anywhere on the table
5. Six *consecutive* forehand serves using backspin
   - Must start from right-hand side of table and be diagonal
6. Six *consecutive* forehand serves using topspin
   - Must start from right-hand side of table and be diagonal
7. Ten-hit rally using any combination of shots
   - May be started with a serve; this does not count as the first hit
   - If started with a bounce, this is not the first hit

## Level II

1. Ten-hit, forehand-to-forehand rally using only the push shot
   - May be started with a serve; this is not the first hit
   - If started with a bounce, this is not the first hit
2. Ten-hit, backhand-to-backhand rally using only the push shot
   - May be started with a serve; this is not the first hit
   - If started with a bounce, this is not the first hit
3. Ten-hit, forehand-to-forehand rally using only the pick shot
   - May be started with a serve; this is not the first hit
   - If started with a bounce, this is not the first hit
4. Ten-hit, backhand-to-backhand rally using only the pick shot
   - May be started with a serve; this is not the first hit
   - If started with a bounce, this is not the first hit
5. Six consecutive returns of a topspin serve using the forehand chop shot
   - Chop shot can be placed anywhere on the table
   - Serve must come from right-hand service court and land in the diagonal court
6. Six consecutive returns of a topspin serve using the backhand chop
   - Chop shot can be placed anywhere on the table
   - Serve must come from right-hand service court and land in the diagonal court
7. Sixteen-hit rally using any combination of shots
   - May be started with a serve; this is not the first hit
   - If started with a bounce, this is not the first hit
8. Six consecutive backhand serves using backspin
   - Must serve from right-hand court
   - Can be placed anywhere on the table
9. Six consecutive backhand serves using topspin
   - Must serve from right-hand court
   - Can be placed anywhere on the table
10. Four out of six slams
    - Ball tossed by partner with slight topspin to bounce 10 to 12 inches (about 25 to 30 cm) high from table
    - After slam, ball caught by partner

*(continued)*

**Figure 12.3** Since the teacher assesses only the final task in each level, while students self- or peer-assess on the previous tasks, teachers are able to hold students accountable for skill development while still monitoring student progress and learning.

## Level III

1. Ten-hit, backhand-to-forehand rally using the push shot
   - May also be forehand-to-backhand
   - Done twice so that each person has a chance to do both forehand and backhand
   - May be started with a serve; this is not the first hit
   - If started with a bounce, this is not the first hit
2. Twenty-hit rally using either the right or left half of the table and only the push shot
3. Ten-hit, backhand-to-forehand rally using the pick shot
   - May also be forehand-to-backhand
   - Done twice so that each person has a chance to do both forehand and backhand hits
   - May be started with a serve; this is not the first hit
   - If started with a bounce, this is not the first hit
4. Ten-hit rally using either the right or left half of the table and only the pick shot

5. Eight out of 10 forehand serves
   - Serve must be diagonal
   - Alternating topspin and backspin
   - Shot must hit a sheet of notebook-size paper (8.5 X 11) placed on the receiver's court
6. Eight out of 10 backhand serves
   - Alternating topspin and backspin
   - Shot must hit a sheet of notebook-size paper (8.5 X 11) placed on the receiver's court
   - Serve must be diagonal
7. Eight-hit rally using only the chop shot
   - May be started with a serve; this is not the first hit
   - If started with a bounce, this is not the first hit
8. Five *consecutive* returns of slam shots with a push or chop shot
   - Both partners must do this
   - Slam shot can be placed anywhere on the table

**Figure 12.3**   *(continued)*

forms of performance-based assessment in the other two units. This way a teacher would only grade portfolios from two classes at any one time, yet all students would assemble a portfolio during the semester.

Another way to avoid having performance-based assessment become a burden is to grade parts of the assessment (e.g., artifacts for a portfolio) when they are actually used with the class instead of requiring the entire performance-based assessment at the end of the unit. Obviously, some assessments should not be broken apart; making this approach is unusable in those cases. Teachers should plan assessments before they begin instruction and not create avoidable burdens for themselves.

## 23. Be Prepared to Revise Assessments

Good teachers tinker with assessments searching for ways to make them more effective or efficient. Most assessments—whether performance-based or traditional—can be improved or fine-tuned. Expecting to write a perfect assessment the first time is unrealistic. Teachers should continually be on the alert for new slants or perspectives with which they can improve an assessment. Because performance-based assessments are written with an open format that allows students to personalize them while remaining within the parameters set by the teacher, some ideas for altering an assessment come from students themselves. Another way to improve assessments is to look at students' errors and misunderstandings. When teachers keep themselves open to different ways of addressing assessments, they find that new and better assessments emerge. Just as a stone polisher continues smoothing the rough edges, teachers need to continually revise and refine assessments, which helps teachers improve the clarity of their vision for what students should know, understand, and be able to do. Each time an assessment is used, teachers should seek to improve and refine it.

## 24. Use Assessments to Showcase Students' Learning and Promote the Physical Education Program

Many performance-based assessments can be used to both assess and showcase students' learning. Additionally, sharing them with people outside of school can increase the authenticity of an assessment. Having students write about what they are learning is an excellent way to both assess students' learning and let others know what is happening in physical education. Students can write articles for school newspapers, create newsletters that go home to parents, or even write to or for the local newspaper. While writing about a game or activity, students demonstrate knowledge of it. Teachers can also require students to do research that provides additional information for an article about class activities. In another approach, physical education parent nights can be used as culminating performances for a variety of activities. Physical educators might sponsor a dance and invite parents to participate with their children in performing dances that students have learned in class. An instructional assessment component could be added by having students teach these dances to the adults. Half-time performances at local sporting event provide other opportunities to showcase student learning. When students know that they will perform for a live audience, they work harder to perfect their skills. All of these ideas can be used to create excellent performance-based assessments that measure students' learning while also promoting the physical education program.

## 25. Teach Students to Benefit From Assessments

Students must understand the purpose of assessment to do their best. When they understand the goals of learning and what they must accomplish if they are to meet these goals, their performance improves. Peer evaluations and self-assessments should be part of the total assessment package for a physical education program. Too many teachers make the mistake of assuming that students can already do these evaluations and thus fail to teach students how they should be done. As a result, the assessments are less effective than they should be. Teachers should also remember their own early days of teaching, when they may not have found the art of skill analysis very easy. When using peer assessments, it is essential to teach students what to look for and where prominent errors might occur.

Students must also see the whole assessment process as one that is designed to help them become better performers. Students who don't understand that the purpose of an assessment is to give feedback that helps the performer improve may be tempted to give classmates high marks on skill analysis peer assessments, even when the marks are not warranted. Clarifying expectations reduces the ambiguity that often surrounds assessment and helps decrease the stress associated with the evaluation process.

## 26. Allow Adequate Time for Students to Complete Performance Assessments

Effective performance-based assessments—those that are worth doing—require time to complete, and teachers must allot adequate time for students to do their best. It's better to have fewer assessments, on which students can do quality work, than several superficial assessments that do not engage students in the learning process. Short units do not give students adequate time to do their best on assessments. In addition, when assessments are used only during the later stages of a unit, there may not be enough time for students to use the feedback they receive. Students' performance potential is maximized when students are informed about assessments as early as possible and when adequate time is allocated to complete the requirements for an instructional unit.

## 27. Weight More Difficult Assessments More Heavily to Give Proper Credit for Extra Effort

When teachers give students choices about what they must do to meet requirements, teachers must ensure that the projects and products are equivalent with workload and time required to complete them. If they are not equivalent, teachers can weight them, giving more credit to students who take on the harder tasks. Students who are capable of doing more difficult work usually do not take on this challenge unless they are rewarded for their extra effort. By making the difficult assessments worth more, teachers encourage able students to take on more challenging assessments.

## 28. Give Students the Opportunity to Improve or Correct Performance

Many performance-based assessments are formative and provide students with multiple chances for evaluation. Formative assessments provide many benefits. When students know in advance what they will be assessed on, they can prepare for the evaluation. Alexander (1982) found that grading was an excellent way to increase student performance. In one instance, when students were graded on a golf task (putting), their performance trials increased almost exponentially. This kind of accountability can work on multiple days when students are given the opportunity to practice for the assessment (Lund 1992; Shanklin 2004).

Students can best improve their performance if they have the opportunity to make use of specific feedback. Students should be given the opportunity to ask, "How can I get better at doing this?" or "What did I do well, and what can be improved?" A formative approach to assessment gives students the opportunity to hone their skills and make significant improvement.

## 29. Have Students Take Assessments Seriously

While giving students multiple chances to improve performance (i.e., using formative assessment) has merit, students must also understand that a teacher has a limited amount of time available and that this time should not be expended in evaluating subpar performances. If allowed to do so, some students will take the approach that they have nothing to lose, so why not show the teacher their skill? When students are given rubrics by which to self-evaluate and peer-assess, they can help the teacher avoid evaluating inferior student work. Students must understand that they do not have unlimited class

time or attempts to present material for evaluation. Although they should have more than one opportunity to demonstrate their competence, they should also understand that when they give the teacher something to evaluate, it should, in the student's mind, meet the criteria specified for the assessment. If the teacher is actually assessing students for a grade, then students' skill levels should be developed enough for students to pass the assessment. Students must take assessments seriously, rather than diminishing their importance because they know they will have other opportunities to demonstrate competence.

## 30. Develop a System for Assessing Every Student, Even in Large Classes

When a teacher has a very large class, he or she may not be able to assess every student every day. The teacher can assess every student, however, by systematically evaluating a different set of students each day. In this approach, students will know that each day, 6 to 10 of them will be evaluated using the assessment for good behavior. They will not, however, know *which* students will be in that group of 6 to 10 on any given day. Eventually, every student in class will be evaluated, but the teacher will not be overwhelmed in the process. When students know that the teacher has built in this type of accountability, they are more likely to stay on task. The teacher has a clearly stated method to assess students' efforts during class rather than relying on subjective measures with unclear and poorly articulated criteria.

## 31. Avoid Activities That Are Culturally Biased

Early proponents of performance-based assessment advocated its use based in part on the idea that it was free from bias. Evaluators now realize that bias can creep into not only traditional assessments but also into performance-based assessments. Teachers should take care to avoid bias—whether connected to gender, socioeconomic status, ethnicity, disability, or other factors—when they select topics for performance-based assessment projects. Some physical education programs promote bias by including only team sports, which favor students who possess superior strength or power. Research projects may favor students who have home computers and Internet access unless provisions are made to give all students access to this technology. Teachers may unintentionally favor a written performance-based assessment that is word-processed or features colorful graphics. Rubrics for written work must address content as well as writing form, and teachers must carefully avoid bias when they select assessments and write the accompanying rubrics.

## 32. Don't Trust Your Memory When Grading Students

Assessments provide a record of student achievement and therefore must be written. There are a variety of ways to do this, from high-tech computers held in one's palm to low-tech clipboards. Checklists allow teachers to record data quickly and effectively, and analytic rubrics can be used to compare students' results and progress. Most secondary teachers have several classes in which students do similar activities and drills, and it is difficult if not impossible to remember performances by every student. With this in mind, when teachers establish a systematic way to record students' performances, they are more likely to have an accurate picture of students' achievement as well as data to use when assigning grades.

## 33. Make Sure the Pieces Fit

Assessments must fit together so that the entire body of student learning is measured. Assessments should not just address the psychomotor domain. Although that is physical education's primary contribution to a school curriculum, it is not the only contribution. Physical education also contributes cognitive knowledge and important affective-domain learning, as well as fitness and wellness components. Assessments should address all of these areas of a physical education program without shortchanging any of them. For example, if a written test covers only a handout used to supplement class information, it omits much of the cognitive learning that occurred during the unit. While this handout information may be important, the knowledge covered in class should also be assessed. Performance-based assessments give teachers an opportunity to assess all information covered in class. How-

ever, the assessments must fit together without leaving gaps in the measurement process.

## 34. Share Your Ideas With Colleagues

Creating assessments and their accompanying rubrics is a time-consuming process, but if teachers share ideas with colleagues, they can make the process much less intimidating. Within a learning community, teachers can share assessments, use colleagues as sounding boards for new ideas, and work with them as a team to develop and refine new assessment ideas. Specifically, teachers can share assessment ideas through

- Internet resources, such as PE Central, PE Talk, and PELINKS4U
- State, regional, and national conferences
- Colleagues within your district
- Former classmates from college
- Student teachers
- Mentor teachers
- Classmates in post-baccalaureate courses
- College professors
- Departmental colleagues

Trying to remember performances from every student during a grading a period is a difficult if not impossible task.

Conferences offer opportunities to get and present new assessment ideas, both through formal presentations and through informal sessions that occur during breaks and meals. Many conferences encourage physical education teachers to present lessons showing others what has worked for them in their own gymnasiums. In talking about assessment with others, teachers see new ideas emerge. Working with others also makes creating assessments a more enjoyable process.

## 35. Be Part of the Solution, Not Part of the Problem

Physical education can make a valuable contribution to a school curriculum when it is properly taught and administered. Physical education programs must be strong if they are to continue playing a part in school curriculums. Recent attention has been given to the obesity epidemic and the lack of physical activity among youth in the United States (National Association for Sport and Physical Education 2006). Problems also occur in a school culture when students fail to respect the rights of others or fail to interact

Assessments must fit together so that the entire picture of student learning is measured.

with one another in a positive manner. Physical education can exert a positive influence on many school problems; it can address such concerns in ways that no other subject area makes possible. Physical education programs must be deliberate in their teaching and must be accountable to the larger school program. Measuring and documenting what students learn in the gym can increase the status of physical education within a school. This is not to say that assessment is the golden key to elevating the importance of physical education in a school. Teachers must use assessment and appropriate data to document the positive results of their teaching in much the same way as teachers in other subject areas.

## CONCLUSION

Assessment can be either a burden or an opportunity to help students learn. We have chosen the latter approach because we see a strong connection between assessment and learning. The performance-based assessments described in this book provide teachers with a fresh way to look at student achievement. So much of physical education is performance-oriented that these new forms of assessment seem to be tailor-made for physical education.

In their visionary article, Hensley et al. (1987) state that "much of what was being delivered in our professional training is not being put to use and that hundreds of published tests lie dormant because they are inappropriate for the typical classroom setting" (61). We sincerely believe that the assessment practices we suggest address many of the concerns outlined in that article. Furthermore, we feel strongly that the assessments described here are appropriate for use in gymnasium settings. We encourage teachers to use performance-based assessments to provide students with feedback about their learning and, when appropriate, to contribute to student grade reports. The instructional process can be greatly enhanced through self-assessment, peer assessment, and evaluation done by teachers. Although Hensley et al. concluded that the proposed changes might sound "too radical, too abstract, too optimistic, or simply out of this world" (62), we disagree. The climate for change in assessment practices is ripe, and there is no better time than now to accept the challenges and the opportunities that follow. Exciting new assessments are being introduced that are both valid and reliable.

We strongly encourage readers to try these ideas in their classes as a means to enhance instruction and student learning. The thought of implementing them may be a bit overwhelming, which is why we suggest identifying an assessment buddy to work with in starting the process. An assessment buddy might be a colleague in one's physical education department or at another school, a college friend, or a fellow professional meet via the Internet. Once teachers begin to use performance-based assessments, we think they will discover that the assessments are fun to use. Performance-based assessments also address some of the assessment problems that have plagued physical education for years. With refinement and revision, assessments can become tasks that are meaningful both to teachers and their students.

We recognize that implementing a new assessment agenda is not an easy process, but, as with any journey, the first step is probably the hardest. Teachers should start by trying some of the ideas found in this book and then modify them to fit the needs of their own programs. When teachers keep initial attempts at performance-based assessment simple, they are more likely to succeed. The results can be positive and rewarding. It's time to take that first step and begin climbing the stairs to a new way to assess student learning.

# Glossary

**adventure education event tasks**—Activities that can be completed within a single instructional period and typically involve a cooperative challenge.

**affective domain**—Attributes concerning how students act and feel (e.g., self-concept, effort, respect for others, assisting classmates and teachers).

**alternative assessment**—Another term for performance-based assessment.

**analytic rubric**—Means of scoring an assessment that lists the various points or dimensions and allows the scorer to determine a degree of quality for each item (two types: qualitative and quantitative, which is also called numerical).

**application task**—Learning or assessment task in which the student is required to apply learned skills, strategies, or knowledge, often in authentic situations.

**artifact**—Document that demonstrates student learning related to a specific goal or standard in an evaluation portfolio.

**authentic assessment**—Another term for performance-based assessment.

**backward mapping**—Method of planning wherein the teacher first identifies the final goal that students are expected to achieve, then designs learning experiences that allow students to do so.

**Bloom's Taxonomy**—System for classifying learning into levels ranging from simple to complex.

**central organizer**—Statement that focuses unit content on a specific theme, concept, problem, skill, or issue during the planning process known as backward mapping.

**characteristic**—See descriptor.

**checklist**—Type of performance list that identifies characteristics or behaviors that are part of a performance; scored as either present or not present with no judgment about the level of quality.

**checkpoint**—Assessment done several times that allows students to track progress and learning related to a given skill or activity (also referred to as progress checkpoints).

**cognitive knowledge**—Knowledge related to the application, comprehension, evaluation, or synthesis of information related to a given subject area.

**competent bystander**—Student who exhibits good behavior but avoids participating in class activities.

**content standards**—Stated expectations for what a student should know and be able to do for a given subject or content area.

**continuous performance-based assessment**—Assessment approach in which assessments are integrated with learning and practice activities across the unit of instruction so that the students and the teacher receive feedback on student performance.

**criteria**—The elements contained in a rubric or scoring guide that identify factors necessary for evaluating performance.

**culminating assessment**—A final performance or product that provides evidence about whether students have achieved unit goals and standards.

**culminating performance**—A final demonstration of skill, intended to capture the key dimensions of learning from a unit during which students are expected to apply their learning from the unit of study in an authentic or realistic situation for a designated audience. Also called a culminating assessment.

**cumulative portfolio**—Portfolio that includes documents representing student learning across multiple units and time.

**curriculum backward planning map**—Guideline for planning a unit of study that begins with the identification of broad goals and standards that students should achieve.

**descriptor**—Element that represents one of the primary attributes used to define excellence when developing a rubric. Also called a characteristic or trait.

**developmental rubric**—A rubric that can be used to judge performance across all levels from a beginner to expert.

**essay**—Performance assessment technique that has students create a written product, such as a brochure, speech, dialogue, or performance critique (e.g., a dance review).

**essential questions**—Third component of the major focus of the curriculum planning map; questions that students should be able to answer throughout, and at the end of, a unit in order to achieve the unit goals.

**evaluation portfolio**—Portfolio submitted for evaluation that contains artifacts demonstrating competency in a subject or area; accompanied by a written narrative explaining the significance of each included item.

**event tasks**—Performance tasks that can be completed within a single instructional period and usually involve physical activity (e.g., playing a game, creating a game or routine, choreographing a dance, skipping rope, performing a dance).

**exemplar**—Student work sample used to demonstrate an acceptable performance.

**extension tasks**—Progression of learning tasks involving a change in the situation, the criteria, or the task itself in order to make it harder or easier and thus facilitate the extension of learning.

**five-step, standards-based planning process**—Planning guideline model that uses backward mapping planning strategies, overall broad goals, and standards, in which the top step identifies standards that students should achieve. The teacher then moves down the steps in planning to identify the culminating assessment, essential questions, essential knowledge, skills, strategies, and learning and assessment activities and critical resources that students must learn to arrive at the top of the staircase to achieve goals and standards.

**formative assessment**—Assessment used during the learning process and designed to provide students with feedback about areas in which they need to achieve additional learning so that they have an opportunity to correct or improve their final product. Often used with the phrase "assessment for learning."

**game play**—Engagement by students in an application task related to a competitive activity; can include both small-sided and full-sided games.

**game-play rubric**—Set of criteria used by a teacher to evaluate students' ability to participate in a game or gamelike activity.

**generalized rubric**—Universal rubric used to assess a variety of performances that are related conceptually (e.g., writing samples, game play for invasion sports).

**group portfolio**—Portfolio developed through a group effort in which each member of a small group contributes artifacts and on the basis of which students are evaluated for cooperation.

**holistic rubric**—Rubric in which levels of performance are described in paragraphs that each address several dimensions or traits. Used most often for evaluating culminating events or summative performances.

**instructional alignment**—Curricular planning technique in which teachers test for what they teach. Goals for student learning, instruction, and assessments are interrelated and support each other.

**integrated assessment tasks**—Assessment tasks that are completed along with learning or practice activities to give students and teachers feedback about learning and progress.

**interview**—A type of assessment during which students are questioned by teachers to determine the extent of student learning; best used when evaluating a small group of students.

**journal**—A type of assessment that requires students to write and reflect on various topics (provided by the teacher or chosen by students) and allows teachers to look at student learning for components in the affective domain.

**level**—Indicates a certain quality of performance or degree of student mastery over subject matter on an analytic or holistic rubric.

**multidimensional assessment**—Portfolio in which the student documents the attainment of two or more goals or standards.

**multiple-independent-component question**—Type of open-response inquiry that asks several questions about the same prompt; contains at least two questions or parts, each independent of the others.

**multiyear portfolio**—Portfolio developed by students to demonstrate learning across many years (e.g., the middle grades—sixth, seventh, and eighth).

**narrative**—Type of parental report that contains a written description of a student's achievement in a subject area; used more widely at the elementary level than at the secondary level.

**norm-referenced**—A method of comparing student learning with the achievement of others who are equivalent in age or other characteristics and were assessed in similar circumstances.

**numerical analytic rubric**—See quantitative analytic rubric.

**open-response question**—Assessment technique that allows students to apply knowledge learned in class to solve a problem set in a real-world scenario. Multiple solutions are possible thus requiring students to use higher-order thinking skills to create a solution.

**peer evaluations or assessments**—Assessment strategy in which students evaluate the performance of a classmate and provide him or her with feedback (written or verbal).

**performance-based assessment**—Assessment focused on student performance of a task typical of a performance or simulation of one that someone in the field might do. Assessment and instruction are usually intertwined, making it impossible to separate the two; students are given the criteria along with the assessment.

**performance standards**—Standards that specify a level of quality for performance for student learning and indicate the type of evidence needed to confirm that a student has satisfied the standard.

**point system performance list**—Scoring guide consisting of a list of weighted characteristics by which to judge a performance or product and determine a final or overall score. There is no judgment made about level of quality on a certain trait or characteristic, but the weighting indicates which descriptors are most important.

**portfolio**—Collection of materials or artifacts that, considered collectively, demonstrate student competence or mastery of a content and skill area, and achievement of goals and standards.

**process criteria**—Criteria that refer to how the performance or product is completed (used in physical education to represent the critical elements of a given skill).

**product criteria**—Criteria that refer to what a student produces or does (e.g., 10 tennis serves, 5 free throws, or 3 forward rolls).

**progress criteria**—Criteria used to determine student achievement toward a goal or standard (used to measure student improvement).

**progressive assessment**—A process whereby student progress is assessed from the performance of simple to more complex skills (i.e., those with increasing complex situations or settings).

**progressive learning activities**—Learning activities that build on previous activities to extend the difficulty of the task by changing the way the task is performed, the situation in which it is performed, or the criteria for performance.

**prompt**—Scenario presented with a performance-based assessment that provides a setting for responding to the question (usually a real-world situation).

**qualitative analytic rubric**—Analytic rubric that describes a level of quality for each trait assessed using a verbal description of that trait (useful for doing formative assessment of student learning).

**quantitative analytic rubric**—Analytic rubric that requires the scorer to determine a level of quality for each assessed trait on the basis of a number that is grounded in a word or phrase such as *sometimes, often, usually,* or *never* (useful for assessing game-play ability).

**refinement task**—Learning task in which the teacher directs the student's focus of learning to a particular learning cue or critical element of a skill performance to refine the performance of that particular element.

**reliability**—The measure of consistency for an assessment.

**representative portfolio**—Portfolio that includes artifacts documenting student learning across one unit of instruction.

**response-to-provided-information question**—Open-response question that provides students with information (e.g., data from a fitness test, excerpt from a journal article, diagram of a game strategy) to which they must respond.

**role-play assessment**—Assessment technique in which the teacher develops a scenario to assess certain components of learning or activity; often used for assessing affective domain dispositions.

**rubric**—Guidelines or criteria by which a performance or product is judged.

**scaffolded open-response question**—Question containing a sequence of increasingly difficult tasks or questions in which each task depends on the response generated by the previous one.

**self-evaluation**—Assessment technique in which students evaluate their performance against a set of criteria provided by the teacher or an expert source.

**single-dimension open-response question**—Question that requires students to respond to a single idea or concept; often requires students to draw a conclusion or take a position, then justify that position.

**single-dimensional assessment**—Portfolio in which students document learning that represents the attainment of a single goal or standard.

**standards-based assessment**—Assessment designed to demonstrate that a student has achieved a level of performance designated by a content standard or performance standard.

**standards-based instruction**—Curriculum designed to enable students to meet instructional standards in which the teacher uses a backward mapping planning strategy to look first at the final goal of instruction, then design learning experiences that allow students to reach the goal.

**standards-based instructional format**—Curriculum developed to allow students to gain competence as called for in published standards that are typically criterion-referenced.

**student-choice open-response question**—Question format that allows students to select the question they wish to address (available questions measure similar content and are of similar difficulty, but may differ in activity or subject area).

**student log**—Document in which students track performance by recording the incident each time it occurs and, when appropriate, the time spent doing the activity or behavior (i.e., duration).

**student performance**—Method of assessing student achievement that requires students to demonstrate competence by presenting a piece that typically requires several days or weeks to prepare.

**student project**—Assessment technique in which students create a concrete product to demonstrate their learning or achievement regarding a topic or subject (e.g., video of workout routine, piece of equipment designed to exercise certain muscles).

**subjectivity**—Degree of judgment used in assigning a score to a student's assessment performance.

**summative assessment**—Final assessment of student learning; typically comes at the conclusion of a unit of study. Also referred to as a culminating assessment.

**task-specific rubric**—Rubric written specifically for an individual assessment task and includes criteria specific to that assessment.

**teaching to the test**—Approach in which teachers know the content of an upcoming test and prepare students to do well on it (suggests a focus on preparing students for the test rather than covering content they will need to know in the adult world and thus carries a negative connotation).

**thematic portfolio**—Assessment portfolio that focuses on a specific theme (e.g., improvement of personal fitness, development of cooperation and teamwork, skills, attitudes, self-expression through movement).

**traditional assessments**—Tests typically used for assessment, such as written tests (e.g., multiple-choice, true-false, matching formats), skill tests (e.g., a serving test in tennis), and fitness tests (e.g., sit-and-reach, 1-minute sit-up test).

**trait**—See descriptor.

**transparency**—The degree to which an assessment provides information about the procedure used to complete the assessment.

**validity**—Measurement technique designed to ensure that an assessment measures the construct it is supposed to measure.

**working portfolio**—Portfolio in which students can gather diverse information demonstrating mastery of learning objectives; place where artifacts are kept in preparation for selecting materials to include in the evaluation portfolio.

# Bibliography

Alexander, K.R. 1982. *Behavior analysis of tasks and accountability in physical education.* PhD diss., Ohio State University.

American Alliance for Health, Physical Education, Recreation and Dance. 1999. *Physical best activity guide: Secondary level.* Reston, VA: AAHPERD.

———. 2005. *Physical Best Activity Guide: Secondary Level.* 2nd ed. Champaign, IL: Human Kinetics.

Arter, J. 1996. Performance criteria: The heart of the matter. In *A Handbook for Student Performance Assessment,* ed. R.E. Blum and J.A. Arter, vi-2:1-8. Alexandria, VA: ASCD.

Arter, J. and J. McTighe. 2001. *Scoring rubrics in the classroom: Using performance criteria for assessing and improving student performance.* Thousand Oaks, CA: Corwin Press, Inc.

Baumgartner, T. and A. Jackson. 1999. *Measurement for evaluation.* New York: McGraw-Hill.

Black, P., and D. Wiliam. 1998. Inside the black box: Raising standards through classroom assessment. *Phi Delta Kappan,* 80 (2): 139-48.

———. 2004. Working inside the black box: Assessment for learning in the classroom. *Phi Delta Kappan,* 86(1): 9-21.

Bloom, B., G. Madaus, and J.T. Hastings. 1981. *Evaluation to improve learning.* New York: McGraw-Hill.

Bracey, G. 2008. Research: Assessing NCLB. *Phi Delta Kappan,* 781-782.

Brown, J. 2004. *Tennis: Steps to success.* 3rd ed. Champaign, IL: Human Kinetics.

Buck, M. 2002. *Assessing heart rate in physical education.* Reston, VA: NASPE.

Burke, K., R. Fogarty, and S. Belgrad. 1994. *The mindful school: The portfolio connection.* Palatine, IL: IRI/Skylight.

Burton, A., and Miller, D. 1998. *Movement skill assessment.* Champaign, IL: Human Kinetics.

Callahan, C. 1997. *Using performance tasks and rubrics to differentiate instruction.* Read by author. Cassette recording no. 297069. Alexandria, VA: ASCD.

Csikszentmihalyi, M. 1997. *Finding flow: The psychology of engagement with everday life.* New York: BasicBooks.

———. 2000. The contribution of flow to positive psychology. Ed. J. E. Gillham, *The Science of Optimism and Hope: Research essays in honor of Martin E. P. Seligman.* Philadelphia: Templeton Foundation Press, 387-395.

Cohen, S.A. 1987. Instructional alignment: Searching for a magic bullet. *Educational Researcher,* 16 (8): 16-20.

The Cooper Institute. 2007. *Fitnessgram/Activitygram test administration manual.* 4th ed. Champaign, IL: Human Kinetics.

Corbin, C., and R. Lindsey. 2007. *Fitness for life.* Champaign, IL: Human Kinetics.

Cotten, D., and M. Cotten. 1985. Grading: The ultimate weapon? *Journal of Physical Education, Recreation & Dance,* 56 (2): 52-53.

Cunningham, G. 1998. *Assessment in the classroom: Constructing and interpreting tests.* Washington, DC: Falmer Press.

Danielson, P. 1992. *Artificial morality: Virtuous robots for virtual games.* London: Routledge.

Department for Education and Employment (DfEE)/Qualifications and Curriculum Authority (QCA). 2000. *Physical Education: The National Curriculum for England, Key stages 1-4.* London: TSO (The Stationery Office).

Dick, E., H. Buecker, and K. Wilson. 1999. *Designing standards-based units of study.* Training manual prepared for the Oldham County Summer Institute for Teachers, 14-17 June.

Dodge, B. 2009. "What Is a WebQuest?" www.webquest.org.

Doolittle, S., and T. Fay. 2002. *Authentic assessment of physical activity for high school students.* Reston, VA: NASPE.

Fredrickson, J.R., and A. Collins. 1989. A systems approach to educational testing. *Educational Researcher,* 18 (9): 27-32.

French, K., J. Rink, L. Rikard, A. Mays, S. Lynn, and P. Werner. 1991. The effects of practice progressions on learning two volleyball skills. *Journal of Teaching Physical Education,* 10 (3): 261-74.

Graham, G., S. Holt-Hale, and M. Parker. 2001. *A reflective approach to teaching physical education.* 5th ed. Mountain View, CA: Mayfield.

———. 2007 *Children moving: A reflective approach to teaching physical education.* 7th ed. Mountain View, CA: Mayfield.

Griffin, L., S. Mitchell, and J. Oslin. 1997. *Teaching sport concepts and skills: A tactical games approach.* Champaign, IL: Human Kinetics.

Guskey, T. 1996a. *Alternative ways to document and communicate student learning.* Read by author. Cassette recording no. 296211. Alexandria, VA: ASCD.

———. 1996b. Three kinds of criteria. *Educational Update,* 38 (6): 1, 4-7.

Guskey, T. and J. Bailey. 2001. *Developing grading and reporting systems for student learning.* Eds. Thomas R. Guskey and Robert J. Marzano. Thousand Oaks, CA: Corwin Press, Inc.

Harrison, J., C. Blakemore, and M. Buck. 2001. *Instructional strategies for secondary school physical education.* 5th ed. New York: McGraw-Hill.

Harvey, J. 2003. The matrix reloaded. *Educational Leadership,* 61 (3): 18-21.

Haywood, C., and C. Lewis. 2006. *Archery: Steps to success.* 3rd ed. Champaign, IL: Human Kinetics.

Hellison, D. 2003. *Teaching responsibility through physical activity.* 2nd ed. Champaign, IL: Human Kinetics.

Hensley, L. 1997. Alternative assessment for physical education. *Journal of Physical Education, Recreation & Dance,* 68 (7): 19-24.

Hensley, L., L. Lambert, T. Baumgartner, and J. Stillwell. 1987. Is evaluation worth the effort? *Journal of Physical Education, Recreation & Dance,* 58 (6): 59-62.

Herman, J., P. Aschbacher, and L. Winters. 1992. *A practical guide to alternative assessment.* Alexandria, VA: ASCD.

———. 1996. Setting criteria. In *A Handbook for Student Performance Assessment,* ed. R.E. Blum and J.A. Arter, vi-4:1-19. Alexandria, VA: ASCD.

Hill, B., and C. Ruptic. 1994. *Practical aspects of authentic assessment: Putting the pieces together.* Northwood, MA.: Christopher Gordon.

Hopple, C.J. 2005. *Elementary physical education teaching & assessment.* 2nd ed. Champaign, IL: Human Kinetics.

Horvat, M., M. Block, and L. Kelly. 2007. Developmental and adapted physical activity assessment. Champaign, IL: Human Kinetics.

Jennings, J. 1995. School reform based on what is taught and learned. *Phi Delta Kappan,* 76 (10): 765-69.

Jensen, E. 1998. *Teaching with the brain in mind.* Alexandria, VA: Association for Supervision and Curriculum Development.

Kelly, L. E., and Melograno, V. J. 2004. *Developing the physical education Curriculum: An achievement-based Approach.* Champaign, IL: Human Kinetics

Kentucky Department of Education. 1993. *Transformations: Kentucky's curriculum framework.* Vol. II. Frankfurt: Kentucky Department of Education.

———. 2008. *How to develop a standards-based unit of study.* Frankfurt: Kentucky Department of Education.

Kimeldorf, M. 1994. *A teacher's guide to creating portfolios.* Minneapolis: Free Spirit.

Kirk, M.F. 1997. Using portfolios to enhance student learning and assessment. *Journal of Physical Education, Recreation & Dance,* 68 (7): 29-33.

Kulinna, P.H., W. Zhu, M. Behnke, R.O. Johnson, D. McMullen, M.E. Turner, and G. Wolff. 1999. Six steps in developing and using fitness portfolios. *Teaching Elementary Physical Education,* 10 (5): 15-17, 28.

Lambert, L. 1999. *Standards-based assessment of student learning: A comprehensive approach.* Reston, VA: NASPE.

———. 2007. *Standards-based assessment of student learning: A comprehensive approach.* 2nd ed. Reston, VA: NASPE.

Lazzaro, W. 1996. Empowering students with instructional rubrics. In *A Handbook for Student Performance Assessment,* ed. R.E. Blum and J.A. Arter, vi-3:1-9. Alexandria, VA: ASCD.

Lewis, A. 1995. An overview of the standards movement. *Phi Delta Kappan,* 76 (10): 744-50.

Lieberman, L. and Houston-Wilson. 2002. *Strategies for inclusion: A handbook for physical educators.* Champaign, IL: Human Kinetics.

Lund, J. 1992. Assessment and accountability in secondary physical education. *Quest,* 44:352-60.

———. 1997. Authentic assessment: Its development and applications. *Journal for Physical Education, Recreation & Dance,* 68 (7): 25-28, 40.

Lund, J. and J. Shanklin (in press). The impact of accountability on student response rate in a secondary physical education badminton unit. *Physical Educator.*

Luxbacher, J.A. 2005. *Soccer: Steps to success.* 3rd ed. Champaign, IL: Human Kinetics.

Mager, R. 1984. *Preparing instructional objectives: A critical tool in the development of effective instruction.* 2nd ed. Belmont, CA: Pittman Learning, Inc.

Marmo, D. 1994. "Sport"folios: On the road to outcomes-based education. Paper presented at the national convention of the American Alliance for Health, Physical Education, Recreation and Dance, Denver.

Marzano, R. 2000. *Transforming classroom grading.* Alexandria, VA: Association for Supervision and Curriculum Development.

———. 2006. *Classroom assessment and grading that work.* Alexandria, VA: Association for Supervision and Curriculum Development.

Marzano, R., D. Pickering, and J. McTighe. 1993. *Assessing student outcomes: Performance assessment using the dimensions of learning model.* Alexandria, VA: ASCD.

Melograno, V.J. 1994. Portfolio assessment: Documenting authentic student learning. *Journal of Physical Education, Recreation & Dance,* 65 (8): 50-55, 58-61.

———. 1999. *Preservice professional portfolio system.* Reston, VA: NASPE.

———. 2000. *Portfolio assessment for K-12 physical education.* Reston, VA: NASPE.

———. 2006. *Professional and student portfolios for physical education.* 2nd ed. Champaign, IL: Human Kinetics.

Metzler, M. 2005. *Instructional models for physical education.* 2nd ed. Scottsdale, AZ: Holcomb Hathaway, Publishers, Inc.

Mitchell, R. 1992. *Testing for learning: How new approaches to evaluation can improve American schools.* New York: Free Press.

Mitchell, S., and J. Oslin. 1999. *Assessment in games teaching.* Reston, VA: NASPE.

Mitchell, S., J. Oslin, and L. Griffin. 2006. *Teaching sport concepts and skills: A tactical games approach.* 2nd ed. Champaign, IL: Human Kinetics.

Mohnsen, B.J. 2000. *Using technology in physical education.* Champaign, IL: Human Kinetics.

National Association for Sport and Physical Education. 1995. *Moving into the future: National standards for physical education.* Reston, VA: NASPE.

———. 2001. *Shape of the nation report.* Reston, VA: NASPE.

———. 2004. *Moving into the future: National standards for physical education.* 2nd ed. Reston, VA: NASPE.

———. 2005. *Physical education for lifelong fitness: The Physical Best teacher's guide.* 2nd ed. Champaign, IL: Human Kinetics.

———. 2006. *Shape of the nation report.* Reston, VA: NASPE.

National Commission on Excellence in Education. 1983. *A nation at risk: The imperative for educational reform.* A report to the nation and the secretary of education. Washington, DC: GPO.

O'Sullivan, M., and M. Henninger. 2000. *Assessing student responsibility and teamwork.* Reston, VA: NASPE.

Owens, D., and L. Bunker. 2005. *Golf: Steps to success.* Champaign, IL: Human Kinetics.

Pangrazi, R. 2001. *Dynamic physical education for elementary school children.* 13th ed. Allyn & Bacon: Boston.

Pangrazi, R., A. Beighle, and C. Sidman. 2007. *Pedometer power: Using pedometers in school and community.* 2nd ed. Champaign, IL: Human Kinetics.

Popham, W. J. 1997. What's wrong—and what's right—with rubrics. *Educational Leadership,* 55 (2): 72-75.

———. 2001. *The truth about testing.* Alexandria, VA: Association for Supervision and Curriculum Development.

———.2003. *Teach better, test better: The instructional role of assessment.* Alexandria, VA: Association for Supervision and Curriculum Development.

———. 2005. *Classroom assessment: What teachers need to know.* 4th ed. Boston, MA: Pearson Education, Inc.

———. 2008. *Transformative assessment.* Alexandria, VA: Association for Supervision and Curriculum Development.

President's Council on Physical Fitness and Sports. 2007. *The president's challenge physical activity and fitness awards program manual.* Atlanta: U.S. Department of Health and Human Services.

Rink, J.E. 2000. Physical education and the physically active lifestyle. Paper presented at the NASPE Conference for standards 3 and 4, Linking Physical Activity and Fitness. Baltimore, MD.

———. 2006. *Teaching physical education for learning.* 5th ed. Boston: McGraw-Hill.

———. 2009. *Designing the physical education curriculum: Promoting active lifestyles.* New York: McGraw-Hill.

Rowlands, A.V., R.G. Eston, and D.K. Ingledew. 1999. Relationship between activity levels, aerobic fitness, and body fat in 8- to 10-year-old children. *Journal of Applied Physiology,* 86 (4): 1428-35.

Scriffiny, P. 2008. Seven reasons for standards-based grading. *Educational Leadership,* 66 (2): 70-74.

Shanklin, J. 2004. *The impact of accountability on student response rate in a secondary physical education badminton unit.* Unpublished master's thesis. Muncie, IN: Ball State University.

Siedentop, D. 2001. *Introduction to physical education, fitness, and sport.* 4th ed. Mountain View, CA: Mayfield.

Siedentop, D., and D. Tannehill. 2000. *Developing teaching skills in physical education.* Mountain View, CA: Mayfield.

Stiggins, R. 1997. *Student-centered classroom assessment.* 2nd ed. Englewood Cliffs, NJ: Prentice Hall.

———. 2001. *Student-involved classroom assessment.* 3rd ed. Upper Saddle River, NJ: Prentice Hall.

———. 2007. *Classroom assessment for student learning.* New Jersey: Pearson Education, Inc.

Strand, B. and R. Wilson. 1993. *Assessing sport skills.* Champaign, IL: Human Kinetics.

Tomlinson, C. 1999. *The differentiated classroom: Responding to the needs of all learners.* Alexandria, VA: Association for Supervision and Curriculum Development.

Tousignant, M. 1981. *A qualitative analysis of task structures in required physical education.* PhD diss., Ohio State University.

Tudor-Locke, C. 2002. Taking steps toward increased physical activity: Using pedometers to measure and motivate. *Research Digest,* 3 (17): 1-8. President's Council on Physical Fitness and Sports. U.S. Department of Health and Human Services.

United States Gymnastics Federation. 1992. *I can do gymnastics: Essential skills for beginning gymnastics.* Indianapolis: Master Press.

U.S. Department of Health and Human Services. 1996. *Physical activity and health: A report of the surgeon general.* Atlanta: U.S. Department of Health and Human Services, Centers for Disease Control and Prevention. National Center for Chronic Disease Prevention and Health Promotion.

Vickers, J. 1990. *Instructional design for teaching physical activities: A knowledge structures approach.* Champaign, IL: Human Kinetics.

Welk, G.J., and M.D. Meredith, eds. 2008. *Fitnessgram/ Activitygram reference guide.* Dallas: Cooper Institute.

Westfall, S. 1998. Setting your sights on assessment: Describing student performance in physical education. *Teaching Elementary Physical Education,* 9 (6): 5-9.

Wiggins, G. 1989a. A true test: Toward more authentic and equitable assessment. *Phi Delta Kappan,* 69: 703-13.

———. 1989b. Teaching to the (authentic) test. *Educational Leadership,* 46 (9): 41-47.

———. 1996. What is a rubric? A dialogue on design and use. In *A Handbook for Student Performance Assessment,* ed. R.E. Blum and J.A. Arter, vi-5: 1-13. Alexandria, VA: ASCD.

———. 1998a. *Educative assessment: Designing assessments to inform and improve student performance.* San Francisco: Jossey-Bass.

———. 1998b. *Sophisticated and naive vs. right and wrong: How to teach and assess for intellectual progress.* Read by author. Cassette recording no. 298303. Alexandria, VA: ASCD.

Wiggins, G. and J. McTighe. 1998. *Understanding by design.* Alexandria, VA: ASCD.

———. 2005. *Understanding by design.* 2nd ed. Alexandria, VA: ASCD.

Wilde, B.E. 2002. *Activity patterns of high school students assessed by a pedometer and a national activity questionnaire.* Mesa: Arizona State University.

Wilde, B.E., C.L. Sidman, and C.B. Corbin. 2001. A 10,000 step count as a physical activity target for sedentary women. *Research Quarterly for Exercise & Sport,* 72 (4): 411-14.

Wilson, S., and K. Roof. 1999. Establishing a portfolio process for K–8 learners. *Teaching Elementary Physical Education,* 10 (5): 10-14.

Winnick, J., and F. Short. 1999. *The Brockport Physical Fitness Test Manual.* Champaign, IL: Human Kinetics.

# Index

Note: The italicized *f* and *t* following page numbers refer to figures and tables, respectively.

# About the Authors

**Jacalyn Lea Lund, PhD,** is an associate professor and chair in the department of kinesiology and health at Georgia State University in Atlanta. She has been a teacher educator since 1989 and had 16 years of teaching experience in the public schools prior to that. She has presented on assessment at numerous workshops and has taught numerous classes on assessment in physical education.

Dr. Lund has been a member of the National Association for Sport and Physical Education (NASPE) for more than 30 years. She was on the committee that developed the 1995 NASPE content standards for physical education and has served as NASPE president. In 2009 she received a Service Award from the National Association of Kinesiology and Physical Education in Higher Education. She loves spending time with her family, dancing, reading, and, as she puts it, "having her dogs take her for a walk."

**Mary Fortman Kirk, PhD,** is a professor of physical education at Northern Kentucky University, where she coordinates health and physical education programs. She also taught physical education at the high school level for 10 years. Kirk has given many presentations on portfolios and alternative assessment at conferences, including AAHPERD, NASPE, and the National Association for Physical Education in Higher Education. She was appointed by the Kentucky commissioner of education to serve on the state task force for the development of physical education assessment and performance assessment of new teachers.

Kirk earned an MA in motor learning and physical education from Michigan State University in 1973 and a PhD in motor development and teacher preparation from Ohio State University in 1989. She is the author of two books on pre-sport development programs for the National Alliance for Youth Sports and the Girl Scouts of the USA.

# CD-ROM User Instructions

## SYSTEM REQUIREMENTS

You can use this CD-ROM on either a Windows-based PC or a Macintosh computer.

### Windows

- IBM PC compatible with Pentium processor
- Windows 2000/XP/Vista
- Adobe Reader 8.0
- 4x CD-ROM drive

### Macintosh

- Power Mac recommended
- System 10.4 or higher
- Adobe Reader
- 4x CD-ROM drive

## USER INSTRUCTIONS

### Windows

1. Insert the *Performance-Based Assessment for Middle and High School Physical Education, Second Edition* CD-ROM. (Note: The CD-ROM must be present in the drive at all times.)
2. Select the "My Computer" icon from the desktop.
3. Select the CD-ROM drive.
4. Open the file you wish to view. See the "00Start.pdf" file for a list of the contents.

### Macintosh

1. Insert the *Performance-Based Assessment for Middle and High School Physical Education, Second Edition* CD-ROM. (Note: The CD-ROM must be present in the drive at all times.)
2. Double-click the CD-ROM icon located on the desktop.
3. Open the file you wish to view. See the "00Start" file for a list of the contents.

For customer support, contact Technical Support:
Phone: 217-351-5076 Monday through Friday (excluding holidays) between 7:00 a.m. and 7:00 p.m. (CST).
Fax: 217-351-2674
E-mail: support@hkusa.com